CONTEMPORARY MODELS
IN VOCATIONAL PSYCHOLOGY

A Volume in Honor of Samuel H. Osipow

CONTEMPORARY MODELS IN VOCATIONAL PSYCHOLOGY

A Volume in Honor of Samuel H. Osipow

Frederick T. L. Leong
The Ohio State University

Azy Barak
University of Haifa

CARROLL COLLEGE LIBRARY
WAUKESHA, WISCONSIN 53186

2001

LAWRENCE ERLBAUM ASSOCIATES, PUBLISHERS
Mahwah, New Jersey   London

Lawrence Erlbaum Associates, Inc., Publishers
10 Industrial Avenue
Mahwah, New Jersey 07430

Cover design by Kathryn Houghtaling Lacey

Library of Congress Cataloging-in-Publication Data

Contemporary models in vocational psychology : a volume in honor of Samuel H.
Osipow / [edited by] Frederick T.L. Leong, Azy Barak.
     p. cm.
   Includes bibliographical references and indexes.
   ISBN 0-8058-2666-1 (cloth : alk. paper) – ISBN 0-8058-2667-X (pbk. : alk. paper)
     1.   Vocational guidance—Psychological aspects. 2. Career development—Psychological
Aspects. I. Osipow, Samuel H. II. Leong, Frederick T. L. III. Barak, Azy.

   HF5381 .C68717 2000
   158.6—dc21
                                                                          00-050379

Books published by Lawrence Erlbaum Associates are printed on acid-free paper,
and their bindings are chosen for strength and durability.

Printed in the United States of America
10   9   8   7   6   5   4   3   2   1

Contents

1. Some Introductory Notes on Innovations in Career Psychology   1
    Inspired by the Legacy of Samuel H. Osipow
    Frederick T. L. Leong and Azy Barak

2. The PIC Model for Career Decision Making: Prescreening,   7
    In-Depth Exploration, and Choice
    Itamar Gati and Itay Asher

3. Career Self-Efficacy   55
    Nancy Betz

4. Samuel H. Osipow's Contributions to Occupational Mental Health   79
    and the Assessment of Stress: The Occupational Stress Inventory
    Arnold R. Spokane and Deborah Ferrara

5. A Cognitive View of the Nature of Vocational Interests: 97
    Implications for Career Assessment, Counseling, and Research
    Azy Barak

6. Cross-Cultural Assessment of Interests   133
    Elchanan I. Meir and Aharon Tziner

7   Cross-Cultural Perspective on Super's Career Development   167
    Theory: Career Maturity and Cultural Accommodation
    Frederick T. L. Leong and Felicisima C. Serafica

8. Women's Career Development: A Postmodern Update   207
    Louise F. Fitzgerald and Lenore W. Harmon

9. Career Assessment: Changes and Trends   231
    Judy M. Chartrand and W. Bruce Walsh

10.   Career Counseling: The Evolution of Theory   257
      Linda Mezydlo Subich and Kelly Simonson

11.   Career Services Within the University   279
      Jane L. Winer

12.   Toward a Comprehensive Theory of Career Development: 295
      Dispositions, Concerns, and Narratives
      Mark L. Savickas

Author index   321
Subject Index   331

CONTEMPORARY MODELS IN VOCATIONAL PSYCHOLOGY

A Volume in Honor of Samuel H. Osipow

Some Introductory Notes on Innovations in Career Psychology Inspired by the Legacy of Samuel H. Osipow

Frederick T. L. Leong
The Ohio State University

Azy Barak
University of Haifa

This collection of innovative scientific chapters was sparked by the retirement of Samuel H. Osipow from Ohio State University in Columbus, Ohio. Osipow, a prominent teacher, researcher, and author, has left his stamp in nearly every area of career psychology: career development theory, career decision-making models, vocational assessment, cross-cultural and minority groups issues, counseling interventions, counseling services provision, organizational consultation, professional intervention ethics, research methodology, and teaching. His active involvement in this broad variety of areas and his dynamic activity—18 books and more than 200 articles published, plus numerous paper presentations—have earned him a central place in the Hall of Fame of career psychology. In addition to his scientific activities, Osipow has continually been involved in academic teaching, supervision, administration, and professional organizations. Osipow was the chairperson of the Department of Psychology at the Ohio State University for 13 years, president of the American Psychological Association's (APA) Division of Counseling Psychology, and chairperson of numerous committees and task forces at APA and other bodies, such as the APA Committee on Women in Psychology and the APA Council of Editors. He was the founder and the first editor of *The Journal of Vocational Behavior* (1970–1975), and he edited the *Journal of Counseling Psychology* (1975–1981) and *Applied and Preventive Psychology* (1993–1999). An examination of his specific deeds and activities indeed leads to the conclusion that he has turned over stones and cultivated these fields in an attempt to facilitate constructive change.

Osipow represents a highly functional perspective: While identifying with and emphasizing cognitive-behavioral theory, he has recognized the place of rival explanations and has been open to alternative viewpoints to his own. In adopting his scientific position and rationale, Osipow has actively contributed to conceptualizing numerous specific topics in career psychology. These contributions included continuous critical reviews of existing career development theories and a cry for their integration and convergence; the role of perceptions of and attributions concerning occupations and occupational titles; adaptation of behavioral and cognitive-behavioral strategies to counseling practice; models of vocational indecision; assessment of career decision making, including processes, barriers, and outcomes; evaluation of and coping with occupational stress; issues related to the career psychology of women; various topics related to the development and crystallization of vocational interests; interrelationship of personality and career choice and development; cognitive factors related to career decision making and choice; the role of occupational and task-specific self-efficacy beliefs; work adjustment; unemployment; vocational and career education; issues in the career development of disabled persons; training of counseling psychologists; psychological consultation in business and industry; and professional identity issues in counseling psychology. This list reflects not only the level of Osipow's activity and involvement, but also his determination, motivation, identity, and dedication to career and counseling psychology. The recognition he has received, reflected in various awards and grants, is a result of these attributes. (For a comprehensive review of Osipow's career, see Simon, 1998.)

In preparing this volume, we collected original contributions from a number of outstanding scientists in the field of career psychology who have been associated with Osipow either as career-long colleagues (e.g., Betz, Harmon, Walsh) or as his students first and colleagues later (e.g., Fitzgerald, Spokane, Winer). Each of these individuals not only contributed a valuable manuscript to this book, but also associated the article with Osipow's work. As a result, this book contains a collection of scholarly, innovative chapters that presents comprehensive view of career psychology and reflects Osipow's involvement in the field.

Chapter 2 analyzes the limitations of existing models of career decision making. Based on this analysis and Gati's program of research on this topic, the authors present a prescriptive–systematic model for career decision making. The PIC model consists of three stages–prescreening, in-depth exploration, and choice. Each stage is presented in detail and compared to the other stages. The chapter concludes with a presentation of research that is relevant to the PIC model, as well as what implications the PIC model holds for the future of career decision making and counseling.

A review of career self-efficacy is presented in chapter 3. Betz was one of the first researchers to adopt the self-efficacy construct for career psychology by conceptualizing both its intervening role in career-related attitudes and behaviors and its measurement. Her analysis associates career self-efficacy with proximate conceptualizations, such as Super's self-concept model and Holland's typological approach. In addition, she reviews the findings on career self-efficacy and on important vocational-related factors, such as interests and decision making. However, central to the chapter, Betz further develops her previous propositions on the centrality of career self-efficacy by explaining career-related attitudes and behaviors of minority group members and by noting its implication for career counseling.

Chapter 4 examines the validity and the utility of Osipow's Occupational Stress Inventory (OSI), an instrument designed to assess occupationally induced stress and the role of coping strategies on well-being. The OSI was first developed in 1981 and revised in 1983 and 1987. OSI is a theoretically derived instrument with three subscales designed to tap role stressors, role strains, and coping roles in the context of a work environment: Occupational Environment Scale (OES), Personal Strain Questionnaire (PSQ), Personal Resources Questionnaire (PRQ). Beginning in 1981, more than 60 studies, including validity studies, support the notion that OSI is a psychometrically sound practical device for use in variety of research and practical settings. In addition, the authors provide empirical evidence for its internal consistency using three individual profile samples. Occupational stress and strain intervention, as well as prevention strategies, are outlined in the three OSI workshop modes (interpretive, full-day, and half-day). Finally, critical reviews concerning the OSI are recognized, followed by helpful guidelines for future research.

Chapter 5 presents a cognitive model of interest, which is a departure from the dominant trait/disposition approach. The chapter begins with illustrations of the pervasiveness of cognitions in one's expressed interests and the assumptions and evaluations we make about others' interests. Interests are conceptualized as emotional manifestations (or feelings) of cognitive processes. The feelings reflect degree of attraction or aversion toward a stimulus, and they originate from a person's thoughts concerning the stimulus. Barak proposes three cognitive determinants of interest (perceived abilities, expected success, and anticipated satisfaction) and presents both correlational and experimental evidence to support his model. Development of interests and implications for career assessment, counseling and research are discussed. Barak views the individual as an active and responsible creator of his or her destiny, and since interests are cognitively determined, career counseling is a constructive dynamic process to help the client modify and restructure his or her emotions of attraction to and repulsion from activities and occupations consistent with his or her personal strengths and weaknesses. The model is also compared and contrasted with two other cognitive approaches: social cognitive career theory and social learning theory of career decision making. Barak concludes by suggesting the possibility of an integrated comprehensive cognitive career psychology theory.

Chapter 6 discusses cross-cultural assessment of interests. Meir and Tziner summarize ways in which cultural differences may influence the expression and assessment of vocational interests. The authors briefly discuss interests and other determinants in career choice and performance, such as abilities, before focusing on interests. Interests are defined as "the extent of attraction to act in, to be engaged in, or to receive training for any task, job, or occupation" (p. 00). The role of interests in occupational choice and satisfaction (i.e., congruence) and the origin of interests are also discussed. In terms of assessment of vocational interests, the authors also discuss evidence regarding the structural similarity if interests across cultures and the importance of using appropriate norm groups. They distinguish between measures that rely on comparisons of an individual's score to the norm group (Is this person's interest high compared to others?) and those that rely on intra-individual comparisons (Is this person's interest high compared to his or her other interests?). Despite the vast number of difficulties noted in attempting to assess interests cross-culturally, the authors provide several rules and concrete practical suggestions for using and/or constructing interest inventories cross-culturally. They conclude with their conviction that accurate cross-cultural interest assessment is possible and that the rewards for doing so are considerable.

Chapter 7 concentrates on cross-cultural perspectives of career development. Leong and Serafica begin by reviewing the publications relating to career development cross-cultural research published since the 1960s in the *Journal of Vocational Behavior* and the *Career Development Quarterly*. The authors attempt to draw conclusions as to how these studies reflect on minority groups' career development and career choice. They then present original generalizations relating to the concept of career maturity in the context of ethnic minorities. Then, Leong and Serafica, in adopting Leong's previously published integrative cross-cultural model of counseling and psychotherapy and applying it in the context of Super's developmental theory, analyze how the research findings that emerged in the first section of the chapter reflect on the second. Their review provides implications for and at the same time strengthens both the cross-cultural validity of Super's model and Leong's emphasis on cultural accommodation.

Existing literature in women's career development is reviewed from the postmodernism perspective in chapter 8. The authors describe the changing face of the female workforce in United States. Then, they discuss measurement interests, parental influences on women's career development, individual factors, the role of marriage and career barriers. They end with the description of the new, emergent portrait of the woman in 2000 in light of all the recent developments in postmodernist thought. This conceptualization of the emergent woman is an extension and elaboration of the pioneering work of Osipow's work in this area.

Chapter 9 discusses career assessment in relation to societal and technological evolutions and revolutions and examines the way these affect several highly relevant issues relating to vocational behavior and organizations. Understanding that a discussion of emerging assessments in a changing world would be meaningless without analyzing the process of change of work and the workplace, the authors first present a broad yet focused review of these topics in light of recent changes that the world is experiencing. Chartrand and Walsh later discuss the structure and role of various assessment devices, including innovative approaches, in light of these changes. They conclude their chapter with an important critique of how these career assessment changes reflect on career counseling and career-related research.

Chapter 10 provides an in-depth analysis of the evolution of career counseling theory. The authors review several early career counseling models, as well as emerging theories of counseling. They show how recent approaches differ from previous methods in relating differently to several psychological factors (e.g., environmental, social, emotional) and also in the way they refer to diagnosis, the counseling process, and client empowerment. The authors analyze the change in perspectives and their implications for counseling.

The challenges in providing career services within the university setting are addressed in chapter 11. The author discusses positive and negative forces that impact career services from three different perspectives: the applied or practitioner perspective, the academic or faculty perspective, and the administrative perspective. The author analyzes the interaction of these three perspectives within the context of the university setting. The last section discusses the problems and potential solutions to providing effective career services to university students.

Chapter 12 expands on Savickas' long-held ideas on the convergence of career development theories by examining and confronting the concept of career maturity as a major factor in career development theory. Savickas challenges common assumptions and myths frequently held by researchers and professionals in career psychology. He proposes an alternative viewpoint that lays the ground for new theorizing. He identifies four major factors—termed levels of analysis (i.e., vocational personality types, career concerns, career narratives, mechanisms of development)—that should be used as foundations for integrating career theories into a comprehensive model of careers. Merging existing individual theories into a comprehensive framework by using the principles proposed may enhance our understanding of career development.

The chapters contained within this volume deal with significant theoretical and practice issues in vocational psychology. In presenting the various contemporary models, the authors present exciting new ideas and cutting-edge materials for both the researcher and practitioner in vocational psychology. From Gati's new model of career decision making to supplant existing models to Betz's discussion of recent developments in career self-efficacy; from Spokane and Ferrara's review of the OSI and occupational stress assessment to Barak's cognitive approach to vocational interests, the chapters highlight new and emergent perspectives in vocational psychology. Significant new developments in cross-cultural issues in vocational psychology are also presented by Meir and Tziner, as well as Leong and Serafica. As Fitzgerald and Harmon present a new perspective on women's career development in light of postmodernism, Chartrand and Walsh highlight significant new directions in career assessment given major changes in the workplace, and Subich and Simonson trace the evolution of career counseling and how the practice of career counseling will change. Winer offers new solutions to providing career services in a university setting, while Savickas proposes a comprehensive framework for merging divergent developments in career development theories. It is fitting that the unifying theme of this volume concerns "change" because the authors have prepared their chapters in honor of Osipow, a pioneer in vocational psychology who has significantly changed the field over the last four decades. Osipow has made these significant changes as a professor, journal editor, scholar, theoretician, practitioner, and mentor. We dedicate this volume to Sam in honor of the all the positive changes he has made in our lives and our professional careers. We hope that this volume will facilitate positive changes and development in the field of vocational psychology and serve as a tribute to Sam's professional legacy.

REFERENCES

Simon, J. (1998). Samuel H. Osipow: Commitment, caring, and innovation. *The Counseling Psychologist, 26,* 607–623.

Chapter 2

The PIC Model for Career Decision Making: Prescreening, In-Depth Exploration, and Choice

Itamar Gati
Itay Asher
The Hebrew University of Jerusalem

People make many decisions every day. Some of these decisions are made as part of one's daily routine, whereas others are perceived as being more important and require more attention. Most career-related decisions belong to the latter kind because they typically have significant long-range implications on people's lifestyle, the friends with whom they socialize, the avocational activities in which they engage, and hence on their quality of life. Therefore, career decisions are among the most important decisions one has to make, and they are significant for both the individual and the society as a whole.

The term *career decision making* has become prevalent in recent years. However, most of the research and discussions on career decision making have not focused on how career decisions are actually made (i.e., how the information is collected and processed by the individual), nor on how they should be made. Rather, they have focused on issues indirectly related to the process of career decision making, such as career indecision and indecisiveness, career decision-making self-efficacy, career decision-making styles, and so on. Additionally, stages in career decision making are often confused with stages and substages in career development (e.g., Miller-Tiedeman & Tiedeman, 1990). In this chapter, *career decision making* refers to the process people go through when they search for viable career alternatives, compare them, and then choose one.

Making a career decision is a complex task, and the deliberation involved often leads to discomfort, anxiety, and confusion (Osipow, Walsh,

& Tosi, 1980). Although some people make such decisions easily, others face difficulties and sometimes seek professional help. Additionally, individuals can be characterized along a continuum ranging from unsystematic (or spontaneous) to systematic career decision makers (e.g., Johnson, 1978). At one end are those individuals who tend to follow "the path of least resistance" (Osipow, 1969, 1990). These individuals do not have well-defined career goals, and typically follow the first accessible career path open to them, thus letting external events play the leading role in determining their vocational future. At the other end are individuals who make decisions systematically, after a thorough examination of the alternatives, often with the help of career counselors or computer-assisted career guidance systems (CACGSs), or after consultation with parents, spouse, and friends.

An individual's career decision-making style is an important factor affecting the process and outcome of career decision making. Harren (1979) distinguished three career decision-making styles: rational, intuitive, and dependent; Scott and Bruce (1995) distinguished five decision-making styles: rational, avoidant, intuitive, dependent, and spontaneous; Sagiv (1999) distinguished between counselees who look for tools and those who seek answers. These, as well as the other classifications of career decision-making strategies and styles reviewed by Phillips and Pazienza (1988), differ in the degree to which the individual is willing to take responsibility for the outcome of the decision and in the degree to which the individual uses a rational strategy or implicitly relies on intuition in the decision-making process.

Numerous studies have demonstrated the advantages of systematic decision making (e.g., Blustein & Phillips, 1988, 1990; Harren, Kass, Tinsley, & Moreland, 1979; Hesketh, 1982; Leong & Morris, 1989; Lunneborg, 1978; Mau & Jepsen, 1992; Phillips, Pazienza, & Ferrin, 1984). However, several researchers (e.g., Brown, 1990; Gelatt, 1989; Krieshok, 1998; Krumboltz, 1992; Phillips, 1994, 1997) questioned the possibility of using rational models in career decision making and discussed alternative models. In an attempt to meet this challenge, we describe and discuss a three-stage model, labeled the PIC model (prescreening, in-depth exploration, and choice), which is derived from decision theory but is adapted to the unique features of career decision making. PIC can be regarded as a prescriptive–systematic (rather than normative–rational) model for making career decisions. The proposed model emphasizes the role of career counselors as decision counselors (Jungerman & Schutz, 1992) whose aim is to facilitate career decision making and to promote better decisions.

In the first section of this chapter, we review traditional models of career choices and discuss some of their problems. Then, we discuss why and how we think decision theory should be utilized as a framework for developing new models or refining old ones. The next section presents the basic concepts underlying the proposed PIC model and its three major stages. This section is followed by a review of some empirical research related to the PIC model. Finally, we discuss the role of intuition in the career decision-making process, compare the PIC model with the person–environment (P–E) fit approach and normative decision theory, and explore implications for research and counseling.

THEORETICAL BACKGROUND

The Person–Environment Fit Approach and Its Problems

Parsons (1909) laid the foundation for the P–E fit perspective, which has dominated vocational psychology and career counseling for many years (e.g., Holland, 1985, 1997; Lofquist & Dawis, 1991; Osipow, 1987). The basic assumption of this approach is that congruence between an individual's characteristics and the characteristics of his or her chosen occupation results in higher indexes of well-being, such as satisfaction, stability, and achievement (e.g. Dawis & Lofquist, 1984; Holland, 1985, 1997; Spokane, 1987; Walsh & Holland, 1992). Reviewing the P–E fit models, Osipow (1987) summarized the challenges faced by this approach in three questions: "How do we assess people? How do we measure their environment? How do we compare the two, regarding the degree and quality of fit?" (p. 334).

Vocational interests (e.g., Holland, 1985, 1997; Meir, 1995; Osipow, 1983; Roe, 1956; Spokane, 1985, 1987; Osipow & Fitzgerald, 1996) are the most prevalent means of characterizing and comparing persons and environments in research, as well as in counseling. According to Holland (1985), career alternatives whose three-letter codes (based on Holland's Occupational Codes; Gottfredson & Holland, 1989) match the three-letter code of the individual, derived from his or her responses to an interest inventory (e.g., the *Vocational Preference Inventory, Self-Directed Search, Strong-Campbell Interest Inventory*), are chosen for further exploration.

Despite the popularity of vocational interests, the ways interests are measured and interpreted have been questioned on theoretical and empirical grounds. First, the relations among the various forms of interest expressions (e.g., manifested, tested, expressed, and inventoried; Crites, 1969) and their relative utility continue to be controversial (e.g., Borgen, 1986; Osipow & Fitzgerald, 1996; Slaney & Slaney, 1986). Second, there is a question of how many types should be used to characterize individuals and environments, and whether this number should be fixed (i.e., always using a three-letter code; Holland, 1985) or variable (Gati, 1985; Gati & Blumberg, 1991; see also the *Strong Vocational Interest Blank* interpretive report; Strong, Hansen, & Campbell, 1985). Third, there is no agreement as to which measure of congruence should be used for the assessment of P–E fit. (For reviews and comparisons of measures, see Assouline and Meir, 1987; Brown & Gore, 1994; Camp and Chartrand, 1992; Gati, 1985; Young, Tokar, & Subich, 1998.) Fourth, there are disagreements on the structure of vocational interests (Gati, 1991; Meir, 1973; Rounds & Tracey, 1996; Tracey & Rounds, 1993), as well as on whether and how to take this structure into account in the interpretation of the individual's interests and the assessment of congruence (e.g., Brown & Gore, 1994; Gati, 1985, 1989). Fifth, reviews of research on P–E congruence reported correlations around .30, less than might be expected (e.g., Assouline & Meir, 1987; Holland, 1997; Spokane, 1985). Additionally, the use of interests for screening the "world of work" and locating "promising alternatives" does not seem to be sufficiently refined. For example, there are several hundred occupations with a Holland *IRE* (Investigative, Realistic, Enterprising) code and a general educational Level 4 in the *Dictionary of Holland occupational codes* (Gottfredson & Holland, 1989). Finally, the over-emphasis on the concept of congruence has often led to a rigid matching between individuals' interests or needs and their environment, instead of encouraging individuals to be active players in their career decision-making process (Barak, chap. 5, this volume).

There are additional instruments for assessing the individual's vocational interests. Some of these instruments yield lists of occupations that match the individual's interests directly (e.g., the *Strong Interest Inventory*, *Kuder Occupational Interest Survey*). Other inventories provide the individual with occupational categories that match their interests (e.g., *Unisex Edition of the American College Testing Interest Inventory*, *Vocational Preference Inventory*); these categories can subsequently be used to get lists of specific occupations. To complement the picture obtained from interest inventories, some comprehensive programs also include guidelines for further career exploration and planning. However, these additional guidelines often assume that the individual's interests are given and that further steps should be based on them.

The Theory of Work Adjustment (TWA; Dawis & Lofquist, 1984), which is based on needs, is another variation of the P–E fit approach. This theory emphasizes the concept of *correspondence*, which is defined as the degree to which the individual and the environment meet each other's requirements (Lofquist & Dawis, 1991). Among the advantages of this approach are that it uses 20 needs (instead of, e.g., Holland's six personality types) in the assessment of P–E correspondence, and it distinguishes between satisfaction and satisfactoriness. However, this approach also leads to a rigid matching between the individual and his or her environment. Additionally, because it relies on a fixed set of needs, there is little flexibility in the search for this matching. Finally, TWA focuses mainly on adjustment to the work environment and the choice of a job and less on the career decision making process of choosing a study major, college, or occupation (during which one cannot take into account considerations like "co-workers" and "company policies").

Normative Decision Theory (NDT) and Its Problems

To make an informed career decision, the individual not only needs all the relevant information, but he or she has to be capable of using it optimally. The complexity of this process raises the need for guidance during the process itself. Decision theory focuses on the study of how decisions are actually made and how they should be made. Thus, decision theory can provide a well-defined framework for guiding a systematic and analytic career decision-making process (Gelatt, 1962; Jepsen & Dilley, 1974; Kaldor & Zytowsky, 1969; Katz, 1966). In particular, it provides a framework for a dynamic, interactive process, instead of the more rigid matching that underlies the traditional P–E fit approach.

Attention to the decision-making approach for occupational choices has increased in recent years, and cognitive approaches are playing a greater role in understanding the processes involved in career decision making (Neimeyer, 1988; Osipow, 1987; Peterson, Sampson, Reardon, & Lenz, 1996; Walsh & Osipow, 1988). Comprehensive reviews and discussions of decision-making theory as used for career choice may be found in Brown (1990); Carson and Mowsesian (1990); Gati (1986, 1990a, 1996); Jepsen and Dilley (1974); Mitchell and Krumboltz (1984); Phillips (1994, 1997); Phillips and Pazienza (1988); Pitz and Harren (1980); and Slaney (1988).

Bell, Raiffa, and Tversky (1988) distinguished three types of decision models: normative, descriptive, and prescriptive. Normative decision models specify how rational choices should be made. Descriptive models describe and explain how people choose among actual options in real-life situations. Prescriptive models outline the suggested steps involved in making better decisions, acknowledging that the decisions made may not necessarily be the best ones in terms of the normative models.

Normative decision models (e.g., the expected utility model or the multiattribute utility model) outline the course of action that should be taken in order to maximize the probability of achieving a specified goal. The basic feature of these models is that the advantages of the alternatives compensate for their disadvantages. According to expected utility theory, the outcomes associated with each alternative can be characterized in terms of two parallel sets (Pitz & Harren, 1980). One set includes the utility attributed by the decision maker to each of the outcomes associated with each alternative, and the other set includes the probability of achieving each specific outcome. The expected utility is the sum of the utilities attributed to the various outcomes associated with choosing a particular option, weighted by their respective probabilities. Normative models have also been applied with some adaptations to career decisions (e.g., the expected utility model, Katz, 1966; the multiattribute utility model, Zakay & Barak, 1984).

However, because of people's cognitive limitations, as well as time and monetary constraints, normative decision-making models (and their adaptations to career decision making) are impractical in real-life situations. First, when the number of potential alternatives is large (as is the case in many career decision-making situations), these models are inapplicable without a computerized system and database. Moreover, it may be claimed that normative decision-making models are too rational, too abstract, and too quantitative for the deliberating individual. They involve too much computations, often based on forced quantification which is not intuitively appealing. Thus, for most individuals, these models are too arbitrary and too complex.

Indeed, evidence exists that, despite of the apparent theoretical advantages of the expected utility model, it is not adequate as a descriptive model (e.g., Tversky, 1975). First, people often violate the expectation principle by overweighting certain outcomes (i.e., when no uncertainty is involved) in comparison to outcomes that are merely probable (Kahneman & Tversky, 1979). Second, people actually appear to make different choices under seemingly identical conditions (e.g., Kahneman & Tversky, 1984; Tversky & Kahneman, 1981). Finally, the need to simplify complex decision problems leads people to adopt rules (heuristics) in which not all options are evaluated (e.g., Tversky & Kahneman, 1974).

The Need for a Prescriptive Model

These disadvantages of normative decision-making models have probably contributed to the low popularity of their applications to career decision making, both in theory and in practice. Hence, there seems to be a need for prescriptive models that can provide a framework for making career decisions while overcoming, circumventing, or at least minimizing the problematic characteristics of the normative models. However, because of the characteristics of career decisions, no decision theory-based model can be adopted as is but should be adapted according to the unique features of career decisions (Gati, 1986).

Like other types of decision making, career decision making has the following features: There is an individual who has to make a decision, there are several alternatives from which to select, and the decision maker has certain aspects or criteria which can be used to compare and evaluate the various alternatives to locate the most suitable one. The need to determine the trade-offs among conflicting objectives (e.g., quality vs. price) increases the complexity of making decisions. This complexity is further augmented by the uncertainty involved in many decisions—even the probability of occurrence of each outcome is often unknown.

In addition to these features, which characterize most decisions, career decisions have additional unique features. First, the number of alternatives to choose from—such as educational pathways (e.g., study majors, colleges), vocational opportunities (e.g., occupations, jobs, potential employers for a recent MBA graduate)—is very large (Osipow, Walsh, & Tosi, 1980). Second, there is an extensive amount of information available (e.g., in occupational information libraries, CACGSs, encounters with incumbents in relevant occupations) on each alternative. One of the factors that contribute to this flood of information is the within-occupational variance in most occupations (Gati, 1986; Katz, 1993; Matarazzo, 1986; Meir & Yaari, 1988; Super, 1953). Third, a large number of criteria or attributes (e.g., length of training, work environment, degree of independence, income, type of relationship with people) are required to adequately characterize occupations and the individual's preferences in a detailed and meaningful way (Gati, 1998; Gati, Garty, & Fassa, 1996; Katz, 1993; Lofquist & Dawis, 1978). Finally, significant others (e.g., parents, spouse, friends) and, in many cases, a career counselor as well, often explicitly or implicitly affect the individual's career decision-making process.

Considering these characteristics of career decisions, a desirable feature of any prescriptive model is to reduce the amount of information that needs to be processed—with as little loss as possible in terms of the expected utility of the chosen alternative. One way to achieve this goal is by separating the decision process into distinct stages—for instance, distinguishing between screening and choice (Beach, 1993; Beach & Potter, 1992). In cases where there are many potential alternatives, unacceptable ones are first screened out if they are incompatible with the decision maker's specifications. Then, if more than a single alternative survives the screening, the best of the remaining ones is chosen (Beach, 1993). Research by Beach and his colleagues has supported their claim that these two stages differ in terms of the strategies used to collect information and the ways the information is used (Beach, 1993, 1998; Potter & Beach, 1994).

Moreover, taking into account the vast amount of information on one hand and the limited cognitive and material resources of the individual

(Pitz & Harren, 1980) on the other, deliberating individuals and their career counselors should give up the unattainable goal of maximizing expected utility (e.g., Katz, 1966; Zakay & Barak, 1984). Rather, they should aim at optimizing the career decision-making process. Furthermore, the guidelines for this process should not assume complete rationality, but only *bounded rationality* (Simon, 1957), which means aiming at the realistic goal of making a good enough or *satisficing* choice (Phillips, 1994). The proposed PIC model, introduced in the next section, attempts to provide a prescriptive framework for making better career decisions, considering the unique features of career decisions and the limited resources of humans.

THE PIC MODEL FOR THE CAREER DECISION-MAKING PROCESS

In this section we outline PIC, a three-stage model for making career decisions, which is a revised and elaborated version of previous proposals and discussions (Gati, 1986, 1989, 1990a, 1993, 1996; Gati, Fassa, & Houminer, 1995). Before describing the PIC model, some basic terms are defined. Next, issues related to readiness, which involves the preconditions for beginning the process, are briefly discussed. Then, the three stages of PIC—prescreening, in-depth exploration, and choice—are described. Next, we discuss issues associated with the implementation of the decision. Finally, we review and compare the three stages of the PIC model.

Basic Concepts

Career-Related Aspects. The term *career-related aspects* (Gati, 1986, 1998; Pryor, 1981, 1982) refers to all the relevant variables that can be used to characterize both individuals and career alternatives, and that may be considered during the process of career decision making (e.g., income, length of training, contribution to society, working indoors or outdoors, finger dexterity). Actually, career-related aspects can be seen as forming a universe that includes various vocational variables, including vocational interests (e.g., Holland, 1985, 1997; Roe, 1956), needs (e.g., Lofquist & Dawis, 1984), work values (e.g., Bridges, 1989; Katz, 1966; Zytowski, 1970), work characteristics (e.g., Manhardt, 1972), abilities (e.g., Dawis & Lofquist, 1984; Gottfredson, 1986), personal styles (Harmon et al., 1994), career constructs (e.g., Neimeyer, 1992), and work roles and styles (Jackson, 1977). Characterizing persons and environments using many career-related aspects can lead to a better P–E fit than using only a single category of vocational variables (Gati, Garty, & Fassa, 1996; Rounds, 1990).

Core Aspects of Career Alternatives. Not all aspects are equally important to the characterization of a particular occupational alternative; rather, they vary in relevance and significance (Borgen, 1986; Gati, 1989). Gati et al. (1996) suggested the term *core aspects*, which refers to those aspects that are crucial for characterizing the essence of an occupation. For example, "unconventional working hours" and "using verbal ability intensively" are among the salient characteristics of a newspaper reporter. Thus, the aspects "working hours" and "using verbal ability" may be considered as core aspects of this occupation (whereas "finger dexterity," for example, may not). These two aspects may be less significant, or even irrelevant, for the characterization of another occupation (e.g., mathematician). Defining the core aspects of occupations is important: Occupational choice satisfaction was found to have a higher correlation with the fit between individuals' preferences and the characteristics of their occupation when only the occupation's core aspects were considered than when all aspects were considered (Gati, Garty, & Fassa 1996; Okon, Meir, & Gati, 2000). The core aspects of an occupation can be derived from the judgments of incumbents, vocational psychologists, and occupational information experts, which are summarized in a description of the occupation (e.g., in the Dictionary of Occupational Titles, Occupational Outlook Handbook, and the databases of computer-assisted career information systems).

The Relative Importance of Aspects for the Individual. People's cognitive limitations and limited resources (e.g., time and money) do not allow them to consider all aspects when screening or comparing alternatives (either simultaneously or sequentially). Therefore, it is necessary to locate a subset of aspects that are most important to the individual in the given situation. In order to avoid unrealistic choices, the selection of relevant aspects must take into account physical or external constraints (e.g., disabilities, location of the spouse's workplace).

Within-Aspect Levels. The variations within each aspect can be divided into a number of distinct qualitative or quantitative levels (e.g., for "prestige": very high prestige, above average, average, below average, and low prestige). Most occupations are characterized by more than one level due to within-occupational variance (e.g., Gati, 1986; Katz, 1993; Matarazzo, 1986; Meir & Yaari, 1988; Super, 1953).

Within-Aspect Preferences. The individual's within-aspect preferences are expressed, first, in the level reported as the *optimal*, and second, in the additional level(s) that are regarded as *acceptable*. These additional levels reflect the individual's willingness to compromise with respect to a given aspect (Gati, 1993). The *range of acceptable levels* includes the optimal level and the additional, acceptable level(s), if any. All other levels are considered *unacceptable*. For example, one may regard "working only indoors" as optimal, but be willing to consider as acceptable alternatives which are characterized as "working mainly indoors."

The relative importance of an aspect and the within-aspect preferences are not independent. For example, aspect importance is expected to be negatively correlated with the range of acceptable levels (i.e., the higher the aspect's importance, the smaller the willingness to compromise). However, Gati, Shenhav, and Givon (1993) found that although aspect importance and within-aspect preferences were correlated, the correlations were low. These findings highlight the need to distinguish between aspect importance and within-aspect preferences. Some theoretical constructs (e.g., values, Schwartz, 1996), as well as assessment tools (e.g., the Minnesota Importance Questionnaire, Rounds et al., 1981; the values questionnaire in System of Interactive Guidance and Information, Katz, 1993), tend to confound aspect importance and within-aspect preference. Such confounding is reflected in questions such as "How important is prestige to you?" (which assumes that "high prestige" is the individual's optimal level). The distinction is particularly important in those aspects where the relative importance of an aspect does not indicate the preferred level. For example, high importance for the aspect of "length of training" does not necessarily imply a preference for one of the extreme levels (e.g., "length of training" may be very important to an individual because of a preference for an intermediate length of training (e.g., a 2-year training period).

Structured and Unstructured Information.   The information about each career alternative can be divided into two types (Katz, 1993). Structured information in an occupational database refers to categorical or numerical information that is organized in "fields." The information about each alternative includes a profile of the characteristic level(s) in each aspect (e.g., for a bank teller—working "only indoors," "less than a year" of training, "low" variety, "below average" status, etc.). Structured information enables the individual to search a given database and to find alternatives with the given specification (e.g., length of training beyond high school is one year or less, no need to work with computers).

Unstructured information refers to "soft" data that cannot be mapped into well-defined within-aspect levels (e.g., verbal descriptions of occupations, videoclips of the tasks carried out during routine work, face-to-face encounters with incumbents in an occupation). Such information may be prone to bias and highly dependent on the perceptions of the information providers and the judgments of the database editors and developers (i.e., what to include and how to transform the information collected into the texts included in the database). Both structured and unstructured information are relevant and need to be considered during the career decision-making process. Structured information is useful for a rapid screening of alternatives when their number is large, whereas unstructured information is important for understanding of the "real" nature of the alternatives and making refined comparisons among them.

Sensitivity Analysis. Sensitivity analysis is the investigation of the effects of certain possible changes in the input to the process on its outcome—for example, whether a reasonable change in the individual's preferences (e.g., a willingness to consider other occupations characterized by a medium status level) or in the information about a career alternative (e.g., that it involves working not only indoors, but also partly outdoors), will affect whether a particular alternative is regarded as suitable. A decision is regarded as sensitive to a certain change in the input, if such a change leads to a different outcome. Sensitivity implies that it is crucial to check the validity of the critical information, whereas insensitivity increases the individual's confidence in the decision made. The need for sensitivity analysis arises at the end of each stage of the process.

Readiness for Making a Career Decision

Before starting the career decision-making process, the deliberating individual must ask him or herself the following questions:

- Do I know what steps are involved in making a career decision systematically?
- Am I willing to spend the resources (e.g., time, energy, money) necessary for making a career decision?
- Am I willing to be honest with myself and find out about my strengths and weaknesses?
- Am I ready to cope with the possible conflicts?
- Do I need help in making the decision? If so, do I know where to get it?
- Am I ready to take responsibility for the decision I am about to make?

Many of these questions are associated with career maturity (Crites, 1978; Super, 1953), which was defined by Betz (1988) as "the extent to which the individual has mastered the vocational development tasks, including both knowledge and attitudinal components, appropriate to his or her stage of career development" (p. 80). Readiness also includes dealing with dysfunctional beliefs and thoughts (Krumboltz, 1994; Sampson et al., 1998) and irrational expectations (Nevo, 1987), such as "there is a perfect occupation for me" or "the counselor will find me the right occupation." It is highly desirable to divest oneself of irrational expectations before beginning the career decision-making process. A thorough discussion of difficulties associated with lack of readiness can be found in Gati, Krausz, and Osipow (1996).

The Three Stages of the PIC Model

The essence of the career decision-making process is finding the alternative(s) that are most compatible with the individual's preferences and capabilities. In most cases, it is impractical to explore all potential career alternatives intensively. Hence, we suggest dividing the career decision-making process into three major stages with different goals, processes, and outcomes:

1. Prescreening the potential set of alternatives through a structured search based on the individual's preferences, resulting in a small and thus manageable set of *promising alternatives*;
2. In-depth exploration of the promising alternatives (including examining the possibility of actualizing them), resulting in a few *suitable alternatives*;
3. Choice of the *most suitable alternative*, based on an evaluation and a comparison of all the suitable alternatives.

These three stages are described in the following sections.

Prescreening the Potential Alternatives

In many career-decision situations, the number of potential career alternatives is large (e.g., the number of study majors, two-year colleges, jobs for graduates in computer sciences). The goal of the prescreening stage is to reduce the number of alternatives to a small (e.g., seven or less; see Miller, 1956) and thus a manageable set of promising alternatives, which deserve further attention in the following stages. Such a limited set of promising alternatives enables the individual to collect comprehensive information on each alternative and to process the collected information efficiently. This stage must be carried out carefully to minimize the possibility of discarding potentially suitable alternatives, because any alternative that is not considered "promising" at this stage will be ignored and will not receive further attention.

The prescreening process suggested here is based on the elimination-by-aspects strategy (Tversky, 1972) adapted to vocational decision making and labeled *sequential elimination* by Gati (1986). The basic idea is to locate a small set of promising alternatives by discarding alternatives that are incompatible with the individual's preferences. Specifically, sequential elimination is based on testing the alternatives' compatibility, one aspect at a time, with the sequence of the aspects reflecting their relative importance. Thus, this stage is carried out by within-aspect, across-alternatives comparisons (see Fig. 2.1). This search process permits the individual to proceed fairly easily, yet systematically, even if the initial set of potential alternatives is large. The proposed prescreening stage is divided into five steps (see Fig. 2.2).

Selecting the Relevant Aspects to be Used in the Search.   The search for promising alternatives is based on the individual's preferences in the aspects relevant to him or her (e.g., work environment, length of training, working hours, type of relationship with people). Because of cognitive and material limitations, it is impractical to consider all possible aspects; hence, the individual must choose a subset of the universe of aspects on

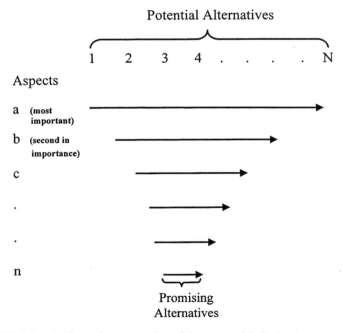

FIG. 2.1.   A schematic presentation of the sequential elimination process (within-aspect, across-alternatives).

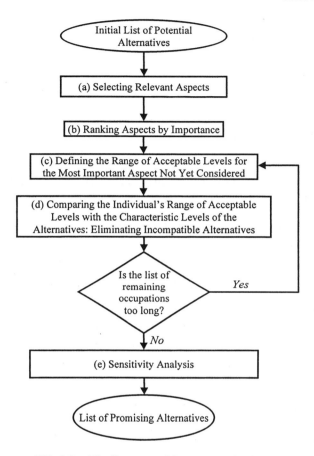

FIG. 2.2.   The five steps of the prescreening stage.

which to focus. Individuals can arrive at such a list of relevant aspects by themselves, based on their life experience and aspirations. However, this step can be facilitated if a list of the potentially relevant aspects is presented to the individual (e.g., by a counselor, a guidebook, a CACGS). This first step is critical because the set of alternatives found to be compatible with the individual's preferences at the end of the search depends on the set of aspects used during the search (Gati, 1994; Katz, 1993).

Ranking the Aspects by Importance.   The sequential elimination is supposed to halt when the number of remaining alternatives is reduced to a small list. Therefore, in many cases, not all the aspects identified as relevant will be considered during the sequential elimination process. Hence, the relevant aspects should be ranked in order of importance, so that the sequential search process can be carried out accordingly (i.e., the search begins with the most important aspect, continues with the second in importance, and so on). In the absence of such a ranking, the search may stop without considering the most important aspects.

Defining the Range of Acceptable Levels for the More Important Aspects. For each aspect considered during the sequential search, the individual's preferences are elicited first by selecting the level regarded as optimal (i.e., the most desirable variation or level in that aspect); then, additional, less desirable but still acceptable level(s) are selected. For example, an individual can consider working "only indoors" as the optimal work environment, but he or she may be willing to compromise on "mainly indoors" or "about equal time indoors and outdoors."

Comparing the Individual's Range of Acceptable Levels With the Characteristic Levels of the Alternatives. The process of sequential elimination begins by screening all potential alternatives and comparing their characteristics with the individual's preferences in the most important aspect. Alternatives that are incompatible with the individual's preferences (i.e., the characteristic levels of an alternative do not overlap even partially with the acceptable range of the individual) are eliminated (see Fig. 2.3, Cases c and d). Note that in cases of "almost overlap" (see Fig. 2.3d), even a small change in the individual's willingness to compromise (e.g., also regarding Level 3 as acceptable) is sufficient to yield a partial overlap and hence prevent the elimination of the alternative. The process is repeated for the remaining aspects (in descending order of importance); it stops when the number of remaining "promising" alternatives is manageable. The use of a range of levels (instead of a single representative level) to characterize career alternatives may prevent the elimination of alternatives in cases where an alternative's single, most typical level does not match the individual's preferences.

Sensitivity Analysis: Checking the Sensitivity of the Results to Possible Changes in Preferences. This step involves reexamining the inputs during the prescreening stage and its outcomes. More specifically, after locating a small set of promising alternatives, it is desirable to reexamine the preceding steps and their outcomes in order to reduce the chances of missing a potentially suitable alternative. This reexamination may involve returning to previous steps and (a) checking whether the reported preferences (e.g., the range of acceptable levels in a particular aspect) still seem acceptable or whether it might be preferable to change them; (b) understanding why certain alternatives, which were considered intuitively appeal-

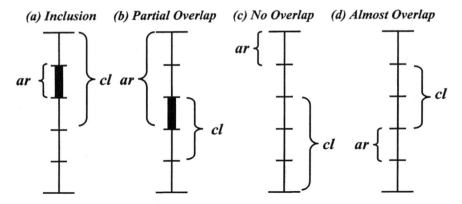

FIG. 2.3. Four examples of a within-aspect compatibility test: A comparison between the acceptable range for the individual (*ar*), and the characteristic levels of an alternative (*cl*).

ing by the individual before the systematic search, were eliminated during the sequential elimination process; (c) locating alternatives which were discarded due to only a small discrepancy in a single aspect, and, for each such alternative, examining the validity of the information with respect to the critical aspect (i.e., the aspect which was the only reason for eliminating the alternative) and considering the possibility of compromising that aspect that was found to be critical.

In-Depth Exploration of the Promising Alternatives

The goal of this stage is to locate a few alternatives that are not only promising but indeed suitable for the individual. The desirable output of the in-depth exploration stage is a list with a few suitable alternatives. These alternatives are regarded as suitable from two perspectives: first, each suitable alternative matches the individual's preferences, and second, the individual meets its requirements. During this stage, the individual is expected to collect additional, mainly unstructured, information on each of the promising alternatives, which can complement the information considered during prescreening. This information is crucial for a better understanding of the essence of each promising alternative, because career alternatives are "more than a simple sum of their features." This stage is also the time for self-exploration (e.g., Blustein, 1989, 1992; Blustein & Phillips, 1988), because core aspects of a certain promising alternative (e.g., working under stress) may raise important questions regarding the individual's fit with the demands of the alternative (e.g., "How well can I perform under highly stressful conditions?").

Because of the nature of the information needed for determining suitability, this stage involves a within-alternative, across-aspects evaluation. Such comprehensive information gathering, however, is possible only after the number of alternatives to be considered has been reduced to a manageable set. If the previous, prescreening stage was conducted efficiently, the input for the in-depth exploration stage is a small list of alternatives that are partially compatible with the individual's preferences. The small number of alternatives makes the task of collecting and processing the additional information feasible.

During the in-depth exploration stage, each alternative is examined with respect to the two facets of suitability (see Fig. 2.4). One facet focuses on whether the alternative indeed suits the individual and the other on

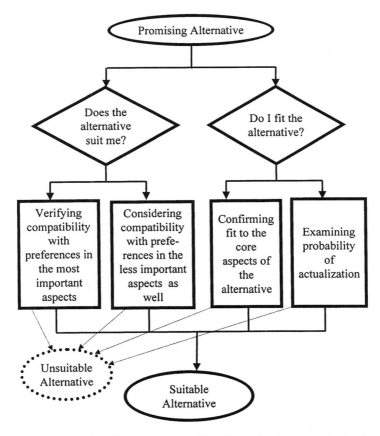

FIG. 2.4.   A suitability test for a promising alternative during the in-depth exploration stage.

whether the individual fits the alternative. The search for answers to these two questions is probably carried out simultaneously during the collection and processing of the information about each of the promising alternatives.

The question of whether an alternative indeed suits the individual involves two suitability conditions. One is verifying the compatibility of each promising alternative with the individual's preferences in the aspects regarded as the most important by him or her, and the other is considering each alternative's compatibility with the individual's preferences in the less important aspects (which were probably not considered during pre-screening). Because the promising alternatives survived elimination in pre-screening, it is clear that they are at least partially compatible with the preferences of the individual in his or her important aspects. However, "zooming in" on the alternative makes it possible to evaluate the relative degree of compatibility in those important aspects, for example, the degree of overlap between the preferred level(s) of work environment (e.g., only indoors) and the characteristic levels (e.g., mainly and only indoors) in a given alternative. Moreover, it is assumed that the individual's preferences may be adjusted during the in-depth exploration, both in terms of optimal level and in terms of what is regarded as acceptable, in light of the additional, more concrete information.

The other facet of suitability involves the individual's fit to a specific alternative, and also comprises two suitability conditions. One is using the collected information to locate the core aspects of each promising alternative and seeing whether the individual indeed meets the requirements specified by these core aspects (e.g., whether the individual is willing to work in shifts—a core aspect of paramedic). Indeed, people often do not realize how important an abstract aspect (e.g., regularity of working hours) is for them, until they zoom in on the core characteristics of career alternatives. The other condition of suitability involves the examination of the probability of actualizing each alternative, considering the individual's previous studies, grades, and achievements (as well as other possible constraints, e.g., time and money) on the one hand and the prerequisites of each alternative regarded as promising (e.g., minimal SAT or ACT score) on the other. Finally, the individual is expected to explore ways of increasing the probability of actualization of certain promising alternatives (e.g., taking a coaching course before being tested again on the SAT or the ACT).

The order in which the suitability conditions are examined is affected by the sequence of the incoming information and its salience rather than the aspect's importance to the individual. Specifically, the suitability test is carried out by considering additional, unstructured verbal or multimedia information. Unstructured information about the alternatives can be found in occupational libraries (e.g., using the *DOT, OOH*), in computerized career information systems (Hinkelman, 1997), and on the Internet (Carson & Cartwright, 1997; Sampson, Kolodinsky, & Greeno, 1997). Additionally, "soft" information should be collected from people who are studying these subjects or working in these occupations (while being aware of the subjectivity and, hence, potential biases of such information). The individual's further self-exploration should focus on capabilities and motivational factors. Career counselors can undoubtedly help in this exploration.

Considering the four suitability conditions often results in a further elimination of alternatives: In case an alternative is found incompatible with respect to even one of the four conditions of suitability, it is regarded as unsatisfying, and discarded from further consideration (see Fig. 2.5). Consequently, the list of the suitable alternatives will probably be shorter than the list of promising alternatives (which thus reduces the complexity of the choice in the next stage). As in the case of prescreening, the suitability tests must be carried out carefully in order to prevent a categorical rejection of an alternative which is suitable. Therefore, when a promising alternative is labeled unsuitable (for whatever reason), it is recommended that the information which caused its elimination be verified and that compromising in the critical aspect be considered. Such a compromise

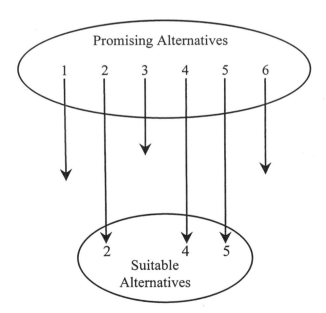

FIG. 2.5. A schematic presentation of the in-depth exploration stage (within-alternative, across aspects).

may prevent the elimination of an alternative that has many advantages which compensate for its disadvantage(s).

Choice of the Most Suitable Alternative

The goal of the third stage is to choose the most suitable alternative for the individual, considering his or her preferences and capabilities, and, if necessary, to select additional, second best alternative(s). This stage involves further processing of the structured and unstructured information that was gathered during the previous stages. The small number of suitable alternatives facilitates the overall evaluation of each one and the necessary detailed comparisons between them. The suggested procedure for the choice stage depends on the number of suitable alternatives and the degree of uncertainty involved in actualizing the most suitable one (see Fig. 2.6).

Choosing the Most Suitable Alternative.

We speculate that many individuals, intentionally or unintentionally, try to end the second stage with a single suitable alternative, and gather information accordingly (e.g., by focusing on favorable features of a preferred alternative and by disregarding unfavorable information about it). This assumption is based on findings from studies of confirmation bias (e.g., Klaynman & Ha, 1987). In such cases, of course, there is no need to compare alternatives, and the individual can directly proceed to the next steps of this stage.

In other cases, however, two (or more) alternatives will be found suitable at the end of the in-depth exploration stage. In such cases, the individual has to compare the suitable alternatives in order to choose the most suitable one. This is done by focusing on those features that distinguish them. A systematic comparison necessarily involves the assessment of compensations in which trade-offs between the aspects are considered, and the alternatives' advantages are contrasted with their disadvantages. In light of the problems with quantitative compensatory models (e.g., the expected utility model or the multiattribute utility model) mentioned earlier, it is proposed that a qualitative, yet systematic, compensatory model, such as Janis and Mann's (1977) balance sheet procedure, or Montgomery's (1989) search for dominance structure, be used.

Specifically, Janis and Mann (1977) suggested that deliberating individuals should list important aspects and then evaluate alternatives by marking their pros and cons (as plus [+] or minus [−] signs, which may vary in magnitude) in each aspect. The alternatives are then compared and ranked according to the overall subjective evaluation of their advantages and disadvantages. An alternative approach is Montgomery's (1989) search for dominance strategy. Montgomery suggested that, because of

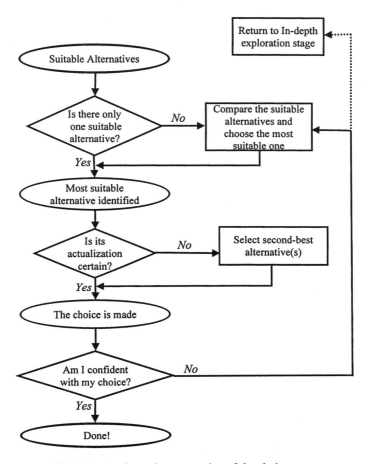

FIG. 2.6.   A schematic presentation of the choice stage.

the typical ease of choice in cases when one alternative dominates others (i.e., is as good as the others in some aspects and better than the others in at least one aspect), people attempt to compare alternatives in such a way that dominance will emerge. According to Montgomery, individuals make approximate, "local" comparisons of the advantages by combining some characteristics of one alternative which are equivalent to some combination of characteristics of the other. For example, the advantage of alternative x over y in terms of the expected higher income may be about equivalent to the advantage of alternative y in terms of better work environment and higher variety. At the end of this process, the individual remains with the "net" advantages of one of the alternatives over the other(s). Note that whereas Janis and Mann's procedure requires only a qualitative evaluation of each alternative in each aspect (+ or −), Montgomery's strategy also involves (although implicitly) quantitative assessments.

The answer to the natural question, "Which of these two models should be used?", depends on several factors. Theoretically, Montgomery's strategy is better than Janis and Mann's procedure for three reasons: First, it considers the size of any existing gap between the individual's optimal level and the characteristic level of a given alternative; second, the relative importance of the aspects is explicitly considered; and third, potential biases (attributable to the dependence among the aspects; e.g., Gati, Fassa, & Mayer, 1998) are much higher in Janis and Mann's (1977) procedure than in Montgomery's (1989).

However, in some cases, Janis and Mann's (1977) procedure may be preferable for practical reasons. For example, when the number of suitable alternatives is greater than two, applying Montgomery's (1989) dominance search strategy may become too cumbersome because this strategy applies to pairs of alternatives. Janis and Mann's balance sheet procedure may be more efficient in such cases because it permits assigning an overall score (e.g., the number of pluses (+) minus the number of minuses (−) for each alternative), and using the simple rule of choosing the one with the highest overall score. Second, Montgomery's strategy is more complex and appears to require greater cognitive skills. Therefore, it may be less suitable for individuals with lower information-processing capabilities, particularly when the number of aspects is relatively large. Future research comparing choice models may highlight the relative effectiveness of these two strategies and may lead to the discovery of additional qualitative, yet systematic, compensatory models.

Selecting Additional Suitable Alternatives. Career decisions are usually made under uncertainty. Specifically, the actualization of a preferred alternative is often uncertain. For instance, the probability of getting a job depends not only on fulfilling minimum requirements, but on the number and quality of other applicants. Thus, the choice of a single alternative in such an important decision may turn out to be a risky gamble. Therefore, after having chosen the preferred, "most suitable" alternative, the individual must assess the probability of actualizing this alternative, using previously gathered information.

If no uncertainty is involved in the actualization (e.g., the individual meets the admission requirements for the training course to be a car mechanic), there is no need to select a second best alternative. If it seems that uncertainty is involved, however, it is highly recommended that the individual go back and search for additional, still suitable alternative(s) that may be regarded as "second best." In cases where the probabilities of actualization of the first and the second best alternatives are relatively low, selecting a "third best," and even a "fourth best," would be advisable.

Furthermore, even in the case when only one alternative was found to be suitable but its actualization is uncertain, the individual may need to go back and reexamine the suitability of promising alternatives which were regarded as "unsuitable" during the in-depth exploration stage. This may involve willingness to compromise more in certain aspects, or willingness to invest more resources in order to increase the chances for actualizing a particular alternative.

Reflecting on the Decision Process

Completing the choice stage ends the systematic career decision-making process, providing the individual with a most suitable alternative, and, in many cases, additional, second best alternatives. If the individual began the process with a long list of potential alternatives, and many aspects were considered during earlier stages, then it is plausible that the overall differences between the suitable alternatives (which survived not only the prescreening but also the in-depth exploration stage) will be small. Thus, it is no longer crucial whether the alternative selected as "best" is, in fact, only second best in terms of overall suitability (i.e., multiattribute utility). Nevertheless, the implementation of the decision may be delayed, impeded, or not carried out if the individual does not truly feel that he or she has made the right decision. Therefore, individuals should be encouraged to review their decision process to be sure that they made the decision correctly and to choose the alternative which is best for them.

The Implementation of the Decision

The implementation of the decision includes the measures that need to be planned and carried out to actualize the individual's chosen alternative. In cases involving uncertainty, these may include taking actions aimed at increasing the chances of actualizing the most suitable alternative. For example, the individual may decide to complete his or her high school studies, as this is a prerequisite for a particular training course leading to the chosen occupation. Sometimes, when uncertainty is involved in the actualization of the alternatives, it is better to try to implement some of them simultaneously (e.g., apply to more than one college). However, in some situations, this may be impossible. In such cases, the individual should try first to actualize the most suitable alternative, and if this attempt fails, proceed according to the rank order of second best alternatives (Gati, 1990b).

Problems or delays in implementation may occur because of lack of readiness or deficiencies in the way the decision was made (Gati, Krausz, & Osipow, 1996). Lack of readiness may be reflected in an unwillingness to take the responsibility for the decision. Delays in implementation may sometimes indicate lack of confidence in the decision. Such delays indicate that the individual needs additional time to reflect on the process itself and on his or her input to it. Individuals with implementation difficulties should be encouraged to actively seek the causes of their lack of confidence. Awareness of the insensitivity of the decision to reasonable changes in the information (e.g., realizing that the chosen alternative will remain the most suitable even if the individual changes his or her preferences in a given aspect in the future) should help the individual to overcome his or her resistance to implementing the decision.

Comparison Among the Three Stages of the PIC Model

In this section, we compare the three stages of the PIC model, highlighting their common and distinctive features.

The "Direction" of Search. A basic difference between the prescreening stage and the in-depth exploration stage is that in the former the search is carried out within-aspect across alternatives, whereas in the latter, it is carried out within-alternative across aspects. The choice stage can be carried out either way, depending on the number of suitable alternatives and the procedure used to compare and evaluate them. This difference in the direction of the search stems from the nature of the stages. Although it is more "natural" for the individual to compare alternatives, because the goal is to select an alternative, such a comparison is clearly impossible when the number of alternatives is large. Because the goal of the prescreening stage is to eliminate alternatives, it is reasonable that screening should be carried out within aspects. Only when the number of alternatives is reduced to a manageable set of promising alternatives can the individual explore them intensively one by one (i.e., within-alternative across aspects).

The Foci of Attention. The goal of prescreening is rejecting unacceptable alternatives, and focusing on those levels of the aspects that are regarded as unacceptable by the individual. During in-depth exploration, however, the goal is to examine the suitability of each of the promising alternatives, and to focus attention on the acceptable levels of the aspects (i.e., checking whether the alternative's characteristics are indeed within the acceptable range). The goal of the choice stage is to choose the best alternative; hence, the focus of attention is on the optimal level for the individual (and the degree to which an alternative matches that level).

Combinations of Preferences and Capabilities. According to the PIC model, the prescreening of alternatives should be carried out with a focus on the individual's preferences ("What do I want?") rather than his or her capabilities or skills ("What can I do?"). We believe that focusing on preferences during prescreening (while taking absolute constraints into account) enhances the motivation for decision making and opens new horizons for the individual. Specifically, the use of preferences can avoid a premature foreclosure due to perceived difficulties (e.g., lack of skills or capabilities, previous schooling, or other relevant prerequisite) or temporary barriers which can be overcome ("If I really want to be a lawyer, it may be worth spending an extra year on improving my undergraduate grades").

On the other hand, if the individual's capabilities lag much behind his or her aspirations, then the compromise involved in the decision may be large, and the individual may experience disappointment and frustration. This, in turn, may lead to lack of motivation to continue the decision-making process or to actualize the alternative found to be most compatible with the individual's preferences and capabilities. However, there are indications that most individuals (psychopathological cases excluded) have a relatively valid self-perception of their abilities (e.g., Katz, 1993; Lunneborg, 1982; Prediger, 1997), which prevents them from stating preferences completely incongruent with their skills (e.g., preference for using finger dexterity by someone who is "all thumbs"). Indeed, people tend to like what they are good at (Barak, 1981; Barak, Librowsky, & Shiloh, 1989; Barak, Shiloh, & Haushner, 1992).

During the in-depth exploration stage, the individual is faced with the need to explore his or her capabilities and check whether they match the requirements of the promising alternatives (i.e., the core aspects of each alternative, as well as the prerequisites needed for its actualization). Thus, this stage involves verifying not only that the alternative matches the individual's preferences ("Does the alternative indeed suit me?") but also that the individuals' capabilities suffice ("Do I fit the alternative?"). Similarly, during the choice stage, the individual has to compare and evaluate the suitable alternatives, taking both preferences and capabilities into account.

Dealing With Compromise in the Three Stages. During prescreening, compromise is manifested in the individual's willingness to widen the range of acceptable levels in the most important aspects. During in-depth exploration, compromise is manifested in the individual's examination of whether the overall compromise associated with a particular alternative is not "too hard to swallow"; that is, whether the sum of within-aspect compromises does not exceed the individual's overall acceptable degree of compromise (Gati, 1993). Compromise is also manifested in the individual's willingness to invest the additional resources to increase the chances of actualization (e.g., to invest time and money in a coaching course for the SAT or the ACT). During the choice stage, compromise is manifested in the individual's willingness to lower the relative weight of certain aspects and to regard almost suitable alternatives as acceptable.

Dealing With Uncertainty in the Three Stages. Uncertainty, like compromise, is an integral part of most career decisions. Uncertainty is generally regarded as undesirable but unavoidable; hence, individuals tend to take measures in order to minimize it. During prescreening, uncertainty concerning the individual's future preferences can be taken into account by the regarding as acceptable not only the optimal level, but also additional level(s). During in-depth exploration, the information gathered can be used to decrease uncertainty about the individual's fit with a promising alternative and the alternative's suitability. During the choice stage, uncertainty in actualization can be dealt with by selecting second best alternative(s) and, if possible, by planning to implement several suitable alternatives simultaneously (e.g., applying to several universities).

RESEARCH RELEVANT TO THE PIC MODEL

In this section, we review a few studies that tested some of the assumptions underlying the PIC model, supported its descriptive validity, and examined the prescriptive utility of the model. First, evidence for screening processes and their utility in decision making is presented. Next, research findings regarding the concept of career-related aspects and their potential utility during the career decision-making process are summarized. Finally, the results of studies which compared different career decision strategies are reviewed.

Prescreening Processes

Payne (1976) used the "information board" paradigm (turning over cards to get information concerning a specific aspect and a particular alternative) and analyses of verbal protocols to study information-collection patterns and decision-making strategies. Payne found that when the number of alternatives was small (e.g., 2), subjects employed a strategy of collecting the same amount of information about each of the alternatives. Such a strategy is compatible with a compensatory model. However, as the number of alternatives to be considered increased (from 2 to 12), subjects shifted to decision strategies that involved eliminating some alternatives on the basis of only a few aspects. This pattern indicated that, when faced with many alternatives, subjects tended to adopt decision strategies that would permit them to eliminate some of the available alternatives as quickly as possible on the basis of a limited amount of information.

Paquette and Kida (1988) compared a few decision strategies as employed by decision makers under differing levels of task complexity (ranging from 2 to 9 alternatives, and 5 aspects). The task required that the subjects, who were professionals, evaluate financial data and select the firm with the highest bond ratings. They found that with greater task complexity (5 and 9 alternatives), an elimination-by-aspects or a mixed strategy (combination of elimination and then compensation) required significantly less time than the more complex compensatory strategy. Neither of these strategies resulted in reduced accuracy (i.e., whether the objectively "best" option was selected).

Gati and Kibari (2000) analyzed the pattern of vocational information search using the same paradigm (an information board of 40 career alternatives × 34 career-related aspects). Participants reported their preferences by responding to a questionnaire in which they were required to rate the importance of the 34 aspects for their decision and to indicate their preferences in each of these aspects, either before or after using the information board. This questionnaire made it possible to evaluate the utility of each alternative for each of the participants, using the multiattribute utility model. In general, the pattern of information seeking was compatible with that expected according to the PIC model. Specifically, the percentage of systematic steps increased during the process, and the relative frequency of within-aspect steps decreased, whereas that of the within-alternative steps increased. Furthermore, participants who used a process resembling the PIC selected an alternative which fitted their preferences better than that selected by those who did not use such a process.

Gati, Saka, and Krausz (2000) examined the effect of using Making Better Career Decisions, a CACGS designed to facilitate prescreening of career alternatives, that follows the steps outlined in the PIC model. A comparison of the responses of users to the *Career Decision-making Difficulties Questionnaire* (Gati, Krausz, & Osipow, 1996) before and after the dialogue with the system revealed the expected effect. Specifically, difficulties related to lack of knowledge about how to make a career decision, and lack of information about self and occupational alternatives significantly decreased, whereas only negligable changes were observed in other difficulty categories (e.g., lack of motivation, dysfunctional beliefs, external conflicts).

Beach and his colleagues (Beach, 1993, 1998; Beach & Potter, 1992; Beach & Strom, 1989) provided empirical evidence for the distinct nature of the prescreening and choice stages of the decision-making process in several areas, including career decision making. According to Beach (1993), alternatives are prescreened with a noncompensatory compatibility test (i.e., alternatives are eliminated if they violate preferences in relevant aspects). In one of these studies, Beach and Strom (1989) asked subjects to assume the role of a recent graduate looking for a job, using a standard description of the job seeker's preferences in 16 career-related aspects, and an array of potential jobs. Their results supported the hypothesis that screening relies almost exclusively on violations of preferences. Further results indicated that the subjects regard screening and choice as two distinct tasks.

A study by Gati and Tikotzki (1989) provided empirical support for the descriptive validity of the prescreening stage of the PIC model in real-life career decision situations. They analyzed the monitored dialogues of 384 career counselees with a computer-assisted career information system. They found that most users (96%) employed a noncompensatory strategy during all or at least a part of the dialogue, both for locating promising alternatives compatible with their preferences and for exploring and collecting information on these alternatives. Specifically, the patterns of transitions between modules of the system indicated that many options considered at a previous stage of the dialogue were not considered at the following stage. This pattern can be interpreted as showing that individuals tend to use a prescreening strategy based on eliminating alternatives; then, using the obtained information, individuals decide that there is no reason to collect more information on some of the career options considered at a previous stage. Thus, the results of the studies by Beach and his colleagues, as well as those of Gati and Tikotzki, suggest that incorporating a systematic prescreening stage into the career decision-making process is compatible with the strategies individuals tend to use naturally when facing many alternatives.

The Advantages of Using Career-Related Aspects

The aspects-based approach provides a basis for eliciting and using the individual's preferences in the career decision-making process. A detailed description and discussion of the aspects-based approach can be found in Gati (1998). Following is a brief review of some of the major findings.

Aspects and Dimensions. Benyamini and Gati (1987) found that using 13 aspects rather than the two dimensions suggested by Prediger (1982) as underlying his world-of-work map (people–things and data–ideas) more than doubled the percentage of variance accounted for in the perceived occupational structure of the subjects (from 35% to 76%). These results support the claim that people perceive occupations in terms of a large set of career-related aspects, and not only a few characteristics, as Prediger's two-dimensional map implies. The results also suggest that individuals take more considerations into account than sex-type, prestige, and fields of interests, as implied by Gottfredson's (1981) circumscription and compromise theory.

Aspects and Interests.   Gati and Winer (1987) investigated the relations between vocational interests (measured by the Ramak interest inventory, Meir & Barak, 1974) and the ideal occupation (elicited in terms of career-related aspects) of 96 career counselees. Intrasubject analyses indicated that the participants' vocational interests, as expressed in their ratings of the relative attractiveness of occupational fields, were reflected in the fields' perceived proximity to the individual's ideal occupation. (The median of within-subject correlations was .53.)

Core Aspects Are What Matters.   Meir and Yaari (1988) and Rounds, Dawis, and Lofquist (1987) investigated the congruence hypothesis within occupations. Their findings suggest that not all aspects contribute to P–E fit to the same degree. Gati, Garty, and Fassa (1996) elicited the career-related preferences of 360 professionals (30 in each of 12 occupations) in 30 career-related aspects, and asked them to report their degree of satisfaction with their occupational choice. The correlation between occupational choice satisfaction and P–E fit, assessed using all 30 aspects, was .27. This finding is similar to those studies in which P–E fit was measured using vocational interests (e.g., Assouline & Meir, 1987; Holland, 1985; Spokane, 1985). However, when P–E fit was assessed using only the core aspects, the correlation with occupational choice satisfaction was greater (.85). Similarly, Okon, Meir, and Gati (2000) found that two core aspects of teachers (i.e., "working with children and adolescents" and "teaching and instructing") predicted occupational choice satisfaction better than all 40 aspects taken together. These findings provide empirical support for the potential advantage of using career-related aspects and, in particular, core aspects (instead of vocational interests) for assessing P–E fit.

Empirical Comparisons Between Career Decision-Making Strategies

Mau and Jepsen (1992) taught students either the sequential elimination strategy or the expected utility strategy. Their findings suggested that teaching either strategy to students with a rational decision-making style affected their career decision-making process. When those students used the sequential elimination strategy, they showed less anxiety and indecision and greater certainty in their choice than those who used the expected utility strategy. In contrast, students who used the expected utility strategy exceeded the others in the complexity of reasons for their choices.

Lichtenberg, Shaffer, and Arachtingi (1993) compared the sequential elimination and the expected utility strategies, and found that the choices made using a sequential elimination strategy or without the use of a formal strategy were similar. This was interpreted as indicating that the sequential elimination strategy may be more natural for decision makers than the expected utility strategy. As hypothesized, the expected utility of careers selected using the sequential elimination strategy was significantly lower than that of those selected using the expected utility strategy, but the absolute difference was relatively small (.94 for sequential elimination in comparison to 1.00, by definition, for expected utility). However, the within-subject design, the lack of distinction between aspect importance and within-aspect preferences, and the use of elimination until only a single alternative remained, all decrease the generalizability of the results of this study.

Zakay and Tsal (1993) explored the effects of forced decision-making strategies on postdecision confidence. First, they found that even when the number of alternatives was small (i.e., three), only 32% of the subjects used a compensatory strategy in comparison to 37% who used a noncompensatory strategy consistently. In the second stage of the experiment, they taught the subjects one of two decision strategies—compensatory or sequential elimination. They found that forcing a decisional strategy incompatible with the subject's intuitive preference decreased postdecision confidence.

DISCUSSION

The PIC model is proposed as a framework for a dynamic and flexible decision-making process in which the individual plays an active role during all stages of decision making. The PIC model allows individuals to enter the process at different stages. For example, an individual who has already formulated a small list of promising alternatives (and wishes to skip systematic prescreening, which could help verify the adequacy of this list) may start immediately with the in-depth exploration stage. Moreover, the PIC model allows individuals to move back and forth in the decision-making process. For example, if individuals discover during the in-depth exploration stage that a particular aspect is more important for them than previously judged, they can return to the prescreening stage and again carry out the sequential elimination process, according to their revised preferences.

Although the PIC model is described here as a three-stage process, to be carried out at a particular time, it is important to explicitly acknowledge that career decisions can be made throughout the individual's lifetime. Even after a systematic choice of a major or a field of study, the individual constantly encounters new incoming information. People's life experience can lead them to update their preferences in two ways: by modifying the relative importance they attribute to the various aspects and by changing the specific levels they regard as optimal or acceptable. Although in some cases, time brings about a greater willingness to compromise (i.e., to widen the range of acceptable levels), in others, the individual's willingness to compromise decreases. At the same time, people's perceptions of the world of work (and in particular the course of study or career they have selected) change. In addition, changes in the salience of the various life roles (Super, 1990) often affect the individual's career-related preferences. For example, parents of young children probably attribute more importance to aspects such as "amount of travel" and "working hours" in their career decision than they will in later stages of life. These aspects usually receive less attention when young adults are at the stage of choosing their college major.

Furthermore, it is important to acknowledge the fact that the PIC model deals with career choice from a cognitive point of view (see also Barak, chap. 5, this volume), without much elaboration of the affective facets of career decision making and career counseling. The role of affect in readiness for the decision-making process, during the three stages of the process and then during implementation, deserves further attention, which exceeds the scope of this chapter. Nevertheless, we believe that some of the emotional problems and indecisiveness may be attributed to the lack of a framework for approaching career decision making. We believe that the PIC model can provide a guiding framework. In the following sections, we deal with the relations between PIC and other approaches for career decision making, including intuitive career decision making, P–E fit models, and normative decision theory (NDT). We end by discussing the research and counseling implications of the PIC model.

Intuition in Career Decision Making

Intuition is an important guide for most decisions, including career choices. However, intuition appears to be affected by incomplete and biased information (e.g., prejudice and stereotypes). Most vocational psychologists and career counselors would probably agree with the claim that intuition is not enough for making good career decisions, yet it should not be ignored either. Therefore, although any suggested prescriptive model should be thorough and systematic, it should also allow (or even encourage) individuals to pay attention to their intuition during the process.

Note that intuition is almost always present at the beginning of the process. Informal observations suggest that most individuals do not start the decision-making process without any direction; in fact, some of them even have a few specific alternatives, or even a single alternative, in mind. However, even in these cases, it is highly recommended that a systematic prescreening be carried out, starting from a large array of potential alternatives. First, this may help to locate additional suitable alternatives of which the individual was not aware. Second, if alternatives which were previously only intuitively considered as promising emerge in a systematic search, the individual's confidence in regarding those alternatives as worth further exploration should increase. If, however, an intuitively promising alternative does not emerge as such in the systematic search, the reason why it was eliminated should be investigated. One possibility is a gap between the individual's explicit preferences used during prescreening and the implicit preferences that underlie his or her intuitions. In such cases, the individual can reconsider his or her preferences and decide whether to change them in order to avoid eliminating this alternative. Another possibility is that the difference is caused by the individual's inaccurate perception of this career alternative.

We speculate that the role of intuition during the in-depth exploration stage is more subtle, and is manifested in directing the individual's attention to certain parts of the information collected. As previously discussed, during this stage, the individual may develop a preference for one of the alternatives, and search for information that may support it and justify choosing it. Awareness of such potential biases may decrease their impact.

Intuitions also play an important role during the choice stage, in cases where the individual has to choose from among a few suitable alternatives. Because all the alternatives under consideration at this point were found to be suitable for the individual after a systematic exploration, a natural tendency may be to follow one's intuition. However, even in such cases, systematic comparison is important for confirming the individual's intuition. If the intuitively favored alternative also emerges as the most suitable in the systematic comparison during the choice stage, then the individual's confidence in choosing that alternative should increase. If not, the individual should look for the causes of the difference between intuition and the outcome of the systematic process. It may be assumed that in most cases the difference will be due to the fact that certain aspects considered intuitively were assigned different weights during the systematic comparison. If the individual tends to choose according to his or her intuition, then the chosen alternative (and particularly its disadvantages) should be compared to the alternative that was found to be best in the systematic comparison.

Comparison of the P–E Fit Approach
and the PIC Model

Both P–E fit and the PIC model are aimed at increasing the fit between the individual and his or her work environment. The focus of P–E fit approach is on the outcome, where the goal is the best fit (typically using interests, needs, or values). The focus of PIC, however, is not only on the outcome—locating the most suitable alternative—but also on the process used for arriving at it. Prescreening based on aspects, rather than solely on interests or needs, makes it possible to take into account a larger and a more flexible set of considerations. Furthermore, the P–E fit approach implies a single-step prescreening, without explication of the additional steps required to locate the "best" alternative. In contrast, PIC prescribes a multistep, systematic and interactive process, in which the individual takes an active role, focusing on assuring compatibility. Furthermore, PIC allows the individual to return to previous stages and encourages dynamic simulations. Finally, the notion of the "core aspects" of alternatives provides a promising way to improve congruence.

One of the differences between PIC and the traditional approaches to P–E fit is the use of career-related aspects, rather than interests only, for prescreening career alternatives. We suggest that the use of aspects for prescreening is preferable for three reasons. First, some aspects refine the vocational interests of the individual by focusing on different components of each type or field, thus providing a better differentiation among occupations which belong to the same field (Gati, 1998; Gati, Fassa, & Mayer, 1998). For example, although preferences for "the field of technology" and "using technical ability" are correlated with preferences for working with "materials" and with "tools and instruments," certain individuals may prefer only the first two and avoid the last two; moreover, some occupations seem to fit this particular pattern (e.g., electronic engineer). Second, other aspects go beyond vocational interests and seem to be fairly independent (e.g., Rounds, 1990). These aspects include prestige, work values, personal styles (e.g., Harmon et al., 1994), and aspects such as "length of training," "income," "professional advancement" and "amount of travel," which are often included in CACGSs (Gati, 1996; Katz, 1993). Thus, information concerning these aspects, which cannot be considered when one focuses only on interests, distinguishes individuals (or occupations) which are characterized by the same interests (e.g., the same three-letter code). Third, the use of aspects provides a convenient means for taking the individual's development and changing needs into account. The claim that interests reflect personality (e.g., Holland, 1985) assumes that, like other personality characteristic, a person's interests tend to be relatively stable throughout his or her life. The focus on preferences, in contrast, enables the person to shape a different image of his or her "ideal alternative" at different times.

It may be claimed that prescreening should begin with the consideration of the individual's vocational interests, and then continue by considering additional aspects, until the set of promising alternatives is reduced to a manageable size (E. Meir, personal communication, 1998). In fact, because of the many alternatives that match any given interest profile, counselors typically encourage their counselees to consider additional factors. This approach stems from the assumption that using interests first is an effective way to eliminate irrelevant career alternatives.

However, one of the basic features of the prescreening stage as suggested in the PIC model is that the elimination process is carried out starting from the most important aspect, and continues along the importance rank-order of the aspects for the individual. Therefore, starting the prescreening with interests means forcing a specific order of importance on the individual, in which interests are the most important aspects. It may be claimed, that for certain individuals, other aspects (e.g., prestige, sex-type; Gottfredson, 1981) are more important than interests. Indeed, Gati, Osipow, and Givon (1995) reported great variability among individuals in the relative importance of 43 aspects (including interests). Therefore, in the proposed PIC model, it is the individual who decides on the relative importance of the aspects for him or her.

Comparison of NDT and the PIC Model

According to both NDT and PIC, the choice is the outcome of a systematic, analytic decision process. However, these two approaches differ in the way this goal is achieved. The basic tenet of NDT is rationality, whereas that of PIC is "bounded rationality" (Simon, 1957). Thus, the notion of maximization in NDT is replaced by optimization in PIC. The one-step computation of overall utility (or expected utility) in NDT is replaced by sequential tests of compatibility. This allows the individual to monitor the process and its outcomes (e.g., by asking why a particular alternative is incompatible with his or her preferences) and make adjustments, if necessary. In the typical application of NDT-based models, the focus is on the comparison between the optimal level for the individual and the most characteristic level of the alternative. In the PIC model, however, within-occupational variance is explicitly considered in the comparison between the individual's preferences and the alternatives' characteristics. In addition, PIC allows the individual to express within-aspect preferences not only in terms of the optimal level but also as a range of acceptable levels (and thus to explicitly express willingness to compromise). Quantitative assessments in NDT are replaced by qualitative assessments in PIC, in a way that still permits a structured search during pre-screening. Finally, although PIC is also a systematic model, it is more natural and less complex than most NDT models, and it is applicable even when the number of potential alternatives is large.

One of the assumptions underlying compensatory models (e.g., multi-attribute and expected utility) is "independence" among aspects (Bell & Raiffa, 1988). However, a recent study by Gati, Fassa, and Mayer (1998) demonstrated that this assumption is clearly violated in career decisions. To uncover the structure of aspects, they used factor and cluster analyses of two large data sets (the occupational database of a CACGS, which included information on 300 occupations, and the career-related preferences of 2,000 counselees reported during their monitored dialogues with the system). Both the factor and the cluster analyses showed that the two aspect structures are highly similar. More importantly, the observed positive correlations between the aspects and the variance in the size of the correlations showed that the aspects are not independent. This conclusion holds for both individuals' preferences and the characteristics of occupations. This dependence implies that the results of compensatory model-based calculations will necessarily be biased, because correlated aspects will be given higher weight than they deserve.

Implications

Research Implications

In this section we propose possible ways to further examine some features of the PIC model, compare it with the traditional models, and investigate the possible differential contribution of teaching the PIC model to individuals with different career decision-making styles.

The PIC Model.   Prescreening is the first stage of the PIC model. The major research question regarding the prescreening stage involves the utility of sequential elimination, using career-related aspects, for this stage. Specifically, the advantages and disadvantages of using career-related aspects, rather than only interests, for screening career alternatives need to be examined. The individual's satisfaction with the list of promising alternatives and a professional counselor's judgment regarding the quality of such a list may serve as possible criteria for such a comparison. Research should aim at finding the characteristics of a "good" prescreening. From a theoretical viewpoint, and assuming the availability of a computerized database, one can compare prescreening based on sequential elimination with that based on a multiattribute utility model. From a more practical viewpoint, there is a question of what is the "best" size for the set of promising alternatives at the end of this stage, and what is the optimal degree of homogeneity of the alternatives included in the list of promising alternatives.

In contrast to the two-step process described by Beach and Potter (1992), the PIC model explicitly prescribes an additional stage, the in-depth exploration stage, between screening and choice. Future research should examine the descriptive validity of this proposed stage. First, its "vertical" (i.e., within-alternative, across-aspects) character should be examined; second, there is a question of whether the four suitability conditions adequately represent all relevant categories of information needed for determining whether a promising alternative is indeed suitable; third, the relative salience of the four suitability conditions has to be examined.

Additional questions involve the choice stage. First, it is important to empirically investigate the relative frequency of cases where the in-depth exploration stage ends with only a single option (and hence there is no need for a formal procedure for comparing suitable alternatives). If there is a need to choose among several suitable alternatives, then there is a question of what the best procedure is for comparing them: Is there a need for a formal model at all and, if so, which of the models should be applied? Finally, the PIC model suggests in some cases that a ranked list of suitable alternatives should be prepared, in order to deal with the uncertainty involved in actualizing the most suitable one. However, it may be claimed that such a ranking decreases the individual's motivation to implement the most suitable alternative. Therefore, future research should examine the utility of using a ranked list in cases involving uncertainty.

The PIC Model Versus Traditional Models.   The major question for comparing the utility of the various models of career decision making is "How do we measure the quality of the decision?" Katz (1979) highlighted the importance of evaluating the process used to make the decision, whereas Krumboltz et al. (1982) defined quality in terms of the degree to which the chosen alternative matches the individual's goals. It seems that quality should be assessed with respect to both criteria. However, because different measures may best fit different models, we speculate that PIC should be compared separately with P–E fit and NDT-based models. Such a comparison, however, may be problematic when the definition of "best match" is theory-dependent. Nevertheless, research should aim at comparing the practical utility of career decisions based on different models, using concurrent and longitudinal research designs. It is desirable that such a comparison utilize various criteria (e.g., occupational choice satisfaction, stability, success).

The Differential Contribution of Teaching the PIC Model to Individuals With Different Career Decision-Making Styles. The effects of teaching PIC on career indecision should be empirically investigated. Specifically, it may be hypothesized that teaching PIC can decrease difficulties stemming from a lack of knowledge about the career decision-making process (Gati, Krausz, & Osipow, 1996) and increase career decision-making self-efficacy (Taylor & Betz, 1983). It may be claimed, however, that the PIC model is of greatest help to individuals with a rational decision-making style, who are already inclined to systematic decision making. Indeed, previous research (e.g., Mau & Jepsen, 1992) has demonstrated that individuals with a rational career decision-making style benefit more from instruction in a systematic model. Thus, the contribution of PIC to individuals with intuitive and dependent styles, in terms of Harren's (1979) classification, needs to be assessed.

Counseling Implications

The proposed PIC model, derived from decision theory, implies that one of the major roles of career counselors is to serve as decision counselors. Adopting the framing of "decision counseling" assumes that one of the goals of career counseling is to facilitate the active decision-making process of deliberating individuals, rather than having the counselor find the best match. In addition, decision counseling implies fostering effective decision making—guiding individuals through the process, while taking into account each individual's career decision-making style, cognitive limitations, and material constraints. This guidance implies tailoring the process to each individual's problems, difficulties, and characteristics. In this section, we discuss the implications of the proposed framework for face-to-face counseling as well as the use of CACGSs, highlighting possible roles of career counselors in each of the proposed stages.

Assessing and Increasing Readiness. Typically, part of the first counseling session is devoted to an initial diagnosis, which includes assessing the client's career readiness. This assessment may include evaluating the client's general level of career indecision (e.g., with the Career Decision Scale; Osipow, Carney, & Barak, 1976), or examining his or her specific difficulties in making the decision (e.g., with the *Career Decision-making Difficulties Questionnaire*; Gati, Krausz, & Osipow, 1996). In addition, the assessment may include some (informal and subjective) assessment of the general level of the client's cognitive abilities (particularly verbal communication skills) and career decision-making style (Harren, 1979; Johnson, 1978). This information is crucial for conducting an effective counseling process that is tailored to the specific needs of the client.

At the same time, the counselor may find that some intervention is needed before the decision-making process starts in order to raise the client's level of readiness for the process. Such intervention may be aimed at one or more of the following issues:

1. Dealing with general indecisiveness. This is not a trivial challenge, and may require more intense and longer intervention, which, however, has the potential of helping the client in many areas of life requiring decision making.
2. Dismantling dysfunctional beliefs and thoughts (Krumboltz, 1994; Sampson et al., 1998) and irrational expectations (e.g., Nevo, 1987) concerning the career decision-making process and the career counseling process. We speculate that it is important to elicit the client's dysfunctional beliefs during the "expectations-matching" phase and deal with them one by one, as they arise.
3. Explaining the decision-making process to the client. This includes explaining the basic rationale of the systematic procedure, and its advantages over a haphazard choice, explicating relevant terms underlying the PIC model, describing the three stages of the PIC model, and presenting their specific steps.

Guiding and Monitoring the Career Decision-Making Process.   One of the roles of a career counselor is to monitor the career decision-making process of the client. This monitoring, however, is different in each of the three stages. During the prescreening stage, the counselor is expected to encourage the client to explicate his or her optimal preferences, yet consider compromise in terms of within-aspect levels. If the client has problems explicating preferences, the counselor can help by directing the client to recall relevant past experiences and his or her feelings in those situations. During the in-depth exploration stage, the counselor may facilitate the career decision-making process by introducing the four suitability conditions and directing the client to various sources of information. During the choice stage, the counselor may need to suggest a systematic method of comparing suitable alternatives (e.g., using Janis & Mann's, 1977, balance sheet procedure, or Montgomery's, 1989, search for dominance structure). Finally, the counselor should encourage the client to reflect on the decision-making process and its outcome, in order to increase his or her confidence in the final choice. This may be a crucial condition for the successful implementation of the decision.

Facilitating Implementation.   After the client has reached a decision and is satisfied with it, the counselor has to ensure that the client knows what to do in order to actualize the chosen alternative. In addition, the counselor should emphasize the advantage of the list of ranked alternatives, in case the preferred alternative cannot be actualized.

The Potential Contribution of CACGSs During the Three Stages of the PIC Model. Increasingly more career counselors incorporate the use of CACGSs into the face-to-face career counseling process and use such systems as an integral part of their interaction with their clients. Indeed, CACGSs can be useful in decision counseling. Specifically, CACGSs can be extremely helpful during prescreening, for locating promising alternatives from the large number included in the CACGS' database. CACGSs can also be used for the in-depth exploration of these promising alternatives. For example, CACGSs can provide structured and unstructured information about the core characteristics and requirements of the alternatives on the one hand as well as information concerning the individual's chances of actualizing the alternative on the other. CACGSs can also guide the deliberating individual to additional sources of information. We believe that the presently available CACGSs cannot help when the individual reaches the choice stage. Any CACGS is based on a formal model, which specifies the algorithms for comparing and evaluating the career alternatives. Such models, however, cannot validly represent the process individuals use to compare and evaluate suitable alternatives; hence, the resulting numerical values cannot adequately represent the outcomes of such processes. Thus, we suggest that choice be made without the use of a computer. Rather, a significant other or a career counselor may provide better help to the individual at this stage than a computer.

The counselor's awareness of the unique advantages and disadvantages of the particular CACGS used is crucial in preparing the client for the dialogue and incorporating its outcomes into the counseling process. Of course, no computer can replace the human qualities of a counselor. The face-to-face personalized contact and human support provided by counselors is needed for helping clients resolve internal conflicts between incompatible preferences and external conflicts with significant others, and acknowledge and accept their own weaknesses and disadvantages. Personal counseling may also be needed for providing refined judgments and sensitive evaluations, restructuring the decision, and reframing the compromises involved in order to reduce their negative consequences (Gati, Houminer, & Aviram, 1998; Gati, Houminer, & Fassa, 1997). Finally, counselors have a unique contribution in helping their clients explore ways for increasing the prospects of realizing the chosen alternative.

Implications for Teaching Career Decision Making
in High Schools and Colleges

Jepsen (1991) claimed that teaching individuals how to address problems is at least as important in career guidance as discovering what solution they should apply. The PIC model appears to be a potential framework for teaching decision making in high schools and colleges. First, PIC suggests explicit procedures for gathering and processing information. Second, PIC seems easier to comprehend than quantitative normative decision theory-based models. Finally, instruction in the PIC model can be helpful to students in other decisions as well.

It is proposed that instruction should focus on four issues. First, the advantages and the basic rationale of the systematic procedure (instead of a haphazard choice) should be highlighted. Second, the necessity of dealing with compromise and uncertainty must be emphasized. Third, terms such as *alternatives, aspects, relative importance, within-aspect levels, optimal level,* and *acceptable range* need to be presented and explained. Finally, the stages and specific steps of the process have to be presented.

Jepsen (1991) raised the possibility of using computers for instructing individuals in career decision making. He highlighted the advantages of computers in providing a private, interactive environment, fitting the needs of every student, sustaining the student's attention to task, and saving instruction time. Such instruction may be explicit, as part of a distinct dedicated module, or implicit, as a part of the individual's dialogue with a CACGS. In fact, teaching career decision making has been incorporated into several computer-assisted career decision-making systems (e.g., DISCOVER, 1996; Gati, 1996; Katz, 1993).

Conclusion

In this chapter, we outlined a possible "prescription" for a systematic career decision-making process, in which the deliberating individual plays not only an active role but the leading one. The PIC model appears to be most appropriate for career choices with a relatively large number of alternatives, such as selecting a college or university, a major, or a job after graduation. However, the PIC model may be appropriate, with slight changes, for other decision situations with many potential alternatives (e.g., buying a car, house, or selecting a vacation site).

The proposed PIC model aims at facilitating decision making and promoting better decisions. Specifically, PIC appears preferable to the prevalent, P–E fit models such as Holland's and the TWA on the one hand and NDT based models on the other. In addition, PIC appears to be more natural and understandable to individuals. It is more compatible with people's cognitive limitations and finite material resources, and apparently resembles the way individuals act intuitively when faced with the need to choose from a very large set of career alternatives.

The growing rate of change in the world of work increases the number of career decisions individuals have to make during their lifetime. The need to make a career decision can originate from an external source (e.g., because of downsizing) or from an internal motive (e.g., changes in preferences and needs). These decisions can be made either casually or systematically. According to the proposed PIC model, in each such decision situation, the individual should reexamine his or her preferences and capabilities, based on previous life experience, and use this information systematically in the decision-making process. Using PIC, we believe, can help individuals achieve the goal of making better career decisions.

ACKNOWLEDGMENTS

The ideas expressed in this chapter benefited from many valuable discussions with Samuel H. Osipow during the two research projects supported by the US-Israel Binational Science Foundation (1992–1995, 1995–1998). We thank Nurit Adler, Tamar Amir, Amia Barak, Azy Barak, Beni Benjamin, Tali Ever-Hadani, Naomi Fassa, Naomi Goldblum, Shoshana Hellman, Leah Israelovitz, Liat Kibari, Fred T. L. Leong, Elchanan I. Meir, Ofra Nevo, Naomi Okon, Dale Prediger, Gal Ram, Lilach Sagiv, Noa Saka, Laurence Shatkin, and Shoshana Shiloh for their helpful comments on an earlier version of this chapter.

REFERENCES

Assouline, M., & Meir E. I. (1987). Meta-analysis of the relationship between congruence and well-being measures. *Journal of Vocational Behavior, 31*, 319–332.

Barak, A. (1981). Vocational interests: A cognitive view. *Journal of Vocational Behavior, 19*, 1–14.

Barak, A., Librowsky, I., & Shiloh, S. (1989). Cognitive determinants of interests: An extension of a theoretical model and initial empirical examinations. *Journal of Vocational Behavior, 34*, 318–334.

Barak, A., Shiloh, S., & Haushner, O. (1992). Modification of interests through cognitive restructuring: Tests of a theoretical model in preschool children. *Journal of Counseling Psychology, 39*, 490–497.

Beach, L. R. (1993). Broadening the definition of decision making: The role of prechoice screening of options. *Psychological Science, 4*, 215–220.

Beach, L. R. (1998). *Image theory: Theoretical and empirical foundations.* Mahwah, NJ: Lawrence Erlbaum Associates.

Beach, L. R., & Potter, R. E. (1992). The pre-choice screening of options. *Acta Psychologica, 81*, 115–126.

Beach, L. R., & Strom, E. (1989). A toadstool among the mushrooms: Screening decisions and image theory's compatibility test. *Acta Psychologica, 72,* 1–12.

Bell, D. E., & Raiffa, H. (1988). Risky choice revisited. In D. E. Bell, H. Raiffa, & A. Tversky (Eds.), *Decision making* (pp. 99–112). New York: Cambridge University Press.

Bell, D. E., Raiffa, H., & Tversky, A. (1988). Descriptive, normative, and prescriptive interactions in decision making. In D. E. Bell, H. Raiffa, & A. Tversky (Eds.), *Decision making* (pp. 9–30). New York: Cambridge University Press.

Benyamini, Y., & Gati, I. (1987). Perception of occupations: Aspects versus dimensions. *Journal of Vocational Behavior, 30,* 309–329.

Betz, N. E. (1988). The assessment of career development and maturity. In W. B. Walsh & S. H. Osipow (Eds.), *Career decision making* (pp. 77–136). Hillsdale, NJ: Lawrence Erlbaum Associates.

Blustein, D. L. (1989). The role of career exploration in the career decision making of college students. *Journal of College Student Development, 30,* 111–117.

Blustein, D. L. (1992). Applying current theory and research in career exploration to practice. *Career Development Quarterly, 41,* 174–184.

Blustein, D. L., & Phillips, S. D. (1988). Individual and contextual factors in career exploration. *Journal of Vocational Behavior, 33,* 203–216.

Blustein, D. L., & Phillips, S. D. (1990). Relation between ego identity statuses and decision-making styles. *Journal of Counseling Psychology, 37,* 160–168.

Borgen, F. H. (1986). New approaches to the assessment of interests. In W. B. Walsh & S. H. Osipow (Eds.), *Advances in vocational psychology: The assessment of interests* (pp. 83–125). Hillsdale, NJ: Lawrence Erlbaum Associates.

Bridges, J. S. (1989). Sex differences in occupational values. *Sex Roles, 20,* 205–211.

Brown, D. (1990). Models of career decision making. In D. Brown, L., Brooks, & Associates (Eds.), *Career choice and development* (2nd ed., pp. 395–421). San Francisco, CA: Jossey-Bass.

Brown, S. D., & Gore, P. A. (1994). An evaluation of interest congruence indices: Distribution characteristics and measurement properties. *Journal of Vocational Behavior, 45,* 310–327.

Camp, C. C., & Chartrand, J. M. (1992). A comparison and evaluation of interest congruence indices. *Journal of Vocational Behavior, 41,* 162–182.

Carson, A. D., & Cartwright, G. F. (1997). Fifth-generation computer-assisted career guidance systems. *Career Planning and Adult Development Journal, 31,* 19–40.

Carson, A., & Mowsesian, R. (1990). Some remarks on Gati's theory of career decision-making models. *Journal of Counseling Psychology, 37,* 502–507.

Crites, J. O. (1969). *Vocational psychology.* New York: McGraw-Hill.

Crites, J. O. (1978). *Career Maturity Inventory theory and research handbook.* Monterey, CA: CTB/McGraw-Hill.

Dawis, R., & Lofquist, L. (1984). *A psychological theory of work adjustment.* Minneapolis: University of Minnesota Press.

DISCOVER [computer program]. (1996). Iowa City, IA: ACT.

Gati, I. (1985). Description of alternative measures of the concepts of vocational interest: Crystallization, congruence, and coherence. *Journal of Vocational Behavior, 27,* 37–55.

Gati, I. (1986). Making career decisions: A sequential elimination approach. *Journal of Counseling Psychology, 33,* 408–417.

Gati, I. (1989). Person-environment fit research: Problems and prospects. *Journal of Vocational Behavior, 35,* 181–193.

Gati, I. (1990a). Interpreting and applying career decision-making models: A comment on Carson and Mowsesian. *Journal of Counseling Psychology, 37,* 508–514.

Gati, I. (1990b). Why, when, and how to take into account the uncertainty involved in career decisions. *Journal of Counseling Psychology, 37,* 277–280.

Gati, I. (1991). The structure of vocational interests. *Psychological Bulletin, 109*, 309–324.

Gati, I. (1993). Career compromises. *Journal of Counseling Psychology, 40*, 416–424.

Gati, I. (1994). Computer-assisted career counseling: Dilemmas, problems, and possible solutions. *Journal of Counseling & Development, 73*, 51–56.

Gati, I. (1996). Computer-assisted career counseling: Challenges and prospects. In M. L. Savickas & B. W. Walsh (Eds.), *Handbook of career counseling theory and practice* (pp. 169–190). Palo Alto, CA: Davies-Black.

Gati, I. (1998). Using career-related aspects to elicit preferences and characterize occupations for a better person-environment fit. *Journal of Vocational Behavior, 52*, 343–356.

Gati, I., & Blumberg, D. (1991). Computer versus counselor interpretation of interest inventories: The case of the Self-Directed Search. *Journal of Counseling Psychology, 38*, 350–366.

Gati, I., Fassa, N., & Houminer, D. (1995). Applying decision theory to career counseling practice: The sequential elimination approach. *Career Development Quarterly, 43*, 211–220.

Gati, I., Fassa, N., & Mayer, Y. (1998). An aspect-based approach to person-environment fit: A comparison between the aspect structure derived from characteristics of occupations and that derived from counselees' preferences. *Journal of Vocational Behavior, 53*, 28–43.

Gati, I., Garty, Y., & Fassa, N. (1996). Using career-related aspects to assess person-environment fit. *Journal of Counseling Psychology, 43*, 196–206.

Gati, I., Houminer, D., & Aviram, T. (1998). Career compromises: Framings and their implications. *Journal of Counseling Psychology, 45*, 505–514.

Gati, I., Houminer, D., & Fassa, N. (1997). Framings of career compromises: How career counselors can help. *Career Development Quarterly, 45*, 390–399.

Gati, I., & Kibari, L. (2000). *Strategies used to search for information for making a career decision.* Unpublished manuscript, Department of Psychology, Hebrew University, Jerusalem.

Gati, I., Krausz, M., & Osipow, S. H. (1996). A taxonomy of difficulties in career decision making. *Journal of Counseling Psychology, 43*, 510–526.

Gati, I., Osipow, S. H., & Givon, M. (1995). Gender differences in career decision making: The content and structure of preferences. *Journal of Counseling Psychology, 42*, 204–216.

Gati, I., Saka, N., & Krausz, M. (2000). *The effect of using a computer-assisted career guidance system on career decision-making difficulties.* Unpublished manuscript, Department of Psychology, Hebrew University, Jerusalem.

Gati, I., Shenhav, M., & Givon, M. (1993). Processes involved in career preferences and compromises. *Journal of Counseling Psychology, 40*, 53–64.

Gati, I., & Tikotzki, Y. (1989). Strategies for the collection and processing of occupational information in making career decisions. *Journal of Counseling Psychology, 36*, 430–439.

Gati, I., & Winer, D. (1987). The relationship between vocational interests and the location of an ideal occupation in the individual's perceived occupational structure. *Journal of Vocational Behavior, 30*, 295–308.

Gelatt, H. B. (1962). Decision-making: A conceptual frame of reference for counseling. *Journal of Counseling Psychology, 9*, 240–245.

Gelatt, H. B. (1989). Positive uncertainty: A new decision-making framework for counseling. *Journal of Counseling Psychology, 36*, 252–256.

Gottfredson, L. S. (1981). Circumscription and compromise: A developmental theory of occupational aspirations. *Journal of Counseling Psychology, 28*, 549–579.

Gottfredson, L. S. (1986). Occupational aptitude patterns map: Development and implications for a theory of job aptitude requirements (Monograph). *Journal of Vocational Behavior, 29*, 254–291.

Gottfredson, G. D., & Holland, J. L. (1989). *Dictionary of Holland occupational codes* (2nd ed.). Odessa, FL: Psychological Assessment Resources.

Harmon, L. W., Hansen, J. C., Borgen, F. H., & Hammer, A. L. (1994). *Strong Interest Inventory applications and technical guide.* Palo Alto, CA: Consulting Psychologists Press.

Harren, V. A. (1979). A model of career decision making for college students. *Journal of Vocational Behavior, 14,* 119–133.

Harren, V. A., Kass, R. A., Tinsley, H. E., & Moreland, J. R. (1979). Influence of gender, sex-role attitudes, and cognitive complexity on gender-dominant career choices. *Journal of Counseling Psychology, 26,* 227–234.

Hesketh, B. (1982). Decision making style and career decision-making behaviors among school leavers. *Journal of Vocational Behavior, 20,* 223–234.

Hinkelman, J. M. (1997). Introduction to the special issue: Computer-assisted career guidance and information systems. *Career Planning and Adult Development Journal, 13,* 7–8.

Holland, J. L. (1985). *Making vocational choices: A theory of vocational personalities and work environments* (2nd ed.). Englewood Cliffs, NJ: Prentice-Hall.

Holland, J. L. (1997). *Making vocational choices* (3rd ed.). Odessa, FL: Psychological Assessment Resources.

Jackson, D. N. (1977). *Manual for the Jackson Vocational Interest Survey.* Port Huron, MI: Research Psychologists.

Janis, I. L., & Mann, L. (1977). *Decision making.* New York: The Free Press.

Jepsen, D. A. (1991, August). *Turning career decision making models into career interventions.* Paper presented at the annual meeting of the American Psychological Association, San Francisco, CA.

Jepsen, D. A., & Dilley, J. S. (1974). Vocational decision-making models: A review and comparative analysis. *Review of Educational Research, 44,* 331–349.

Johnson, C. S. (1978). Individual styles of decision making: A theoretical model for counseling. *The Personnel and Guidance Journal, 56,* 530–536.

Jungermann, H., & Schutz, H. (1992). Personal decision counseling: Counselors without clients? *Applied Psychology: An International Review, 41,* 185–200.

Kahneman, D., & Tversky, A. (1979). Prospect theory: Analysis of decision under risk. *Econometrica, 47,* 263–291.

Kahneman, D., & Tversky, A. (1984). Choices, values, frames. *American Psychologist, 39,* 341–350.

Kaldor, D. B., & Zytowski, D. G. (1969). A minimizing model of occupational decision-making. *Personnel and Guidance Journal, 47,* 781–788.

Katz, M. R. (1966). A model for guidance for career decision making. *Vocational Guidance Quarterly, 15,* 2–10.

Katz, M. (1979). Assessment of career decision making: Process and outcome. In A. M. Mitchell, G. B. Jones, & J. D. Krumboltz (Eds.), *Social learning and career decision making* (pp. 81–100). Cranston, RI: Carroll Press.

Katz, M. R. (1993). *Computer-assisted career decision making.* Hillsdale, NJ: Lawrence Erlbaum Associates.

Klaynman, J., & Ha, Y. W. (1987). Confirmation, disconfirmation, and information in hypothesis testing. *Psychological Review, 94,* 211–228.

Krieshok, T. S. (1998). An anti-introspectivist view of career decision making. *Career Development Quarterly, 46,* 210–229.

Krumboltz, J. D. (1992). The wisdom of indecision. *Journal of Vocational Behavior, 41,* 239–244.

Krumboltz, J. D. (1994). The career beliefs inventory. *Journal of Counseling and Development, 72,* 424–428.

Krumboltz, J. D., Rude, S. S., Mitchell, L. K., Hamel, D. A. & Kinneir, R. T. (1982). Behaviors associated with "good" and "poor" outcomes in a simulated career decision. *Journal of Vocational Behavior, 21,* 349–358.

Leong, F. T., & Morris J. (1989). Assessing the construct validity of Holland, Daiger, and Power's measure of Vocational Identity. *Measurement and Evaluation in Counseling and Development, 22,* 117–125.

Lichtenberg, J. W., Shaffer, M., & Arachtingi, B. M. (1993). Expected utility and sequential elimination models of career decision making. *Journal of Vocational Behavior, 42,* 237–252.

Lofquist, L. H., & Dawis, R. V. (1978). Values as secondary to needs in the Theory of Work Adjustment. *Journal of Vocational Behavior, 12,* 12–19.

Lofquist, L. H., & Dawis, R. V. (1984). Research on work adjustment and satisfaction: Implications for career counseling. In S. D. Brown & R. W. Lent (Eds.), *Handbook of counseling psychology* (pp. 216–237). New York: Wiley.

Lofquist, L., & Dawis, R. (1991). *Essentials of person-environment correspondence counseling.* Minneapolis: University of Minnesota.

Lunneborg, C. E. (1982). Systematic biases in brief self-ratings of vocational qualifications. *Journal of Vocational Behavior, 20,* 255–275.

Lunneborg, P. W. (1978). Sex and career decision-making styles. *Journal of Counseling Psychology, 25,* 299–305.

Manhardt, P. J. (1972). Job orientation of male and female college graduates in business. *Personnel Psychology, 25,* 361–368.

Matarazzo, J. D. (1986). Computerized clinical psychological test interpretations: Unvalidated plus all mean no sigma. *American Psychologist, 41,* 14–24.

Mau, W. C., & Jepsen, D. A. (1992). Effects of computer-assisted instruction in using formal decision-making strategies to choose a college major. *Journal of Counseling Psychology, 39,* 185–192.

Meir, E. I. (1973). The structure of occupations by interest: A smallest space analysis. *Journal of Vocational Behavior, 3,* 21–31.

Meir, E. I. (1995). Elaboration of the relation between interest congruence and satisfaction. *Journal of Career Assessment, 3,* 236–241.

Meir, E. I., & Barak, A. (1974). A simple instrument for measuring vocational interests based on Roe's classification of interests. *Journal of Vocational Behavior, 4,* 33–42.

Meir, E. I., & Yaari, Y. (1988). The relationship between congruent specialty choice within occupation and satisfaction. *Journal of Vocational Behavior, 33,* 99–117.

Miller, G. A. (1956). The magical number seven, plus or minus two: Some limits on our capacity for processing information. *Psychological Review, 63,* 81–97.

Miller-Tiedeman, A., & Tiedeman, D. V. (1990). Career decision making: An individualistic perspective. In D. Brown, L. Brooks, & associates (Eds.), *Career choice and development* (2nd ed., pp. 308–337). San Francisco, CA: Jossey-Bass.

Mitchell, L. K., & Krumboltz, J. D. (1984). Research on human decision making: Implications for career decision making and counseling. In S. D. Brown & R. W. Lent (Eds.), *Handbook of counseling psychology* (pp. 238–282). New York: Wiley.

Montgomery, H. (1989). From cognition to action: The search for dominance in decision making. In H. Montgomery & O. Svenson (Eds.), *Process and structure in human decision making* (pp. 23–49). New York: Wiley.

Neimeyer, G. J. (1988). Cognitive integration and differentiation in vocational behavior. *The Counseling Psychologist, 16,* 440–475.

Neimeyer, G. J. (1992). Personal constructs in career counseling and development. *Journal of Career Development, 18,* 163–173.

Nevo, O. (1987). Irrational expectation in career counseling and their confronting arguments. *Career Development Quarterly, 35,* 239–250.

Okon, N. R., Meir, E. I., & Gati, I. (2000). The relationship between congruence and well-being measures among teachers. *Eyunim B'Chinuch* (in Hebrew), *4,* 217–237.

Osipow, S. H. (1969). Cognitive styles and vocational-educational preference and selection. *Journal of Counseling Psychology, 16,* 534–546.

Osipow, S. H. (1983). *Theories of career development* (3rd ed.). Englewood Cliffs, NJ: Prentice-Hall.

Osipow, S. H. (1987). Applying person-environment theory to vocational behavior. *Journal of Vocational Behavior, 31*, 333–336.

Osipow, S. H. (1990). Careers: Research and personal. *The Counseling Psychologist, 18*, 338–347.

Osipow, S. H., Carney, C. G., & Barak, A. (1976). A scale of educational-vocational undecidedness: A typological approach. *Journal of Vocational Behavior, 9*, 233–243.

Osipow, S. H., & Fitzgerald, L. F. (1996). *Theories of career development* (4th ed.). Boston, MA: Allyn & Bacon.

Osipow, S. H., Walsh, W. B., & Tosi, D. J. (1980). *A survey of counseling methods*. Homewood, IL: Dorsey Press.

Paquette, L., & Kida, T. (1988). The effect of decision strategy and task complexity on decision performance. *Organizational Behavior and Human Decision Processes, 41*, 128–142.

Parsons, F. (1909). *Choosing a vocation*. Boston, MA: Houghton Mifflin.

Payne, J. W. (1976). Task complexity and contingent processing in decision making: An information search and protocol analysis. *Organizational Behavior and Human Decision Processes, 16*, 366–387.

Peterson, G. W., Sampson, J. P., Reardon, R. C., & Lenz, J. G. (1996). A cognitive information processing approach to career problem solving and decision making. In D. Brown, & L. Brooks (Eds.), *Career choice and development* (3rd ed., pp. 423–475). San Francisco, CA: Jossey-Bass.

Phillips, S. D. (1994). Choice and change: Convergence from the decision-making perspective. In M. L. Savickas & R. W. Lent (Eds.), *Convergence in career development theories* (pp. 155–163). Palo Alto, CA: Consulting Psychologist Press.

Phillips, S. D. (1997). Toward an expanded definition of adaptive decision making. *Career Development Quarterly, 45*, 275–287.

Phillips, S. D., & Pazienza, N. J. (1988). History and theory of the assessment of career development and decision making. In W. B. Walsh & S. H. Osipow (Eds.), *Career decision making* (pp. 1–31). Hillsdale, NJ: Lawrence Erlbaum Associates.

Phillips, S. D., Pazienza, N. J., & Ferrin, H. H. (1984). Decision-making styles and problem-solving appraisal. *Journal of Counseling Psychology, 31*, 497–502.

Pitz, G. F., & Harren, V. A. (1980). An analysis of career decision making from the point of view of information processing and decision theory. *Journal of Vocational Behavior, 16*, 320–346.

Potter R. E., & Beach, L. R. (1994). Imperfect information in prechoice screening of options. *Organizational Behavior and Human Decision Processes, 59*, 313–329.

Prediger, D. J. (1982). Dimensions underlying Holland's hexagon: Missing link between interests and occupations? *Journal of Vocational Behavior, 21*, 259–287.

Prediger, D. J. (1997, August). *Self-rated and objectively measured abilities are not equivalent: Thank Goodness*. Paper presented at the annual meeting of the American Psychological Association, Chicago, IL.

Pryor, R. G. L. (1981). Tracing the development of the Work Aspect Preference Scale. *Australian Psychologist, 16*, 241–257.

Pryor, R. G. L. (1982). Values, preferences, needs, work ethics, and orientation to work: Towards a conceptual and empirical integration. *Journal of Vocational Behavior, 20*, 40–52.

Roe, A. (1956). *The psychology of occupations*. New York: Wiley.

Rounds, J. B. (1990). The comparative and combined utility of work value and interest data in career counseling with adults. *Journal of Vocational Behavior, 37*, 32–45.

Rounds, J. B., Jr., Henly, G. A., Dawis, R. V., Lofquist, L. H., & Weiss, D. J. (1981). *Manual for the Minnesota Importance Questionnaire: A measure of vocational needs and values*. Minneapolis: Department of Psychology, University of Minnesota.

Rounds, J., & Tracey, T. J. (1996). Cross-cultural structural equivalence of RIASEC models and measures. *Journal of Counseling Psychology, 43*, 310–329.

Rounds, J. B., Dawis, R. V., & Lofquist, L. H. (1987). Measurement of person-environment fit and prediction of satisfaction in the theory of work adjustment. *Journal of Vocational Behavior, 31*, 297–318.

Sagiv, L. (1999). Searching for tools versus asking for answers: A taxonomy of counselee behavioral styles during career counseling. *Journal of Career Assessment, 7*, 19–34.

Sampson, J. P., Kolodinsky, R. W., & Greeno B. P. (1997). Counseling on the information highway: Future possibilities and potential problems. *Journal of Counseling and Development, 75*, 203–212.

Sampson, J. P., Peterson, G. W., Lenz, L. G., Reardon, R. C., & Saunders, D. E. (1998). The design and use of a measure of dysfunctional career thoughts among adults, college students, and high school students: The Career Thoughts Inventory. *Journal of Career Assessment, 6*, 115–134.

Schwartz, S. (1996). Value priorities and behavior: Applying a theory of integrated value systems. In C. Seligman & J. M. Olson (Eds.), *The psychology of values: The Ontario symposium* (Vol. 8, pp. 1–24). Mahwah, NJ: Lawrence Erlbaum Associates.

Scott, S. G., & Bruce, R. A. (1995). Decision-making style: The development and assessment of a new measure. *Educational and Psychological Measurement, 55*, 818–831.

Simon, H. A. (1957). *Models of man: Social and rational.* New York: Wiley.

Slaney, R. (1988). The assessment of career decision making. In W. B. Walsh & S. H. Osipow (Eds.), *Career Decision Making* (pp. 33–76). Hillsdale, NJ: Lawrence Erlbaum Associates.

Slaney, R., & Slaney, F. M. (1986). Relationship of expressed and inventoried interests of female career counseling clients. *Career Development Quarterly, 35*, 24–33.

Spokane, A. R. (1985). A review of research on person-environment congruence in Holland's theory of careers. *Journal of Vocational Behavior, 26*, 306–343.

Spokane, A. R. (1987). Conceptual and methodological issues in person–environment fit research. *Journal of Vocational Behavior, 31*, 217–221.

Strong, E. K., Hansen, J. C., & Campbell, D. P. (1985). *Strong Vocational Interest Blank.* Palo Alto, CA: Consulting Psychologists Press.

Super, D. E. (1953). A theory of vocational development. *American Psychologist, 8*, 185–190.

Super, D. E. (1990). A life-span, life-space approach to career development. In D. Brown, L. Brooks, & Associates (Eds.), *Career choice and development* (2nd ed., pp. 197–261). San Francisco: Jossey-Bass.

Taylor, K. M., & Betz, N. E. (1983). Applications of self-efficacy theory to the understanding and treatment of career indecision. *Journal of Vocational Behavior, 22*, 63–81.

Tracey, T. J., & Rounds, J. (1993). Evaluating Holland's and Gati's vocational interest models: A structural meta-analysis. *Psychological Bulletin, 113*, 229–246.

Tversky, A. (1972). Elimination by aspects: A theory of choice. *Psychological Review, 79*, 281–299.

Tversky, A. (1975). A critique of expected utility theory: Descriptive and normative consideration. *Erkenninis, 9*, 163–173.

Tversky, A., & Kahneman, D. (1974). Judgment under uncertainty: Heuristics and biases. *Science, 185*, 1124–1131.

Tversky, A., & Kahneman, D. (1981). The framing of decisions and the psychology of choice. *Science, 211*, 453–458.

Walsh, W. B., & Holland, J. L. (1992). A theory of personality types and work environments. In W. B. Walsh & K. H. Craik (Eds.), *Person-environment psychology: Models and perspectives* (pp. 35–69). Hillsdale, NJ: Lawrence Erlbaum Associates.

Walsh, W. B., & Osipow, S. H. (Eds.) (1988). *Career decision making.* Hillsdale, NJ: Lawrence Erlbaum Associates.

Young, G., Tokar, D. M., & Subich, L. M. (1998). Congruence revisited: Do 11 indices differentially predict job satisfaction and is the relation moderated by person and situation variables? *Journal of Vocational Behavior, 52*, 208–223.

Zakay, D., & Barak, A. (1984). Meaning and career decision making. *Journal of Vocational Behavior, 24*, 1–14.

Zakay, D., & Tsal, Y. (1993). The impact of using forced decision-making strategies on post-decisional confidence. *Journal of Behavioral Decision Making, 6*, 53–68.

Zytowski, D. G. (1970). The concept of work values. *Vocational Guidance Quarterly, 18*, 176–186.

Chapter 3

Career Self-Efficacy

Nancy Betz
The Ohio State University

This chapter will place self-efficacy theory in the framework of self-concept and self-esteem, which are fundamental variables in career behavior. This is particularly appropriate because Samuel H. Osipow, whose contributions to vocational psychology are recognized by the publication of this volume, has published research on the self-concept and self-efficacy in vocational behavior. Following an overview of self-concept in the study of vocational behavior, research on domains of career self-efficacy are reviewed.

THE SELF-CONCEPT IN VOCATIONAL BEHAVIOR

The importance of the self-concept to career development has long been recognized by vocational psychologists. One of the first theorists to explicitly incorporate the self-concept into vocational theory was Donald Super, whose work helped to define the field of vocational psychology and career development. Super originally suggested the importance of the self-concept in a 1949 speech made in Fort Collins, Colorado, and later in a 1951 article. Major statements in 1953 and 1963 defined the "vocational self-concept" (Super, 1963, p. 20) and posited that the process of vocational development was that of implementing the vocational self-concept. Much later, Super (1990) emphasized the metadimensions of self-esteem and self-efficacy in influencing how effectively the vocational self-concept can be implemented.

Although Super's theory has generated a vast body of research on self-concept implementation, vocational maturity, and career exploration behavior (see a recent comprehensive review of Osipow & Fitzgerald, 1996), Korman and Osipow particularly emphasized the concept of self-esteem. In an attempt to elaborate on and refine some of the postulates of Super's theory, Korman (1967) postulated that self-esteem operates as a moderator of the vocational choice process in that individuals with high self-esteem would seek those vocational roles that would be congruent with one's self-perceived characteristics, whereas this would be less likely the case for those individuals with low self-esteem (Korman, 1967, p. 65). In a series of studies, Korman (1969) found that high self-esteem individuals were more likely to implement their vocational self-concepts in their occupational choices than were low self-esteem individuals and that high-esteem individuals were more likely to make choices which fulfilled their needs than were low self-esteem individuals.

Osipow and his colleagues pursued similar ideas. For example, Resnick, Fauble, and Osipow (1970) examined the relationship between self-esteem (as measured by the Tennessee Self-Concept Scale) and vocational crystallization, as indicated by the number of high scores (above the 75th percentile) on the Kuder Preference Record. Although high self-esteem individuals did not have more high scores than did low self-esteem individuals, high-esteem individuals of both sexes expressed more certainty about their career plans.

Leonard, Walsh, and Osipow (1973) found that high self-esteem individuals were more likely to make a second vocational choice (an alternative choice if they could not implement their first choice) consistent with their primary vocational preference as measured by Holland's Vocational Preference Inventory. In contrast, individuals low in self-esteem were as likely to make inconsistent as consistent vocational choices.

Holland, in his theory (1997) and the instruments he developed (e.g., the Self-Directed Search), has long acknowledged the essential role of the self-concept if career decisions are to be informed and adaptive. Holland's Self-Directed Search (Holland, 1994) contains a section for self-estimates of ability as part of the overall assessment of the six Holland types (Realistic, Investigative, Social, Enterprising, Artistic, and Conventional). In a 1991 symposium, Holland expressed the view that individuals with low self-esteem may not act on their interests and suggested that interventions designed to increase an individuals's range of experiences would be useful in increasing self-efficacy.

Thus, the potential importance of the self-concept and self-esteem to vocational behavior has long been recognized. More recently research attention has focused on a related, although more specific, construct of career self-efficacy. Although related, the constructs of self-esteem, the self-concept, and self-efficacy have different substantive meanings and different practical (counseling) implications. As defined by theoreticians in the area (e.g., Blaskovich & Tomaka, 1991), the self-concept is a broadly inclusive construct that can describe cognitive, behavioral, and affective elements. For example, an individual's self-concept might include the belief that he or she is intelligent, kind, good at drawing but poor at dancing, as someone who would make a good doctor but a poor teacher.

The construct of self-esteem refers both to a more global and evaluative aspect of the self-concept. According to Blascovich and Tomaka (1991), self-esteem is "the overall affective evaluation of one's own worth, value, or importance. The concept of self-esteem goes by a variety of names (e.g., self-worth, self-regard, self-respect, self-acceptance). It is the sum of evaluations across salient attributes of one's self or personality" (p. 115). Thus, self-esteem is a global self-evaluation. The best known measures of self-esteem, for example, the Rosenberg (1965) Self-Esteem Inventory and Coopersmith (1975) Self-Esteem Inventory were developed to measure global self-esteem.

Self-efficacy, on the other hand, refers to one's beliefs concerning his or her ability to perform a given behavior or class of behaviors. The concept of self-efficacy is behaviorally specific rather than general. The concept of self-efficacy must, therefore, have a behavioral referent to be meaningful. We can refer to perceived self-efficacy with respect to mathematics, initiating social interactions, investing in stocks, or fixing a flat tire.

The design of interventions to increase self-efficacy with respect to given behavioral domain is built into the theory itself, via Bandura's four sources of self-efficacy information. In contrast, interventions for the improvement of problems of low self-esteem are less obvious from theories or definitions of the constructs, except in a few cases, for example Carl Rogers' (1957) specification of the therapeutic core conditions (empathy, unconditional positive regard and genuineness) as means of improving the client's self-ideal congruence (i.e., self-acceptance). From the standpoint of career behavior, self-concepts, self-esteem, and self-efficacy are important to consider, but self-efficacy theory may contain within it the most straightforward, usable implications for interventions.

SELF-EFFICACY THEORY

Self-efficacy theory may be viewed as one approach to the more general study of the applicability of social learning or social cognitive theory (e.g., Krumboltz, Mitchell, & Jones, 1976; Krumboltz & Nichols, 1990; Lent, Brown, & Hackett, 1994) to vocational behavior.

As proposed by Bandura (1977), self-efficacy expectations refer to a person's beliefs concerning his or her ability to successfully perform a given task or behavior. They are postulated by Bandura to be major mediators of behavior as indicated by at least three behavioral indicators: (a) approach versus avoidance behavior, (b) quality of performance of behaviors in the target domain, and (c) persistence in the face of obstacles or disconfirming experiences. Low self-efficacy expectations regarding a behavior or behavioral domain lead to avoidance of those behaviors, poorer performance, and a tendency to give up at the first sign of difficulty. In the context of career development, *approach behavior* often refers to an individual's willingness to choose a given educational or career option—self-efficacy beliefs can, thus, act as either facilitators of a given career choice if they are strong or barriers to career choices when they are low or weak. Beyond the consideration of career options, low self-efficacy expectations could serve as barriers to the implementation of a possible choice by hampering performance and persistence in demanding educational programs.

Additionally, Bandura (1977) specified four sources of information through which self-efficacy expectations are learned and by which they can be modified. These sources of information include:

1. performance accomplishments, that is, experiences of successfully performing the behavior in question;
2. vicarious learning or modeling;
3. verbal persuasion, for example, encouragement and support from others, and
4. lower levels of emotional arousal, that is, lack of anxiety, in connection with the behavior.

Thus, the theoretical context of the self-efficacy construct provides not only a means for understanding the development of self-efficacy beliefs, but the means for their modification through interventions incorporating positive applications of the four sources of efficacy information.

In the next sections, domains of career self-efficacy that have received the most extensive research attention will be briefly reviewed. Focus is on constructs, measures, and representative research. The domains covered include occupational self-efficacy, including self-efficacy for scientific and technical careers; mathematics self-efficacy; self-efficacy with respect to basic dimensions of career behavior, such as those represented by the Holland types and by Osipow's Task Specific Occupational Self-Efficacy Scale; and career decision-making self-efficacy.

CAREER SELF-EFFICACY: CONSTRUCTS, MEASURES, AND ILLUSTRATIVE FINDINGS

Occupational Self-Efficacy

The first study examining the applicability of self-efficacy theory to career development was that of Betz and Hackett (1981). Their 20-item Occupational Self-Efficacy Scale was developed to measure students' perceptions of self-efficacy with respect to the educational requirements and job duties of 20 commonly known occupations. The instrument was originally developed to test the postulate (Hackett & Betz, 1981) that the underrepresentation of women in many nontraditional (i.e., male dominated) career fields was due in part to women's low expectations of career-related self-efficacy with respect to male-dominated career fields. Accordingly, the concept of traditionality/nontraditionality was used to select occupational titles for inclusion in the instrument and as a basis for scoring the instrument. Based on percentages of women and men in the occupation, 10 traditionally female dominated (denoted "traditional") and 10 traditionally male-dominated ("nontraditional") occupations were selected. "Social worker" and "engineer" are examples of traditional and nontraditional occupations, respectively.

Consistent with prediction, significant gender differences were found in occupational self-efficacy expectations when traditionality of the occupation was taken into account. Men's occupational self-efficacy was essentially equivalent for traditionally male-dominated and traditionally female-dominated occupations; women's self-efficacy expectations were significantly lower than men's for male-dominated occupations, and significantly higher than men's for female-dominated occupations. Further, these gender differences in self-efficacy were predictive of gender differences in the range of traditional and nontraditional occupations considered, suggesting that low perceptions of efficacy with respect to gender nontraditional careers reduces the likelihood of including them among one's range of options.

The assessment of general occupational self-efficacy as pioneered by Betz and Hackett (1981) has been used in many subsequent studies, with most showing gender differences in occupational self-efficacy (Layton, 1984; Matsui, Ikeda, & Ohnishi, 1989; Mitchell, 1990; Post-Kammer & Smith, 1985; Williams & Betz, 1994; Zilber, 1988). The largest and most robust difference is the higher male self-efficacy with respect to male-dominated occupations. Other studies (e.g., Layton, 1984; Rotberg, Brown, & Ware, 1987) have replicated the findings that self-efficacy is related to the range of career options considered.

Although research on general occupational self-efficacy supported the theoretical validity of self-efficacy expectations as a predictor of "choice" behavior, optimal application of Bandura's theory to career behavior suggested the development of domain-specific measures of self-efficacy.

Self-Efficacy for Scientific/Technical Careers

Research by Lent, Brown, and Larkin (1984, 1986) focused on the persistence of students in science and engineering occupations. Lent et al. (1984, 1986) investigated the relationship between self-efficacy estimates and the degree of persistence and academic success of students enrolled in the Institute of Technology at the University of Minnesota. In their first study, Lent et al. (1984) adapted Betz and Hackett's (1981) assessment procedure to measure self-efficacy with regard to 15 scientific and technical occupations. Using a relatively small sample of students who had declared college majors in engineering, Lent et al. found significant differences in several measures of academic performance and persistence between students with high versus low scientific/technical self-efficacy. Generally, students with higher confidence in their abilities relative to scientific/technical occupations achieved higher grades and persisted longer in their majors. Moderate and significant correlations were also reported between technical/scientific self-efficacy and objective measures of mathematics aptitude and high school achievement. However, no gender differences in scientific/technical self-efficacy were found.

In a subsequent study, Lent et al. (1986) conducted a partial replication and extension of their earlier study with a larger sample. In this study, a second measure of scientific/technical self-efficacy was developed, assessing efficacy beliefs with regard to "academic milestones," that is, specific accomplishments critical to academic success in science and engineering majors, such as completing the mathematics requirements and remaining enrolled in the college of technology. Like the previous study, results from this study indicated an absence of gender differences in efficacy expectations, but scientific/technical self-efficacy was significantly predictive of grades in technical courses, persistence in a major, and range of career options. Brown, Lent, and Larkin (1989) and Hackett, Betz, Casas, and Roche-Singh (1992) also reported an absence of gender differences in scientific/technical self-efficacy, as well as the strong predictive power (in terms of grades in science/engineering curricula) of academic self-efficacy.

Thus, several studies indicate that scientific/technical self-efficacy is predictive of the postulated outcomes of performance and persistence in majors in those areas. The lack of gender differences in self-efficacy is likely due to the fact that the young women in these samples had chosen, versus avoided, science and engineering majors, suggesting higher science and engineering self-efficacy expectations initially in comparison to women in general.

Mathematics Self-Efficacy

The importance of a math background to a range of educational and career options has led it to be called the "critical filter" to career development (Sells, 1982), yet many students, especially women, avoid taking math courses (Betz, 1997; National Science Foundation, 1990).

Early research examining cognitive barriers to the study of math emphasized the concept of math anxiety (see Betz, 1978). In 1983, Betz and Hackett published the first measure of mathematics self-efficacy expectations and proposed that because self-efficacy theory includes a specification of the components of interventions (i.e., the four sources of efficacy information), it may be a more useful concept than that of math anxiety.

The original research of Betz and Hackett (1983) used a three-part measure of math self-efficacy. The items assessed self-efficacy with respect to everyday math tasks (e.g., balancing a checkbook), math courses (e.g., calculus), and math problems. Large gender differences in math self-efficacy were found, with males being significantly more confident than were females. In addition, math self-efficacy expectations were related to students' preferences for, versus avoidance of, careers in the sciences. Hackett (1985) used path analysis to test the hypothesis that mathematics-related self-efficacy mediates the effects of gender and mathematics preparation and achievement on the math-relatedness of college major choice. Results were consistent with a self-efficacy approach to career development in that gender, gender-role socialization, high school mathematics preparation, and mathematics achievement were all found to influence math self-efficacy, which, in turn, was significantly predictive of math-related major choice.

Following these early studies, a considerable body of empirical research has consistently supported the existence of large gender differences in math self-efficacy (Lent, Lopez, & Bieschke, 1991), the predictive relationship of math self-efficacy to math performance and achievement (e.g., Siegel, Galassi, & Ware, 1985), and the importance of math self-efficacy to the science- or math-relatedness of career choices (Hackett & Betz, 1989; Lapan, Shaughnessy, & Boggs, 1996; Post-Kammer & Smith, 1986).

Recent research has focused on the sources of math self-efficacy, and its results may have important implications for the design of treatment programs. Matsui, Matsui, and Ohnishi (1990) studied math self-efficacy in 163 Japanese college students. Men reported significantly higher math self-efficacy than did women, and three sources of efficacy information, that is, performance accomplishments (high school math grades), vicarious learning (seeing others perform math), and emotional arousal (less math anxiety) contributed to greater math self-efficacy.

Lent, Lopez, and their colleagues (Lent, Brown, Gover, & Niijer, 1996; Lent et al., 1991; Lent, Lopez, Brown, & Gore, 1996; Lopez & Lent, 1992) have also examined the sources of math self-efficacy. Lent et al. (1991) reported that all four sources of efficacy information (performance accomplishments, vicarious learning, social persuasion, and emotional arousal) were significantly related to math self-efficacy, although after controlling for performance accomplishments the latter three sources did not explain additional variance. Further, their research indicated that gender differences in math self-efficacy are mediated by differential efficacy-building experiences in the two sexes, that is, differential experience with the four sources of efficacy information, especially past performances. Lent et al. reported that Bandura's (1986) concept of outcome expectations (beliefs that a given behavior will lead to a certain outcome) was also useful in the prediction of career choice and recommended the more frequent inclusion of outcome, as well as efficacy, expectations in research on cognitive factors related to career choice and development.

To further clarify and refine understanding of the dimensionality of the source of math self-efficacy information, Lent, Lopez, Brown, and Gore (1996) used confirmatory factor analysis to test two-, three-, four-, and five-factor models of the structure of their measures of the sources of math self-efficacy. Their results, obtained from both high school and college samples, support Bandura's four-factor model of the sources of self-efficacy, but also suggest a more parsimonious heirachical model in which performance accomplishments, social persuasion, and emotional arousal are highly correlated because they are all based on direct, personal experience, whereas vicarious learning is an indirect source of efficacy information. However, when peer versus adult modeling were differentiated, the latter was more closely related to the other sources of efficacy information. Lopez, Lent, Brown, and Gore (1997) reported that perceived past performance was a much stronger predictor of math self-efficacy than was measured ability and that social persuasion was related to math self-efficacy for students enrolled in elective math classes.

Most recently, Luzzo, Hasper, Albert, Bibby, and Martinelli (1998) reported the superiority of performance accomplishments in increasing math/science self-efficacy in undecided college students. The performance accomplishments intervention, involving a number series task structured so that participants successfully "passed," led to increased math-science course self-efficacy both posttreatment and at a follow-up conducted four weeks after the conclusion of treatment. The vicarious learning intervention, a videotaped presentation of an African-American man and a European-American woman describing their successful pursuit of math-science careers, did not have significant effects on self-efficacy. However, students who received both the performance accomplishments and vicarious learning interventions reported significantly higher math-science interests at the 4-week follow-up than did other students.

Lent, Brown, Gower, and Nijjer (1996) used thought listing analysis to examine the sources of information that students used in appraising their mathematics self-efficacy. The most commonly cited sources were personal performance experiences. Based on their research, Lent et al. (1996) and Brown and Lent (1996) suggested that challenging clients' interpretations of past performance data or structuring new mastery experiences (e.g., remedial or refresher courses) would be most useful, and that social support and anxiety management be considered useful only as performance itself is strengthened. They also suggest the utility of adult role models to administer these interventions.

SELF-EFFICACY WITH RESPECT TO HOLLAND'S THEMES

There are now several measures of self-efficacy of one or more of the six Holland (1997) types; these six themes, Realistic, Investigative, Artistic, Social, Enterprising, and Conventional (RIASEC), have been among the major individual differences variables used in career theory, assessment, and counseling.

Lapan, Boggs, and Morrill (1989) developed a measure of self-efficacy with respect to the RIASEC areas in order examine the degree to which gender differences in self-efficacy mediated gender differences in interests. Lapan et al. (1989) introduced and described each theme as an occupational category, below which examples of occupations in that category were given (e.g., pharmacist, computer programmer, mathematician, and physicist for the Investigative theme). Lapan et al. found significant gender differences in favor of males on Realistic and Investigative self-efficacy, though not on self-efficacy with respect to Artistic, Social, Enterprising, or Conventional themes. Self-efficacy was found to play a major role in mediating gender differences in Investigative and Realistic interests.

Rooney (1991) cluster-analyzed the items of the Task Specific Occupational Self-Efficacy Scale (TSOSS; Rooney & Osipow, 1992) and was able to assign 225 of the 230 items to one of the six Holland theme areas. Number of items per cluster ranged from 18 (Enterprising) to 56 (Realistic). Males were significantly more confident with respect to Realistic and Investigative, and females were significantly more confident in the Social area.

Lenox and Subich (1994) also developed measures of self-efficacy with respect to Holland's themes. Six 5-item scales were developed using activities representing each theme. Only the Realistic, Investigative, and Enterprising scales were investigated further, however, because the Artistic, Social, and Conventional scales were characterized by restriction in range. Like previous research findings, women were less confident than men in relationship to Realistic and Investigative. The Skills Confidence Inventory (SCI; Betz, Borgen, & Harmon, 1996) is a 60-item measure of self-efficacy, with 10 items assessing self-efficacy for each of the six RIASEC areas. As described in Betz, Borgen, et al. (1996) and Betz, Harmon, and Borgen (1996), the SCI was developed using samples of about 1,100 employed adults and 700 college students. Each confidence scale consists of 10 activities, tasks, or school subjects associated with the relevant Holland theme.

Gender differences on the SCI varied according to the sample studied. In the original normative studies, college men reported significantly more confidence on the Realistic, Investigative, Enterprising, and Conventional themes, whereas college women reported significantly greater Social confidence. These findings are consistent with other findings that suggest males are more confident with respect to the Realistic and Investigative themes (Lapan et al., 1989; Lenox & Subich, 1994; Rooney, 1991) and that females report greater confidence with respect to the social theme (Rooney, 1991). The male advantage on Enterprising is consistent with somewhat higher scores of males on measures of the Holland interest themes (e.g., the Strong Interest Inventory), and the advantage on Conventional is probably due to the increased emphasis on computer and accounting skills, similar to that of the revised Conventional General Occupational Theme on the 1994 revision of the Strong Interest Inventory.

Fewer gender differences were evident among 1,147 employed adults. Gender differences (in favor of men) were found only for Realistic and Enterprising confidence. In further within-occupation analyses, gender differences on the RIASEC themes were found for only 9 of 126 possible comparisons (Betz, Borgen, Kaplan, & Harmon, 1998). Fewer gender differences are evident in research using samples where choices have already been made, for example, Lent et al.'s (1984, 1986) Institute of Technology students and Hackett et al.'s (1992) students in engineering majors. Research by Betz, Borgen, et al. (1996) and Betz, Harmon, et al. (1996) shows gender similarity within occupational groups. Since higher self-efficacy is postulated to lead to "approach" behavior, we would expect greater similarity in confidence among those who have made similar choices. Further, the SCI adult normative sample consisted of employees, both male and female, who were relatively satisfied and successful in their jobs, thus suggesting relatively high confidence in relevant theme areas. Even so, gender differences persisted in Realistic and Enterprising Confidence in the sample as a whole.

Recent research using measures of self-efficacy with respect to the Holland themes has focused on the relationships between interest in and self-efficacy expectations with respect to a given Holland theme (e.g., Betz, Borgen, et al., 1996, Lenox & Subich, 1994) and, in particular, the joint use of these in career assessment and counseling. The theoretical relationships between interests and efficacy are discussed later.

TASK-SPECIFIC OCCUPATIONAL SELF-EFFICACY

Also measuring several basic dimensions of vocational interest is the Task-Specific Occupational Self-Efficacy Scale (TSOSS; Rooney & Osipow, 1992; Osipow, Temple, & Rooney, 1993). The original version of the TSOSS consisted of 230 occupationally-relevant skills items selected from the 66 *Guide for Occupational Exploration* (GEO) categories from the *Dictionary of Occupational Titles* (U.S. Department of Labor, 1981). Specific items included "Indicate your confidence in your ability to gain the trust and confidence of people" and "Use hand tools."

A short form of the TSOSS was developed (Osipow, Temple, & Rooney, 1993) based on factor analysis of the original 230-item scale. Based on this analysis, a 60-item short form including four factors was derived. The factors were described as follows: (a) Verbal, interpersonal skills (Verbal); (b) Quantitative, logical, and business skills (Quant); (c) Physical strength and agility (Physical); and (d) Aesthetic skills (Aesthetic). In a recent review, Osipow and Temple (1996) suggested that the short form, with its four interpretable subscales, is more useful than the long form, which provided only an overall self-efficacy score.

Although gender differences were not reported in the original research, there was evidence that gender moderated the relationship between self-efficacy and career indecision for the first two factor scores, with self-efficacy significantly and inversely related to indecision for men but not for women (Osipow et al., 1993; Temple, 1991). The authors speculated that, based on research on the career development of women (e.g., Fassinger, 1990), females may have more factors to consider in making career decisions than do males. Thus, one factor, such as self-efficacy, can have a stronger predictive effect in males. In order to examine this hypothesis, Temple and Osipow (1994) predicted that the choice behavior of women high on a measure of sex-role egalitarianism would be more similar to that of men, giving stronger predictive power to a single factor such as self-efficacy. Temple and Osipow (1994) reported that college women high on the measure of sex-role egalitarianism reported significantly higher self-efficacy with respect to the first two factors and the TSOSS total (short form) score than did women low on sex-role egalitarianism, but that degree of sex-role egalitarianism did not substantially moderate the efficacy-indecision relationship. For Factor 1, a significant r in the high egalitarian group (r = .32) is not significantly different from an r of .27 in the low egalitarian group.

Williams and Betz (1994) and Betz, Schifano, and Kaplan (1999) reported statistically significant gender differences on the TSOSS factors, with college men (N = 108) scoring significantly higher on the Quantitative and Physical factors in comparison with college women (N = 159). No gender differences on the Verbal or Aesthetic factors were found. Lee (1994) studied women students enrolled in four universities in Korea. She found that women in engineering and natural science majors scored significantly higher on TSOSS Factor 2 (Quantitative) and significantly lower on both Factors 1 (Verbal) and 4 (Aesthetic), in comparison to other groups of college women, thus providing some evidence for the criterion-related validity of the TSOSS short form.

Although several other validity studies are reviewed by Osipow and Temple (1996), their overall conclusion based on some small validity r's and an unstable factor structure was that the 60-item form needed revision. Accordingly, Temple (1996) examined several revisions of the instrument, focusing on an attempt to increase the range of scores. This attempt was successful for two of the three revisions examined, but Osipow and Temple (1996) suggest the need for additional validity studies and for possible additional revisions for the purpose of continuing scale refinement.

More promising evidence of validity was reported by Betz et al. (1999). They examined the relationships of TSOSS scores to SCI scores. They reported that relationships among similarly named scores, that is, TSOSS Verbal/interpersonal with SCI Social, TSOSS Quantitative with SCI Investigative, TSOSS Physical with SCI Realistic, and TSOSS Aesthetic with SCI Artistic were high, ranging from .50 (Verbal with Social) to .80 (Aesthetic with Artistic). Both TSOSS Verbal/interpersonal and SCI Social were negatively related to career indecision, thus suggesting that self-perceived social/interpersonal confidence plays a facilitative role in career decision making. Correlations between Verbal/interpersonal confidence and indecision were also reported by Temple (1991) in men and by Temple and Osipow (1994) in women.

Although Osipow and Temple (1996) did not discuss the particular uses of the TSOSS with women clients, the fact that the scale assesses basic dimensions of career-related behavior, at least two of which may be gender-related, suggests possible uses similar to those suggested for the measures of self-efficacy with respect to the Holland themes. For example, scores on the four TSOSS factors can be compared with actual ability data or grades to determine the realism of the individual's self-perceived abilities. Further, the extent to which low levels of confidence are preventing the individual from exploring career options, particularly if some degree of interest is present (see Betz, 1999), should be discussed in counseling. Interventions based on self-efficacy theory can then be implemented, if appropriate.

CAREER DECISION MAKING SELF-EFFICACY

In addition to career self-efficacy measures designed to predict the type of options considered versus avoided, or the nature of the choices made, self-efficacy theory has also been applied to the process of career decision making. The most widely used measure of this type is the Career Decision-Making Self-Efficacy Scale (CDMSE; Taylor & Betz, 1983) designed to measure an individual's degree of belief that he or she can successfully complete tasks necessary to making career decisions. The basis for scale construction was the five Career Choice Competencies postulated in Crites' (1978) model of career maturity and assessed in the Career Maturity Inventory (Crites, 1978). Thus, the item content included behaviors pertinent to: (a) accurate self-appraisal (b) gathering occupational information (c) goal selection (d) making plans for the future, and (e) problem solving. There is a 50-item version, including 10 items for each competence domain (Taylor & Betz, 1983) and, a shorter 25-item form (Betz, Klein, & Taylor, 1996), containing 5 items for each domain of decision-making behavior. As reviewed by Betz and Luzzo (1996) both versions have been shown to be highly reliable and to be strongly related to criterion measures including career indecision, as measured by Osipow, Carney, and Barak's (1976; Osipow, 1987) Career Decision Scale and the Vocational Identity Subscale of Holland, Daiger and Power's (1980) My Vocational Situation.

Several studies have shown CDMSE scores to be related to behavioral (vs. self-report) indicators of educational and career adjustment. Taylor and Popma (1990) reported that the CDMSE significantly differentiated three groups of students categorized on the basis of college major status: declared majors, those with tentative major choices, and undecided students. Mathieu, Sowa, and Niles (1993) reported that career undecided college women had significantly lower CDMSE scores than did women preferring either male-dominated or gender-neutral occupations but that the scores of undecided women did not differ from those of women preferring traditional female occupations. In a related investigation, Nevill and Schlecker (1988) found that women who scored high on the CDMSE were more willing to engage in the career-related activities of nontraditional occupations than were women who scored low on the CDMSE.

Research by Blustein (1989) also provided evidence of the relationship between career decision-making self-efficacy and career exploration behavior. Measures of goal instability and environmental and self-exploratory activities were administered along with the CDMSE to 106 college students. Results of a canonical correlation analysis suggested that career decision-making self-efficacy emerged as a more prominent predictor of exploratory activity than any of the other variables (goal instability, age, and gender).

Peterson (1993) examined the CDMSE as a predictor of academic and social integration which, in turn, were postulated to be related to academic persistence (retention) versus attrition. Using a sample of 678 underprepared college students, Peterson reported that CDMSE scores surpassed all other variables as predictors of overall and academic integration, explaining 18% of the variance of each. Scores on the CDMSE also explained 12% of the variance in social integration. Because of the strength of her findings, Peterson (1993) suggested that interventions designed to increase career decision-making self-efficacy should be strongly considered in programs to increase student retention.

Not surprisingly, given findings regarding its correlates, research is now being focused on the evaluation of counseling interventions designed to increase career decision-making self-efficacy. For example, Foss and Slaney (1986) reported the results of a systematic effort to increase CDMSE scores. In their investigation, college women completed the CDMSE prior to exposure to a videotaped career intervention designed to broaden women's range of perceived career options by reducing gender stereotyping in career planning and education. Results of the study indicated significant increases in participants' CDMSE scores 2 weeks following exposure to the video. Fukuyama, Probert, Neimeyer, Nevill, and Metzler (1988) reported results of an investigation designed to evaluate the effects of a computer assisted career guidance program, DISCOVER, on the career decision-making self-efficacy and career decidedness of undergraduates. Results indicated significant gains in CDMSE scores and a decrease in career indecision following students' exposure to DISCOVER.

More recently, Luzzo and Taylor (1994) evaluated the effects of verbal persuasion on the CDMSE scores of first-year college students. Eighty-eight students completed the CDMSE as a pretest measure and were then randomly assigned to either a treatment or a control group. Students in the treatment group completed the World of Work Inventory (WOWI) and subsequently met with a career counselor to discuss the results. During the feedback session, the counselor verbally persuaded students that they possessed adequate skills and opportunities to engage in effective career decision-making activities. Students in the control group also completed the WOWI but did not receive the verbal persuasion treatment. Results indicate significant gains in CDMSE scores of students who received verbal persuasion, whereas CDMSE scores of students in the control group were unchanged. An evaluation of the effects of attributional retaining on the CDMSE scores of college students was reported by Luzzo, Funk, and Strang (1996). The intervention was an attributional retraining procedure designed to persuade students to attribute low levels of confidence in making career decisions and career-related failures to a lack of effort. Results revealed that the CDMSE scores of students who initially exhibited an external career locus of control significantly increased to a more internal locus following the attributional retraining procedure.

Development and validation of the CDMSE has also led to several investigations evaluating the effects of career counseling workshops and career exploration courses on the career decision-making self-efficacy of college students (Foltz, 1993; McNeill, 1990; Oreshnick, 1991; Shaw, 1988). Results consistently indicate that the CDMSE scores of students who receive a viable intervention tend to increase, whereas CDMSE scores of students who do not receive an appropriate intervention remain relatively stable over time. Thus, in counseling with or programming for undecided college students, an intervention focusing on career decision-making self-efficacy may prove very helpful. Although not the only model of decision-making components, Crites' (1978) system of career choice competencies (on which the CDMSE is based) provided one possible approach to organizing treatment modules. Data on the effectiveness of this type of intervention are convincing enough to strongly recommend its use. Betz (1992) provides some suggestions.

Finally, other researchers have also developed and examined measures of self-efficacy relative to aspects of the process of career decision making and implementation. For example, Solberg and his colleagues (Solberg, Good, Nord, et al., 1994; Solberg, Good, Fischer, Brown, & Nord, 1995) developed a measure of career search efficacy, used with individuals at the point of finding or changing jobs or careers, or reentering the job market. Like career decision-making self-efficacy, interventions focused on career search efficacy may also be very useful for career counseling.

SELF-EFFICACY AND VOCATIONAL INTERESTS

The final topic of this chapter, the possibility that self-efficacy theory may also be useful as a means to increase the range of vocational interests, was also presaged by the work of Samuel H. Osipow. Although Osipow was not the only theorist speculating that interests (or task liking) can be increased through task success (what in Bandura's theory are called performance accomplishments), some of his early research demonstrated precisely that. Osipow and Scheid (1971) administered a task involving choice among paired nonsense syllables and varied experimentally manipulated success ratios from 85/15%, 70/30%, and 50/50%. As predicted, preferences for the task increased most under conditions of greatest success. Similarly, Osipow (1972) reported that preferences for less preferred tasks could be increased with high success ratios in task involvement (see also Campbell & Hackett, 1986; Hackett & Campbell, 1987) for research supporting the relationship of task success to task liking or interests.

Barak and his colleagues (Barak, 1976, 1981, Chap. 5 this volume; Barak, Librowsky, & Shiloh, 1989) formulated a cognitive theory of the development of interests in which perceived abilities are one of the major determinants of interest development. In a study by Barak, Shiloh, and Haushner (1992) children receiving an intervention designed to increase their perceived abilities on a task also showed increased preference for the tasks subject to manipulation. Although their research supports the postulated role of perceived abilities in the development of interests, the model is more comprehensive than the self-efficacy model per se in its inclusion of perceived and believed needs satisfaction (anticipated satisfaction).

More specifically, Barak (1976, 1981, Chap. 5,this volume) conceptualized interests as emotional manifestations of cognitive processing of vocationally relevant information. The three cognitive determinants of interests were postulated to be perceived abilities, expected success, and anticipated satisfaction. This latter factor is conceptually independent of the other two constructs, since anticipated satisfaction from a task may not always coincide with perceived abilities or expected success related to that task. Research on this model, and its counseling implications, are comprehensively reviewed by Barak (Chap. 5, this volume). Barak further discusses the greater similarity of his model to Krumboltz, Mitchell, and Jones' (1976; Krumboltz & Nichols, 1990) social learning theory of career decision making than to career self-efficacy theory because of the former's more comprehensive focus.

Lapan and his colleagues (Lapan, Boggs, & Morrill, 1989; Lapan, Shaughnessy, & Boggs, 1996) have been pursuing research based on the presumption that increasing self-efficacy can increase interests. Lapan and his colleagues (1989) found evidence that lower self-efficacy with respect to Realistic and Investigative areas may explain women's lower Realistic and Investigative interests. And Lapan and his colleagues (1996) used path analysis to support the importance of both math self-efficacy and math interests in predicting entry into math/science majors and in the mediation of gender differences in these decisions.

A social–cognitive model incorporating both self-efficacy and interests is that of Lent, Brown, and Hackett (1994). Their (1994) model highlights three "person" mechanisms—self-efficacy, outcome expectations, and goals—that form the core of a social cognitive approach to career behavior. In contrast to efficacy expectations, which involve the belief that one can successfully perform a behavior, outcome expectations involve beliefs in the *consequences* of performing those behaviors. Efficacy and outcome expectations must be distinguished because "correct" performance does not always lead to the desired outcome.

Efficacy and outcome expectations are postulated to influence the development both of interests and of goals related to the career choice and decision process, with plans, decisions, aspirations, and behavioral choices all involving goal mechanisms. Lent, Lopez, and Bieschke (1993) provided the first empirical test of the social cognitive model. Their results suggested that self-efficacy mediates the effects of prior performance on interests which, in turn, mediate the effect of self-efficacy on choice intentions. Fouad and Smith (1996) tested the social cognitive model with respect to math and science self-efficacy in a sample of inner city middle school students in the midwest. They also reported a strong relationship between self-efficacy and interests which, in turn, related to choice intentions. Finally, Lopez, Lent, Brown, and Gore (1997) reported the results of a comprehensive test of the social cognitive model for predicting math-related interests and performance in a sample of 296 students enrolled in math courses at a predominantly White, middle-class high school. Both self-efficacy and outcome expectations predict subject matter interest, and self-efficacy partially mediates the effects of measured ability on course grades. Thus, they conclude good support for a model in which ability is related to self-efficacy which, in turn, facilitates stronger outcome expectations and greater interests.

Betz (1999) argued that self-efficacy expectations may mediate the development and/or exploration of interests, through the mechanism of the avoidance behavior postulated to be a consequence of low self-efficacy. That is, if an individual avoids an area because of perceived inability to accomplish the behaviors or tasks involved, it is also unlikely that he or she will gain enough familiarity with the task domain to give interests a chance to develop. As an example, assume an individual who is "computer phobic," avoiding learning to use a computer because of fears that "she can't learn to do it." Until she overcomes her avoidance or is helped to do so, she will never have the opportunity to develop an enjoyment of the many capabilities of computers. Betz (1999) suggests means of both assessment and intervention focused on facilitating interest exploration through increased self-efficacy.

Given both empirical and theoretical support for the possible role of increased self-efficacy in increasing interests, studies of interventions designed to do this are needed and are beginning to appear in the literature. As mentioned previously in this chapter, Luzzo et al. (1998) reported that a math-science self-efficacy intervention increased not only math self-efficacy but math/science interests in a sample of undecided college students.

Betz and Schifano (2000) reported that an intervention focused on Realistic self-efficacy was effective not only in increasing Realistic self-efficacy but Realistic interests in college women. In this study, an all-day intervention, including classes on architecture and the construction trades, the use of hand tools and hardware, and building and repairing common household objects, was utilized.

Thus, there is some evidence that efficacy-based interventions may indeed facilitate interest development focusing as well as increased cognitions of personal efficacy. More research in this area, especially that focused on the development and evaluation of interventions, is needed.

SUMMARY

Career self-efficacy theory is used for understanding, assessing, and designing interventions focusing on career behavior. Few would disagree that in the decades since the publication of the Hackett and Betz (1981) article "Applications of self-efficacy theory to the career development of women," the concept and measures of career self-efficacy have gained widespread acceptance as important career related individual difference variables. What may be especially striking, however, is the intellectual contribution of Samuel H. Osipow to this area of research, beginning with his research in the 1970s on the relationship of self-esteem to career behavior, his development of one of the major measures of career self-efficacy, the TSOSS, and, perhaps most significantly, his research in the early 1970s presaging one of the most promising current directions of career self-efficacy research, that of the relationships between efficacy beliefs and interest development. In addition, his Career Decision Scale, the major measure of career indecision, has been a frequent criterion measure in research on career decision-making self-efficacy. Although I did not originally intend to cite him in nearly every section of this chapter, his work spoke for itself.

As attested to by the preparation of this entire volume, and as illustrated in particular in this chapter, the field of vocational psychology has gained immeasurably through the contributions of Samuel H. Osipow. We thank him.

REFERENCES

Bandura, A. (1977). Self-efficacy: Toward a unifying theory of behavioral change. *Psychological Review, 84,* 191–215.

Bandura, A. (1986). *Social foundations of thought and action.* Englewood Cliffs, NJ: Prentice-Hall.

Barak, A. (1976). *Cognitive aspects of vocational interests.* Unpublished doctoral dissertation, Department of Psychology, The Ohio State University, Columbus.

Barak, A. (1981). Vocational interests: A cognitive view. *Journal of Applied Psychology, 75,* 77–86.

Barak, A., Librowsky, I., & Shiloh, S. (1989). Cognitive determinants of interests: An extension of a theoretical model and initial empirical examinations. *Journal of Vocational Behavior, 34,* 318–334.

Barak, A., Shiloh, S., & Haushner, O. (1992). Modification of interests through cognitive restructuring: Test of a theoretical model in preschool children. *Journal of Counseling Psychology, 39,* 490–497.

Betz, N. E. (1978). Prevalence, distribution, and correlates of math anxiety in college students. *Journal of Counseling Psychology, 25,* 441–448.

Betz, N. E. (1992). Counseling uses of career self-efficacy theory. *Career Development Quarterly, 41,* 22–26.

Betz, N. E. (1997). What stops women and minorities from choosing and completing majors in science and engineering? In D. Johnson (Ed.), *Minorities and girls in school* (pp. 105–140). Thousand Oaks, CA: Sage.

Betz, N. E. (1999). Getting clients to act on their interests: Self-efficacy as a moderator of the implementation of vocational interests. In M. L. Savickas & A. R. Spokane (Eds.), *Occupational Interests: Their meaning, measurement, and use in counseling* (pp. 327–344). Palo Alto, CA: Davies-Black.

Betz, N., Borgen, F., & Harmon, L. (1996). *Skills Confidence Inventory Applications and Technical Guide.* Palo Alto: Consulting Psychologists Press.

Betz, N. E., Borgen, F., Kaplan, A., & Harmon, L. (1998). Gender as a moderator of the validity and interpretive utility of the Skills Confidence Inventory. *Journal of Vocational Behavior, 53,* 1–19.

Betz, N. E., & Hackett, G. (1981). The relationship of career-related self-efficacy expectations to perceived career options in college women and men. *Journal of Counseling Psychology, 28,* 399–410.

Betz, N. E., & Hackett, G. (1983). The relationship of mathematics self-efficacy expectations to the selection of science-based college majors. *Journal of Vocational Behavior, 23,* 329–345.

Betz, N., Harmon, L., & Borgen, F. (1996). The relationships of self-efficacy for the Holland themes to gender, occupational group membership, and vocational interests. *Journal of Counseling Psychology, 43,* 90–98.

Betz, N. E., Klein, K., & Taylor, K. (1996). Evaluation of a short form of the Career Decision-Making Self-Efficacy Scale. *Journal of Career Assessment, 4,* 47–57.

Betz, N., & Luzzo, D. (1996). Career assessment and the Career Decision-Making Self-Efficacy Scale. *Journal of Career Assessment, 4,* 313–328.

Betz, N. E., & Schifano, R. (2000). Increasing realistic self-efficacy and interests in college women. *Journal of Vocational Behavior, 56,* 35–52.

Betz, N., Schifano, R., & Kaplan, A. (1999). Relationships among measures of perceived self-efficacy with respect to basic domains of vocational activity. *Journal of Career Assessment, 7, 213–226.*

Blascovich, J., & Tomaka, J. (1991). Measures of self-esteem. In J. P. Robinson, P. R. Shaver, & L. S. Wrightsman (Eds.), *Measures of personality and social psychological attitudes* (pp. 115–160). San Diego, CA: Academic Press.

Blustein, D. L. (1989). The role of goal instability and career self-efficacy in the career exploration process. *Journal of Vocational Behavior, 35,* 194–203.

Brown, S. D., & Lent, R. W. (1996). A social cognitive framework for career choice counseling. *Career Development Quarterly, 44,* 354–366.

Brown, S. D., Lent, R. W., & Larkin, K. C. (1989). Self-efficacy as a moderator of scholastic aptitude-academic performance relationships. *Journal of Vocational Behavior, 35,* 64–75.

Campbell, N. K., & Hackett, G. (1986). The effects of mathematics task performance on math self-efficacy and task interest. *Journal of Vocational Behavior, 28,* 149–162.

Coopersmith, S. (1975). *Coopersmith Self-Esteem Inventory Technical Manual.* Palo Alto, CA: Consulting Psychologists Press.

Crites, J. O. (1978). *Career Maturity Inventory: Theory and research handbook.* Monterey, CA: CTB/McGraw Hill.

Fassinger, R. E. (1990). Causal models of career choice in two samples of college women. *Journal of Vocational Behavior, 36,* 225–240.

Foltz, B. M. (1993). *The effect of a career counseling workshop on the career self-efficacy of non-traditional college students.* Unpublished doctoral dissertation, Clemson University, South Carolina.

Foss, C. J., & Slaney, R. B. (1986). Increasing nontraditional career choices in women: Relation of attitudes toward women and responses to a career intervention. *Journal of Vocational Behavior, 28,* 191–202.

Fouad, N., & Smith, P. L. (1996). Test of a social-cognitive model for middle school students: Math and science. *Journal of Counseling Psychology, 43,* 338–346.

Fukuyama, M. A., Probert, B. S., Neimeyer, G. J., Nevill, D. D., & Metzler, A. E. (1988). Effects of DISCOVER on career self-efficacy and decision making of undergraduates. *Career Development Quarterly, 37,* 56–62.

Hackett, G. (1985). The role of mathematics self-efficacy in the choice of math-related majors of college women and men: A path model. *Journal of Counseling Psychology, 32,* 47–56.

Hackett, G., & Betz, N. E. (1981). A self-efficacy approach to the career development of women. *Journal of Vocational Behavior, 18,* 326–339.

Hackett, G., & Betz, N. (1989). Mathematics performance, mathematics self-efficacy, and the prediction of math-related college majors. *Journal for Research in Mathematics Education, 20,* 261–273.

Hackett, G., Betz, N. E., Casas, J. M., & Rocha-Singh, I. A. (1992). Gender, ethnicity, and social cognitive factors predicting the academic achievement of students in engineering. *Journal of Counseling Psychology, 39,* 527–538.

Hackett, G., & Campbell, N. (1987). Task self-efficacy and task interest as a function of performance on a gender neutral task. *Journal of Vocational Behavior, 30,* 203–215.

Holland, J. S. (1994). *Self-Directed Search Form R: 1994 Edition.* Odessa, FL: Psychological Assessment Resources.

Holland, J. L. (1997). *Making vocational choices: A theory of vocational personalities and work environments* (3rd ed.). Odessa, FL: Psychological Assessment Resources.

Holland, J. L., Daiger, D. C., & Power, P. G. (1980). Some diagnostic scales for research in decision making and personality. *Journal of Personality and Social Psychology, 39,* 1191–2000.

Korman, A. K. (1967). Self-esteem as a moderator of the relationship between self-perceived abilities and vocational choice. *Journal of Applied Psychology, 51,* 65–67.

Krumboltz, J. D., Mitchell, A. M., & Jones, G. B. (1976). A social learning theory of career selection. *The Counseling Psychologist, 6,* 71–81.

Krumboltz, J. D., & Nichols, C. W. (1990). Integrating the social learning theory of career decision-making. In W. B. Walsh & S. H. Osipow (Eds.), *Career counseling* (pp. 159–192). Hillsdale, NJ: Lawrence Erlbaum Associates.

Lapan, R. T., Boggs, K. R., & Morrill, W. H. (1989). Self-efficacy as a mediator of Investigative and Realistic General Occupational Themes on the Strong Interest Inventory. *Journal of Counseling Psychology, 36,* 176–182.

Lapan, R. T., Shaughnessy, P., & Boggs, K. (1996). Efficacy expectations and vocational interests as mediators between sex and choice of math/science college majors: A longitudinal study. *Journal of Vocational Behavior, 49,* 277–291.

Layton, P. L. (1984). *Self-efficacy, locus of control, career salience, and women's career choice.* Unpublished doctoral dissertation, Department of Psychology, University of Minnesota, Minneapolis.

Lee, J. Y. (1994). *The relationship between women's self-efficacy expectations and career decision status at the college level in Korea.* Unpublished doctoral dissertation, The Ohio State University, Columbus.

Lenox, R., & Subich, L. (1994). The relationship between self-efficacy beliefs and inventoried vocational interests. *Career Development Quarterly, 42,* 302–313.

Lent, R. W., Brown, S. D., Gover, M. R., & Niijer, S. K. (1996). Cognitive assessment of the sources of math self-efficacy: A thought listing analysis. *Journal of Career Assessment, 4,* 33–46.

Lent, R. W., Brown, S. D., & Hackett, G. (1994). Toward a unifying social cognitive theory of career and academic interest, choice, and performance. *Journal of Vocational Behavior, 45,* 79–122.

Lent, R. W., Brown, S. D., & Larkin, K. C. (1984). Relation of self-efficacy expectations to academic achievement and persistence. *Journal of Counseling Psychology, 31,* 356–362.

Lent, R. W., Brown, S. D., & Larkin, K. C. (1986). Self-efficacy in the prediction of academic success and perceived career options. *Journal of Counseling Psychology, 33,* 265–269.

Lent, R., Lopez, F., & Bieschke, K. (1991). Mathematics self-efficacy: Sources and relation to science-based career choice. *Journal of Counseling Psychology, 38,* 424–430.

Lent, R., Lopez, F. G., & Bieschke, K. J. (1993). Predicting mathematics-related choice and success behaviors: Test of an expanded social cognitive model. *Journal of Vocational Behavior, 42,* 223–236.

Lent, R. W., Lopez, F. G., Brown, S. D., & Gore, P. A. Jr. (1996). Latent structure of the sources of mathematics self-efficacy. *Journal of Vocational Behavior, 49,* 292–308.

Leonard, R. L., Jr., Walsh, W. B., & Osipow, S. H. (1973). Self-esteem, self-consistency, and second vocational choice. *Journal of Counseling Psychology, 20,* 91–93.

Lopez, F. G., & Lent, R. W. (1992). Sources of mathematics self-efficacy in high school students. *Career Development Quarterly, 41,* 3–12.

Lopez, F. G., Lent, R. W., Brown, S. D., & Gore, P. A. Jr. (1997). Role of social-cognitive expectations in high school students' mathematics related interest and performance. *Journal of Counseling Psychology, 44,* 44–52.

Luzzo, D. A., Funk, D. P., & Strang, J. (1996). Attributional retraining increases career decision-making self-efficacy. *Career Development Quarterly, 44,* 378–386.

Luzzo, D., Hasper, P., Albert, K., Bibby, M., & Martinelli, E. (1998). Effects of self-efficacy enhancing interventions on the math-science self-efficacy and career interests, goals, and actions of career undecided college students. *Journal of Counseling Psychology, 46,* 233–243.

Luzzo, D. A., & Taylor, M. (1994). Effects of verbal persuasion on the career self-efficacy of college freshmen. *California Association for Counseling and Development Journal, 14,* 31–34.

Mathieu, P. S., Sowa, C. J., & Niles, S. G. (1993). Differences in career self-efficacy among women. *Journal of Career Development, 19,* 187–196.

Matsui, T., Ikeda, H., & Oshnishi, R. (1989). Relations of sex-typed socializations to career self-efficacy expectation of college students. *Journal of Vocational Behavior, 35,* 1–16.

Matsui, T., Matsui, K., & Ohnishi, R. (1990). Mechanisms underlying math self-efficacy learning of college students. *Journal of Vocational Behavior, 37,* 225–238.

McNeill, P. (1990). Impact of a problem-solving vocational intervention on career decision-making self-efficacy and career indecision (Doctoral dissertation, University of Florida, 1990). *Dissertation Abstracts International, 51,* 852A.

Mitchell, S. L. (1990). *The relationship between racial identity attitudes, career self-efficacy, and involvement in campus organizations among black students.* Unpublished doctoral dissertation, Department of Psychology, The Ohio State University, Columbus.

National Science Foundation (1990). *Women and minorities in science and engineering.* Washington, DC: Author.

Nevill, D. D., & Schlecker, D. I. (1988). The relation of self-efficacy and assertiveness to willingness to engage in traditional/nontraditional career activities. *Psychology of Women Quarterly, 12,* 91–98.

Oreshnick, C.A. (1991). Enhancing career decision-making self-efficacy via a university career course intervention (Doctoral dissertation, Iowa State University, 1991). *Dissertation Abstracts International, 53*, 1072B.

Osipow, S. H. (1972). Success and preference: A replication and extension. *Journal of Applied Psychology, 56*, 179–180.

Osipow, S. H. (1987). *Career Decision Scale Manual*. Odessa, FL: Psychological Assessment Resources.

Osipow, S. H., Carney, C. G., & Barak, A. (1976). A scale of educational-vocational undecidedness: A typological approach. *Journal of Vocational Behavior, 9*, 233–243.

Osipow, S. H., & Fitzgerald, L. F. (1996). *Theories of career development* (4th ed.). Needham Heights, MA: Allyn & Bacon.

Osipow, S. H., & Scheid, A. B. (1971). The effect of manipulated success ratios on task preference. *Journal of Vocational Behavior, 1*, 93–98.

Osipow, S. H., & Temple, R. D. (1996). Development and use of the Task-Specific Occupational Self-Efficacy Scale. *Journal of Career Assessment, 4*, 445–456.

Osipow, S. H., Temple, R. D., & Rooney, R. A. (1993). The Short Form of the Task Specific Occupational Self-Efficacy Scale. *Journal of Career Assessment, 1*, 13–20.

Peterson, S. L. (1993). Career decision-making self-efficacy and institutional integration of underprepared college students. *Research in Higher Education, 34*, 659–683.

Post-Kammer, P., & Smith, P. L. (1985). Sex differences in career self-efficacy, consideration, and interests of eighth and ninth graders. *Journal of Counseling Psychology, 32*, 551–555.

Post-Kammer, P., & Smith, P. L. (1986). Sex differences in math and science career self-efficacy among disadvantaged students. *Journal of Vocational Behavior, 29*, 89–101.

Resnick, H., Fauble, M. L., & Osipow, S. H. (1970). Vocational crystallization and self-esteem in college students. *Journal of Counseling Psychology, 17*, 465–467.

Rogers, C. R. (1957). The necessary and sufficient conditions of therapeutic personality change. *Journal of Consulting Psychology, 21*, 95–103.

Rooney, R. A. (1991). *The relationship of task-specific occupational self-efficacy and career interests in college women and men*. Unpublished doctoral dissertation, Department of Psychology, The Ohio State University, Columbus.

Rooney, R. A., & Osipow, S. H. (1992). Task-specific occupational self-efficacy scale: The development and validation of a prototype. *Journal of Vocational Behavior, 40*, 14–32.

Rosenberg, M. (1965). *Society and the adolescent self-image*. Princeton, NJ: Princeton University Press.

Rotberg, H. L., Brown, D., & Ware, W. B. (1987). Career self-efficacy expectations and perceived range of career options in community college students. *Journal of Counseling Psychology, 34*, 164–170.

Schifano, R., & Betz, N. (1998, August). *Increasing realistic self-efficacy and interests in college women*. Paper presented at the annual convention of the American Psychological Association, San Francisco, California.

Sells, L. (1982). Leverage for equal opportunity through mastery of mathematics. In S. M. Humphreys (Ed.), *Women and minorities in science* (pp. 7–26). Boulder, CO: Westview Press.

Shaw, T. D. (1988). The effects of a career counseling/intervention program on student-athletes' career decision-making self-efficacy expectations and their vocational identity. (Doctoral dissertation, Southern Illinois University at Carbondale, 1988). *Dissertation Abstracts International, 51*, 461A.

Siegel, R. G., Galassi, J. P., & Ware, W. B. (1985). A comparison of two models for predicting mathematics performance: Social learning versus math-aptitude-anxiety. *Journal of Counseling Psychology, 32*, 531–538.

Solberg, V. S., Good, G. E., Fischer, A. R., Brown, S. E., & Nord, D. (1995). Relative effects of career search self-efficacy and human agency upon career development. *Journal of Counseling Psychology, 42*, 448–455.

Solberg, V. S., Good, G., Nord, D., et al. (1994). Assessing career search expectations. *Journal of Career Assessment, 2,* 111–123.

Super, D. E. (1951). Vocational adjustment: Implementing a self-concept. *Occupations, 30,* 88–92.

Super, D. E. (1963). Self-concepts in vocational development. In D. E. Super (Ed.), *Career development: Self-concept theory* (pp. 1–16). New York: College Entrance Examination Board.

Super, D. E. (1990). A life-span life-space approach to career development. In D. Brown, & L. Brooks, & Associates (Eds.), *Career choice and development* (2nd ed., pp. 197–261). Hillsdale, NJ: Lawrence Erlbaum Associates.

Taylor, K. M., & Betz, N. E. (1983). Applications of self-efficacy theory to the understanding and treatment of career indecision. *Journal of Vocational Behavior, 22,* 63–81.

Taylor, K. M., & Popma, J. (1990). Construct validity of the career decision-making self-efficacy scale and the relationship of CDMSE to vocational indecision. *Journal of Vocational Behavior, 37,* 17–31.

Temple, R. D. (1991). *The relationship between task-specific self-efficacy and career indecision.* Unpublished master's thesis, The Ohio State University, Columbus.

Temple, R. D. (1996). *Revising the Task-Specific Occupational Self-Efficacy Scale.* Unpublished doctoral dissertation, The Ohio State University, Columbus, Ohio.

Temple, R. D., & Osipow, S. H. (1994). The relationship between task-specific self-efficacy, egalitarianism, and career indecision for females. *Journal of Career Assessment, 2,* 82–90.

U. S. Department of Labor (1981). *Selected characteristics of occupations defined in the Dictionary of Occupational Titles.* Washington, DC: U. S. Government Printing Office.

Williams, T., & Betz, N. (1994). The relationships among occupational and task-specific measures of career self-efficacy. *Journal of Career Assessment, 2,* 341–351.

Zilber, S. M. (1988). *The effects of sex, task performance, and attributional styles on task and career self-efficacy expectations.* Unpublished doctoral dissertation, Department of Psychology, The Ohio State University, Columbus.

Chapter 4

Samuel H. Osipow's Contributions to Occupational Mental Health and the Assessment of Stress: The Occupational Stress Inventory

Arnold R. Spokane
Deborah Ferrara
Lehigh University

> *Recognizing that work occupies a substantial portion of the time that people spend in their waking lives, and recognizing that in any context work is a major source of personal stress or satisfaction, it is clear that attention to occupational mental health provides a significant opportunity both to identify potential resources that people can use to enhance their satisfaction and effectiveness, as well as a significant source of difficulty that either has to be addressed through intervention or which can be prevented or minimized by appropriate programmatic interventions at earlier stages.*
>
> —Osipow (1979, p. 65)

There is a quality about Samuel Osipow's scholarly observations that compels us to read each one of his commentaries. Osipow can synthesize literature in an area of interest, and uncover the essential leading edge of that area of inquiry in a way that makes next intellectual steps obvious. This ability to reconfigure research and theory in unique and heuristic ways and to cut to the heart of important issues accounts for the unusual impact of *Theories of Career Development* (Osipow & Fitzgerald, 1996) in spite of a crowded field of competitive books on the same subject. This ineluctable quality characterized his article on convergence in career development theory (Osipow, 1990) that led to a series of remarkably productive conferences sponsored by the now Society for Vocational Psychology on career development theory and practice (e.g., the convergence conference).

As the opening quote reflects, Osipow (1979) opened occupational mental health as a new area of research and practice to counseling psychology that was both a logical extension and application of the core skills and assumptions that characterize counseling psychology, as well as a reinterpretation of the stress literature to focus on the assessment and promotion of individual coping skills in response to stress. Although this recombination of vocational psychology with health psychology and mental health consultation seems obvious in retrospect, Osipow's discussion of these issues in 1979 presaged a shift in health psychology in precisely the directions that Osipow predicted (Keita & Jones, 1990; see also American Psychological Society's Human Capital Initiative)—the promotion of healthy behavior at work and at home.

As he did in each of his major scale development and research projects, Osipow sought out younger colleagues with whom to collaborate. Although these colleagues provided valuable input, support, and assistance to which Sam has always been open, there should be no mistake about the genesis of the seminal ideas in these projects. In each case it was the fertile and incisive intellect that characterized all of Osipow's contributions to counseling psychology.

Our particular collaboration began in 1980 while Sam was on sabbatical leave at the University of Maryland. We met, agreed to work together, and discovered that we shared common interests in the measurement and characterization of occupational environments. Sam already had already begun work on a comprehensive model of the occupational roles that contribute to stress and strain that integrated the literature on social roles, coping, and the behavioral and physical consequences of role stress. I had been tinkering with item content for a physical environment scale. The result of our collaboration was a comprehensive model and scales to measure occupationally induced stress, strain, and coping. Table 4.1 presents this model.

The model was intended to be generic and to apply across occupational fields and levels. Further, the model was intended to illuminate both the negative consequences of stress and to illustrate how more positive outcomes might result in spite of those stresses. Discussions of the precursors of this model are found in Osipow (1991), Osipow and Spokane (1983, 1987).

Six role stresses (overload, insufficiency, boundary, ambiguity, responsibility, and physical environment) were postulated to result in four strains (vocational, physical, interpersonal and psychological). The frequency, intensity, and duration of these stressors were hypothesized to affect the frequency, intensity, duration, pervasiveness, and disruptiveness of any resulting strains. The model presumes that the stress–strain relationship is mediated by four coping resources (social supports, recreational, selfcare, and rational-cognitive), as well as by several fixed individual differences.

TABLE 4.1
Occupational Stress, Coping, and Strain: A Model

Occupational Stress	Coping	Strain
Role Stresses (Types) overload insufficiency boundary ambiguity responsibility for people physical environment	Resources social supports recreational self-care rational/cognitive	Type vocational physical interpersonal psychological
Role Stresses (Degree) frequency intensity duration	Individual Differences personality age gender ethnicity learning history	Degree frequency intensity duration pervasiveness disruptiveness

Note. From S. H. Osipow & A. R. Spokane, copyright © 1983. *A Manual for Measures of Occupational Stress, Strain, and coping,* Marathon consulting and Press, Columbus, Ohio. Reprinted with permission.

DEVELOPMENT AND VALIDATION
OF THE OSI SCALES

When we began our work in 1980, stress management interventions were beginning to proliferate geometrically, but few if any comprehensive and valid assessment devices existed to measure occupationally-induced stress and its consequences on well-being (i.e., strain). Formulations that included the mediating role of individual coping responses on felt strain were still more rare. Consistent with Osipow's original thinking (1979), we reasoned that substantial levels of occupational role stress might be unavoidable, and thus, individual's ability to mobilize personal and interpersonal resources to combat that stress was crucial in determining the effects of that stress. Further, the promotion of coping was very consistent with the professional role and assumptions of the counseling psychologist.

We began by constructing an interlocking set of homogeneous (theoretical) scales and subscales that corresponded to the elements of the working model, thereby constructing three separate scales: the Occupational Environment Scale (OES; Role Stressors), The Personal Strain Scale (PSS; Role Strains), and the Personal Resources Questionnaire (PSQ; Coping Roles). Each scale contains subscales corresponding with those detailed in the model. The scale and subscale development procedures and assumptions that were driven by theoretical considerations, are described in detail in the OSI Manual (Osipow & Spokane, 1987). The original OSI was released in 1981 and revised in 1983 and 1987 (Osipow & Spokane, 1981, 1983, 1987). A fourth revision, is underway now. Essentially, this process involved the identification of scales and subscales consistent with the model and the distillation of logical, theoretical facets defining each of the subscales. Items were then written to tap each of the facets. Definitions of these scales based on the item content are described in Table 4.2.

THREE PROFILE SAMPLES OF THE OSI

The following three examples (females doing the same job—adult literacy instructor) illustrate different OSI profile types:

Profile A , is a typical profile for a worker who has a single elevation on the Occupational Resources Questionnaire (ORQ) but who shows strong coping to offset that elevation. Note that the Role Ambiguity Scale is high, and when over 70 can be viewed as clinically significant, but that spike is the only apparent stressor. This profile suggests that the individual experiences considerable ambiguity about what she is expected to do, how she should spend her time at work, and what her supervisors generally expect of her. We note, however, in Profile A, that all of the Resource Scales (PRQ) are at or *above* the mean, and thus, all of the strain scores (PSQ) are at or *below* the mean. This respondent has a good balance between occupational stressors and coping resources and thus, experiences minimal strain. Even though the stressor scales are modest, this individual may profit from an intervention with her supervisors to clarify her work role—for example, a job description could be written if one is not available—or she could consult with her supervisors to clarify her role.

Profile B shows a very low stressor report, low strain, and moderate to high coping. This individual either experiences little stress, or chooses to report little stress. Profile C shows a similar, but slightly higher Ambiguity spike than that seen on Profile A, and the Ambiguity score is the only elevation apparent on the profile. Coping resources reported by this individual are minimal, thus resulting in high strain scales. We do note moderate elevations on the psychological strain and physical strain scales, indicating some depression, anxiety, unhappiness or irritability, and worries about health and physical symptoms offset by a fair amount of social support from supervisors and family and friends. It is not unusual for respondents with identical jobs to share similar profiles, though the coping resources brought to bear are generally unique, as they are across the three profiles provided here.

Although a complete discussion of the validation of the OSI is beyond the scope of this contribution, a summary follows. Because the OSI is a

TABLE 4.2
Scale Descriptions and Possible High Score Interpretation

Scale Name	Interpretation
Role Overload (RO)	High scorers may describe their work load as increasing, unreasonable, and unsupported by needed resources. They may describe themselves as not feeling well trained or competent for the job at hand, needing more help, and working under tight deadlines.
Role Insufficiency (RI)	High scorers may report a poor fit between their skills and the job they are performing. They may also report that their career is not progressing and has little future. Needs for recognition and success may not be met. They may report boredom and/or underutilization.
Role Ambiguity (RA)	High scorers may report a poor sense of what they are expected to do, how they should be spending their time, and how they will be evaluated. They seem not to know where to begin on new projects and experience conflicting demands from supervisors. They may also report no clear sense of what they should do to "get ahead."
Role Boundary (RB)	High scorers may report feeling caught between conflicting supervisory demands and factions. They may report not feeling proud of what they do, or not having a stake in the enterprise. They may also report being unclear about authority lines and having more than one person telling them what to do.
Responsibility (R)	High scorers may report high levels of responsibility for the activities and work performance of subordinates. They are worried that others will not perform well. They are sought out for leadership and frequently have to respond to other's problems. They may also have poor relationships with people at work or feel pressure from working with angry or difficult employees or the public.
Physical Environment (PE)	High scorers may report being exposed to high levels of noise, wetness, dust, heat, cold, light, poisonous substances, or unpleasant odors. They may also report having an erratic work schedule or feeling personally isolated.
Vocational Strain (VS)	High scorers may report poor attitudes toward their work, including dread, boredom, and lack of interest. They may report making errors in their work or having accidents. They may also report that the quality of their work is suffering. Concentration problems and absenteeism may be in evidence.
Psychological Strain (PSY)	High scorers may report feeling depressed, anxious, unhappy, and/or irritable. They may report complaining about little things, responding badly in routine situations, and having no sense of humor. They may report that things are not "going well."
Interpersonal Strain (IS)	High scorers may report frequent quarrels or excessive dependency on family members, spouses, and friends. They may report wanting to withdraw and have time alone or, conversely, not having time to spend with friends.

(continued)

83

TABLE 4.2
(Continued)

Physical Strain (PHS)	High scorers may report frequent worries about their health as well as a number of physical symptoms (colds, heart palpitations, aches and pains, stomach aches, and erratic eating habits). They may report unplanned weight changes, overuse of alcohol, and disturbances in sleeping patterns. They may also report feeling lethargy and apathy.
Recreation (RE)	High scorers may report taking advantage of the recreational/leisure time coming to them and engaging in a variety of activities which they find relaxing and satisfying. They may also report doing the things they most enjoy in their spare time.
Self-care (SC)	High scorers may report that they regularly exercise, sleep eight hours per day, are careful about their diet, practice relaxation techniques, and avoid harmful substances (e.g., alcohol, drugs, tobacco, coffee).
Social Supports (SS)	High scorers may report feeling that there is at least one person they can count on and who values and/or loves them. They may report having sympathetic people to talk to about work problems and report having help to do important things and/or things around the house. They may also report feeling close to another individual.
Rational/Cognitive (RC)	High scorers may report that they have a systematic approach to solving problems, think through the consequences of their choices, and are able to identify important elements of problems encountered. They may report being able to set and follow priorities, and have techniques to avoid being distracted. They may also report being able to reexamine and reorganize their work schedule. They put their jobs out of their minds when they go home and feel that there are other jobs besides their present one which they can do.

homogeneous or theoretically derived instrument with practical applications as a central feature, validation of the resulting scales has occurred in four distinct but overlapping phases:

- *Initial psychometric validation*—This work consisted of an examination of the internal consistency, item-scale intercorrelations, and test–retest reliability.
- *Model confirmation*—Consisting of confirmatory factor analyses and tests of the OSI model examining relationships between stress, strain, and coping as predicted by the model.
- *Construct validation*—Studies of the relationship of the OSI scales and subscales to other measures and constructs in order to establish a nomological net of their meaning. This included examination of

OSI Profile Form A for Females

Name_____ Age_____

Job Title_____ Date_____

	ORQ Scales						PSQ Scales				PRQ Scales				
T-Score	RO	RI	RA	RB	R	PE	VS	PSY	IS	PHS	RE	SC	SS	RC	
80--	50	.	.	.	43	40	34	.	.	44	48	.	.	.	-80
-	.	.	38	.	.	39	.	44	40	43	.	48	.	.	
-	49	.	37	44	42	38	33	43	.	.	47	47	.	.	
-	48	.	.	43	41	.	.	42	39	42	46	.	.	.	
-	47	.	36	42	.	37	32	41	38	41	.	46	.	.	
75-	46	50	35	.	40	36	.	.	.	40	45	45	.	.	-75
-	.	49	.	41	39	.	31	40	37	39	44	.	.	.	
-	45	48	34	40	.	35	.	39	36	.	.	44	.	.	
-	44	47	.	39	38	34	30	38	.	38	43	43	50	.	
-	43	46	33	38	37	33	.	.	35	37	42	.	.	.	
70-	42	45	32	.	.	.	29	37	.	36	.	42	.	49	-70
-	41	44	.	37	36	32	.	36	34	.	41	41	.	48	
-	.	43	.	36	35	31	28	35	33	35	40	.	.	.	
-	40	42	.	35	.	30	.	.	.	34	39	40	.	47	
-	39	41	30	34	34	.	27	34	32	33	.	39	.	.	
65-	38	40	29	.	.	29	.	33	.	32	38	38	.	46	-65
-	37	39	.	33	33	28	26	32	31	.	37	.	.	45	
-	.	38	28	32	32	27	.	31	.	31	.	37	.	.	
-	36	37	27	31	.	.	25	.	30	30	36	36	50	44	
-	35	36	.	30	31	26	.	30	29	29	35	.	49	.	
60-	34	35	26	.	30	25	24	29	28	28	.	35	48	43	-60
-	33	34	.	29	.	24	.	28	.	.	34	34	.	42	
-	.	33	25	28	29	.	23	.	27	27	.	.	47	.	
-	32	32	24	27	28	23	.	27	.	26	.	33	.	41	
-	31	.	.	26	.	22	22	26	26	25	32	32	45	40	
55-	30	31	23	.	27	21	.	25	25	.	31	.	.	.	-55
-	29	30	.	.	26	.	21	.	.	24	.	31	44	39	
-	28	29	22	24	.	20	.	24	24	23	30	30	43	.	
-	.	28	21	23	25	19	20	.	23	22	29	.	42	.	
-	27	.	.	22	24	.	.	.	.	21	.	29	.	37	
50-	26	26	20	.	.	18	19	.	22	.	28	28	41	.	-50
-	25	25	19	21	23	17	18	.	.	20	27	.	40	36	
-	24	24	.	20	22	16	.	20	21	19	.	27	39	.	
-	.	23	18	19	.	.	17	19	20	.	26	26	.	35	
-	23	22	.	18	21	15	.	18	.	.	25	25	38	34	
45-	.	21	17	.	.	14	16	.	19	17	24	.	37	.	-45
-	21	20	16	17	.	.	.	17	18	16	.	24	36	33	
-	20	19	.	16	19	.	15	16	.	15	23	23	.	.	
-	.	18	15	15	18	12	.	15	17	14	22	.	35	32	
-	19	17	.	14	.	11	14	.	.	.	.	22	34	31	
40-	18	16	14	.	17	10	.	14	16	13	21	21	33	.	-40
-	17	15	13	13	16	.	13	13	15	12	20	.	32	30	
-	16	14	.	12	.	.	.	12	.	11	.	20	.	29	
-	15	13	12	11	15	.	11	11	.	10	19	19	31	.	
-	.	12	11	.	14	.	.	.	.	.	18	.	30	28	
35-	14	11	.	10	.	.	10	10	.	.	.	18	29	.	-35
-	13	10	10	.	13	.	.	.	12	.	17	17	.	27	
-	12	.	.	.	12	.	10	.	.	.	16	.	28	26	
-	11	.	.	.	.	.	.	.	11	.	.	16	27	.	
-	.	.	.	.	11	.	.	.	.	10	15	15	26	25	
30-	10	.	.	.	10	.	.	.	.	.	14	.	.	.	-30
-	.	.	.	.	.	.	.	.	.	.	.	14	25	24	
-	.	.	.	.	.	.	.	.	.	.	13	13	24	23	
-	.	.	.	.	.	.	.	.	.	.	12	12	23	.	
-	.	.	.	.	.	.	.	.	.	.	.	.	.	22	
25-	.	.	.	.	.	.	.	.	.	.	.	11	22	.	-25
-	.	.	.	.	.	.	.	.	.	.	.	10	21	21	
-	.	.	.	.	.	.	.	.	.	.	.	.	20	20	
-	.	.	.	.	.	.	.	.	.	.	.	.	19	19	
20-	.	.	.	.	.	.	.	.	.	.	.	.	18	18	-20

T-Score	RO	RI	RA	RB	R	PE	VS	PSY	IS	PHS	RE	SC	SS	RC
Raw Scores	22	27	31	25	27	13	11	23	13	18	33	34	46	38

Profile Form A. From Psychological Assessment Resources, Inc./P.O. Box 998/Odessa, FL 33556. Copyright © 1981, 1983, 1987 by Psychological Assessment Resources, Inc. Reprinted with permission.

85

OSI Profile Form B for Females

Name_____Age_____

Job Title_____Date_____

T-Score	RO	RI	RA	RB	R	PE	VS	PSY	IS	PHS	RE	SC	SS	RC	
			ORQ Scales					PSQ Scales				PRQ Scales			
80–	50	.	.	.	43	40	34	.	.	44	48	.	.	.	–80
-	.	.	38	.	.	39	.	44	40	43	.	48	.	.	-
-	49	.	37	44	42	38	33	43	.	.	47	47	.	.	-
-	48	.	.	43	41	.	..	42	39	42	46	.	.	.	-
-	47	.	36	42	.	37	32	41	38	41	.	46	.	.	-
75–	46	50	35	.	40	36	.	.	.	40	45	45	.	.	–75
-	.	49	.	41	39	.	31	40	37	39	44	.	.	.	-
-	45	48	34	40	.	35	.	39	36	.	.	44	.	.	-
-	44	47	.	39	38	34	30	38	.	38	43	43	.	50	-
-	43	46	33	38	37	33	.	.	35	37	42	.	.	.	-
70–	42	45	32	.	.	.	29	37	.	36	.	42	.	49	–70
-	41	44	.	37	36	32	.	36	34	.	41	41	.	48	-
-	.	43	31	36	35	31	28	35	33	35	40	.	.	.	-
-	40	42	.	35	.	30	.	.	.	34	39	40	.	47	-
-	39	41	30	34	34	.	27	.	32	33	.	39	.	.	-
65–	38	40	29	.	.	29	.	33	.	32	38	38	.	46	–65
-	37	39	.	33	33	28	26	32	31	.	37	.	.	45	-
-	.	38	28	32	32	27	.	31	.	31	.	37	.	.	-
-	36	37	27	31	.	.	25	.	30	30	36	36	50	44	-
-	35	36	.	30	31	26	.	30	29	29	35	.	49	.	-
60–	34	35	26	.	30	25	24	29	28	28	.	35	48	43	–60
-	33	34	.	29	.	24	.	28	.	.	34	34	.	42	-
-	.	33	25	28	29	23	23	27	27	27	33	.	47	.	-
-	32	32	24	27	28	.	.	.	.	26	.	32	46	41	-
-	31	.	.	26	.	22	22	26	26	25	32	32	45	40	-
55–	30	31	23	.	27	21	.	25	25	.	31	.	.	.	–55
-	29	30	.	25	26	.	21	.	.	24	.	31	44	39	-
-	28	29	22	24	.	20	.	24	24	23	30	30	43	.	-
-	.	28	21	23	25	19	20	23	23	22	29	.	42	38	-
-	27	27	.	22	24	.	.	22	.	.	.	29	.	37	-
50–	26	26	20	.	.	18	19	21	22	20	28	28	41	.	–50
-	25	25	19	21	23	17	18	.	.	20	27	.	40	36	-
-	24	24	.	20	22	16	.	20	21	19	.	27	39	.	-
-	.	.	18	19	.	15	17	19	20	18	26	26	.	35	-
45–	22	22	17	18	.	15	16	18	.	17	25	25	38	34	-
-	22	21	17	.	.	14	.	17	19	17	24	.	37	.	–45
-	21	20	.	17	.	13	15	16	18	16	23	24	36	33	-
-	20	19	.	16	19	.	.	15	.	15	22	23	.	.	-
-	.	18	15	15	18	12	.	.	17	14	.	.	35	32	-
-	19	17	.	14	.	.	14	.	.	.	.	22	34	31	-
40–	18	16	14	.	17	10	.	14	16	13	21	21	33	.	–40
-	17	15	13	12	16	.	13	.	.	12	20	.	32	30	-
-	16	14	.	.	.	.	12	12	.	11	.	20	.	29	-
-	15	13	12	11	15	.	12	11	14	10	19	19	31	.	-
35–	14	11	.	10	.	.	.	10	.	.	18	.	30	28	–35
-	13	10	10	.	13	.	.	.	12	.	17	18	29	.	-
-	12	.	.	.	12	.	10	.	11	.	16	17	.	27	-
-	11	.	.	.	.	.	.	.	11	.	.	16	28	26	-
-	.	.	.	11	.	.	.	.	10	.	15	15	27	25	-
30–	10	.	.	.	10	.	.	.	.	.	14	.	26	.	–30
-	.	.	.	.	.	.	.	.	.	.	13	14	25	24	-
-	.	.	.	.	.	.	.	.	.	.	12	13	24	23	-
-	.	.	.	.	.	.	.	.	.	.	.	12	23	.	-
-	.	.	.	.	.	.	.	.	.	.	.	.	.	22	-
25–	.	.	.	.	.	.	.	.	.	.	.	11	22	.	–25
-	.	.	.	.	.	.	.	.	.	.	.	10	21	21	-
-	.	.	.	.	.	.	.	.	.	.	.	.	20	20	-
-	.	.	.	.	.	.	.	.	.	.	.	.	.	.	-
-	.	.	.	.	.	.	.	.	.	.	.	.	19	19	-
20–	.	.	.	.	.	.	.	.	.	.	.	.	18	18	–20
T-Score	RO	RI	RA	RB	R	PE	VS	PSY	IS	PHS	RE	SC	SS	RC	
Raw Scores	23	23	16	12	21	11	11	13	15	21	30	33	46	42	

Profile Form B. From Psychological Assessment Resources, Inc./P.O. Box 998/Odessa, FL 33556. Copyright © 1981, 1983, 1987 by Psychological Assessment Resources, Inc. Reprinted with permission.

86

OSI Profile Form C for Females

Name_____Age_____

Job Title_____Date_____

		ORQ Scales					PSQ Scales				PRQ Scales			
T-Score	RO	RI	RA	RB	R	PE	VS	PSY	IS	PHS	RE	SC	SS	RC	
80–	50	·	·	·	43	40	34	-	-	44	48	-	·	·	–80
-	-	-	38	·	-	39	·	44	40	43	-	48	-	·	
-	49	·	37	44	42	38	33	43	-	-	47	47	-	·	
-	48	·	·	43	41	-	··	42	39	42	46	-	-	·	
-	47	·	36	42	-	37	32	41	38	41	-	46	-	·	
75–	46	50	35	-	40	36	-	-	-	40	45	45	-	·	–75
-	·	49	-	41	39	·	31	40	37	39	44	-	-	·	
-	45	48	34	40	·	35	·	39	36	·	-	44	-	-	
-	44	47	·	39	38	34	30	38	-	38	43	43	-	50	
-	43	46	31	38	37	33	-	-	35	37	42	-	-	49	
70–	42	45	·	-	-	-	29	37	-	36	-	42	-	49	–70
-	41	44	·	37	36	32	-	36	34	-	41	41	-	48	
-	-	43	31	36	35	31	28	·	33	35	40	-	-	-	
-	40	42	-	35	-	30	-	·	-	34	39	40	-	47	
-	39	41	30	34	34	-	27	34	32	33	-	39	-	-	
65–	38	40	29	-	-	29	-	33	-	32	38	38	-	46	–65
-	37	39	·	33	33	28	26	32	31	-	37	-	-	45	
-	-	38	28	32	32	27	-	31	-	31	-	37	-	-	
-	36	37	27	31	-	-	25	-	30	30	36	36	50	44	
-	35	36	-	30	31	26	-	30	29	29	35	-	49	-	
60–	34	35	26	-	30	25	24	29	28	28	-	35	48	43	–60
-	33	34	-	29	-	24	-	28	-	-	34	34	-	42	
-	-	33	25	28	29	-	23	-	27	27	33	-	·	-	
-	32	32	24	27	28	23	·	27	-	26	-	33	44	41	
-	31	·	-	26	-	22	22	26	26	25	32	32	45	40	
55–	30	31	23	-	27	21	25	25	25	-	31	-	-	-	–55
-	29	30	·	25	26	-	24	-	-	24	-	31	44	39	
-	28	29	22	24	-	20	-	24	24	23	30	30	43	-	
-	-	28	21	23	25	19	20	23	23	22	29	-	42	38	
-	27	27	-	22	24	-	-	22	-	21	-	29	-	37	
50–	26	26	20	-	-	18	19	21	22	-	28	28	41	-	–50
-	25	25	19	21	23	17	18	-	-	20	27	-	40	36	
-	24	24	-	20	22	16	-	20	21	19	-	27	39	-	
-	·	23	18	19	-	-	17	19	20	18	26	26	-	35	
-	23	22	17	18	21	15	16	18	19	·	26	25	38	34	
45–	22	21	17	-	-	14	16	-	19	17	24	-	37	-	–45
-	21	21	16	-	-	13	-	17	18	16	-	-	36	33	
-	20	19	-	16	19	-	15	16	-	15	23	23	-	-	
-	18	18	15	15	18	-	-	15	-	14	22	-	35	32	
-	19	17	-	14	-	11	14	-	-	-	-	22	34	31	
40–	18	16	14	-	-	10	-	14	-	13	21	21	33	-	–40
-	17	15	13	13	16	-	13	13	15	12	20	-	32	30	
-	16	14	-	12	-	-	-	12	-	11	-	20	-	29	
-	15	13	12	11	15	-	12	11	14	10	19	19	31	28	
35–	14	11	11	-	14	-	11	10	13	-	18	-	30	-	–35
-	13	10	10	-	13	-	-	-	12	-	17	17	29	27	
-	12	·	·	·	12	-	10	-	-	-	16	-	28	26	
-	11	·	·	·	·	-	·	-	11	-	-	16	27	-	
30–	10	·	·	·	10	-	·	·	10	-	15	15	26	25	–30
-	·	·	·	·	·	·	·	·	·	·	-	14	·	·	
-	·	·	·	·	·	·	·	·	·	·	13	13	24	23	
-	·	·	·	·	·	·	·	·	·	·	12	12	23	·	
25–	·	·	·	·	·	·	·	·	·	·	-	11	22	22	–25
-	·	·	·	·	·	·	·	·	·	·	-	10	21	21	
-	·	·	·	·	·	·	·	·	·	·	-	-	20	20	
20–	·	·	·	·	·	·	·	·	·	·	-	-	19	19	–20
													18	18	

T-Score	RO	RI	RA	RB	R	PE	VS	PSY	IS	PHS	RE	SC	SS	RC
Raw Scores	21	20	33	17	17	12	21	36	16	30	25	24	47	28

Profile Form C. From Psychological Assessment Resources, Inc./P.O. Box 998/Odessa, FL 33556. Copyright © 1981, 1983, 1987 by Psychological Assessment Resources, Inc. Reprinted with permission.

gender differences as well as replications across occupational samples for confirmation of the generic nature of the scales.
*   *Utility or functional validation*—Inlcuding studies of the effects of
    interventions employing the OSI, and the use of the OSI as an out-
    come measure in other practical applications.

EMPIRICAL EVIDENCE FOR THE OSI SYSTEM

The evidential base for the OSI, which now numbers more than 60 studies, is too extensive to discuss in detail in a single book chapter. We do
attempt to highlight and illustrate some of the more important themes and
outcomes in research on the OSI. The reader is referred to the OSI Manual (Osipow & Spokane, 1987) for a more extensive treatment of these
studies. Studies completed since 1987 are featured in the present review.

In Decker and Borgen (1993), 249 employed women and men completed the OSI, the Minnesota Satisfaction Questionnaire, and a negative
affectivity scale. A hierarchical regression analysis revealed that the
stress–strain link was largest when an organizational triad of subscales
(insufficiency, boundary, ambiguity) was included. Overwork was less of a
contributor to strain and satisfaction than were "poorly defined work
roles." This thorough study also found that stress contributed heavily to
intrinsic and extrinsic job satisfaction, well beyond the variance explain-
able by negative affectivity. Finally, higher levels of coping were most
closely related with interpersonal and physical strain. Generally, in these
analyses, relationships predicted by the model were confirmed, and gender was not a significant determinant of outcomes.

Sowa, May, and Niles (1994) found that male and female counselors ($n =$
125) who reported high levels of stress also reported significantly higher
levels of strain and lower levels of coping—consistent with the predictions
of the model. Similarly, Aitken, and Schloss (1994) gave the OSI to 150 male
and female mental health workers. Correlations between the OSI scales and
the subscales of the Maslach Burnout Inventory (MBI) and measures of anxiety and depression were all in the direction predicted by the OSI model—
Stress and Strain were positively correlated with state and trait anxiety and
depression—whereas coping was negatively related with these three measures. Aitken and Schloss found the strongest associative relationship
between the PSQ and the measures of mental health status.

Pithers and Fogarty (1995) studied 83 vocational teachers and 71 non-
teachers in an attempt to compare levels of occupational stress. Although
there are problems in comparing one occupational sample with another,
especially when there may be sampling differences between the groups,
these vocational teachers reported less stress than comparison groups.

Although complete tabular data were not available, some significant gender differences were noted.

Lagace (1988) gave 138 salesmen and women the role stress subscales from the OSI, as well as measures of job performance and job satisfaction. Few gender differences were found on the subscales with the exception of Role Overload on which the saleswomen scored higher. In a regression analysis, only role insufficiency predicted job satisfaction for the women, whereas for the men both Role Overload and Role Insufficiency were related to job satisfaction.

Stillson, O'Neil, and Owen (1991) used cannonical correlation to study gender role conflict and strain among 134 working White, Black, Asian, and Hispanic men. One discrete group of these men reported low vocational strain but elevated physical strain—a combination that was associated with self-reported success, power, and competition, restrictive emotionality, and work–family conflict.

In a recent study, Buboltz (1997) gave 171 working adults the OSI, the Hoppock Job Satisfaction Blank, and the Career Mastery Inventory (Crites, 1978). Once again, no significant gender differences were found. Multiple regression analysis revealed significant relationships between career mastery and reported occupational stress and strain as well as with coping in theoretically expected directions. The authors concluded that a reciprocal relationship exists between task mastery and stress strain and coping.

A review of the usage patterns and research studies indicates that the OSI appears to be a particularly popular tool for use in understanding occupationally-induced stress among teachers (Bertoch, Nielson, Curley, & Borg, 1989; Kaunitz, Spokane, Lissitz, & Strein, 1986; Pithers & Fogarty, 1995), among child-care workers (Chang, 1992; Kountz, 1990), in business settings (Barber, 1990; Gardner, 1991; Kagan et al., 1995; Lagace, 1988), in healthcare environments (Aitken & Schloss, 1994) and for women clients generally (Long, 1989; Matsui et al., 1995; Pugh, 1989). One particularly practical finding is that strain is greater for workers who do not isolate work stress from family interactions (Kauntiz et al., 1986).

The Japanese Version of the OSI

Japanese interest in occupationally induced stress increased sharply during the 1980s and 1990s. Some of this increase was in reaction to several publicized deaths attributed to a syndrome the Japanese call "Karoshi" or sudden cardiac death. Some of the increase in interest in stress is the result of an aging workforce with increasing numbers of women entering the labor force. A 1993 Japanese interest in and translation of the OSI (Tanaka, Watanabe, & Kosaka, 1993) paved the way for a number of subsequent papers and articles (Matsui & Onglatco, 1992; Matsui, Oshawa, & Onglatco, 1995; Tanaka, Watanabe, & Kosaka, 1994).

A complete description of the efforts to translate and validate the OSI in a Japanese sample is contained in Tanaka et al. (1993). Internal consistencies were similar to those found on the English version. The Japanese version of the OSI was administered to 226 Japanese adults, and a confirmatory factor analysis using a six-factor solution closely replicated the English edition. Complex interactions were found between sex, age, and occupational rank on role stressors and role strains. Tanaka et al. (1994) administered the Japanese version of the OSI to 1085 employed Japanese men and women in 50 occupations. Multivariate analyses revealed higher responsibility and lower overload, ambiguity insufficiency, boundary, and physical environment scores among older workers. Middle-aged respondents reported more interpersonal strain than older or younger participants, and older respondents reported higher use of recreational, self-care, and rational cognitive coping but lower levels of social support than did younger respondents. Matsui et al. (1995) studied work–family conflict among 131 Japanese women. When total Strain from the OSI was used as a dependent measure, a small but significant relationship was found between family work conflict and life strain. Further, family role definition did not buffer the effects of family conflict on strain.

INTERVENTIONS TO PROMOTE COPING
AND REDUCE STRESS AND STRAIN

Although most of the early work on the OSI involved scale construction and validation efforts, Dorn (1991) correctly notes that less attention has been paid to counseling interventions. This does not mean that practical applications have not been conducted, but rather that these practical strategies have not been communicated in the professional literature. This section describes some of those interventions and observes that the more than 2,000 user sites that employ the OSI have developed many more such strategies.

During the past 15 years of development and intervention with the OSI, several novel practical applications have proven useful. These interventions include interpretive workshops, organizational consultations, resource center modules, and various clinical interventions. Each of these interventions has been used repeatedly with success. A description of a few successful applications follows.

The OSI Interpretive Workshop

Our experience with small and large group interpretive workshops has been very gratifying. In general, participants appreciate the feedback from the OSI, and participate readily and with a minimum of threat in such group activities. Further, there is sufficient empirical evidence of the effectiveness of stress interventions generally (Ivanevich, Matteson, Freedman, & Phillips, 1990; Keita, & Jones, 1990) and for OSI-based interpretive workshops specifically (Higgins, 1986; Kagan, Kagan (Klein) & Watson, 1995) for us to feel comfortable recommending these interventions for general use.

Most organizations will need to be encouraged to allot sufficient time to implement an effective stress reduction intervention. Typically, efforts begin with a one-hour seminar over lunch, or a half-day workshop. The following describes a one-day workshop with consultations or "booster" interventions.

Full-Day OSI Workshop

30 min—Brief overview of the problem of stress in the workplace and its effects on human behavior—overview of workshop.

One hour—One-Two-Four-Eight Worksheet on identifying stress and coping strategies (Fig. 4.1).

15 min—Discussion and processing of One-Two-Four-Eight

Break

45 min—Introduction to OSI Model plus case examples

Lunch

One hour—Participants receive OSI profile and scale descriptions Q & A

90 min—Small Group session on Short and long-term action planning to reduce stress and improve coping on an individual and organizational level

One hour—Demonstration of stress reduction techniques—e.g., Jacobsen deep muscle relaxation

Wrapup

This one-day workshop can be conducted as a one-half day intervention as follows:

Half-Day OSI Workshop

30 min—Brief overview of the problem of stress in the workplace and its effects on human behavior—overview of workshop.

One hour—One-Two-Four-Eight Exercise on identifying stress and coping strategies

15 min—Discussion and processing of One-Two-Four-Eight

Break

30 min—Introduction to OSI Model plus case examples

30 min—Participants receive OSI profile and scale descriptions Q & A

One-Two-Four-Eight Exercise on Sources of Stress

One-two-four-eight is a consensus seeking exercise designed to assist an intact working group to identify and clarify needed actions on issues of importance. This exercise is a useful consulting tool for developing cohesiveness in a work team, or for resolving disparate opinions on a difficult topic. One-two-four-eight has proven effective in a wide variety of organizational settings, and for diverse problem types, and also serves as an icebreaker for group interactions.

In our case, we are using 1-2-4-8 to identify sources of stress among literacy educators, and ways of handling that stress successfully. Later participants can use these strategies to improve their personal coping.

The following steps are taken to implement 1-2-4-8.

Step 1: Individuals in the group complete a worksheet identifying sources of stress among literacy educators.

Step 2: After completing the worksheets, each individual pairs up with another participant—hopefully someone they don't know. Each member of the pair introduces him/herself to the other member of the pair. Each member then describes the toughest client they ever had.

Step 3: Next, the two lists are combined on a third worksheet. If there are overlaps in the qualities described (i.e., the same qualities on both lists), a consensus must be reached about the most important component requirements and their order of importance.

Step 4: The pairs form into fours. Each member of a four introduces themselves by indicating one successful instance where they experienced stress and managed to cope effectively with that stress. The "two" lists are then combined into a single list, and where there are overlaps, consensus is reached.

Step 5: The fours form into eights, and members reintroduce themselves, this time describing any useful specific strategies they have tried for reducing the stress in their job. A final consensus list is compiled.

Step 6: The final lists are placed on newsprint and taped on the wall for discussion. The focus of the discussion is on sources of stress and ways for successfully coping with that stress.

One-Two-Four-Eight Worksheet
Identifying Sources of Stress

1. What sources of stress can you identify in your present work environment?

2. What successful strategies have you tried or observed others using for dealing with the stressors that you identified in 1?

FIG. 4.1.   One-two-four-eight exercise on sources of stress and the worksheet.

The goals of these workshops are to sensitize participants to sources of stress in their work environment, to teach them the OSI model as a way of understanding and acting upon these stresses, and finally, to provide individualized feedback on their OSI profile. The full-day workshop also attempts to engage individuals, groups, and organizations in planning efforts aimed at providing assistance, training, or organizational development designed to enhance efforts to cope constructively with work-related stress. As we note in the research section, these efforts appear to produce positive outcomes.

REVIEWS AND CONSTRUCTIVE CRITICISM

Reviews of the 1987 version of the OSI (Bunda, 1992; Cochran, 1992; Colbrow, 1992; Dorn, 1991; Powell, 1991; Swanson, 1991; Yanico, 1985) provide balanced, constructive feedback on the inventory and its uses. These reviews generally conclude that the OSI although it has some limits, is an integrated, psychometrically sound and practical device for use in a variety of research and practical applications. Reviewers find the internal consistency evidence sufficient and the factor structure to be consistent with the hypothesized model. Most reviewers also appreciate the efforts to examine the OSI and its properties in empirical investigations. These same reviewers , however, raise questions about the size and representativeness of the normative sample, a problem which is presently being addressed in a revision of the OSI. Reviewers find the OSI promising, await sufficient evidence to convert the research version to a clinical version, and provide suggestions many of which have been addressed in the upcoming revision.

THE OSI IN THE CONTEXT OF THE EMERGING
FIELD OF HEALTH PSYCHOLOGY

Recent research on the increased risk of fatalities among heart attack victims who are depressed—and the establishment of the link between depression and coronary functioning generally, reminds us of the crucial role that applied and preventive psychology must play in physical, as well as mental health treatment. Adler and Matthews (1994) review of the field of health psychology underscores the importance of individual behavior style in the etiology and progression of a host of immunological responses as well. The OSI, with its underpinning in prevention and its emphasis on multiple levels of intervention (e.g., individual, family, work group, supervisory, and general organizational) embodies the unique perspective and application strategies that counseling psychologists bring to the field of health psychology. There is much to learn not only about how individuals respond to social stressors, the relation of health and personalities, and how we can assist individuals to adopt more healthy behaviors.

Sam Osipow's insightful foray into the field of occupational mental health, then, has resulted in a valid and reliable instrument to measure occupational stress, strain, and coping, as well as an array of practical interventions to reduce the detrimental effects of work-related stressors.

REFERENCES

Aitken, C. J., & Schloss, J. A. (1994). Occupational stress and burnout amongst staff working with people with an intellectual disability. *Behavioral Interventions, 9*, 225–234.

Adler, N., & Matthews, K. (1994). Health psychology: Why do some people get sick and some stay well? *Annual Review of Psychology, 45*, 229–259.

American Psychological Society (APS). (1993). *The human capital initiative: The changing nature of work*. Washington, DC: Author.

Bertoch, M. R., Nielson, E. C., Curley, J. R., & Borg, W. R. (1989). Reducing teacher stress. *Journal of Experimental Education, 57*, 117–128.

Brown, P. R. (1987). *Occupational stress, strain, and coping resources as predictors of military performance*. Unpublished doctoral dissertation, Vanderbilt University, Nashville, TN.

Buboltz, W. C. (1997). *Occupational stress and career development task mastery*. Paper presented at the annual meeting of the American Psychological Association, Chicago, IL.

Bunda, M. A. (1992). Review of the Occupational Stress Inventory. *Mental Measurements Yearbook, 11*, 623.

Chang, S. H. (1992). The effect of stress management intervention on job stress in child careworkers (Doctoral dissertation, Drake University, 1990). *Dissertation Abstracts International, 52*, 2027.

Cochran, L. (1992). Review of the Occupational Stress Inventory. *Mental Measurements Yearbook, 11*, 623–624.

Colbrow, L. (1992). Review of the Occupational Stress Inventory. *Mental Measurements Yearbook, 11*, 623–624.

Crites, J. O. (1978). *Career Mastery Inventory, Theory and Research Handbook*. Mastry, CA: CTB/McGraw-Hill.

Decker, P. J., & Borgen, F. H. (1994). Occupational strain and job satisfaction: Hierarchical prediction by negative affectivity, occupational stress, and coping. *Journal of Counseling Psychology, 40*, 470–478.

Dorn, F. J. (1991). The Occupational Stress Inventory: A picture worth a thousand words about work. *Journal of Counseling and Development, 70*, 328–329.

Gardner, J. K. (1991). *A comparison of the occupational stress and related variables among salespersons, clerical staff, service technicians, and managers of the mid-Ohio district of the Xerox Corporation*. Unpublished doctoral dissertation, The Ohio State University.

Harden, S. (1986). *A comparison of type A and type B behavior pattern stress coping behaviors in working men and women*. Unpublished doctoral dissertation, United States International University, San Diego, CA.

Higgins, N. C. (1986). Occupational stress and working women: The effectiveness of two stress-reduction programs. *Journal of Vocational Behavior, 29,* 66–78.

Ivanevich, J. M., Matteson, M. T. Freedman, S. M., & Phillips, J. S. (1990). Worksite stress management interventions. *American Psychologist, 45,* 252–261.

James, M. M. (1989). Occupational stress among black professionals. Doctoral dissertation, Ohio State University, *Dissertation Abstracts International, 50,* 102.

Kagan, N. I., Kagan (Klein), H., & Watson, M. G. (1994). Stress reduction in the workplace: The effectiveness of psychoeducational programs. *Journal of Counseling Psychology, 42,* 71–78.

Kaunitz, N., Spokane, A. R., Lissitz, R. W., & Strein, W. O. (1986). Stress in student teachers: A multidimensional scaling analysis of elicited stressful situations. *Teaching and Teacher Education, 2,* 169–180.

Keita, G. P., & Jones, J. M. (1990). Reducing adverse reaction to stress in the workplace: Psychology's expanding role. *American Psychologist, 45,* 1137–1141.

Kountz, M. R. (1990). Occupational stress and job satisfaction for direct care workers in residential child care facilities (Doctoral dissertation, California School of Professional Psychology–Fresno). *Dissertation Abstracts International, 51,* 3136.

Lagace, R. R. (1988). Role-stress differences between salesmen and saleswomen: Effect on job satisfaction and performance. *Psychological Reports, 62,* 815–825.

Long, B. C. (1989). Sex-role orientation, coping strategies, and self-efficacy of women in traditional and nontraditional occupations. *Psychology of Women Quarterly, 13,* 307–324.

Matsui, T., Oshawa, T., & Onglatco, M. (1995). Work-family conflict and the stress buffering effects of husband support and coping behavior among Japanese married working women. *Journal of Vocational Behavior, 47,* 178–192

Olson, V. A. (1992). *Closure stress: A study to determine the effect of military base closure on affiliated personnel.* Unpublished master's thesis, Embry-Riddle Aeronautical University, Daytona Beach, FL.

Osipow, S. H. (1979). Occupational mental health: Another role for counseling psychologists. *The Counseling Psychologist, 8,* 65–70.

Osipow, S. H. (1990). Convergence in theories of career choice and development: Review and prospect. *Journal of Vocational Behavior, 36,* 122–131.

Osipow, S. H. (1991). Developing instruments for use in counseling. *Journal of Counseling and Development, 70,* 322–326.

Osipow, S. H., & Fitzgerald, L. F. (1996). *Theories of career development (4th ed.).* Boston: Allyn & Bacon.

Osipow, S. H., & Spokane, A. R. (1981). Measures of occupational stress, strain, and coping (Form E-1). Columbus, OH: Marathon Consulting and Press.

Osipow, S. H., & Spokane, A. R. (1983). Manual for Measures of occupational stress, strain, and coping (Form E-2). Columbus, OH: Marathon Consulting and Press.

Osipow, S. H., & Spokane, A. R. (1987). *Manual for the Occupational Stress Inventory: Research version.* Odessa, FL: Psychological Assessment Resources.

Pithers, R. T., & Fogarty, G. J. (1995). Symposium on teacher stress: Occupational stress among vocational teachers. *British Journal of Educational Psychology, 65,* 3–14.

Powell, T. E. (1991). A review of the Occupational Stress Inventory. *Measurement and Evaluation in Counseling and Development, 24,* 127–130.

Pugh, S. C. (1989). Employment status and job related stress for women in a typical Ohio county. Unpublished master's thesis, Ohio State University, Columbus.

Sowa, C. J., May, K. M., & Niles, S. G. (1994). Occupational stress within the counseling profession: Implications for counselor training. *Counselor Education and Supervision, 34,* 19–29.

Stillson, R. W., O'Neil, J. M., & Owen, S. V. (1991). Predictors of adult men's gender-role conflict: Race, class, unemployment, age, instrumentally-expressiveness, and personal strain. *Journal of Counseling Psychology, 38,* 458–464.

Swanson, J. L. (1991). The Occupational Stress Inventory. (Research version). In D. J. Keyser
    & R. C. Sweetland (Eds.), *Test critiques*. Kansas City, MO: Test Corporation of America.
Tanaka, K., Watanabe, M., & Kosaka, T. (1993). The development of a Japanese Version of
    the Occupational Stress Inventory: Basic and theoretical applicability. *Bulletin of the Fac-
    ulty of Education*, Okayama University, *No. 93*, July 1993, 185–195.
Tanaka, K., Watanabe, M., & Kosaka, T. (1994). *Occupational stress, strain, and coping across the
    life span of Japanese workers.* Paper presented at the 23rd annual conference of the Inter-
    national Congress of Applied Psychology, Madrid, Spain.
Yanico, B. J. (1985). Occupational Environment Scales Form E2. In D. J. Keyser & R. C.
    Sweetland (Eds.), *Test critiques* (Vol. II). Kansas City, MO: Test Corporation of America.

Chapter 5

A Cognitive View of the Nature of Vocational Interests: Implications for Career Assessment, Counseling, and Research

Azy Barak
University of Haifa

The term *cognition* and the related adjective *cognitive* were, for many years, associated with experimental psychology and related areas such as learning, memory, and thinking. These terms were introduced to applied domains of psychology in the 1960s. Sam Osipow was one of the pioneers in adapting these terms into counseling and career psychology, using cognitive-behavioral and cognitive-behavioral-related variables in his early research (Osipow, 1962, 1969, 1972; Osipow & Scheid, 1971) and conceptual writings (Osipow, 1970; Osipow & Walsh 1970a, 1970b).

As Sam's student in the early 1970s, I accepted these new perspectives with much enthusiasm because they opened new and exciting windows for my psychological conceptualizations and philosophy. Sam has greatly inspired my professional development in this respect. He has lead me to an insight—reflecting throughout my career and various areas of scientific involvement—that the way one cognitively processes information has a great impact on one's behavior and emotions and that individuals process information differently; therefore, reality is only secondary in importance to subjective, cognitive (i.e., perceptual and interpretational) processes. In my doctoral dissertation (Barak, 1976), under Sam's supervision, I put together my thoughts and ideas related to my cognitive conceptualization of vocational interests, and empirically tested some of them. I have intermittently continued to develop and examine this model over the years. However, Sam's special viewpoint has inspired my research on topics other than vocational interests with which I have been involved, from counselor's ratings to empathy training, vocational development and choice, career counseling effectiveness, sexual harassment, and even the effects of pornography.

This chapter presents a current summary of my cognitive conceptualization of vocational interests and its implications for interest assessment, career counseling, and related topics, originally influenced by Sam's views. However, this chapter, together with a few other writings, also challenges the common, conservative, but dominant career counseling approaches. Many of the ideas presented here have also been inspired by Sam's quiet resistance to the trait-and-factor school of thought applied to career counseling, as was already made clear in the first edition of his classic *Theories of Career Development* (Osipow, 1968) and recently in a professional colloquium (Osipow, 1998). My views on the concept of vocational interests and career counseling—and other relevant considerations, such as measurement or training—are actually similar to certain others in this area, but challenge most prevailing approaches. I have laid open these ideas, dedicated to Sam, as suggestions and propositions to be further conceptually discussed and empirically examined.

INTRODUCTION

Case 1: Bob, a 3-year-old boy, tells you he would like to be an astronaut when he grows up. And Carol (case 2), a 4-year-old girl, tells you she would like to be a ballet dancer when she is older. Being a nice person, you will probably heed Bob's and Carol's occupational daydreams with much respect and attention but will sensitively disregard them as being relevant, reliable, and valid bits of information on which their careers should be based and planned. Why do we all refer to a child's desire to become a police officer, a fire fighter, a physician, a locomotive driver, a professional basketball player, or a teacher as naive, immature, and childish? Why do we regard occupational interests manifested (e.g., through game activities) or verbally proclaimed by these youngsters as reflecting nothing other than immature ideas?

Case 3: Ted, a 20-year-old man, is a sophomore at a university. He has not decided on a specific study program yet has taken a number of introductory courses in various disciplines. When you had the chance to talk to him, he told you that he wanted to study law. He was interested in the constitution and the legal system; liked to watch Court TV; closely followed O. J. Simpson's criminal and civil trials; admired famous lawyers and judges; and had even read several of their biographies. However, in evaluating his abilities and skills, you found that Ted had poor verbal ability (i.e., vocabulary, oral communication skills, and writing skills) and had mediocre grades both in high school and in his first three semesters in undergraduate studies. In your conversation with him, he also lacked concentration in thinking and seemed to be anxious, and to lack confidence. With this information in mind, would you encourage him to pursue a legal career?

Case 4: Alice, a 19-year-old woman, has just graduated from high school. You had an opportunity to converse with her too and found out that she was interested in going into a computer-related career. She seemed to be enthusiastic about the central place computers had taken in the modern world; about the endless possibilities in pursuing this career path; about the opportunity to develop, explore, and invent in this area, about the great job market, as well as about her personal fascination with a personal computer. This clear interest of hers was especially marked compared to her lack of any special attraction to other occupational fields or careers. She was very indifferent, and even inimical, about activities and tasks related to a variety of other occupations, including business-, technical-, art-, or people-related occupations. However, in closely examining her case, you found out that Alice had extraordinary artistic skills: She draws beautifully, she was a member of an art club and for years, her paintings decorated the school walls. You had a clear impression that Alice is very talented in arts, is highly creative, and considerably productive for her age. Now, let us hear your thoughts: Would you disregard or minimize these talents and encourage her to purse a career in computers?

Let me guess a few of your considerations in trying to analyze the cases of Bob, Carol, Ted, and Alice. First, it seems reasonable that you did not judge the vocational interests manifested by Bob and Carol and those expressed by Ted and Alice similarly, because you have referred to *age* as an important factor. But why is age a relevant consideration in assessing vocational daydreams and plans? It seems that we hold a belief (albeit a valid one) that children's vocational interests, as compared with older people's, are determined by *irrelevant, erroneous, and biased* ideas. Second, we assume that older individuals—especially after a certain age—possess interests that are more *stable* than those of children. Third, you may also presuppose that children would *process information* (as opposed to holding certain content-bound ideas) related to themselves, as well as to the world which surrounds them—differently (apparently in a less intelligent or knowledgeable manner) from older people, thus they might end up with mistaken (or, at least, less accurate) impressions and consequent desires. These three factors (among other considerations) would probably affect anybody who reviews these cases, a professional and a lay person alike. The common implicit theme seems to be that we consider children to possess different, less sophisticated, thinking mechanisms than adults, and hence, we attribute the resulting affects or motivations (namely, interests) to those immature cognitive processes. Therefore, we tend to consider children's occupational interests as being unreliable and invalid data on which to base any career planning, although we tend to do the opposite or, at least, to do it differently, with adults. That is, *we implicitly hold an assumption that thinking-related competencies are an important factor in determining the nature of interests*. We return to this intuitive (but insightful) assumption later.

Another consideration you may have used in evaluating Bob's, Carol's, Ted's, and Alice's career-related ideas has to do with the ways and means vocational interests were expressed. You would apparently regard an interest expressed through oral manifestation differently from one expressed through actual actions, a formal interest assessment instrument, and so on. It seems reasonable to believe that you would think that the more *committing and obligatory* the expressions of interests are, the more truly they reflect internal and authentic motivations. Therefore, it is fair to assume that you attributed more importance to Alice's successful artistic performance, or to Ted's legal-related activities, than to their verbally expressed career attitudes.

Yet a third element you may have considered in assessing Bob's, Carol's, Ted's, and Alice's occupational ideas had to do with comparing their expressed interests versus their abilities and skills. Although in the cases of Bob and Carol, this consideration was simply impossible, due to their young age, it becomes central (or, at least, highly important) in the cases of the two older persons, Ted and Alice. Naturally and logically, you contrasted their verbally expressed vocational interests and—based on your knowledge, experience, or "hunch"—related them to corresponding abilities and skills these individuals possess. Ideally, and consistent with common assumptions in the area of career decision making, you would find it simple to match people with jobs (or professions) where the person's characteristics "fit" what the job has to offer. However, in the earlier examples, this match would not be simple, because Ted's interests and skills, like Alice's, do not seem to fit. In this case, I suppose, you would suggest a profession, or a certain specialty within an occupation, where one can combine interests–desires and abilities–skills. Actually, there are numerous occupational opportunities that focus on rather specific aspects of a vocation, where specific individual expectations may be more fully met.

Note that common to all three major considerations indicated we have automatically tried to apply logic and reason to analyze a person's interests. In other words, we intuitively referred to the *nature of interests*, or what we assume about this nature, in trying to analytically understand their essence and to come up with insightful ideas. It is arguable that we assumed that we implicitly referred to interests as being *active and dynamic* in our analysis. We did not refer to interests as given static data, where a formula could be used to come up with a solution (i.e., career decision), assuming the input is passively preset.

For years, career counselors have been trained to conceptualize a career choice as a sort of combination of "objective" data related to one's characteristics and one's interests, or feelings and thoughts toward (or against) occupations (e.g., occupational values), and their relation to or match with the characteristics of occupations or occupational environments. This matchmaking approach was suggested in the early 1900s (Parsons, 1909) and further conceptualized in the 1920s (Kitson, 1925); 1930s (Paterson & Darley, 1936; Williamson, 1939a, 1939b); 1940s (Berdie, 1949); 1950s (Darley, 1950); and 1960s (Lofquist & Dawis, 1969). The approach was reinforced by Holland's (1973, 1985a, 1997) still-dominating theory of vocational choice, as well as by Dawis and Lofquist's (1984) theory of work adjustment. Generally, it seems that career counselors, encouraged by various ongoing models of career decision making, have been looking for a match or an approximation between a person's profile, that is, his or her capabilities as well as desires on the one hand, and occupational requirements and satisfiers on the other. A balance (or an ideal identity) between a person's talents, abilities, and traits, as well as his or her motives, and the characteristics of a profession (or a specific job) have been thought to be the desired end product of career counseling.

However, the thrust of the current conceptualization is that *vocational interests should generally be regarded as one's emotions* (i.e., subjective feelings or affects) that stem from and are caused by various cognitive mechanisms and processes (i.e., thought patterns and contents). These emotions, when dysfunctional, counterproductive, destructive, or incompatible (with "objective" relevant information) should be *a target for change* and not a source or an input for career decision making. Therefore, it is proposed here that the role of career counseling is to identify clients' strengths and weaknesses through independent, professional observation and to foster, nourish, and reinforce consistent emotions toward them. The role of a career counselor is, thus, not to merely assess client information and put it into a passive and static decision-making formula but to dynamically and actively modify and restructure clients' emotions of attraction to and repulsion from activities and occupations consistent with their personal strengths and weaknesses. It should be noted that we use the term *strengths and weaknesses* as a general term, referring to both cognitive abilities, as well as to physical characteristics or personality traits.

TRADITIONAL APPROACHES TO INTERESTS

Interests have traditionally been thought to be a central concept in career development theory and research (Osipow & Fitzgerald, 1996). This perhaps mirrors people's reference to their individual interests, rather than other personal characteristics such as personality traits or special abilities, in considering career-related choices and subsequent decisions. That is, it is quite common for people to consider their interests as a primary or superior factor on which to base their decisions, apparently well above other factors that objectively have been shown to be of similar value in predicting various career outcome criteria (Walsh & Betz, 1995). Another indicator of the great importance attributed to vocational interests in career decision making is the overwhelming use of interest inventories by counselors over other career-related instruments (Watkins, Campbell, & Nieberding, 1994).

Scientists investigating vocational psychology have proposed various theories and hypotheses as to the nature of interests, their origin, and development. Not surprisingly, these views are as broad and varied as psychological conceptualizations are with any other meaningful psychological construct. One may find that all major psychological schools of thought have been adopted to conceptualize interests, from the traditional psychoanalytic approach, to more current personality theories, to biologically related explanations, and to behavioristic formulations. Similar to the case of the conception and assessment of intelligence, professionals and scholars alike were typically interested in practical subjects such as measuring interests and finding convenient, valid, and an appropriate diagnostics system to efficiently integrate this with counseling. This practical emphasis was preferred over developing better understanding of the concept of interests. And, similarly to the study of intelligence (Cronbach, 1990), the question remains whether one can investigate a psychological entity before conceptually defining it, or if it is impossible to develop conceptualization before collecting empirical observations in a systematic way, which reminds us of the classic chicken and the egg question.

It is not surprising, therefore, that all major interest measurement scales, as well as less central ones, did not deal at all, or did not deal thoroughly, with conceptual issues concerning the nature of interests, and found it quite sufficient to develop operational definitions which survived reliability and external validity testings. Thus, manuals and related publications that describe the development of interest measures address the concept of interest in a rather general and vague fashion, usually in referring to *interests* as "likes" and "dislikes" (of occupations, activities, courses, hobbies, and the like), as if the audience has an accepted and agreed upon understanding of the concept at hand. And indeed, in reviewing the writings describing the common interest measures such as the Strong Vocational Interest Blank and its various revisions and editions (Hansen & Campbell, 1985), the Kuder Occupational Interest Survey (Zytowski & Kuder, 1986), the Jackson Vocational Interest Survey (JVIS; Jackson, 1993), the Vocational Preference Inventory (Holland, 1985b), the Self-

Directed Search (Holland, Fritzsche, & Powell, 1994), the Ramak (Barak & Meir, 1974; Meir & Barak, 1973; see also Meir & Tziner, chap. 6, this volume), and many more, it is clear that while psychometrics received major emphasis, the conceptual discussion and definition of interests was virtually neglected.

However, a few attempts were actually made at understanding the nature of interests. Influenced by the psychodynamic view of personality, several researchers argued that interests reflect basic unconscious needs, motives, conflicts, defense mechanisms and other such psychoanalytically related concepts. Bordin (1953), for instance, claimed that a person's interests reflect his or her personality structure, as determined in early development, influenced by factors such as identification with a father's occupation. More specifically, within the psychodynamic framework, Lang (1964) viewed interests as reflecting object relations, reflecting on the people relatedness nature of career development as well as on specific vocational choice through separation-individualization and differentiation processes. Darley and Hagenah (1955), in the same but somewhat broader framework, suggested that interests indirectly reflect personality structure by the intervening processes of the individual value system, needs, and motivations. Schaffer (1953) put a major emphasis on personal needs, and claimed that interest measurement is actually need measurement. The intensive work of Roe (1956; Roe & Seligman, 1964) proposed that interests—a major construct in her career development theory—are multiply determined: they are a causal product of mother–child relationship, in combination with other personality as well as biological factors.

A number of researchers have proposed learning-based models to explain the development of interests. Berdie (1943, 1944), for example, argued that a study of interests is actually a study of motivational learning, in the context of personality development and genetic factors. Other researchers (Asch, 1952; Brender, 1960; Fryer, 1931) also put heavy emphasis on motivation of various kinds (i.e., intrinsic–extrinsic), and claimed that individual's interests are outer expressions of this motivation factor. Still other researchers (e.g., Strong, 1943, 1951) put more emphasis on learning processes and claimed that interests are habituated activities. Darley and Hagenah (1955), in a comprehensive review of these and other proposals, suggested that interests are multiply determined by personality needs, motivational, and learning mechanisms. They, too, suggested that interests are the end product of such processes, differently structured and weighted in various individuals. Likewise, Fletcher (1966), in analyzing interets, values, and attitudes, viewed all of these as concepts in general and argued that they develop in a similar way to any concept formation. In a thorough discussion, he argued that these concepts develop in a combination of need satisfaction, learning, and consequent generalized dispositions.

Quite a few psychological conceptualizations referred to interests as dispositions or patterns, that is, as an expression or reflection of a total personality structure or type. This approach is well represented by Holland (1966, 1973, 1985a, 1997), who viewed interests as one of the expressions of a personality type, as defined by his RIASEC model [R (Realistic), I (Investigative), A (Artistic), S (Social), E (Enterprising), and S (Social)]. Holland did not attempt to make a distinction between interests and other expressions (e.g., preferences, behaviors) belonging to a certain personality type, but analyzed this concept in the framework of a total or global set of emotional, thinking, and behavioral patterns. Thus, a realistic-type person is generally characterized by a set of behaviors (e.g., repairs appliances or machines), thinking patterns (e.g., concrete and organized planing), and emotional reactions (e.g., dislikes nurturing people), whereas his or her interests are a given byproduct of this pattern. It is impossible to understand the nature, development, or change of interests by this rather schematic approach because it lacks specificity, as well as content-related formulations to enable the understanding of interests as a dynamic phenomenon.

The foregoing sample of views and approaches generally represents the overall picture of psychological approaches to interests. However, given the premise stated in introducing this issue, that interests—from many perspectives—are regarded as a crucial factor in career choice and development by lay people, as well as by professionals, it is suggested that this distinct psychological construct receives a special focus. One of these special attempts was made in the model presented in the next section.

THE COGNITIVE MODEL OF INTERESTS

Overview

The cognitive model of interests was first proposed by Barak (1976, 1981), and has been partially extended in later publications (Barak, Librowski, & Shiloh, 1989; Barak, Shiloh, & Haushner, 1992). Although Barak's approach was different from and independent of existing traditional conceptualizations of interests (Betz, 1992), it was generally derived from cognitive views of work-related attitudes, such as Vroom's (1964) theory of work motivation, Locke's (1965, 1966) model of task liking, Super's (1963) idea of implementation of self-concept in career development, and Osipow's analysis of task preferences (Osipow, 1972; Osipow & Scheid, 1971).

Consistent with cognitive conceptualizations of personality, and unlike traditional models of interests, Barak's approach argued that, in principle, interests are emotional manifestations of cognitive processes which adapt vocational relevant information. Thus, interests are basically emotions or feelings: feelings that reflect the degree of attraction toward an occupation, a task, an activity, or a training course, or aversion thereof. These feelings originate from a person's thoughts concerning stimulus concepts (e.g., an image of a specific occupation). The contents of these thoughts are based on a person's assumptions, beliefs, perceptions, stereotypes, expectations, attributions, memories, or cognitive schemas in general, and other related cognitive mechanisms and processes. The cognitive schemas and elements are distorted, in principle (e.g., Fiske, 1981; Kruglanski, 1980; Kruglanski & Ajzen, 1983), in relation to vocational stimuli, as they are distorted in relation to any other stimuli. Thus, feelings stemming from these processes are based, in principle, on unsubstantiated, partial, wrong, or subjectively biased information and hence could not be considered as a valid guide to one's career choice.

Specifically relevant to career-related thought processes, Barak (1981) identified three specific elements, which he termed the *cognitive determinants of interests*. It is important to stress that these three distinct yet parallel processes were not identified or defined on an arbitrary basis, nor were they based on a practical consideration. As reviewed by Barak (1981), these elements were isolated and highlighted because of extensive accumulated empirical research, as well as related theoretical considerations, which pointed at their significance. Having clarified that, it is not argued here that these are *the only* three relevant or important cognitive determinants of interests, but that they have been found to be conceptually, as well as empirically valid. In addition, the order of the three factors as described shortly is rather random, because each of them is equally important, in principle, to the determination of interests. Moreover, research showed that for different individuals, and for different stimuli, another cognitive determinant could have more weight than any other two.

Perceived Abilities. The first cognitive determinant of interests referred to a person's perceived abilities to perform in certain tasks. This factor refers to the way an individual evaluates his or her potential—either intellectual, physical, or related to personality traits—relative to what she or he believes is needed to do well in accomplishing these tasks. Thus, two different and independent cognitive processes are involved here: what a person believes about his or her own capabilities, and what she or he believes about the requirements needed to perform in a given activity (or a set of activities). The gap, or the correspondence, between these two perceptual elements is responsible for the degree of how well a person believes she or he is able to perform in this activity. Interestingly, but not surprisingly, these two perceptual elements have but little to do with reality for many people. That is, it is well documented that perceived abilities are far from being identical to actual (real) level of abilities (see review by Barak, 1981) and, likewise, it has been shown that perceptions of occupations, for instance, are far from being accurate or valid (e.g., Gerhart, 1988; Osipow, 1962).

As indicated earlier, perceived abilities do not only refer to intellectual abilities, as commonly conceptualized or measured. For instance, Holland et al.'s (1994) Self-Directed Search (SDS) refers to "self-ratings" that basically comprise of intellectual evaluations, and not to other, relevant self-perceptions. However, this narrow definition of self-perceptions was better referred to in Campbell Interest and Skill Survey (Campbell, Hyne, & Nilsen, 1992), which includes different types of abilities in the perceived skills section of the instrument. It is also important to note that "perceived abilities" is a *relative* factor, not an absolute one, as it relates to a given anchoring point. That is, a person may believe that she or he has the math abilities needed to function as a cashier but not to function as a mechanical engineer. In the same vein, perceived abilities are attached to various stimulus contents differently. That is, a person may evaluate his or her abilities differently in relation to a certain activity, a study course, or an occupation, despite the fact they may all have a common denominator and belong to the same vocational field. Whereas Holland et al.'s (1994) SDS, in the two self-ratings sections, ignores this simple factor by asking respondents to rate their abilities independent of a stimulus, Campbell Interest and Skill Survey (Campbell et al., 1992) is correctly asking people to rate their perceived skills in relation to specific content items.

Expected Success. The second cognitive determinant of interests referred to a person's estimation of his or her success in performing in various tasks. Obviously, this factor is somewhat dependent on perceived abilities, because abilities are thought to be a necessary component of success. However, perceived ability is not the only factor in estimating future success in a given activity, because there are also well-known external factors that determine the degree of success. For instance, the factor of expected luck (or fate) is a common one, and this factor plays a major role in people's attitudes, decisions, and motivation (e.g., Kassner, 1990). Another factor refers to situational circumstances which may be random, uncontrolled, and certainly beyond the capacity of a person. This latter factor may include temporal variables such as weather or traffic conditions or more global ones such as political atmosphere, and economics and the job market. As was argued by the Social Learning Theory of Career Decision Making (SLTCDM; Krumboltz, 1979, 1994a; Krumboltz, Mitchell, & Jones, 1976; Krumboltz & Nichols, 1990; Mitchell & Krumboltz, 1990), circumstantial events may prove to be more relevant and more critical in one's career development than is normally considered important. A third factor that may influence expected success refers to functioning of other people. That is, in many tasks, the degree of a person's accomplishment is dependent upon constructive collaboration (or destructive competition) by others (e.g., Sommer, 1995). Hence, what a person believes about others' relevant behavior may become another crucial element in determining his or her degree of expected success level. A fourth factor affecting the level of expected success are personality characteristics that are related to one's own predictions of personal future events. Specifically, personal level of self-confidence may affect a person's certainty in accomplishing a task; individual degree of risk-taking may relate to readiness to be engaged in certain activities; internal versus external locus of control may be correlated with personal predictions of success in interaction with the type of activity involved; and level of pessimism–optimism as a personal trait is certainly related to a person's expectation of success. Obviously, all four factors presented here are, in principle, independent of one's perceived abilities in determining one's level of expected success.

Anticipated Satisfaction. The third cognitive determinant of a person's individual interests referred to his or her anticipated satisfaction from engaging in an activity. This factor too is conceptually independent of the other two cognitive determinants. That is, a person may not believe he or she is capable of performing well in a given task, expect only mediocre performance, and still anticipate a high level of satisfaction. Likewise, a person may perceive him or herself as highly capable of performing a given task, expect a relatively high level of success when performing this task, but still anticipate little satisfaction from engaging in that task.

The reasons why anticipated satisfaction gained from doing something does not necessarily coincide with perceived abilities to do it and expected success in doing it, are numerous, and refer to both situational variables as well as personality dispositions. Situational variables include factors as simple as the weather (e.g., "I can play soccer well in any weather, I believe I can score a goal even if it is wet, but I don't enjoy playing soccer when it is raining because I hate this feeling") or the time of day, or more complicated ones, such as a person's emotional state or mood. Personality dispositions influencing interests, or anticipation of satisfying personal needs, may include basic psychological needs (e.g., need for affiliation) and personal values (Nevo, Nevo, & Zehavi, 1993), as well as cognitive factors such as gender, social, and occupational stereotypes.

The Development of Interests

According to Barak's model, interests get modified as a result of the differential development of the three cognitive determinants. The personal shaping of these determinants is dependent on personal experiences, but not necessarily actual ones. As noted by the SLTCDM in discussing self-observation generalizations—the cognitive concept by which interests are produced according to this approach—experiences that influence the development may be actual, vicarious, or simply imagined. There is no preference or superiority for any of these three sources of gathered cognitive information over the others. Thus, positive (or negative) actual experiences in any given activity or set of activities alone may not determine attraction toward (or repulsion from) these activities if other, competitive cognitive experiences have taken place. Hence, only a thorough cognitive mapping of an individual's experiences, based on all possible sources of cognitive structuring mechanisms, could explain the development of interests. Therefore, according to Barak's model, behavioristic explanations of the development of interests are too simplistic in nature, and only more comprehensive, multilevel investigation may lead to better understanding of the development of an individual's structure of interests.

Research

Several research investigations were carried out to test some hypotheses stemming from Barak's model of the modification of interests. The purpose of the first study (Barak et al., 1989, Study 1), was to examine if and to what degree the three cognitive determinants were actually related to interests. A sample of 144 female and 144 male first-year college students were administered questionnaires aimed at measuring the variables of perceived abilities, expected success, anticipated satisfaction, and interests. The measurement was conducted across three stimulus contents, including various activities, academic courses, and occupations, representing Roe's (1956) eight occupational fields. The findings showed that (a) all three cognitive determinants were highly correlated with interests in all three stimulus contents and all eight occupational fields. The correlations varied from .57 to .87 (all p's < .01); (b) multiple correlations of the three cognitive determinants with interests were in the .80s (all p's < .01); (c) generally, anticipated satisfaction had higher correlations with interests than either perceived abilities or expected success. However, this finding varied among occupational fields and stimulus content; and (d) subsequent analyses showed that in most cases at least (any) two of the cognitive determinants significantly had higher correlations with interests than either one of them. This finding means that interests were indeed correlated with different combinations of the cognitive determinants and not with any one of them. The significance of this point is discussed next.

The purpose of a second study (Barak et al., 1989, Study 2), was to examine the relationships of the cognitive determinants and interests intrapersonally, or within individuals (in contrast to Study 1 which examined these relationships interpersonally, or across individuals), as well as to study the relationships of the cognitive determinants and several cognitive mechanisms. Participants in this study included 116 female and 107 male job applicants with a mean age of 30 years. They were administered a questionnaire consisting of a list of 30 activities, each five representing one of Holland's (1985a) six vocational types, to which they were instructed to respond (separately) according to their interests, perceived abilities, causal internal or external, and stable or unstable, attributions of expected success. Individual rank-order correlations were computed between the order of interests in each of the six fields, and the other variables. Results (similar for both genders) showed that the mean personal correlation between perceived abilities and interests was .59 and approximately 90% of the personal correlations were .35 (the critical significance value for $p < .01$). In addition, personal mean correlations of .48 to .64 were found for the two types of attributions and perceived abilities, while they were in the .30s and .40s with interests. Interestingly, a recent study by Tracy and Ward (1998) found correspondence between interests and competence perceptions consistent with the current view, increasing with age of the research participants. The meaning of these findings is that perceived abilities are highly correlated with interests within individuals, mirroring what was found across individuals in Study 1. In addition, it showed that relevant cognitive mechanisms were indeed correlated with these variables, and higher (as hypothesized) with perceived abilities than with interests. Although the findings in these studies were consistent with the hypotheses derived from Barak's model, they should be considered as necessary but insufficient conditions for its validity. Further, experimentally based research was needed to provide clearer evidence for the model's pertinence, as presented next.

In a third study (Barak et al., 1992), an attempt was made to use Barak's model to modify interests of young children. Assuming that childrens' interests are not crystalized and stable and that childern are less acquainted with a variety of activities than older people, Barak et al. (1992) examined how the restructuring of the cognitive detrminants could modify interests of 40 preschool children in four game activities. The cognitive restructuring manipulation was applied through personal self-talk treatment (Meichenbaum, 1977). This cognitive manipulation was compared with a behavioral reinforcement of 40 other children, and to 20 children who were in a no-treatment control group. Interests were measured before, immediately after, and 2 weeks after manipulations were conducted. The results, for both genders, showed that the children in the cognitive restructuring manipulation group changed their interests according to the desired direction, as opposed to the other two groups who did not change. These results were stable over the 2-week testing period. This finding supported Barak's model. However, a question remains as to what degree *each* of the cognitive determinants was necessary (or sufficient) to cause the modification of interests. For that reason, the following experiment was conducted.

In an unpublished study (Okev, 1993), Barak's et al.'s (1992) study was replicated and extended in two ways. First, instead of four game activities, six activities—representing Holland's (1985a) six vocational types—were used. Second, instead of having a single cognitive restructuring group—based on an intervention that included manipulation of all three cognitive determinants together—separate experimental cognitive restructuring groups of preschool children ($N = 140$; 70 boys and 70 girls) were treated. Each of these groups was exposed to a different manipulation of interests through self-talk in referring to perceived abilities alone; expected success alone; anticipated satisfaction alone; perceived abilities and expected success alone; perceived abilities and anticipated satisfaction alone; expected success and aniticipated satisfaction alone; and all three cognitive determinants (replicating Barak et al.'s, 1992, cognitive restructuring manipulation). Generally, the results showed that manipulating each of the cognitive determinants separately, for both genders, caused significant change in the order of preference for the game activities in the hypothesized direction. These effects remained stable over the 2-week testing period. Further examination of the data showed that each of the cognitive determinants separately was able to affect interests in a similar way; manipulation of any single cognitive determinant was sufficient to cause interest change; and manipulation of two or more cognitive determinants did not cause stronger effects on interest change than manipulation of any single one. These findings supported Barak's model in that it is sufficient to restructure any one of the cognitive determinants alone to cause interest change.

In a second unpublished study (Blau, 1991), a test of Barak's model was done from another prespective. In this study, mathematical and verbal abilities, vocational interests, sex-role, and the three cognitive determinants of 256 (112 men and 144 women, age ranged from 18 to 57) career undecided clients in a counseling agency were tested. Results revealed that

1. as expected, actual (tested) abilities and the cognitive determinants did not correlate, including perceived abilities in specific fields;
2. also as expected, there were no significant relationships between actual abilities and interests;
3. consistent with Barak's model, all three cognitive determinants highly correlated with interests in respective fields;
4. different combinations of the cognitive determinants were included in multiple correlations with intersts in different fields. Overall, each and every cognitive determinant contributed independent variance to the multiple correlation of interests significantly;
5. differences in social and mathematical-related interests between men and women were highly visible. These differences coincided

with the cognitive determinants and not with differences in actual abilities;

6. sex-role did not add any significant variance to the prediction of interests over the three cognitive determinants.

These findings highly supported Barak's model. In addition, they showed how this model is able to explain differential interests between men and women.

Some predictions derived from Barak's model were also tested in a study aimed at examining children's gender-stereotyped interests. In this study (Barak, Feldman, & Noy, 1991), the level of traditionality of 113 preschool children's interests was assessed. It was found, for both boys and girls, that this variable was correlated with the traditionality of their mothers' occupations. This supported the model's hypothesis that distal factors may indeed be responsible for the development of interests rather than relevant or valid factors such as actual abilities or achievements. That is, gender-linked differentiation of interests may be an outgrowth of child-relevant (and possibly distorted) cognitive contents which may lead to occupational conceptions and consequent vocationally related self-schema, resulting in "invalid" or "faulty" interests.

In summary, these studies provided strong support to Barak's model concerning the nature and development of interests. In using very different populations, measures, and research foci, it was consistently found that the cognitive determinants are not only highly correlated with interests, but apparently can cause change in them. In addition, and in line with accumulated research evidence, the studies provided strong support to the basic argument that people's cognitive processes, including perceptions, attributions, expectations, beliefs, stereoypes, and so on, intervene between actual experiences, events, and facts, and subjective affects (i.e., interests). As argued by Barak (1981; Barak et al., 1989; Barak et al., 1992), this may suggest a basic and meaningful approach to career development and related counseling intervention theory (elaborated next).

THE CORRESPONDENCE TO THE SOCIAL COGNITIVE CAREER THEORY AND THE CAREER SELF-EFFICACY MODEL

A similar view on the development, nature, and role of vocational interests was proposed by the career self-efficacy model, more recently entitled the Social Cognitive Career Theory (SCCT) of career development (Lent & Brown, 1996; Lent & Hackett, 1994; Lent, Brown, & Hackett, 1994; see

Betz, chap. 3, this volume). This model which, to some degree, iterates, paraphrases, and expands Barak's model, basically relies on Bandura's (1986) self-efficacy theory. The work on the SCCT was inspired by an innovative theoretical model (Betz & Hackett, 1981; Hackett & Betz, 1981) and the development of the Occupational Self-Efficacy Scale (Betz & Hackett, 1981) which was constructed in purpose to examine the hypothesis that gender differences in career choice and preferences are related to different vocational self-efficacy beliefs of men and women. While supporting this hypothesis, in this particular study, as well as in a series of numerous other ones (e.g., Post-Krammer & Smith, 1986; Rotberg, Brown, & Ware, 1987; Williams & Betz, 1994. See Betz, chap. 3, this volume, for a comprehensive revue), Hacket's and Betz's original idea became a cornerstone in developing a more pervasive approach to implementing the self-efficacy beliefs concept into career development theory. Numerous invesigations tested various career behavior-related topics while attempting to learn the intervening role of relevant career self-efficay beliefs, such as in predicting academic persistence and performance of science and engineering students (Lent, Brown, & Larkin, 1984, 1986), relationships with Holland's (1985a) vocational types (Lapan, Boggs, & Morrill, 1989), or relationships with career decision making (Betz & Luzzo, 1996). A special line of research examined and consistently found positive correlations between career self-efficacy beliefs and corresponding vocational interests. In addition to Lapan et al. (1989), this relationship was supported by numerous studies in various populations using various measures (e.g., Church, Teresa, Rosenbrook, Szendre, 1992; Lapan, Shaughnessy, & Boggs, 1996; Lopez, Lent, Brown, & Gore, 1997). This latter finding closely relates to Barak's view concerning the nature of interests, in that it showed that self-perceptions of abilities and skills in a given occupation or occupational field were highly related to interests.

Based on Hackett and Betz's (1981) pioneering work and subsequent research, as well as on numerous other studies, the SCCT (Lent & Brown, 1996; Lent et al., 1994) and a respective framework for career counseling (Brown & Lent, 1996) were proposed. In this theory, Lent and his associates provided explanations as to how vocational interests, career selection, and occupational persistence and performance are established and pursued as a function of self-efficacy beliefs and outcome expectations. Although past research predominantly and almost exclusively focused on self-efficacy beliefs only, Lent and his associates found that the inclusion of the "outcome expectations" concept was necessary to make their theory more complete and consistent with empirical findings (see also Lent & Hackett, 1994). This presented some shift from Bandura's (1986) theory which highlighted the role of self-efficacy beliefs while downplaying (though discussing) the role of outcome expectations. Several empirical investigations supported various predictions made by SCCT (Bishop & Bieschke, 1998; Fouad & Smith, 1996).

It is clear that SCCT and its predecessor career self-efficacy model view on the formation of interests and their role in career development highly resemble Barak's approach. It is interesting to note, however, that these researchers arrived at their conceptualizations (at least admittedly) independently, and based their arguments on quite different empirical grounds. However, two major differences can still be detected between the two models: (a) whereas SCCT refer to two basic cognitive elements as crucial mechanisms in forming vocational interests, namely, self-efficacy and outcome expectations (both of which, similarly in both models, are considered to be intervening processes of career-related behaviors), Barak's model refers to three such cognitive elements, namely, perceived abilities, expected success, and anticipated satisfaction. This difference should *not* be considered marginal, insignificant, or trivial. It seems that the mechanism of self-efficacy in SCCT is identical to Barak's cognitive determinant of "perceived abilities" (and both relate to Super's, 1963, self-concept element; see Betz, chap. 3, this volume, on this point), although the latter refers to a more operational factor. However, it also seems that "outcome expectations" is too broad a concept, which involves "imagined consequences of performing particular behaviors" with no particularly determined career-related focus or criterion (Lent et al., 1994, p. 85). Barak's proposition of the "expected success" and the "anticipated satisfaction" factors both offers operationalization to the broad concept as well as putting a career-related focus on it. (b) Similarly to SCCT (see Brown & Lent, 1996), Barak (see Barak et al., 1992) proposed that because interests have a pivotal medtiating role between relevant cognitions and career-related goal setting and subsequent behaviors, and because interests, in principle, are distorted, a major career counseling goal is to restructure these cognitions which, in turn, modify interests, in order to help the client to arrive at realistic and functional choices. Whereas SCCT primarily highlights the modification of self-efficacy, using techniques based on Bandura's (1977, 1986, 1989) conceptualization on the development of *self-efficacy beliefs* (Brown & Lent, 1996; Brown, Lent, Ryan, & McPartland, 1996; Lent et al., 1994; Lent & Maddux, 1997. See also Betz, chap. 3, this volume), Barak's approach to the modification of interests is broader. As proposed by Barak et at. (1989), and especially by Barak et al. (1992), modification of distorted (i.e., faulty, in SCCT terms) interests, which may lead to dysfunctional career goals, should be considered as a special case of cognitive therapeutic intervention, and thus should apply any effective cognitive technique possible to restructure the cognitive determinants. In this aspect, Barak's approach is more similar to career counseling applications proposed by SLTCDM (Krumboltz, 1996) than to those recommended by SCCT.

IMPLICATIONS FOR CAREER ASSESSMENT, COUNSELING, AND RESEARCH

The cognitive model of interests proposed by Barak has important implications for career psychology. These implications introduce a quite different approach in various aspects and activities in this field from traditional views and applications. Basically, Barak's approach, similarly to constructivistic and narrative schools of thought, highlights the role of cognitive mechanisms and processes, and views the individual as an active and responsible creator of his or her destiny. Barak's view is fundamentally different from common, traditional career psychology approaches that generally regard individuals as passive followers of their predetermined, prescribed future. Therefore, this approach—unlike the passive matchmaking trait–factor approach (which basically takes a person's ideas "as is" in trying to match them with occupations), and similar to constructivistic and dynamic career counseling approaches (e.g., Spokane, 1991)—refers in a different way to interest assessment and the role and conduct of career counseling.

Assessment of Interests

As already discussed, interests should be regarded as emotions (and consequent motivations) toward real or imagined stimuli. These emotions, like any other emotions, can, in principle, be quantified and compared both within and among individuals. However, it is suggested here that there is a better way to measure these emotions than by simply asking individuals about how they feel. That is, by presenting a stimulus item— made up as an occupational title, description of an activity, or a name of a course—and asking a person to what degree this is interesting, attractive, or appealing—*is tautological in nature.* People may be unaware of their feelings and provide us with just the obvious. From another point of view, people may be subjected to various mental defenses in experiencing or questioning their likes and dislikes. As is commonly practiced in studying emotions in general (depression, anxiety), a more sophisticated approach may be needed, and actually ought to be used, to inquire about *relevant antecedents and correlates* of the emotions under examination. The same way that the Beck Depression Inventory (BDI; Beck, Ward, Mendelson, Mock, & Esbaugh, 1961) surveys respondents' depression-related antecedents and correlates (e.g., desperate thoughts, appetite level, crying behavior, sleeping behavior), and does not ask about depressive feelings per se, *interest measurement should be based on measuring interest-relevant antecedents and correlates, and not on asking about the degree of interest.* This approach is totally different from several interest measures that have been in use for quite a long time (e.g., Strong Vocational Interest Inventory [SVII], and its various revisions, Kuder Occupational Interest Survey [KOIS], Jackson Vocational Interest Survey [JVIS], Ramak, Vocational Preference Inventory [VPI], and resembles some parts of other interest measures (e.g., SDS, CVIS).

The second proposition, related to the assessment of interests implied from the current approach, is that the stimuli (i.e., questionnaire items) to which individuals respond should represent a wide variety of content areas, so as to more validly sample the construct under examination. Unlike some interest measures (e.g., VPI, Ramak) that are based solely on occupational titles, and unlike other interest measures that are primarily composed of a list of activities (e.g., JVIS, KOIS), it is proposed that *an interest measure be constructed by numerous career-relevant stimulus contents*. At the very least, such stimuli should include occupational titles, courses, and activities, but other stimuli (e.g., hobbies) should be considered as well. Given the current process of a rapidly changing world of work and occupations (cf. Chartrand & Walsh, chap. 9, this volume; Krumboltz & Coon, 1995), a stronger emphasis should be assigned to the more core and basic vocationally related activities and tasks rather than to predefined occupations.

Related to the latter aspect, and in accord with other recent writings (e.g., Day & Rounds, 1997; see also Chartrand & Walsh, chap. 9, this volume), it is proposed that the assessment scales used by an interest questionnaire—in contrast to most common methods—should be based on basic occupational-related dimensions, aspects, or values rather than specific occupations or occupational groups. The rapidly changing world of work, emerging cultures, globalization of economy and communications, and intensive international collaborations, in addition to highly developed and still germinating technologies, have accelerated and fostered interdisciplinarity as never before. This growing trend makes it necessary for existing occupations and vocational training to change in order to adjust to these transformations. It is beyond the scope of this chapter to predict these developments, but it seems that career-related assessment should be prepared for the future world of work or it becomes totally obsolete and useless. Because the current approach highlights cognitive structure and mechanisms, it seems obvious that the dimensions of interests be consistent with this view. Thus, and consistent with most recent research on the structure of interests, a quadratic structure of interests made up by the dimensions of people, data, things, and ideas (Prediger & Vansickle, 1992) may be most useful. However, as proposed by Day and Rounds (1997), more detailed and specific basic dimensions of interests may be needed and found functional for the valid description of the construct as well as usage in career counseling. Notwithstanding, rather than *contents* of occupations, a more counseling-meaningful structure may be useful in referring to vocationally-relevant *aspects* (Gati, Shenhav, & Givon, 1993) or *values* (Dawis & Loftquist, 1984) common to questionnaire items, such as prestige, independence, and authority.

In summary, I suggest that an interest assessment measure be constructed in accordance with the foregoing principles. Specifically, consistent with Barak's cognitive view of interests, I recommend that such an interest inventory inquire into the respondents' perceived abilities to, expected success in, and anticipated satisfaction from performance or involvement in a list of items. This list should include a variety of vocational-related content area stimuli, and be interpreted using basic interest, occupational values, or vocational choice aspects as dimensions of measurement.

Career Counseling

Several years ago, Phillips (1992) thoughtfully included the individual's "self-definition" as one of five "ideal components" of career counseling. Her thorough review found that this component of career choice process was characterized with relatively little scientific knowledge. Although career psychology and counseling research have certainly advanced, our knowledge about this crucial factor in career development is still quite limited. This is especially conspicuous in light of the long-lasting theoretical clamor regarding the centrality of the self-definition factor, beginning with Super's (1953) position on the role of self-concept in career development, through the growing research on career self-efficacy from the beginning of the 1980s (cf. Betz, chap. 3, this volume), to the recent formulation of SCCT (Lent et al., 1994). The current model concerning the nature of interests is consistent with this outcry, and regards self-determination of interests as a crucial element in career choice and, therefore, in career counseling.

The cognitive model of interests presented here has direct and important implications for career counseling. The model views interests as a product of particular antecedent beliefs concerning one's capabilities, success, and satisfaction associated with various vocational-related engagements. Because these beliefs might be subjectively biased, distorted, or arbitrary in nature, the consequent interests (i.e., emotions, or affects) should be considered as dysfunctional in terms of an individual's career-related goal attainment. Thus, it is suggested that the basic roles of career counseling are (a) to *assess the realistic value of a client's interests* in terms of their correspondence to actual relevant client's personal characteristics; (b) to *modify the client's interests* which are found to be dysfunctional (i.e., unrealistic, unsubstantiated, unfulfilling), whether underarticulating existing personal characteristics, or overarticulating nonexistant ones; and (c) to *help a client implement* appropriate choices through training or in employment. To some degree this view resembles principles related to career maturity stemming from Super's (e.g., 1963) developmental theory of career choice, where realism of vocational choice was considered essential (Crites, 1981). However, this approach to the definition of career counseling is obviously quite different from that of traditional trait–factor approaches. In contrast to passively and statically recording clients' characteristics, including their expressed or measured vocational interests, and matching them up with occupations or work environments, the current approach calls for an active and dynamic counseling intervention to achieve desired career counseling goals. Thus, the current approach views a counselor as a professional who assumes responsibility for helping clients change their dysfunctional cognitions and consequent interests rather than one who matches up clients with choices for short-term gains.

The present approach should be considered as a crucial addendum, or as complementary to existing cognitive decision-making models in career counseling. For instance, Gati's sequential elimination approach (Gati, 1986; Gati, Fassa, & Houminer, 1995; Gati, Osipow, & Givon, 1995; Gati, Shenhav, & Givon, 1993; see also Gati, chap. 2, this volume) refers to "vocational aspects" as a major input in an individual's process of selecting appropriate occupations. Whereas Gati's approach accepts the individual's input of vocationally relevant aspects or considerations in eliminating possible occupational alternatives, the current model would suggest *adding a new stage* of examining the realism of each aspect as objectively contrasted with that individual's actual characteristics. Weighing occupational aspects solely on the basis of an individual's desires and subjective perceptions and attributions might represent an entirely dysfunctional, eventually frustrating career choice. Rather, *realistic* occupational aspects—those that survive reality testing—may effectively guide clients toward an appropriate career goal. In the same vein, cognitively oriented problem-solving and decision-making approaches (e.g., Sampson, Peterson, Lenz, & Reardon, 1992) which accept clients' data regarding their interests at face value and include them in a career choice process, may mislead some clients who are not aware of the discrepancy between their actual personal characteristics and the perceived ones.

According to the present view, in order to achieve the first career counseling phase or object (related to assessment) as proposed earlier, interest measurement, as well as comprehensive personal diagnostics, should be conducted. A client's conceptualization of the counseling problem may thus be developed, not by merely referring him or her to troubling portions of the environment (Olson, McWhirter, & Horan, 1989) but by extending it to self-cognitive processes as well. Contrasting these bits of information may lead to a second phase *of either choice implementation or modification of interests*. The relevant counseling question then becomes: how to modify one's dysfunctional interests, and what procedures should be practiced to this end. Because the current approach views interests as emotional consequences as a result of cognitive antecedents, any effective cognitive restructuring technique may be considered legitimate. However, unlike SCCT (Lent et al., 1994), which refers to Bandura's (1977, 1986) alleged four sources of shaping self-efficacy beliefs—performance accomplishments, vicarious learning, social persuasion, and physiological reactions—as the sole or major counseling methods of modifying client's beliefs, the current approach would welcome *any* effective relevant counseling method. Nevertheless, because of the cognitive-purposed nature of the intervention, cognitively oriented approaches might be considered more useful. In their research, Barak et al. (1992) and Okev (1993) used Meichenbaum's (1977) self-talk or self-instruction technique to restructure the cognitive determinants of interests and, in turn, to modify interests. Numerous other cognitive restructuring techniques are available to attempt to change clients' thoughts and beliefs which, in turn, may successfully modify interests.

In addition to Ellis' (1962, 1996) well-known Rational Emotive Behavior Therapy (REBT) verbal persuasive techniques, which resemble Bandura's social persuasion method, any cognitive technique, as presented by Beck and colleagues (Beck, 1976; Beck & Weishaar, 1995; DeRubeis & Beck, 1988; Weishaar & Beck, 1986; see also Freeman, 1987, and Haaga & Davison, 1991) may be good for this purpose. In principle, all possible forms of cognitive distortions that were shown to be related to depression, anxiety, personality disorders, or other psychological difficulties and distress, may be responsible for dysfunctional interests too. Thus, "all-or-nothing" or "dichotomous" thinking, catastrophizing and exaggerating, overgeneralization, selective abstraction, disqualifying the positive, arbitrary inference, magnification or minimization, emotional reasoning, "should/must/ought" statements, labeling and mislabeling, personalization—all these destructive cognitive processes may account for the creation and formation of dysfunctional interests or, as explained earlier, interests that are not based, do not reflect, and do not correspond to the existence of specific personal characteristics. Therefore, any effective cognitive restructuring technique may be adapted for the sake of minimizing the proximity of interests (i.e., motivations and emotions) and actual self and real-world data.

The general three cognitive intervention categories as suggested by Beck (e.g., Beck & Weishaar, 1995), namely, collaborative empiricism, Socratic dialogue, and guided discovery, are relevent and applicable to help modify clients' interests. A fuller list of techniques includes interpreting and changing idiosyncratic meaning, questioning the evidence, reattribution, examining options and alternatives, de-catastrophizing, fantasized consequences (see also Zakay & Barak, 1984, in relation to career decision making), advantages and disadvantages, turning adversity to advantage, labeling of distortions, downward arrow, paradox or exaggeration, scaling, replacement imagery, externalization of voices, cognitive rehearsal, daily record of dysfunctional thoughts, three questions (attacking baseless logic of beliefs), cognitive errors, identifying schemata, turn-off technique, repetition, time projection, using metaphors, induced imagery, goal rehearsal, positive imagery, and coping imagery (DeRubeis & Beck, 1988; Freeman, 1987; Weishaar & Beck, 1986). All these techniques may be adjusted and adapted to restructure relevant cognitions, namely, one or more of the three cognitive determinants of interests (i.e., perceived abilities, expected success, and anticipated satisfaction) to produce the individual's functional vocational interests. Other, more social psychological-oriented influence approaches (Dorn, 1990), may also be used to achieve optimal client change.

However, these cognitive methods may not be sufficient to enhance desired interest change, and more behaviorally based techniques may be called into action, reflecting recent changes in cognitive–behavioral therapies (Hollon & Beck, 1994). This is parallel to the use of behavioral or cognitive–behavioral interventions in therapy in an attempt to change clients' emotions and motivations (Kanfer, 1996). These behavioral techniques may include activity scheduling, mastery and pleasure ratings, behavioral rehearsal, social skills training, bibliotherapy, graded task assignments, assertiveness training, in-vivo practice, diversion techniques, and shame-attacking exercises (DeRubeis & Beck, 1988; Ellis, 1996; Freeman, 1987; Weishaar & Beck, 1986). No clear and comprehensive evidence is available yet concerning the effectiveness of these techniques in modifying clients' interests. However, accumulative information on the success of these methods in restructuring undesired cognitions in other problem areas supports the argument that they may be found to be successful in interest change as well.

It should be noted that the present approach highlights cognitive interventions aimed at changing clients' dysfunctional (or faulty) vocational interests, that is, changing the *content-bound* aspect of career-related decisions. This purpose is independent of, and is only complementing, *process-bound* aspects of career-related choices, as reflected by dysfunctional career beliefs (Krumboltz & Vosvick, 1996) and thoughts (Sampson, Peterson, Lenz, Reardon, & Saunders, 1998). From this perspective, the present view—just like Chartrand and Rose's (1996) sociocognitive intervention model—*complements* other existing models to make up for necessary gaps or deficiencies and provide a more full, comprehensive approach.

Research

Although the present approach is based on numerous research investigations, directly related to Barak's model, or on close conceptions, much research is needed to substantiate it. More specifically, it seems that research is especially needed in testing the basic premises of the model and hypotheses derived from it, examining its implications on career development, and its counseling-related propositions and applications.

Much research has been conducted on various cognitive and cognitive-related mechanisms, processes, and procedures in the field of career psychology. However, it seems that past research lacked a comprehensive theoretical framework and purpose. Although SCCT (Lent et al., 1994) recently provided the needed theoretical framework, the current conception may render some additional definitions, explanations, descriptions, and related implications to make it more tangible and palpable. Likewise, the current model may be considered a magnification of several specific portions of SLTCDM (Krumboltz, 1994a, 1996; Krumboltz & Nichols, 1990; Mitchell & Krumboltz, 1990). For instance, with regard to SCCT, replacing the general, abstract term *outcome expectations* with more concrete, operational *expected success* and *anticipated satisfaction* factors, should make the theory more testable and standard. Similarly, but in quite a different way, SCCT's "self-efficacy" could be replaced with "perceived abilities" to reflect more accurate and relevant self-perceptions, referring to personal characteristics in general rather than intellectual abilities alone. These possible contributions of the current model to SCCT may promote its validity and advance its utility. Concerning SLTCDM, it seems that the three cognitive determinants of interests may provide better operationalization the process referred to under the general concept of "self observation generalizations" and thus help its empirical examination. In addition, the current model's focus on the *content* of career-related choice, through the special assessment procedures discussed earlier, rather than the *process* of choice, may make research more applicable and generalizable to actual career counseling situations. Needless to say, these suggestions should be empirically tested.

As already suggested, the current view of the nature of interest necessitates the development of a new method of measuring interests by focusing on their antecedent cognitions across a wide range of stimulus contents and providing results along value-based rather than content-based dimensions. Obviously, developing such an instrument necessitates much research in item selection and testing reliability, validity, and utility. However, according to the present viewpoint, most of the existing common measures of interests are characterized by confining to the same traditional trait–factor assumption on the one hand, and focusing on emotional outcomes (i.e., interests) rather than on their antecedents on the other. Because, according to the current view, diagnostics of the functionality level of a client's interests is an essential step in effective career counseling, the development and use of a differently conceived interest measure seems inevitable and desired. Moreover, as described earlier, rapid changes in the world of work and the foreseen developments make it crucial that an interest measure refer to multiple relevant stimuli rather than be limited to currently existing but eventually changing items (e.g., occupational titles).

A great effort should be made to identify successful methods to modify career-related cognitions and subsequent dysfunctional interests. As already mentioned, consistent with Krumboltz's (1996) approach, and in contrast to the SCCT (Brown & Lent, 1996) propositions, it is suggested that these methods should not be confined to Bandura's (1986) quadratic conception regarding the sources of self-efficacy beliefs, but rather a more comprehensive, open-ended, and general view at counseling interventions should be considered. Using the framework of well established cognitive and cognitive–behavioral psychotherapeutic techniques, developed to modify clients' cognitions in other problem domains, seems desirable in referring to the modification of interests too. However, empirical research is needed to test these assumptions. In addition, adoption of numerous specific cognitive, cognitive–behavioral, and other related techniques seems necessary. These methods have generally been relevant and effective toward changing dysfunctional cognitions, and hence can be effective in altering career-related noxious, toxic, deleterious, and eventually destructive beliefs or, alternatively, to promote and reinforce career-related constructive, valuable, and useful ones. In this context, cognitively oriented methods practiced and postulated by researchers such as Mitchell and Krumboltz (1987), Nevo (1987), Richman (1988, 1993), Elliott (1995), Chartrand and Rose (1996), and London (1997) should be applied to achieve these goals. However, much research is needed to examine the accountability of these methods in the framework of cognitive career counseling.

TOWARD A COMPREHENSIVE COGNITIVE CAREER PSYCHOLOGY THEORY

Osipow and Fitzgerald (1996) reviewed cognitive approaches to career development, and showed how SLTCDM (Krumboltz & Nichols, 1990; Mitchell & Krumboltz, 1990), SCCT (Lent et al., 1994), the Barak's model reviewed here, as well as some other cognitively oriented research and theoretical proposals in this area, may be combined to create an integrated cognitive framework, just as SCCT proposed. Although SCCT provides a very general and quite unified framework, it may lack some substantial ingredients to make it an actual comprehensive cognitive theory of career choice and adjustment. In addition to the need to clarify, operationalize, and specify some basic factors and terms, as mentioned above, it seems that SCCT is too narrow in some of its views and analyses. For instance, as indicated by Osipow and Fitzgerald (1996) in relation to cognitive approaches to career psychology in general, too much emphasis is given to career choice while career adjustment process is underdeveloped. An integration of SCCT with SLTCDM (which, incidentally, specifically addressed work adjustment-related issues; see Mitchell & Krumboltz, 1990), Barak's cognitive model of interests, and some other essential research and theoretical proposals (e.g., Chartrand and Rose, 1996; Neimeyer, Nevill, & Probert, 1985) may provide a more valid and useful approach than any of these individual perspectives.

It is of particular importance to elaborate on SLTCDM in this context, and to note some possible theoretical combinations. The SLTCDM (Krumboltz, 1979, 1994a, 1996; Krumboltz, Mitchell, & Jones, 1976; Krumboltz & Nichols, 1990; Mitchell & Krumboltz, 1990), similarly to SCCT and Barak's model of vocational interest development, puts a major emphasis on career-related cognitions. Generally, SLTCDM considers four classes of factors that influence an individual's career decision making: genetic endowment and special abilities, environmental conditions and events (e.g., job and training opportunities, social policies and labor laws, community influences), learning experiences (instrumental, associative, or vicarious), and task approach skills (e.g., work habits and values). These factors dynamically evolve and interact to subsequently produce two basic sets of cognitions and beliefs, and associated skills and actions. The cognitive sets include self-observation generalizations and world-view generalizations. According to SLTCDM, similarly to the view of the current model, self-observation generalizations are the causal source of career interests and attitudes. According to SLTCDM, the major role of career counseling is to intervene in a client's cognitive system and attempt to change it in order to (a) expand the client's capabilities and interests, rather than base decisions on existing characteristics only; (b) prepare for changing work tasks, rather than to assume that occupation will remain stable; (c) empower to take action, rather than merely to be given diagnosis; and (d) deal with all career problems, rather than with just occupational selection (Krumboltz, 1996). Like SCCT's and Barak's conceptions, SLTCDM considers vocational interests, as well as skills, beliefs, attitudes, values, and other related personal qualities, as subject to change, and proposed numerous relevant interventions for either developing appropriate personal conceptions and preventive measures (i.e., career education) or remedy-related cognitive–behavioral methods (i.e., career counseling).

In order to assess people's work-related beliefs, Krumboltz (1991, 1994b; Krumboltz & Vosvick, 1996) developed the Career Beliefs Inventory (CBI) which measures 25 categories of beliefs (e.g., Career Path Flexibility, Persisting While Uncertain) which have been found in research to interfere with (or block) career decision making. As exemplified in the earlier writings, this diagnosis can be very helpful in identifying cognitions that undermine functional career decision making and development and, therefore, should be used as a central counseling tool. It is important to note, however, that the CBI refers to the *process* of decision-making and not to its *contents*. In other words, although the CBI may shed light on dysfunctional beliefs, attitudes, and values related to the process of making a career decision, it cannot (and is not targeted to) detect problems related to the very content-bound nature of a career decision. SLTCDM acknowledges that the client's vocational interests, for instance, as a product of a person's subjective self-observation generalizations, may be a target for change or reinforcement, as a result of an assessment which finds and defines them as dysfuncional. However, this important factor cannot be identified by the CBI. Moreover, as empirically found by Naylor and Krumboltz (1994; see also Krumboltz 1994c), the CBI scales are *independent of* interests and abilities, and, thus, may add valuable information in counseling, but hence cannot detect the content of functional versus dysfunctional career-related choices or preferences.

It seems that the current viewpoint of interests may complement a needed aspect to make career counseling even more functional. As proposed by Barak, contrasting a client's expressed or measured interests with his or her actual personal capabilities, as well as with opportunities and relevant external conditions, may point at a new counseling direction as a *possible content* of career decisions. This view is fully consistent with SLTCDM, as well as with SCCT, and may contribute to making counseling even more productive and helpful for needy individuals. Observing and confronting discrepancies, distortions, denials, and other possible clients' responses may serve as an important counseling experiential tool and a vehicle for counseling change (Krumboltz & Jackson, 1993). To use Krumboltz's (1993) clinical-like terminology to diagnose personal (rather than vocational–educational) difficulties, Barak's proposal of identifying gaps between self-perceptions and reality may be termed as diagnosing kinds of delusional and anxiety disorders (apparently related to career immaturity). Effectively treating these emotionally based difficulties may contribute not only to improved career-related self-actualization but also to improved mental health.

The preceding analysis shows how Barak's model may compensate, contribute, and complement the model advocated by SLTCDM at understanding career development and practicing career education and career counseling. In other sections of this chapter it was shown how Barak's model may also complement the SCCT conception and make it more operational and applicable. These suggestions, together with numerous other contributions to career psychology underlining cognitive-related conceptions and techniques, including recent constructivistic and narrative approaches (e.g., Peavy, 1992; Savickas, 1991, 1993, 1995), may be collected and integrated to form a new, comprehensive, cognitively bound career psychology theory. Ackerman and associates' (Ackerman, 1996a, 1996b, 1997; Ackerman & Heggestad, 1997; Goff & Ackerman, 1992; Rolfhus & Ackerman, 1996) recent conception related to a new look at the relationships among personality, self-concept, interests, and intelligence, may present another course where a comprehensive cognitive career theory pursue.

SUMMARY

Career psychology has attracted numerous theoreticians and researchers throughout the 20th century in persisting, continuous attempts to understand the nature of individuals' work-related development and adjustment. A permanent theoretical approach characterizing this field, implying relevant practical training and counseling applications, has been the trait–factor conception. This approach has magnified matchmaking between people and occupations (or occupational environments) in what are considered to be relevant and important factors. Although research has generally supported the trait–factor view, in numerous personal cases another conception may be more valid and effective in contributing to personal growth and welfare. Moreover, in the current rapidly changing world of work, of information revolution, evolving cultures, global economy and communications, as well as of other relevant social changes, a more open-ended, flexible, and dynamic approach is needed to reflect these developments.

The current chapter presents a cognitive conception regarding the nature and development of career-related interests, developed by Barak (1976, 1981; Barak, Feldman, & Noy, 1991; Barak, Librowski, & Shiloh, 1989; Barak, Shiloh, & Haushner, 1992), and analyzed its possible implications for career assessment, counseling, and research. It was shown how this model resembles, in several major components, two other, independently developed, theoretical approaches to career psychology, namely, the Social Cognitive Career Theory (Lent, Brown, & Hackett, 1994), and Social Learning Theory of Career Decision Making (Krumboltz, 1994a, 1996). The chapter also presents ways in which Barak's model may contribute to the improvement of each of these two theories, and make them more counseling- and research-ready. Finally, based on these points, an idea has been expressed to develop an integrated, comprehensive, cognitive, career psychology theoretical framework which may better serve scientists and practitioners alike.

ACKNOWLEDGMENT

The help of Jolyn Ballandais in preparing this chapter is highly appreciated.

REFERENCES

Ackerman, P. L. (1996a). A theory of adult intellectual development: Process, personality, interests, and knowledge. *Intelligence, 22*, 227–257.

Ackerman, P. L. (1996b). Intelligence as process and knowledge: An integration for adult development and application. In W. A. Rogers & A. D. Fisk (Eds.), *Aging and skilled performance: Advances in theory and applications* (pp. 139–156). Mahwah, NJ: Lawrence Erlbaum Associates.

Ackerman, P. L. (1997). Personality, self-concept, interests, and intelligence: Which construct doesn't fit? *Journal of Personality, 65*, 171–204.

Ackerman, P. L., & Heggestad, E. D. (1997). Intelligence, personality, and interests: Evidence for overlapping traits. *Psychological Bulletin, 121*, 219–245.

Asch, S. E. (1952). *Social psychology.* Englewood Cliffs, NJ: Prentice-Hall.

Bandura, A. (1977). Self-efficacy: Toward a unifying theory of behavioral change. *Psychological review, 84*, 191–215.

Bandura, A. (1986). *Social foundations of thought and action: A social cognitive theory.* Englewood Cliffs, NJ: Prentice-Hall.

Bandura, A. (1989). Human agency in social cognitive theory. *American Psychologist, 44*, 1175–1184.

Barak, A. (1976). *Cognitive view of vocational interests.* Unpublished doctoral dissertation, Department of Psychology, Ohio State University, Columbus.

Barak, A. (1981). Vocational interests: A cognitive view. *Journal of Vocational Behavior, 19*, 1–14.

Barak, A., Feldman, S., & Noy, A. (1991). Traditionality of children's interests as related to their parents' gender stereotypes and traditionality of occupations. *Sex Roles, 24*, 511–524.

Barak, A., Librowsky, I., & Shiloh, S. (1989). Cognitive determinants of interests: An extension of a theoretical model and initial empirical examinations. *Journal of Vocational Behavior, 34*, 318–334.

Barak, A., & Meir, E. I. (1974). The predictive validity of a vocational interest inventory— "Ramak": A seven-year follow-up. *Journal of Vocational Behavior, 4*, 377–387.

Barak, A., Shiloh, S., & Haushner, O. (1992). Modification of interests through cognitive restructuring: Test of a theoretical model in preschool children. *Journal of Counseling Psychology, 39*, 490–497.

Beck, A. T. (1976). *Cognitive therapy and the emotional disorders.* New York: International Universities Press.

Beck, A., Ward, C., Mendelson, M., Mock, J., & Esbaugh, J. (1961). An inventory for measuring depression. *Archives of General Psychiatry, 4*, 561–571.

Beck, A. T., & Weishaar, M. E. (1995). Cognitive therapy. In R. J. Corsini & D. Wedding (Eds.), *Current psychotherapies* (5th ed.). Itasca, IL: Peacock.

Berdie, R. F. (1943). Likes, dislikes, and vocational interests. *Journal of Applied Psychology, 27*, 180–189.

Berdie, R. F. (1944). Factors related to vocational interests. *Psychological Bulletin, 41*, 137–157.

Berdie, R. F. (1949). Counseling: An educational technique. *Educational and Psychological Measurement, 9*, 89–94.

Betz, N. E. (1992). Career assessment: A review of critical issues. In S. D. Brown & R. W. Lent (Eds.), *Handbook of counseling psychology* (2nd ed., pp. 453–484). New York: Wiley.

Betz, N. E., & Hackett, G. (1981). The relationship of career-related self-efficacy expectations to perceived career options in college women and men. *Journal of Counseling Psychology, 28*, 399–410.

Betz, N. E., & Luzzo, D. (1996). Career assessment and the Career Decision-Making Self-Efficacy Scale. *Journal of Career Assessment, 4*, 313–328.

Bishop, R. M., & Bieschke, K. J. (1998). Applying social cognitive theory to interest in research among counseling psychology doctoral students: A path analysis. *Journal of Counseling Psychology, 45*, 182–188.

Blau, S. (1991). *The effects of cognitive determinants on differential formation of male and female interests*. Unpublished master's thesis, Department of Psychology, Tel Aviv University.

Bordin, E. S. (1953). A theory of vocational interests as dynamic phenomena. *Educational and Psychological Measurement, 3*, 49–65.

Brender, M. (1960). Toward a psychodynamic system of occupational classification. *Journal of Counseling Psychology, 7*, 96–100.

Brown, S. D., & Lent, R. W. (1996). A social cognitive framework for career choice counseling. *Career Development Quarterly, 44*, 354–366.

Brown, S. D., Lent, R. W., Ryan, N. E., & McPartland, E. B. (1996). Self-efficacy as an intervening mechanism between research training environments and scholarly productivity: A theoretical and methodological extension. *The Counseling Psychologist, 24*, 535–544.

Campbell, D. P., Hyne, S. A., & Nilsen, D. A. (1992). *Manual for the Campbell Interest and Skill Survey*. Minneapolis, MN: National Computer Systems.

Chartrand, J. M. (1996). Linking theory with practice: A sociocognitive interactional model for career counseling. In M. L. Savickas & W. B. Walsh (Eds.), *Handbook of career counseling theory and practice* (pp. 121–134). Palo Alto, CA: Davies-Black.

Chartrand, J. M., & Rose, M. L. (1996). Career interventions for at-risk populations: Incorporating social cognitive influences. *Career Development Quarterly, 44*, 341–354.

Church, A. T., Teresa, J. S., Rosenbrook, R., & Szendre, D. (1992). Self-efficacy for careers and occupational consideration in minority high school equivalency students. *Journal of Counseling Psychology, 39*, 498–508.

Crites, J. O. (1981). *Career counseling: Models, methods, and materials*. New York: McGraw-Hill.

Cronbach, L. J. (1990). *Essentials of psychological testing* (5th ed.). New York: Harper & Row.

Darley, J. G. (1950). Conduct of the interview. In A. H. Brayfield (Ed.), *Readings in modern methods of counseling* (pp. 265–272). New York: Appleton-Century-Crofts.

Darley, J. G., & Hagenah, T. (1955). *Vocational interest measurement*. Minneapolis: University of Minnesota Press.

Dawis, R. V., & Lofquist, L. H. (1984). *A psychological theory of work adjustment*. Minneapolis: University of Minnesota Press.

Day, S. X., & Rounds, J. (1997). "A little more than a kin, and less than a kind": Basic interests in vocational research and career counseling. *Career Development Quarterly, 45*, 207–220.

DeRubeis, R. J., & Beck, A. T. (1988). Cognitive therapy. In K. S. Dobson (Ed.), *Handbook of cognitive-behavioral therapies*. New York: Guilford.

Dorn, F. J. (1990). Career counseling: A social psychological perspective. In W. B. Walsh & S. H. Osipow (Eds.), *Career counseling: Contemporary topics in vocational psychology* (pp. 193–223). Hillsdale, NJ: Lawrence Erlbaum Associates.

Elliott, K. J. (1995). Anthetic dialogue: A new method for working with dysfunctional beliefs in career counseling. *Journal of Career Development, 22,* 141–148.

Ellis, A. (1962). *Reason and emotion in psychotherapy.* New York: Lyle Stuart.

Ellis, A. (1996). *Reason and emotion in psychotherapy: A comprehensive method of treating human disturbances* (Revised). Secaucus, NJ: Carol Publishing Group.

Fiske, S. T. (1981). Social cognition and affect. In J. H. Harvey (Ed.), *Cognition, social behavior, and the environment* (pp. 227–264). Hillsdale, NJ: Lawrence Erlbaum Associates.

Fletcher, F. M. (1966). Concepts, curusity, and careers. *Journal of Counseling Psychology, 13,* 131–138.

Fouad, N. A., & Smith, P. L. (1996). A test of a social cognitive model for middle school students: Math and science. *Journal of Counseling Psychology, 43,* 338–346.

Freeman, A. (1987). Cognitive therapy: An overview. In A. Freeman & V. B. Greenwood (Eds.), *Cognitive therapy: Applications in psychiatric and medical settings.* New York: Human Sciences Press.

Fryer, D. (1931). *The measurement of interests.* New York: Holt.

Gati, I. (1986). Making career decisions: A sequential elimination approach. *Journal of Counseling Psychology, 33,* 408–417.

Gati, I., Fassa, N., & Houminer, D. (1995). Applying decision theory to career counseling practice: The sequential elimination approach. *Career Development Quarterly, 43,* 211–220.

Gati, I., Osipow, S. H., & Givon, M. (1995). Gender differences in career decision making: The content and structure of preferences. *Journal of Counseling Psychology, 42,* 204–216.

Gati, I., Shenhav, M., & Givon, M. (1993). Processes involved in career preferences and compromises. *Journal of Counseling Psychology, 40,* 53–64.

Gerhart, B. (1988). Sources of variance in incumbent perceptions of job complexity. *Journal of Applied Psychology, 73,* 154–162.

Goff, M., & Ackerman, P. L. (1992). Personality-intelligence relations: Assessment of typical intellectual engagement. *Journal of Educational Psychology, 84,* 537–552.

Haaga, D. A. F., & Davison, G. C. (1991). Cognitive change methods. In F. H. Kanfer & A. P. Goldstein (Eds.), *Helping people change* (4th ed., pp. 248–304). Elmsford, NY: Pergamon.

Hackett, G., & Betz, N. E. (1981). A self-efficacy approach to the career development of women. *Journal of Vocational Behavior, 18,* 326–329.

Hansen, J. C., & Campbell, D. P. (1985). *Manual for the Strong-Campbell Interest Inventory* (4th ed.). Palo Alto, CA: Consulting Psychologists Press.

Holland, J. L. (1966). *The psychology of vocational choice.* Waltham, MA: Blaisdell.

Holland, J. L. (1973). *Making vocational choices: A theory of careers.* Englewood Cliffs, NJ: Prentice-Hall.

Holland, J. L. (1985a). *Making vocational choices: A theory of vocational personalities and work environment.* Englewood Cliffs, NJ: Prentice-Hall.

Holland, J. L. (1985b). *Vocational Preference Inventory manual.* Odessa, FL: Psychological Assessment Resources.

Holland, J. L. (1997). *Making vocational choices: A theory of vocational personalities and work environments* (3rd ed.). Odessa, FL: Psychological Assessment Resources.

Holland, J. L., Fritzsche, B. A., & Powell, A. B. (1994). *The Self-Directed Search technical manual.* Odessa, FL: Psychological Assessment Resources.

Hollon, S. D., & Beck, A. T. (1994). Cognitive and cognitive-behavioral therapies. In A. E. Bergin & S. L. Garfield (Eds.), *Handbook of psychotherapy and behavior change* (4th ed., pp. 428–466). New York: Wiley.

Jackson, D. N. (1993). *Jackson Vocational Interest Survey manual.* Port Huron, MI: Sigma Assessment Systems.

Kanfer, F. H. (1996). Motivation and emotion in behavior therapy. In K. S. Dobson & Craig, K. D. (Eds.), *Advances in cognitive-behavioral therapy* (Vol. 2, pp. 1–30). Thousand Oaks, CA: Sage.

Kassner, M. W. (1990). Attributions about subjectively defined career success in different occupations. *Journal of Business and Psychology, 5,* 37–46.

Kitson, H. D. (1925). *The psychology of vocational adjustment.* Philadelphia, PA: Lippincott.

Kruglanski, A. W. (1980). Lay epistemo-logic—Process and Contents: Another look at attribution theory. *Psychological Review, 87,* 70–87.

Kruglanski, A. W., & Ajzen, I. (1983). Bias and error in human judgment. *European Journal of Social Psychology, 13,* 1–44.

Krumboltz, J. D. (1979). A social learning theory of career decision-making. In A. M. Mitchell, G. B. Jones, & J. D. Krumboltz (Eds.), *Social learning theory and career decision making* (pp. 19–49). Cranston, RI: Carroll.

Krumboltz, J. D., Mitchell, A. M., & Jones, G. B. (1976). A social learning theory of career selection. *The Counseling Psychologist, 6,* 71–80.

Krumboltz, J. D. (1991). *Manual for the Career Beliefs Inventory.* Palo Alto, CA: Consulting Psychologists Press.

Krumboltz, J. D. (1993). Integrating career and personal counseling. *Career Development Quarterly, 42,* 143–148.

Krumboltz, J. D. (1994a). Improving career development theory from a social learning perspective. In M. L. Savikas & R. W. Lent (Eds.), *Convergence in career development theories: Implications for science and practice* (pp. 9–31). Palo Alto, CA: Consulting Psychologists Press.

Krumboltz, J. D. (1994b). The Career Beliefs Inventory. *Journal of Counseling and Development, 72,* 424–428.

Krumboltz, J. D. (1994c). Potential value of the Career Beliefs Inventory. *Journal of Counseling and Development, 72,* 432–433.

Krumboltz, J. D. (1996). A learning theory of career counseling. In M. L. Savickas & W. B. Walsh (Eds.), *Handbook of career counseling theory and practice* (pp. 55–80). Palo Alto, CA: Davies-Black.

Krumboltz, J. D., & Coon, D. W. (1995). Current professional issues in vocational psychology. In W. B. Walsh & S. H. Osipow (Eds.), *Handbook of vocational psychology: Theory, research, and practice* (2nd ed., pp. 391–426). Mahwah, NJ: Lawrence Erlbaum Associates.

Krumboltz, J. D., & Jackson, M. A. (1993). Career assessment as a learning tool. *Journal of Career Assessment, 1,* 393–409.

Krumboltz, J. D., Mitchell, A. M., & Jones, G. B. (1976). A social learning theory of career selection. *The Counseling Psychologist, 6,* 71–80.

Krumboltz, J. D., & Nichols, C. W. (1990). Integrating the social learning theory of career decision making. In W. B. Walsh & S. H. Osipow (Eds.), *Career counseling: Contemporary topics in vocational psychology.* Hillsdale, NJ: Lawrence Erlbaum Associates.

Krumboltz, J. D., & Vosvick, M. A. (1996). Career assessment and the Career Beliefs Inventory. *Journal of Career Assessment, 4,* 345–361.

Lang, K. (1964). Interest. In J. Gould & W. Kolb (Eds.), *Dictionary of the social sciences.* New York: Free Press.

Lapan, R. T., Boggs, K. R., & Morrill, W. H. (1989). Self-efficacy as a mediator of Investigative and Realistic General Occupational Themes on the Strong Interest Inventory. *Journal of Counseling Psychology, 36,* 176–182.

Lapan, R. T., Shaughnessy, P., & Boggs, K. (1996). Efficacy expectations and vocational interets as mediators between sex and choice of math/science college majors: A longitudinal study. *Journal of Vocational Behavior, 49,* 277–291.

Lent, R. W., & Brown, S. D. (1996). Social cognitive approach to career development: An overview. *Career Development Quarterly, 44,* 310–321.

Lent, R. W., Brown, S. D., & Hackett, G. (1994). Toward a unifying social cognitive theory of career and academic interest, choice, and performance [Monograph]. *Journal of Vocational Behavior, 45*, 79–122.

Lent, R. W., Brown, D., & Larkin, K. C. (1984). Relation of self-efficacy expectations to academic achievement and persistence. *Journal of Counseling Psychology, 31*, 356–362.

Lent, R. W., Brown, D., & Larkin, K. C. (1986). Self-efficacy in the prediction of academic success and perceived career options. *Journal of Counseling Psychology, 33*, 265–269.

Lent, R. W., & Hacket, G. (1994). Sociocognitive mechanisms of personal agency in career development: Pantheoretical prospects. In M. L. Savickas & R. W. Lent (Eds.), *Convergence in career development theories: Implications for science and practice* (pp. 77–102). Palo Alto, CA: Consulting Psychologists Press.

Lent, R. W., & Maddux, J. E. (1997). Self-efficacy: Building a sociocognitive bridge between social and counseling psychology. *The Counseling Psychologist, 25*, 240–255.

Locke, E. A. (1965). The relationship of task success to task liking and satisfaction. *Journal of Applied Psychology, 49*, 370–385.

Locke, E. A. (1966). The relationship of task success to task liking: A replication. *Psychological Reports, 18*, 552–554.

Lofquist, L. H., & Dawis, R. V. (1969). *Adjustment to work*. New York: Appleton-Century-Crofts.

London, M. (1997). Overcoming career barriers: A model of cognitive and emotional processes for realistic appraisal and constructive coping. *Journal of Career Development, 24*, 25–38.

Lopez, F. G., Lent, R. W., Brown, S. D., & Gore, P. A., Jr. (1997). Role of social-cognitive expectations in high school students' mathematics related interest and performance. *Journal of Counseling Psychology, 44*, 44–52.

Meichenbaum, D. (1977). *Cognitive-behavioral modification: An integrative approach*. New York: Plenum Press.

Meir, E. I., & Barak, A. (1974). A simple instrument for measuring vocational interests based on Roe's classification of occupations. *Journal of Vocational Behavior, 4*, 33–42.

Mitchell, L. K., & Krumboltz, J. D. (1987). The effects of cognitive restructuring and decision-making training on career indecision. *Journal of Counseling and Development, 66*, 171–174.

Mitchell, L. K., & Krumboltz, J. D. (1990). Social learning approach to career decision making: Krumboltz's theory. In D. Brown & L. Brooks (Eds.), *Career choice and development: Applying contemporary theories to practice* (2nd ed., pp. 145–196). San Francisco, CA: Jossey-Bass.

Naylor, F. D., & Krumboltz, J. D. (1994). The independence of aptitudes, interests, and career beliefs. *Career Development Quarterly, 43*, 152–160.

Neimeyer, G. J., Nevill, D. D., & Probert, B. (1985). Cognitive structures in vocational development. *Journal of Vocational Behavior, 27*, 197–201.

Nevo, O. (1987). Irrational expectations in career counseling and their confronting arguments. *Career Development Quarterly, 35*, 239–250.

Nevo, O., Nevo, B., & Zehavi, A. D. (1993). Gossip and counselling: The tendency to gossip and its relation to vocational interests. *Counselling Psychology Quarterly, 6*, 229–238.

Okev, G. (1993). *Modification of interests through restructuring of three cognitive determinants in different combinations and each one separately: A test of a theoretical model in preschool children*. Unpublished master's thesis, Department of Psychology, Tel Aviv University.

Olson, C., McWhirter, E., & Horan, J. J. (1989). A decision-making model applied to career counseling. *Journal of Career Development, 16*, 107–117.

Osipow, S. H. (1962). Perceptions of occupations as a function of titles and descriptions. *Journal of Counseling Psychology, 9*, 106–109.

Osipow, S. H. (1968). *Theories of career development*. New York: Appleton-Century-Crofts.

Osipow, S. H. (1969). Cognitive styles and educational-vocational preferences and selection. *Journal of Counseling Psychology, 16*, 534–546.

Osipow, S. H. (1970). Some cognitive aspects of career development. In E. Evans (Ed.), *Adolescence: Readings in behavior and development* (pp. 111–123). Chicago, IL: Dryden.

Osipow, S. H. (1972). Success and preference: A replication and extension. *Journal of Applied Psychology, 56*, 179–180.

Osipow, S. H. (1998, March). *Recent developments in career development theories.* Paper presented in a colloquium, Department of Psychology, University of Haifa, Israel.

Osipow, S. H., & Fitzgerald, L. F. (1996). *Theories of career development* (4th ed.). Boston, MA: Allyn & Bacon.

Osipow, S. H., & Scheid, A. B. (1971). The effects of manipulated success ratios on task preferences. *Journal of Vocational Behavior, 1*, 93–98.

Osipow, S. H., & Walsh, W. B. (1970a). *Strategies in counseling for behavior change.* Englewood Cliffs, NJ: Prentice-Hall.

Osipow, S. H., & Walsh, W. B. (Eds.). (1970b). *Behavior change in counseling: Readings and cases.* Englewood Cliffs, NJ: Prentice-Hall.

Parsons, F. (1909). *Choosing a vocation.* Boston, MA: Houghton Mifflin.

Paterson, D. G., & Darley, J. G. (1936). *Men, women, and jobs.* Minneapolis: University of Minnesota Press.

Peavy, R. V. (1992). A constructivist model of training for career counselors. *Journal of Career Development, 18*, 215–228.

Phillips, S. D. (1992). Career counseling: Choice and implementation. In S. D. Brown & R. W. Lent (Eds.), *Handbook of counseling psychology* (2nd ed., pp. 513–547). New York: Wiley.

Prediger, D. J., & Vansickle, T. R. (1992). Locating occupations on Holland's hexagon: Beyond RIASEC. *Journal of Vocational Behavior, 40*, 111–128.

Post-Krammer, P., & Smith, P. L. (1986). Sex differences in math and science career self-efficacy among disadvantaged students. *Journal of Vocational Behavior, 29*, 89–101.

Richman, D. R. (1988). Cognitive career counseling for women. *Journal of Rational Emotive and Cognitive Behavior Therapy, 6*, 50–65.

Richman, D. R. (1993). Cognitive career counseling: A rational-emotive approach to career development. *Journal of Rational Emotive and Cognitive Behavior Therapy, 11*, 91–108.

Roe, A. (1956). *The psychology of occupations.* New York: Wiley.

Roe, A., & Seligman, M. (1964). *The origin of interests.* Washington, DC: American Personnel and Guidance Association.

Rolfhus, E. L., & Ackerman, P. L. (1996). Self-report knowledge: At the crossroads of ability, interest, and personality. *Journal of Educational Psychology, 88*, 174–188.

Rotberg, H. L., Brown, D., & Ware, W. B. (1987). Career self-efficacy expectations and perceived range of career options in community college students. *Journal of Counseling Psychology, 34*, 164–170.

Sampson, J. P., Peterson, G. W., Lenz, J. G., & Reardon, R. C. (1992). A cognitive approach to career services: Translating concepts into practice. *Career Development Quarterly, 41*, 67–74.

Sampson, J. P., Peterson, G. W., Lenz, J. G., Reardon, R. C., & Saunders, D. E. (1998). The design and use of a measure of dysfunctional career thoughts among adults, college students, and high school students: The Career Thoughts Inventory. *Journal of Career Assessment, 6*, 115–134.

Savickas, M. L. (1991). The meaning of work and love: Career issues and interventions. *Career Development Quarterly, 39*, 315–324.

Savickas, M. L. (1993). Career counseling in the postmodern era. *Journal of Cognitive Psychotherapy: An International Quarterly, 7*, 205–215.

Savickas, M. L. (1995). Constructivist counseling for career indecision. *Career Development Quarterly, 43*, 363–373.

Schaffer, R. H. (1953). Job satisfaction as related to need satisfaction in work. *Psychological Monographs, 67*(14, Whole No. 364).

Sommer, S. M. (1995). Social competition: Identifying new perspectives and strategies for task motivation. *International Journal of Conflict Management, 6,* 239–256.

Spokane, A. R. (1991). *Career intervention.* Englewood Cliffs, NJ: Prentice-Hall.

Strong, E. K., Jr. (1943). *Vocational interests of men and women.* Stanford, CA: Stanford University Press.

Strong, E. K., Jr. (1951). Permanence of interest scores over 22 years. *Journal of Applied Psychology, 35,* 89–92.

Super, D. E. (1953). A theory of vocational development. *American Psychologist, 8,* 185–190.

Super, D. E. (1963). Self concepts in vocational development. In D. E. Super, R. Starishevsky, N. Matlin, & J. P. Jordaan (Eds.), *Career development: Self-concept theory.* New York: College Entrance Examination Board.

Tracy, T. J. G., & Ward, C. C. (1998). The structure of children's interests and competence perceptions. *Journal of Counseling Psychology, 45,* 290–303.

Vroom, V. H. (1964). *Work and motivation.* New York: Wiley.

Walsh, W. B., & Betz, N. E. (1995). *Tests and assessments* (3rd ed.). Englewood Cliffs, NJ: Prentice-Hall.

Watkins, C. E., Campbell, V. L, & Nieberding, R. (1994). The practice of vocational assessment by counseling psychologists. *The Counseling Psychologist, 22,* 115–128.

Weishaar, M. E., & Beck, A. T. (1986). Cognitive therapy. In W. Dryden & W. L. Golden (Eds.), *Cognitive-behavioral approaches to psychotherapy* (pp. 324–339). New York: Harper & Row.

Williams, T., & Betz, N. E. (1994). The relationships among occupational and task-specific measures of career self-efficacy. *Journal of Career Assessment, 2,* 341–351.

Williamson, E. G. (1939a). *How to counsel students.* New York: McGraw-Hill.

Williamson, E. G. (1939b). The clinical method of guidance. *Review of Educational Research, 9,* 214–217.

Zakay, D., & Barak, A. (1984). Meaning and career decision-making. *Journal of Vocational Behavior, 24,* 1–14.

Zytowski, D. G., & Kuder, F. (1986). Advances in the Kuder Occupational Interest Survey. In W. B. Walsh & S. H. Osipow (Eds.), *Advances in vocational psychology: Vol. I: The assessment of interests* (pp. 288–306). Hillsdale, NJ: Lawrence Erlbaum Associates.

Chapter 6

Cross-Cultural Assessment of Interests

Elchanan I. Meir
Tel Aviv University

Aharon Tziner
Netanya Academic College

This chapter might seem superfluous to readers who are familiar with recent literature on interest measurement in the context of cross-cultural comparisons, such as the excellent articles by Hansen (1987), Rounds and Tracey (1996), and Hesketh and Rounds (1995). Hansen (1987) states that "Development of interest inventories in other countries [outside the U.S.] or with ethnic cultures in the United States, in most cases, is prohibitive; the task is too expensive, too impractical, and in some instances, simply impossible because of the unavailability of adequate sample sizes for acceptable test construction and validation" (p. 173). This statement implies either that in small cultures counseling should not be based on any measurement of vocational interests or that interest measurement in these cultures should employ tools and measures adapted from larger cultures—a problematic strategy due to cross-cultural differences, as is discussed later. Our experience in interest measurement has convinced us otherwise. Both construct and predictive validity findings in cultures outside the United States indicate that abandoning the construction and use of interest inventories beyond American borders would be unjustified and might even be called negligent.

Several projects carried out in Israel between 1950 and 1963 were designed to construct instruments for the adequate measurement of interests. All these attempts failed, and consequently, no research reports were published (as often happens with unsuccessful projects). A change was marked by Meir's (1968, 1975) development of the Hebrew interest inventories, Ramak and Courses, based on Roe's (1956) occupational classification. However, the attempt to construct equivalent interest inventories in English targeted for the American culture, failed and was characterized by Osipow (1991) as an effort . . . that turned out to be extraordinarily difficult. "We found that occupational titles are perceived in different ways cross-culturally. . . . Cross-cultural adaptation is extremely difficult" (p. 323). Nevertheless, despite the difficulties, more meticulous methodology later produced promising findings (Meir, Rubin, Temple, & Osipow, 1997).

We would like to share with the reader the methodology that yielded these positive results and by means of which, we are confident, others may also overcome the methodological and empirical difficulties noted by Hansen (1987). As Osipow (1991) states, "One often learns more from one's failures than from the successes" (p. 323).

Cultural differences seem to have a considerable impact on interests. Cultures differ in regard to the popularity, legitimacy, and status of various occupations, training processes, demand for personnel, distribution of employees in general and by gender, etc. The Bible itself contains an interesting illustration of this principle. The Biblical patriarchs (e.g., Abraham, Jacob, Moses, David) were shepherds and are described in the Old Testament with the utmost reverence. Yet their neighbors frowned upon their "occupation," . . . "for every shepherd is an abomination unto the Egyptians" (Genesis, 46:34), so that we may assume that even in Biblical times, the various cultures did not display equivalent interest in the occupation of shepherd. Cultures also differ in the ways that occupational interests are allowed to be expressed, as illustrated by the sanctions imposed in certain subcultures against expressing an interest in becoming an army officer, a nuclear physicist, or a nightclub singer.

Furthermore, an eminent member of a certain occupation (e.g., opera singer, actor, or journalist) in a given culture may affect the status and associations evoked by the relevant occupational titles, so that in one culture, the image aroused by a given title may be that of an ordinary employee, whereas in another, it may be associated with unique expertise. As Rounds and Tracey (1996) stated ". . . the possible different underlying meaning[s] ascribed by each culture to the methods and items [lead] to the possible differences in the structural properties of the measures" (p. 310).

INTERESTS AND OTHER DETERMINANTS
IN CAREER CHOICE AND PERFORMANCE

Six factors determine one's performance, satisfaction and stability in any activity, role, task, job or occupation (Meir, 1990). These are:

1. Abilities—the general and specific aptitudes needed to master the training for and proficiency in the job or occupation (e.g., mechanical comprehension);
2. Interests—the level of aspiration and the distribution of level of interest for the various activities, tasks, jobs, or occupations (e.g., technological interests with a high level of aspiration);
3. Environmental Conditions—opportunities and labor market, environmental and social climate, financial resources, norms and values, etc.;
4. Health—physical and mental health, including physique and sensory and motor skills;
5. Personality Characteristics—e.g., management qualities, the Big Five; and
6. Achievements—knowledge and skills gained through formal and informal studies, training and experience (e.g., mastery of foreign languages).

These factors are not totally independent; for example, several studies have shown (Holland, 1996a) a relationship between personality attributes and certain types of interests, and belief in self-efficacy may be classified under more than one of the determinants. Moreover, instruments measuring Abilities and Achievements involve right or wrong answers, while the responses relating to Interests and Personality Characteristics are descriptive, and Environmental Conditions and Health may preclude certain careers rather than indicating any suitable occupation. Nevertheless, presenting the six determinants as orthogonal makes it easier to interpret the results for the counselee and for him or her to assimilate the scores, as well as facilitating personnel decisions or other vocational psychology issues.

Although all six are necessary factors that must be taken into account in making career choice decisions, the first two, Abilities and Interests, are the most important. Whereas abilities are largely hereditary (Jensen, 1986), interests are exclusively, or almost exclusively, an outcome of environmental experiences, as demonstrated by meta-analyses of abilities (e.g., Hunter, 1986) and vocational interests (Assouline & Meir, 1987; Tranberg, Slane, & Ekeberg, 1993) as predictors of occupational performance, satisfaction, and stability. Issues relating to cultural differences in abilities are discussed in a review by Campbell (1996), but similar issues regarding occupational interests seem to warrant further elaboration.

Definition of Interests

Several definitions have been proposed for vocational or occupational interests (see the chapter by Barak, chap. 5, this volume, and Hesketh and Rounds, 1995). We would like to begin by presenting our own approach to this question as a basis for the forthcoming sections.

Every definition of *vocational* or *occupational interests* (we use these terms interchangeably) must include the following two components: (a) level of need or preference and (b) constant characteristics. Thus, neither a compulsory activity (e.g., preparing an income tax return) nor readiness to participate in an occasional activity (e.g., a search for survivors of a sunken ship), even if they require continuous activity for a long duration, represents an expression of interests. On the other hand, interests may exist even if the person cannot execute or express them (e.g., due to a lack of adequate financial resources or opportunities). Nor does the existence of interests indicate their origin, which might be an attraction toward an activity or the avoidance of alternatives, strong ambition with a need to supervise, give orders, and be dominant, or a desire not to make decisions, or take responsibility. Interests may indicate a preference for unchanging requirements and stable conditions, or an affinity for change and a readiness to embark continuously on new adventures, to take risks, to modify expectations or to develop self-sufficiency of all kinds.

The definition of occupational interest also includes an indication of the *level* of relatively constant attraction toward the various occupations or categories (groups) of occupations. Our definition of *interests* is, therefore, the extent of attraction to act in, to be engaged in or to receive training for any task, job or occupation. Thus, at any moment, every individual has a given level of interest in every activity, role, task, and occupation. The level may vary from a negative attraction (presumably most psychologists have a negative interest in repairing the electrical wiring of the building they are in), through zero (i.e., no interest or indifference), to a positive attraction. Because the general understanding of the meaning of the term *interest* relates to the positive, the scale of measurement in all common interest measurements ranges from *No Interest, Indifference*, or *Very Little Interest* to positive expressions, with expressions of negative attraction or avoidance excluded.

External gratification also affects the interest level, giving rise to the question "To what extent should the rewards associated with any activity be included in the definition and measurement of interest?" Should the interest be defined and measured on the assumption that rewards are equal for the various activities, which may seem unrealistic, or should it include some reference to the external gratification, which may distort the measurement of fundamental or real interest? Perhaps the level of external gratification should be left to the individual's own imagination. One might argue that any discussion of interests that disregards the level of the gratifications involved (e.g., salary, status) is unfeasible from the nonprofessional (e.g., counselee) point of view. The answers to these questions have empirical implications. If interests are to be measured without reference to gratification, the instructions in the empirical instrument might be phrased something like: "Indicate to what extent you would choose each of these academic subjects as one of three additional courses required for your degree," or "Assuming the salary is the same, indicate whether or not you would like to be engaged in each of the following occupations." There are environments, such as the kibbutz (a communal settlement in Israel in which income and resources are divided among the members according to need rather than contribution), in which such a formulation is not solely hypothetical. If interests are to be measured with reference to gratification, the previous instruction might read: "How much are you willing to invest (in money, time, etc.) to enroll in each of the following academic courses," or "What is your interest in" without specifying the "price" of any choice. Although the first type of item might be preferred because it refers more explicitly to the "real" or "pure" interest, it is the second type that is closer to the traditional method generally used in measuring interests. For example, in Holland's (1985a) Self-Directed Search (SDS) respondents are instructed to indicate their "competencies" and the responses are entered into the scoring regardless from the opportunity for skill utilization in any job.

Occupational interests also includes aspiration level. Some people have a need to act in an occupational capacity that requires more responsibility, longer training, and the utilization of unique or high-level skills, whereas others need to feel free from responsibility, preferring an occupational capacity that does not involve the requirement to make decisions, and/or a long process of training or education. Those with a high level of aspirations derive satisfaction from managerial positions and are less satisfied if their job does not include such a function, while those with a low level of aspirations may feel depressed if required to manage others and are more satisfied if they can merely perform given tasks according to specific requirements. An expression of low level of aspirations can also emerge from past experience of discrimination, resulting in "foreclosed horizons or a tendency to set one's sights lower than necessary" (Bowman, 1995, p. 153). Level of aspiration is, thus, part of interests to the extent that it is one's preference to be given a certain level of responsibility, and not simply a result of forces in the labor market or a lack of alternatives. However, the inclusion of aspiration level under interests holds true for talented subjects, as well as for those whose abilities or aptitudes are low, or to put it in other words: Aspiration level appears under interests independently of whether the requirements of the occupations are suited to, above, or below one's aptitudes. It may be assumed that incongruence between aptitudes or level of aspiration and the requirements of an occupation would be a source of frustration similar to incongruence between field of interests and actual occupational field.

The Role of Interests

The basic assumption underlying the measurement of interests is that interests in accord, or "congruent," with occupation can predict a higher level of satisfaction, persistence (or stability), and achievements. This is, in effect, the essence of the "congruence hypothesis" (Holland, 1973, 1985b, 1997b). It does not mean that satisfaction, stability, or achievements can emerge in spite of incongruence between interests and occupation, but that if congruence does exist, a higher level of satisfaction, stability, and achievements can be expected. Congruence may be the result of a suitable occupational choice, arrived at with or without the help of vocational counseling, of *post-factum* crystallization of interests around an initially incongruent occupation, or even of accidentally embarking on a congruent profession.

Even in the era of modern technology, there are jobs that entail monotonous repetitive activity. This can hardly be expected to accord with the interests of people with a desire for skill utilization, a high aspiration level, or an interest in specific tasks associated with certain occupations and not with others. In such cases, the satisfaction derived from the congruence between interests and requirements will not be found within the framework of the occupation, and the individual may seek it out in his or her avocational choice. The match of interests and leisure or avocational activity may serve to replace the satisfaction lacking in the person's occupation. When occupation is in accord with interests, the congruence of avocational activity may add to the occupational congruence to produce an even higher level of satisfaction, persistence, and achievements (Meir & Melamed, 1986; Meir, Melamed, & Abu-Freha, 1990; Meir, Melamed, & Dinur, 1995; Melamed, Meir, & Samson, 1995).

Numerous studies have sought to examine the congruence hypothesis. Holland and Gottfredson (1990) published an annotated bibliography with several hundred references, Spokane (1985) and Edwards (1991) published reviews of congruence studies, and Assouline and Meir (1987) and Tranberg, Slane, and Ekeberg (1993) performed meta-analyses of 53 and 17 studies, respectively, on the relation between congruence and satisfaction or congruence and other dependent variables. Only a relatively small number of these studies did not find support for the congruence hypothesis (e.g., Bates, Parker, & McCoy, 1970; Elton & Rose, 1981).

Congruence between interests and occupation is a predictor of satisfaction and perhaps also of stability and achievements. However, the efficiency of the prediction expressed by the correlation coefficients is generally low. The mean correlations between congruence and satisfaction found in the aforementioned meta-analyses (Assouline & Meir, 1987; Tranberg et al., 1993) were .21 and .20, respectively. The breakdown of these correlations indicated that for certain measures of congruence and types, the mean correlations reached the .40 to .50 level, although the mean correlations between congruence and stability and congruence and achievements were much lower: .15 and .06, respectively (Assouline & Meir, 1987).

Because the foregoing reviews and meta-analyses include studies carried out in different cultures and with different tools (inventories) and measures, it seems obvious that the positive relation between congruence and satisfaction exists cross-culturally. Thus, wherever they live, people who are "congruent" (in Holland's, 1985b, 1997b terms), will feel more satisfied with their occupational choice and career, will produce more and better, and will persist in their job. It is also in line with the congruence hypothesis that where career is congruent with interests, people will suffer less from burnout and accidents, manifest a lower level of disobedience and absenteeism, and so on. Meir (1989) has suggested the following Mapping Sentence: "Level of congruence ———→ Well-Being," meaning that every measure of congruence, fit or accordance between interests, abilities, values, etc., on the one hand, and environment, expectations, requirements, norms, etc. on the other, will correlate positively with positively connotated variables that reflect well-being (e.g., satisfaction, performance, stability) and negatively with negatively connotated variables that express lack of well-being (e.g., burnout, anxiety, accidents).

THE ORIGIN OF INTERESTS

Interests might have their origin in earlier experience. Roe (1957) based her occupational classification on assumptions regarding the influence of the family climate on interests. In studies on twins, Lykken, Bouchard, McGue and Tellegen (1993) and Waller, Lykken, and Tellegen (1995) suggested a hereditary factor which influences interests. However, "it is still widely believed that variance in interests is largely influenced by environmental factors" (Bouchard, 1997, p. 381). Gati (1991) claimed that "although there is evidence for the contribution of genetic factors to interests, these factors account for less than 5% of the interest variance" (p. 312). Yet, according to Bouchard (1997), "this view is in serious error" (p. 381) and "it seems clear that the heritability of well-measured vocational interests is in the range of 0.40 to 0.50" (p. 382).

Because cultures differ vastly by employment distribution (e.g., the proportion of employees in rural occupations), then either cultures differ by the frequency of employees who happen to have a vocational career that is incongruent with their interests, or the difference in interest distribution is produced by the combination of heritage and environment. If interests are largely a result of heritage, how can we explain the fact that in recent centuries the percentage of people employed in rural occupations (e.g., agriculture, animal husbandry) has decreased from some 75% to around 4% in Western cultures but not in some Far Eastern cultures. A similar issue is the occupational distribution among immigrants in their "new" culture. As Leong (1995) stated, "the extent to which an individual has become knowledgeable about and incorporates the culture of the dominant ethnic group . . . is bound to influence his or her occupational interests, aspirations" (p. 84). A possible explanation of the hereditary effect on interests is that hereditary is related to the level of occupations rather than to their field. Level includes the various kinds of abilities (e.g., verbal, artistic, manual), the need for achievement, an interest in dominance, innovation, efficiency, etc., some of which are already known to be inherited.

It may be assumed that in liberal or democratic cultures there will be more tolerance for children not following their parents' careers. In other societies, a discontinuity of occupational choice might mean a real loss in economic terms or reputation. For example, in rural cultures, the tribe, or family, may lose control of their land if children do not continue their parents' agricultural career, so that social pressure might be expected to ensure that at least one member of each family will continue to work the land. Similar pressure might be found in the case of religious careers or in families who have gained a reputation for certain skills (e.g., making violins).

Hofstede's (1994) studies of value differences among people in more than forty countries have revealed four core values likely to differentiate cultures. They are power distance, individualism—collectivism, masculinity—femininity, and uncertainty avoidance.

Power distance refers to the extent to which the less powerful members of a culture accept the fact that power is distributed unequally. In large power distance cultures, members are expected to respect and obey people in positions of authority. Employees in such cultures are afraid to challenge their superiors and express a preference for a non consultative style of decision making. Conversely, in small power distance cultures, individuals are treated more or less as equals, and initiative is both encouraged and rewarded.

In *individualistic* cultures, a premium is placed on personal time, freedom, and challenge, and interpersonal bonds are loose. In *collectivistic* cultures, in contrast, importance is attached to loyalty to the group, and the sense of individual achievement is derived through the attainment of group interests. Hence training and skill utilization are valued to the extent that they enhance the well-being of the group.

In cultures of a *masculine* character, importance is attached to creating opportunities for high earnings, recognition, advancement, and challenging work. In such cultures, the family socializes for ambition, assertiveness, and competition. Cultures of a *feminine* character emphasize having a good working relationship with direct superiors, cooperation, and employment security. Here the family socializes for modesty and solidarity.

Finally, in high *uncertainty avoidance* cultures, as little as possible is left to chance, and individuals are socialized to feel comfortable only in structured environments. In low uncertainty avoidance cultures, uncertainty does not generate intolerable anxiety. Moreover, people grow up acquiring patterns for dealing with unexpected changes and adjusting to low structured environments.

As for the bearing of this cultural taxonomy on occupational interests, we may expect, for instance, the aspiration level or level of achievement need to be higher in high power distance cultures than in low power cultures. Consequently, individuals would be more attracted to occupations involving authority, responsibility, and decision making, and this would be reflected in the distribution of interests. Similarly, in collectivistic cultures, we may anticipate a greater preference for occupations involving work with people (e.g., sales personnel, social workers, nurses, and so on) than in individualistic cultures, where preferences for sophisticated manipulation of data or objects (e.g., computer programming, chemists, mathematicians, and the like) may dominate. In masculine cultures, individuals would be expected to develop affinities for entrepreneurship and would opt for occupations allowing for high degrees of competition and demonstration of excellence, such as in competitive sports, the military, or private business (e.g., sales agents, managerial positions). On the other hand, in feminine cultures, individuals would tend to gravitate into occupations requiring team work and collaboration (e.g., teachers, welfare jobs), and into the public sector, where steady employment is relatively assured and working for the community is valued. In high uncertainity avoidance cultures, interests in occupations in the exact sciences (e.g., technology, biology, medicine) may be expected to be more pervasive than in low uncertainity cultures, where greater preference would probably be expressed for human and social occupations (e.g., psychologists, writers, educators, musicians).

These ideas could be formulated as hypotheses to be examined in appropriate cultures. Unfortunately, the relevant data is neither available nor readily accessible. An adequate study would have to produce both a cultural classification according to Hofstede (1994), and a comparison between the cultures on identical measures. However, as shown in the following, interest inventories differ by language, and even the same wording may have different meanings in different cultures or sub cultures. Thus, a cross-cultural comparison cannot be made on any kind of scores on identical stimuli, but only on groups of occupations, such as high level, science, or physical labor. The comparison would also require comparable samples, that is, matching by gender, age, educational level, urban vs. rural, economic level, industrialization in the labor market, etc. Such data does not seem to exist. It might be possible to draw adequate comparisons from the cross-cultural meta-analysis by Rounds and Tracey (1996) if labels such as individualistic versus collectivistic could be found to fit the cultures investigated.

The value system in a given culture may also affect the attractiveness of certain occupations or even fields of occupations. It might be postulated that the shift from an underdeveloped to a modern industrialized culture engenders a parallel shift towards greater interest in the technological/industrial field of occupations, along with a decrease in interest in the physical labor associated with agricultural occupations. Karayanni (1987) describes the situation of Israeli Arabs "no longer choosing their careers according to the will and needs of the social system" (Karayanni, 1987, p. 84), though "the structure of opportunities lags considerably behind" (Karayanni, p. 89).

The motive behind interests may be either to enjoy the activity itself or to indirectly gain the gratifications that ensue from that activity (e.g., salary or status). Interests may also derive from the desire to avoid negative reinforcements, such as punishment or scorn for not obeying the prevailing norms (e.g., obligatory army service, volunteering for community projects, or doing one's share of household chores). Agreement, or refusal, to perform social or religious obligations, even temporarily, may affect the career of many members in any society and consequently produce the difference in the economic distribution of careers, as illustrated by the frequency of military occupations.

ITEMS IN INTEREST INVENTORIES

Super and Crites (1962) define "four major interpretations of the term interest, connected with as many different methods of obtaining data" (p. 377): (a) Expressed Interests—the subject states that he or she likes or dislikes something; (b) Manifest Interests—observation of the level of the subject's participation in an activity or occupation; (c) Tested Interests—

revealing by means of an objective test, the accumulation of relevant information mastered by the subject; and (d) Inventoried Interests—the subject's expression of preference for each item in a list. Here the answers "are added in order to yield a score which represents, not a single subjective estimate as in the case of expressed interests, but a pattern of interests which research has shown to be rather stable" (Super & Crites, 1962, p. 380). At the Conference of The Society for Vocational Psychology (May, 1997), Crites added a fifth interpretation: (e) Machine Experimental Measure—e.g., how long the subject is willing to view a picture of a certain content. The most popular method for measuring interests is the inventoried method, preferred because it can be subject to item analysis, reliability, and validity examination and also is less expensive to develop, administer, and score.

The inventoried method better fits our definition of interests because it makes it possible to measure the level of interest toward an adequate sample of alternatives rather than relying on a limited list of options. Moreover, inventories can serve as a basis for cross-cultural translation and adaptation. We therefore limit our discussion here to inventoried interests, not least because all other methods for measuring interests in different cultures are very rarely employed.

There are several kinds of interest inventories. They differ by the content of the items (e.g., occupational titles, self-evaluation of competencies, leisure activities); the scale on which responses are given, (e.g., Y vs. N or Y ? N scales); length, free or forced choice; grouping by headings or random arrangement, and the like. What is of interest to our cross-cultural comparison, however, is not the form of the scale, but the content of the items.

In defining his 12 principles for constructing interest inventories, Kuder (1970) criticizes the use of occupational titles as items, stating "If a person really knows enough about occupations to answer questions about them, it is pertinent to ask whether he needs the information which the interest inventory is designed to yield" (p. 218). Admittedly, there is no assurance that a respondent has the correct idea or image of the content of a given item, or that different respondents share the same image, even if it is wrong. Much effort has been devoted to producing "culture fair" ability tests, but "the message given by them all [major U.S. textbooks] is consistently the same: Culture fairness has run its course or never really existed" (Brislin, Lonner, & Thorndike, 1973, p. 109).

Nevertheless, we would argue that the same criticism might apply to all sorts of items. For example, school subjects (Electricity, Biology, History) do not reflect what employees in the respective occupations really do. Items that require self- evaluation of competencies are, by definition, measures of abilities rather than of interests; items that require the subject to choose between alternative activities might be the result of a misunderstanding of both alternatives and an avoidance-avoidance forced choice rather than an expression of attraction. Answers to items after a movie showing the contents of a certain workplace, activity, or occupation might be influenced by identification with the featured actor or the result of the film director's ability.

Other arguments might also be raised against the use of occupational titles in interest inventories. For example, certain occupations were once open solely to professionals with long training and experience and are now open to semiskilled workers. On the other hand, the high cost of sophisticated instrumentation, as well as considerations of safety, may dictate that low-level employees not be allowed to use such equipment without close supervision. In other words, over time and with technological development, occupations change in terms of content, the tasks involved, status, norms and values, required training, certification and instrumentation. As a result, no matter how accurate the image of a given occupation, it may prove obsolete after several years. At the Conference of The Society for Vocational Psychology (May, 1997), Borgen demonstrated how the occupation of horticulturist moved closer to carpet laying because of modern grass breeding. Therefore, a positive, negative, indifferent, or doubtful response to an occupational title, or any other kind of item in an interest inventory, is bound to the current image of that item for the unsophisticated respondent or counselee.

Occupations also differ in regard to the tasks involved in various cultures. For instance, in certain cultures, physicians make house calls as a major part of their job; in other cultures routine cases are tended to at the doctor's office, and more severe cases are treated solely in hospitals, making house calls very rare. Thus, Holland's (1985a, 1994) Self-Directed Search Inventory administered to English speakers in the United States is not identical to the version administered to English speakers in Canada (Holland, 1996b).

Moreover, cultures differ by the percentage of males and females engaged in the various occupations. Female bus drivers and dentists are more common in Eastern Europe than in the United States. This fact may have an obvious impact on the distribution of vocational interests by gender. It requires a very high level of self-confidence and temerity to be among the very few male kindergarten teachers, male beauticians, or female astronauts or female combat pilots. Indeed, the special public attention aroused by an extraordinary gender occupational choice may either strengthen that choice or stimulate its avoidance.

Furthermore, language is an expression of culture, and culture has a significant impact on the development of language. For our purposes, we note that in some languages, every occupational title is either masculine or feminine (e.g., German, Hebrew), whereas in others, almost all such labels are "unisex." (In English, even the few exceptions, such as actor–actress, air steward–stewardess or hostess, have recently been altered to avoid gender references.) This alone refutes the assumption that the translation of items from one language to another and back will retain the same meaning. The gender of the stimulus item in the interest inventory may affect the respondent's image of or attitude toward that item in cultures where occupational titles contain a linguistic indication of gender. In such languages, an artificial modification of the occupational title to avoid gender meaning (e.g., stage acting instead of stage actor) may provoke misunderstanding or resistance to the bizarre characterization.

Translating or adapting an interest item found to be highly valid in one culture to another culture thus appears to be a prodigious task. Moreover, it is more difficult than for items in ability tests. In the latter, the researcher must simply solve the problem of finding an equivalent for an item asking for the size of the U.S. population or "how many weeks there are in a year?" (In the Jewish calendar, every cycle of 19 years contains seven leap years, each with four additional weeks). In the case of interests, however, the problem is not one of equivalent differentiation and difficulty, but rather of content as such: Does the item in the new culture reflect the same level and field as in the original culture? For example, in the United States, the occupation of registered nurse was rated close to that of x-ray technician (Prediger & Vansickle, 1992), presumably because both are paramedical professions, whereas in Israel registered nurse was rated a service occupation (Hener & Meir, 1981). Similarly, in Russian, a counselor is known as a *defectolog* (a label that may discourage some readers from working as counselors in that culture), and in certain societies, a ladies' hairdresser is suspected of having monosexual tendencies. Of course, prevailing images such as these affect the subject's interest and readiness to consider these occupations.

The socioeconomic status of occupations also differs by cultures. The status of a certain occupation may be very high in one culture and much lower in another. Naturally, status of an occupation has an impact on the interest of people not yet engaged in it; generally, low-status occupations are universally less attractive. This status derives from a variety of cultural factors, such as tradition, religious or social values, or the depiction of employees in the various occupations in the media. Differences in the cultural image of occupations similarly emerge from the dimension of level. Tourist guides in Israel, for instance, must have at least 14 years of education, while in some other cultures, the educational requirements are much lower. Furthermore, Hesketh and Rounds (1995) pointed out that individualistic versus collectivistic orientation could account for cross-cultural differences. For instance, as previously discussed following Hofstede

(1994), in a collectivistic culture we would anticipate a considerably greater preference for occupations serving to promote the interests and well-being of the society as a whole than in individualistically oriented cultures. Hansen (1987) also suggested that cultural differences may stem from traditional family structure and the societal values of various cultural entities. Yet, for cross-cultural assessment to be feasible, translated items must provide the same stimuli as the original items, and their inferred meaning must be equivalent.

An illustration with which the psychologists among us can identify is our very own occupation. According to Hansen and Campbell (1985), psychology is an Investigative–Artistic occupation (p. 3 in summary of results), whereas in Israel the correlations between responses to this occupational title and field scores on Service and General-Cultural (in Roe's, 1956, classification) far exceed the correlations with either Science or Arts and Entertainment (Meir, 1975).

Military activities may serve as another example. In some cultures (e.g., Israel), military activities are an expression of a risk-taking attitude because of the image of the combat soldier. In other cultures, particularly those in which army service is obligatory and universal, the army is perceived as an organization offering a variety of occupations, many of them with a technical, organizational, scientific, or even artistic nature (e.g., tank crew, paymasters, intelligence, and marching band members, respectively). Yet, in Hansen and Campbell (1985), the theme code of military activities is Realistic. Moreover, an item such as YMCA director would have no meaning in non-Christian cultures.

Illustrations of cultural differences can also be found in Karayanni's (1987) empirical study. For example, in the Hebrew version of the Ramak, · a salesperson in a book shop belongs to the field of Business (in Roe's, 1956, classification), while in its literal translation for Arabs living in the same country, it yielded a higher correlation with the field of General Culture because "the sale of books in Arab culture used to be the work of educated people" (p. 88); the item was replaced by salesperson in a furniture shop. Similarly, the correlation between the score on "math problems in evolution research" (Courses inventory) and Science was below expectations because the word for "math" in Arabic means both mathematics and sports.

Thus, the problem of developing an interest inventory in one culture based on successful experience in another is not solely a question of the four stages proposed by Hansen (1986), namely: translation, back translation, bilingual testing to identify comparability, and "testing a population in another country to determine the predictive accuracy of the Strong in that culture compared to the accuracy with a similar population in the United States" (p. 26). Accordingly, Brislin et al. (1973) claimed that "adapted translations may be faulty" (p. 115). In fact, translations of the Strong (1943) Vocational Interest Blanks into German, Dutch, Spanish, French and other languages have not always shown the proper concern for cross validation. Hansen's (1986) conclusion that "the Spanish version of the Strong . . . has been used to study the generalizability of Holland's theory to other cultures with results that support the hypothesis that the theory is cross-culturally robust" (p. 27) was based on studies of American samples, where the meaning and the cultural images of words are perhaps more homogeneous than in cross-cultural comparisons. As proposed by Leong (1995) "very few validity studies have been done to determine if Holland's classification system . . . or the Strong . . . is appropriate for Asian Americans as a group" (p. 85). According to Brown (1995), there is some evidence for the use of Holland's interest inventories among African Americans, while this is not the case with Strong's inventory. According to Bowman, "one should not confuse popularity of a vocational instrument with effectiveness" (p. 149). Lacking a body of data for the other culture, we can only adopt the questionable assumption that men or women in a particular occupation have roughly similar interests beyond cultures. This assumption seems glaringly untenable. How far, for instance, can the leisure activity of cricket be conveyed in Israel where "Cricket Club" does not even exist as an entry in the Yellow Pages? The same applies, of course, to all occupations that deal with gold mines, coal mines, fishery and sailing, dockyards, and so on—occupations that simply do not exist in a great number of cultures. These differences go beyond those of employee distribution by gender, such as the frequency of males employed as registered nurses or "driving a truck or tractor" (an item in Holland's (1996) Self-Directed Search Form E).

Generalization and cross-cultural adaptation is even more suspect if the method calls for scores on a specific list of basic scales or occupations which are not conceived as representative samples in other cultures, as in the case of Johannson's (1986) Career Assessment Inventory. The success of this instrument within the American culture for which it was designed can be attributed to the fact that it is used with counselees whose aspiration level or abilities are restricted to the nonacademic level, so that the subject's responses to all items refer to the combination of field and level.

Even within one culture, it seems unavoidable that respondents to an interest inventory will have different perceptions of any given item. What associations does the phrase "stage actor" arouse in your own mind, for instance? The creative work involved in bringing a role to life, the type of people with whom an actor works, or the applause at the end of the performance and the accompanying fame and glory? Familiarity with an occupation or with a certain person engaged in it may create differing images, with either positive or negative connotations, at different levels. Even pupils who should know the contents of the teaching occupation better than anyone else still relate to the label "teacher" with the image of a certain teacher in mind, or consider solely the tasks vis-à-vis pupils, disregarding the necessary preparation for class and the work load associated with evaluating students' homework and exams. Given this situation, the task of translating items appears even more daunting.

Let us illustrate the difficulty of translation in reference to the issue of producing culture fair ability tests. Allalouf and Sireci (1998) investigated the differential item functioning (DIF) between Hebrew and Russian examinees on four types of verbal items. They found that on equivalent translated items, the Russian speaking examinees performed better on 82% of the DIF analogies items, where no difference was found on sentence completion, logic, or reading comprehension items. The authors embrace the explanation by Angoff and Cook (1988) that translated verbal items with greater context are more likely to retain their meaning.

In short, the problem of generating items in one culture based on positive experience in another is not solely a question of translation and back translation. In order to preserve the connotations of a given item, it must be tested in full in the new culture on a variety of dimensions, including distribution in the working population, gender of the item, occupational and sociological level, legitimacy in terms of values and norms, and so on.

SCORING AND NORMS

According to our definition of interests, the assessment of occupational interests requires measuring the attraction toward all occupations or activities, or an adequate sample of them. This will produce a profile of scores, each reflecting the interest level of the respondent toward the various occupations or groups of occupations. Interest level for reasons such as career counseling can then be determined according to the within-individual distribution of scores. There is no significance to the sum of all interest scores toward all occupations. The only meaningful reference is to the profile and the within-subject variance among the scores in that profile. Although some interest inventories are based on norms, in others, the comparison is solely intrapersonal (each score compared with other scores of the same participant). This raises another question: Is it relevant for purposes of interest measurement to know the level of interest in the comparison group (e.g., culture, peer group, gender)? Some methods measure interests without reference to any kind of norm (e.g., Holland, 1973, 1985b), whereas comparison is at the very heart of the method and interpretation of others (e.g., Kuder, 1988; Strong, 1943).

The measurement of interests differs essentially from the measurement of abilities. In measuring mental abilities, the respondent's success in solving a series of items is always compared with that of his or her comparison group. If the majority of the group succeeds in solving the same series of items as the respondent, his or her ability is considered moderate or less. What is significant here is the comparison between the individual's scores and those of the comparison group, rather than the variance among the scores of that individual on the test battery. Thus, in mental ability measurement, a score will be considered high only if that or higher scores are very rare in the comparison group. In contrast, in interest measurement, a score will be considered high if it is sufficiently higher than the other scores of the same individual on the other items or scales. In other words, a very popular occupation means that a large number of respondents express interest in it. That interest may remain high for an individual respondent and will not be diminished by the fact that many others also express interest in the same occupation. Popularity may even serve to increase the individual's level of interest. Although popularity may create competitive conditions that make it impossible for the respondent to pursue his or her interests, this does not necessarily detract from them.

Interest inventories based on norms are subject to obsolescence of either the items (e.g., a change in the content or image of the items or in their frequency within the culture) or the comparison group (i.e., the popularity of the items). For this reason, Strong's Vocational Interest Blank (1943, SVIB) has been revised several times for the same culture for which it was originally designed (Walsh & Osipow, 1986). Interest inventories that do not make use of norms can be updated with greater ease and can also be more readily adapted to other cultures. If updating a norm-based inventory requires examining the applicability of both items and norms for a non norm-based inventory, only the items need to be examined. This means introducing an adequate representation of new items and deleting those that have become obsolete or have changed their characteristics to such an extent that they no longer represent the categories they once did. Updating norms, on the other hand, involves collecting current data on the distribution of responses to both versions of the inventory in the relevant comparison group.

The basis for interpreting scores on the SVIB and similar inventories is how "eminent people" of the same gender in the relevant occupation (scale) differ from "men in general" or "women in general." Inventories developed on the basic assumptions of Strong (1943) cannot be transferred from one culture to another without an immense project of data collection on representative samples to support the construction of equivalent items. This is a particularly difficult task in small cultures with limited financial resources, where a reasonable number of "eminent people" in many of the occupational scales is virtually impossible! Criticism of the adequacy of samples is also voiced within cultures (e.g., African-American males and females), as stated by Carter and Swanson (1990) and Leong (1995). Although it might be suggested that individuals in occupations based on natural law (e.g., mechanical engineering) manifest a greater similarity of interests across cultures than do individuals in occupations based on human laws (e.g., lawyers, psychologists), this is still of little value for our purposes. Chu (1975) noted that cultural factors play an important role in generating a difference in interests among American and Chinese students. It is this problem that motivated Hansen's (1987) sweeping skepticism of cross-cultural inventories with which we began this chapter.

The need for an appropriate comparison group where norms are used to interpret interest inventories can be illustrated by the fact that the first author (an Orthodox Jewish male) found "minister" to be the seventh suggestion in his Report Form based on his responses to the Kuder's Occupational Interest Scale (1988, KOIS) in comparison to his gender, and the first suggestion in comparison to females. In other words, interest inventories based on interpersonal comparisons cannot be translated and adapted to different cultures without conducting a careful investigation to form an adequate basis for comparison. For systems that use only intrapersonal comparisons, it is sufficient to find adequate items for the interest inventory. Of course, if the items do not precisely represent the required categories, the validity of the inventory will suffer.

The issue of comparing one individual's responses to those of other respondents requires additional discussion. As early as 1961, Cronbach offered the following example: "A student may indicate that he likes 25 computational activities out of 80 such activities listed in a particular questionnaire. This, on its face, appears not to indicate much liking for computational work. But since our culture views computation more often as work than as fun, this raw score of 25 places the student near the 80th percentile for high-school boys. Though he may not be strongly attracted to computation, he evidently finds it much less distasteful than most boys do. He is a much-better-than-average prospect for a vocation which combines computational duties with duties in which he would have a positive interest" (1961, pp. 405–406). If this student were competing for a job characterized by a lot of computational activities, the employer might prefer him over other candidates because he is relatively less resistant to the computational tasks involved. Yet, if the same student were a client in career counseling, it might be argued that because there are so many other occupational options, why should he have to suffer the obligation to perform the 55 computational activities that do not interest him? Any answer that makes reference to the comparison with his peers would be irrelevant in this setting. In other words, if he moved to a different environment or culture where his score put him in the 15th percentile, would he not suffer from the same level of incongruence as in the first culture? If I like ice cream, or the color blue, what does it matter to me (aside from the financial implications) whether the others in my environment dislike it or have an uncontrollable addiction to it? Obviously, for career counseling, what matters are the within-individual differences in the counselee's profile rather than the differences between his or her preferences and those of the norm group.

There are also technical constraints in arriving at adequate comparison groups. Unorganized workers and the self-employed are not easily located or persuaded to respond to interest inventories, so that in most cases, the norm group presumably suffers from inadequate sampling, especially in small cultures. That might explain in part why among female American college students ($n = 4283$), 57% were found to have Social as their first letter code in Holland's (1985b) typology and another 27% to have Social as their second letter code, whereas among women employees aged 20–24 ($n = 1446$), Social was the first letter code for only 20% and the second letter code for another 38%, a total of 84% vs. 58% (data from Holland's presentation, May 1997a, Conference of The Society for Vocational Psychology). These figures indicate the gap between the distribution of interests and the realities of the labor market.

THE STRUCTURE OF OCCUPATIONS

Several cross-cultural studies of vocational interests have examined the extent to which the underlying structure of occupations is universal. This structure is of both theoretical and practical significance. In theoretical terms, it serves as a means for examining the construct validity of the typology and the instruments. In practical terms, it allows counselors to enhance in their clients alternatives which are closer to their vocational preferences rather than those which are more distant in psychological content, as revealed by the statistical relationship and overall configuration. Cross-cultural comparisons can also be of interest from the theoretical point of view: Does the same structure of occupations exist despite economic, industrial, and social differences? If the answer is positive, findings in one culture may be more applicable to others, which might be of particular importance for small cultures where it can be exceeding difficult to find adequate data. As Rounds and Tracey (1996) stated, "Without equivalent structures, mean score comparisons across cultures are pointless: the differences or similarities are essentially uninterpretable" (p. 310).

The structure of occupations has been studied repeatedly, and two meta-analyses have been published: Tracey and Rounds (1993), who examined the structure according to Holland's (1985b, 1997b) typology and Tracey and Rounds (1994), who employed Roe's (1956) occupational classification. A cross-cultural comparison of the structure of occupations was also conducted by Rounds and Tracey (1996), with a meta-analysis of 18 different cultures, in addition to the U.S. benchmark and U.S. ethnic groups, on a total of 96 correlation matrices. The purpose of this study was "to examine the cross-cultural equivalence of Holland's (1985b) model of vocational interests (p. 310) . . . to evaluate the extent to which constructs developed to characterize personality in one culture can be applied across many diverse cultures" (p. 311).

According to Holland's system (1973, 1985b), six personality types labeled R (Realistic), I (Investigative), A (Artistic), S (Social), E (Enterprising), and C (Conventional), with six equivalent environmental types, form a hexagonal configuration, abbreviated RIASEC. Several intercorrelation matrices (e.g., Holland, 1972) support Holland's notion of the circular configuration of RIASEC, albeit with some deviations. Rounds and Tracey (1993) concluded their review on 77 U.S. RIASEC correlation matrices based on a variety of samples by stating that "the circumplex structure itself is the crucial distinguishing feature" (p. 875). The hypothesis that the six types are equidistant from each other ("circumplex") has not received unequivocal support. Among the studies supporting this arrangement are those of Fouad, Cudeck, and Hansen (1984) and Fouad and Dancer (1992) on Mexican and American subjects and Khan et al. (1990) on Pakistani subjects.

In another series of studies, Meir (e.g., 1973, 1975) showed that the eight occupational fields in Roe's (1956) classification similarly form a circular configuration: Business–Organization–General Culture–Service–Arts and Entertainment–Outdoor–Technology. This finding was based on Smallest Space Analysis (SSA) of the responses of 22 Israeli samples (one consisting of Arab respondents, Meir, Sohlberg, & Barak, 1973) to either the Ramak or the Courses interest inventories (in Hebrew), both based on Roe's (1956) occupational classification. A variation of the Ramak and Courses for counselees with a negative response attitude (response scales being Reject, Doubtful, Agree rather than Yes, Doubtful, No) and using Israeli soldiers as respondents (Meir, Bar, Lahav, & Shalhevet, 1975) also revealed a circular configuration. The same configuration of occupational fields was found in a combination of the Hebrew adaptation of Holland's SDS and the Ramak (Meir & Ben-Yehuda, 1976) administered to Israeli participants, and again in a combination of the VPI, Ramak and Courses (the latter two adapted into English) with American students as participants (Meir, Rubin, Temple, & Osipow, 1997). A translated version of the Ramak into Spanish (Peiser & Meir, 1976) for immigrants to Israel from Latin American countries revealed a similar, though not entirely circular, arrangement. Finally, a translated version of the Ramak into German, with the necessary modifications (Meir & Stauffer, 1980) was administered twice to Swiss participants at a gap of about one year. The SSA of the $2 \times 8 = 16$ fields also revealed a close to circular arrangement of the fields.

Thus, the circular arrangement emerges whether it is based on Holland's (1973, 1985b) typology into six personality types and responses on either the VPI or the SDS interest inventories, or on any adaptation of these interest inventories into other languages. It also emerges when Roe's (1956) classification into eight occupational fields is employed, with responses on either the Ramak or Courses interest inventories. Moreover, the same arrangement emerges whether the data analysis method is principal component analysis, SSA, randomization test, or confirmatory factor analysis.

Nevertheless, according to more recent research (Rounds & Tracey, 1996), the circular arrangement is not universal. The authors report on a cross-cultural meta-analysis performed on 20 U.S. ethnic group matrices, 76 international matrices and a U.S. benchmark sample of 73 matrices, and conclude that "the cross-culture structural equivalence of Holland's circular order was not supported" (p. 310). Although the circular structure appeared when the participants were either nonethnic Americans, Icelandic (contradictory data in the paper), or Israeli, the structure of the six Holland types was not circular on samples from Guyana, Canada, Papua, New Guinea, Malaysia, Taiwan, New Zealand, Pakistan, Australia, Mexico, Columbia, France, Brazil, Paraguay, Indonesia, Portugal, or Japan (ranging in order from an extremely low correspondence index to the value of .6). For most of these cultures, a higher correspondence index was found for the "alternative 3 class partition," that is, a typology into three classes: R and I; A; and S, E, and C. For the others, Gati's (1979) three group partition—R and I; A and S; and (3) E and C—was found to be superior. Assuming that Rounds and Tracey's (1996) meta-analysis does not suffer from the inclusion of small or non representative samples, or any other methodological flaws, their conclusion must be adopted: a circular configuration of occupations is adequate in some cultures (United States, Israel, Iceland) and not in others, and the "alternative three-class partition," namely R and I ; A; and S, E, and C, is the better fit for the data as a generalization for all cultures. Furthermore, Gati's (1991) "three-group partition" into R and I, A and S, E and C is cross-culturally a better fit than Holland's (1985b) circular arrangement, RIASEC.

Two aspects of this study may be of interest for the cross-cultural assessment of interests. The first is the question of whether it is fundamentally a necessary condition for an interest device in any culture to confirm one of the three structures (circular, "alternative 3 class partition" or "Gati's group partition") as a prerequisite for its use. In other words, if a new interest measurement instrument fails to yield any of the three structures, would its use be considered unethical? According to Rounds and Tracey (1996), "cross-cultural structural equivalence of the constructs must be established . . . before a measure developed in one culture can be used for counseling and research purposes in a second culture and before meaningful cross-cultural comparisons can be made" (p. 311). This question would be equally valid if the circular arrangement were confirmed cross-culturally.

The second issue is the limitation already stated by Rounds and Tracey (1996). The partition into either of the three groups of types incorporates considerably fewer statements of order. Whereas the circular arrangement contains 72 statements regarding the proximity of types, the "alternative 3 class partition" and the "Gati 3 group partition" contain only 44 and 36 such statements, respectively. Thus, both of the three partition models contribute less to our understanding of the structure of occupations and to the counselor's work than does the circular arrangement. Perhaps, for the time being, it would be best to admit that while the structure of occupations is not identical across cultures, the circular arrangement has received considerable support and incorporates many more predictions and is therefore the preferable reference. Figure 3 (p. 321) in Rounds and Tracey's (1996) paper indicates that in some cultures the differences in the level of fitness of the various models are not impressive. It might even be argued that the circular arrangement was found to be less suitable to the findings at least in part because it incorporates more predictions and thus has a better chance of showing deviations.

It could be claimed that the only necessary and sufficient condition that an interest inventory must meet is its predictive validity in regard to a relevant external criterion in a follow-up study. Admittedly, adequate data for this purpose is generally difficult to obtain. Nevertheless, cross-cultural uniqueness or diversity of occupational configuration cannot replace longitudinal validation.

We illustrate this argument by means of one such empirical longitudinal investigation that has been conducted, a seven-year follow-up study by Barak and Meir (1974) on participants' responses to the Ramak. These researchers found correlations of .40 and .26 on 158 males and 202 females, respectively, between the interest scores on the chosen occupational field and satisfaction with that choice seven years later. In a further analysis of the same data, Peiser and Meir (1978) found that the greater the proximity between the chosen occupational field (on the circular arrangement!) and the respondent's highest field score on the original test, the higher the satisfaction with the occupational choice after seven years.

It is worth noting that because occupations in this study were classified into eight fields according to Roe's (1956) classification, and not only into six as in Holland's (1985b) typology, the number of order predictions was higher by far, incorporating 288 predictions, or statements, of order on the circular arrangement of the eight occupational fields out of 378 possible comparisons (Tracey & Rounds, 1994). Indeed, in a previous meta-analysis by Tracey and Rounds (1994) on 24 correlation matrices, the circular arrangement was found to be the best fit for the configuration of Roe's (1956) eight occupational fields. This finding, however, does not refute Rounds and Tracey's (1996) contention that, cross-culturally, the circular arrangement of occupations has not been confirmed, because all the correlation matrices in the earlier study were derived from the scores of either American or Israeli participants.

Thus, the data allow for two possible conclusions: (a) the structure of occupations is circular in some but not all cultures, whereas the partition into three groups is valid cross-culturally, the conclusion that Rounds and Tracey (1996) have adopted; or (b) the structure of occupations is circular cross-culturally if measured using Roe's (1956) classification into eight fields. These two alternative explanations invite a cross-cultural test of Roe's (1956) occupational classification and its possible cross-cultural circular configuration which would include samples that are non-American, non-Israeli and non-Icelandic.

A third possibility also exists: that the circular arrangement of both Holland's (1985b) six types and Roe's (1956) eight fields do fit the data cross-culturally, and the reason why this was not confirmed in some cultures is that the findings were based on problematic interest inventories. We would like to elaborate on this possibility. As stated earlier, the measurement of interests by means of interest inventories requires a very careful selection of suitable items. If this is not done, subjects' responses on any item might lead to inaccurate conclusions. If the items are not chosen in such a way as to control both level and field, negative responses might be given to items because of their level rather than their content (field).

In order to examine the latter possibility empirically, Rounds and Tracey (1996) separated their matrices into Holland-based interest inventories that were simply translated and those that were translated and modified. They reached the same conclusion for both categories. Yet, even in the modified inventories, the dimension of level might not have been taken into account. Thus, the Investigative type might emerge in the configuration as closer to Enterprising than to Conventional, in contradiction to the RIASEC hypothesis, because Investigative and Enterprising represent a higher socioeconomic level, while Conventional (the field expected to be located between them) consists of lower level items. As already stated, due to cultural differences, translated items do not necessarily represent similar occupational levels. This is equally true for fields: In constructing an interest inventory a deviation in the expected arrangement might be generated by selecting items which, although they belong to the relevant field, are loaded to "desired" proxy fields. For instance, Social will move closer to Investigative, rather than Artistic, if "medical service" replaces the title "speech therapist." For the moment, however, this is a speculation that calls for empirical support.

Another question still remains unanswered: If we could measure by paired comparisons the perceived structure of all occupations for a certain respondent, and also by adequate measurement find his or her "place" in that structure, would this mean that the occupations around this placement best fit that individual? It may well be that the perception of proxies among occupations is unrelated to a person's interests or to other determinants which may argue against fitness to that occupation. This might be even more conspicuous if the individual possessed more than a single focus of interests.

It would seem that the data in studies of occupational interests are particularly sensitive to faulty design. To illustrate, in their SSA of Holland's six types, Fouad and Dancer (1992) found that R was somewhat outside the conservative circle. As suggested by the authors, as well as by Holland and Gottfredson (1992) and Subich (1992), this might be because their participants were engineers, for whom the salient distinction among occupations is whether or not they are close to R. It has already been suggested that "misshaped polygons rather than perfect hexagons are often obtained, possibly due to defects of theory, assessment or samples" (Holland & Gottfredson, 1992, p. 165). This may also supply an answer to Hansen's (1992) query as to why African-American and Mexican respondents perceive the structure of occupations in a different way than do White Americans. Perhaps it is merely due to biased samples and deficient tools.

CONCLUSION

As the first concluding note of this chapter, we concur with Bowman's (1995) statement that "a lack of awareness on the counselor's part of the potential biases evident in the inventories used may result in the dissemination of misleading information to ethnic minority career clients at best, or potentially damaging information at worst" (p. 147). However, the fact that despite the difficulties outlined above, significant correlations have been found between measures derived from interest inventories and external criteria indicates that there is something more in the measure of interests than merely the single response, which can be so severely criticized. In view of the problems involved, we would nevertheless recommend the following rules for constructing and employing interest inventories.

1. Items in an interest inventory should be carefully chosen to avoid misunderstanding.
2. Appropriate methods of testing (e.g., item analysis) can aid in selecting better items. In this context, better items would be those that are free from cultural bias within the examined culture.
3. Because any item might be ambiguous to certain respondents, interpretation should rely on groups of items rather than on single responses.
4. The form of items can be random or organized, with or without headings, on scales of "Y ? N" ; "L I D" ; or "Y N" as paired comparisons or free choice, with or without a restriction on the number of items to which the respondent is allowed to respond positively, etc. Because conclusions are based on within-respondent differences of scores, it is assumed that the respondent's attitude will not be affected by the form of presentation.
5. "The proof of the pudding is in the eating"—the quality of items, sums of scores, profiles and inventories should be subjected to appropriate reliability and validity tests.

We refer readers to the six rules formulated by Meir and Gati (1981) and presented next.

PRACTICAL TIPS

Presumably, at this point readers are fairly convinced that cultural aspects hinder the adaptation to another culture of methods or tools on vocational interests developed in one culture. Contrary to Hansen (1987), however, we would like to conclude this discussion on a more optimistic note, offering practical suggestions as to how interest inventories can be developed and examined so as to produce a fairly high level of reliability and validity even in small cultures. These suggestions are based both on a theoretical strategy and on successful empirical experience in Israel.

The first step in developing an interest inventory is to decide on the number of levels and fields to use. The number of levels should be small, as it may be very difficult to discriminate reliably between more than four. Although according to Roe (1956), there are six occupational levels, in Israel, for example, only four were reliably differentiated (Meir, 1968): professional and managerial, semiprofessional, skilled workers, and semi- and unskilled workers. We would recommend starting with these four levels.

The decision as to the number of fields is more difficult. Holland (1973, 1985b) began with six fields with impressive success, to judge by the large number of studies that adopted his method. However, his division suffered from low differentiation, especially among females (with Social emerging as the first letter code for about 50%, and as the second letter code for another 30%). Roe (1956) began with eight occupational fields, (using a separate field for Outdoor and making a distinction between Service and General-Cultural, with the former being more person-to-person oriented and the latter more individual-to-group or community oriented), and we believe this categorization to have its advantages. The combination of four levels (the horizontal dimension) and eight fields (the vertical dimension) means a starting point of 12 definitions and 32 possible clusters of occupations. This has the clear advantages of economy and simplicity. Because the structure of fields appears to be hierarchical in the vertical dimension and circular in the horizontal, theoretically any other number of occupational levels or fields could be adopted providing that proper definitions reliably discriminate between any two. The actual structure of the occupational fields in the culture for which the new interest inventory is being developed is irrelevant at this stage.

The second step is to construct or select the appropriate items. Each new item should fulfill the following conditions: (a) have a clear meaning for "naive" respondents as to content; (b) be neither too attractive nor too repulsive in meaning and associations; (c) be unbiased in its gender meaning (unless separate inventories for males and females are to be developed); (d) adequately represent the occupational clusters and definitions of level and field determined in the first step, and be perceived as such by "naive" respondents. Items need not necessarily represent the actual labor market and employee distribution (indeed there is little chance that employment distribution will coincide with the distribution of interests among candidates for the labor market); and (e) be of a constant number to represent each combination of level and field (e.g., three items for each combination of level and field, that is, $3 \times 4 \times 8 = 96$ items if all four levels and eight fields are represented in the inventory). Because participants generally refrain from responding positively to low level items, the level of semi- and unskilled occupations, in all fields, can be left out of the inventory (reducing accordingly the number of items). We would recommend that this step of selecting the appropriate items for the new inventory be performed by a panel of 3 to 5 experts who are familiar with both the occupational world (fields and levels) and the associations attached to various wordings in the given culture. The scale on which respondents indicate their interest can be dichotomous (e.g., Yes and No), or of three (e.g., Yes, Doubtful, and No) or more ranks.

The third step in constructing a new interest inventory is the theoretical examination of the instrument. A different panel should classify the chosen items, presented to them in random order, into levels and fields. An item should be included in the experimental version of the inventory only if the members of the second panel agree on its classification into both level and field, and this classification is in accord with the intention of the first panel. At this stage, some items will undoubtedly have to be rejected and replaced by new items which must again be subjected to a similar test. Because during the empirical examination of the items (see step four) even more items may have to be rejected and replaced, we recommend that the first panel select at least one or two alternative items for each combination of level and field. Moreover, the second panel must determine the content validity of the group of items for each combination of level and field, that is, they must judge the extent to which all the items pertaining to the same cluster represent the population of occupations in that cluster. If the items within a given cluster are too similar, they might not adequately represent the entire population of occupations that belong to that cluster in the occupational world. For example, the developers of the English version of the Ramak (Meir, Rubin, Temple, & Osipow, 1997) selected social worker, psychologist, and physical therapist to represent the professional and managerial level in Service (in Roe's, 1956, classification), and electronics technician, automobile mechanic, and electrician to represent the semiprofessional level of Technology (in the same classification), believing each group to be sufficiently indicative of its category.

Step four is the empirical examination of the items in the inventory. We recommend that the inventory be administered to a sample of potential counselees with a heterogeneous educational background (providing they can respond to a pencil and paper test) with assumed different interests. In other words, the respondents should not be culled from one educational program (e.g., engineering students or medical staff). The instructions should emphasize that what is being measured is the level of interest in each of the items, independent of any potential fulfillment of that interest, and that there is no limit to the number of positive responses. Following administration, the inventories should be scored according to the scale chosen (e.g., 1 for Yes, 0 for No; or 2, 1, and 0 for Yes, Doubtful, No, respectively). Thus, each respondent will receive a score on each cluster of occupations that is equal to the sum of his or her scores on the items in it. The scores will range from zero—*no interest in any of the items in the cluster*—*to a figure equaling the number of items in the cluster multiplied by the highest score on the scale.* The higher the score, the higher the interest level of the respondent in occupations of a particular cluster. The cluster scores are then summed up horizontally to arrive at level scores and vertically to produce field scores. The sum of the level scores and field scores must, of course, be the same. This figure indicates the total interest, or general baseline, of the individual respondent towards all items in the inventory.

At this stage, the scores should be subjected to reliability tests: horizontally for each of the level scores and vertically for each of the field scores using the conservative split-half or Cronbach alpha methods. Other reliability tests can be designed to achieve test–retest reliabilities, and if more than a single inventory is constructed the equivalent test reliability should also be measured. It must be emphasized that the reliability of all these measures should be tested separately for each level and for each field. The series of reliability measures can be represented in brief by means of their median and range.

An even more crucial test of the new interest inventory is item analysis. Meir and Gati (1981) suggested six rules for determining the fitness for an item of an interest inventory. These are, in brief:

1. the mean score on an item should not be too extreme;
2. the standard deviation of responses on any item should not be too low;
3. all within-field (and within-level) items should correlate positively among themselves;
4. the correlation between each item and its field score should be high enough;
5. the correlation between any item and any other field score should be low enough; and
6. there should be enough of a difference between the correlation of an item with its own field score and its correlation with any other field score.

Of course, decisions have to be made to determine the meaning of "enough" for the last three requirements. Meir and Gati (1981) suggested that for (6), for example, the difference between the square of the correlation coefficient of an item with its field and the square of its correlation with any of the other fields be at least 10%.

To illustrate, an experimental version of the Ramak interest inventory (based on Roe's (1956) occupational classification) contained 99 items to be marked on a scale of Y ? N (Yes, Doubtful, No) with scores of 2, 1, and 0, respectively. Each field score was derived from nine items: three each for professional-managerial, semi-professional, and skilled workers. The responses of a sample of 128 respondents showed that for the item Psychologist, (a) the mean score was 1.06, and (b) its standard deviation was .92. In other words, the mean was around the "?" response, with a distribution of about 50% responding Y and another 50% responding N. (Statistically the highest possible standard deviation is half the range, a situation that occurs when the sample is divided equally between the two extreme scores.) The correlation between the score on Psychologist and the field score of Service was .63, while the correlations between Psychologist and the other seven field scores were .23, .13, .49, .41, 11, .22, and −.21 with Business, Organization, General–Cultural, Arts and Entertainment, Outdoor, Science, and Technology, respectively. This proves empirically that, at least in this sample, the image of Psychologist is linked much more closely to Service than to any of the other fields in Roe's (1956) classification of occupations. In contrast, the item Systems Analyst yielded a mean score of .75 with $SD = .82$, and correlations of .08, .32, .19, 04, .16 .33, .50 and .47 with Business, Organization, General–Cultural, Service, Arts and Entertainment, Outdoor, Science, and Technology, respectively. The small difference between the last two correlations made it impossible to include this item under either Science or Technology, and therefore it had to be dropped from the final version of the inventory.

The fifth step in developing a new interest inventory is to examine its validity. There are five possible methods for doing so:

1. Correlating it with existing proven inventories (if any happen to be available, why put so much effort into developing a new one?!);
2. Analyzing the structure of the scores to see whether the internal correlations fit the known structure of correlations (e.g., the circular arrangement of fields; the hierarchical order of levels);
3. Determining whether people engaged in a certain field score higher on that than on any of the other fields, and also higher than people engaged in other fields;
4. Examining the concurrent validity, that is whether there is a positive correlation between field scores and well-being measures (e.g., satisfaction, stability, or achievement) or negative correlations between field scores and well-being measures with negative connotations (e.g., burnout, absenteeism);
5. Examining the predictive validity by using the same method as above but with a gap of several years between the measurement of interests and that of the well-being measures. This obviously requires time, resources, facilities, and overcoming the difficulty of locating the respondents after several years.

Step six of the elaboration process of the new interest inventory is designed to assess its cross-cultural equivalence. Following Marsella and Leong (1995), it is necessary to conduct the examination with respect to linguistic, conceptual, scaling, and normative aspects. Linguistically, the items of an interest inventory should be translated into languages representing different ethnocentric groups in a way that insures cultural validity. On the conceptual level, use of ethnosemantic procedures is recommended in order to achieve similarity across cultures in the nature and the connotative meaning of the items tapping the levels and fields of interests. Moreover, Marsella and Leong (1995) contend that in many non-Western cultures, Yes-Doubtful-No or Likert/Thurstone scales appear inappropriate, either because situational factors determine the right preferences/behaviors or because scaling in a linear/graduated manner is incongruent with the way in which they conceive their world and life experiences. For instance, in an individualistically oriented culture, a respondent might express interest in engineering professions if these are perceived as leading to personal achievement. Conversely, if the culture is collectivisically oriented, he or she might prefer medical or welfare promoting professions.

Finally, normative equivalence should be insured, the implication being that norms should be established for interest inventories with respect to various ethnocultural groups. Step seven is necessary if the new interest inventory is designed for normative comparisons between respondents as in Kuder (1988) or Strong (1943) and is not required if the design of the new interest inventory is for intraperson comparisons, such as Holland's (1985a, 1994) SDS or Meir et al.'s (1997) Ramak and Courses.

To conclude, the six or seven steps are meant to convey the message that the process of designing a good interest inventory should be guided by solid theoretical considerations rather than by trial-and-error. Indeed, Osipow (1991) reached the same conclusion following the initial failure to produce an English version of the Ramak by translating the original Hebrew items, and the subsequent success when the choice of items was based on appropriate theory and definitions.

We hope that this discussion, along with the practical tips we have offered, will encourage researchers to undertake the daunting task of cross-cultural interest measurement. Although the investment in terms of time and effort may be high, we believe the "interest" that may accrue from it will be no less considerable.

ACKNOWLEDGMENT

The authors thank Itamar Gati for his comments on a draft of this chapter.

REFERENCES

Allalouf, A., & Sireci, S. G. (1998). *Detecting sources of DIF in translated verbal items*. Report No. 245. Jerusalem: National Institute for Testing and Evaluation.

Angoff, W. H., & Cook, L. L. (1988). *Equating the scores of the Prueba de Aptitud Academica and the Scholastic Aptitude Test* (College Board Report No. 88-2). New York: College Entrance Examination Board.

Assouline, M., & Meir, E. I. (1987). Meta-analysis of the relationship between congruence and well-being measures. *Journal of Vocational Behavior, 31*, 319–332.

Barak, A., & Meir, E. I. (1974). The predictive validity of a vocational interest inventory "Ramak": seven year follow-up. *Journal of Vocational Behavior, 4*, 377–387.

Bates, G. L., Parker, H. J., & McCoy, J. F. (1970). Vocational rehabilitants' personality and work adjustment: A test of Holland's theory of vocational choice. *Psychological Reports, 26*, 511–516.

Borgen, F. (1997, May). *Future of interest assessment.* Paper presented at the meeting of the Society for Vocational Psychology, Bethlehem, PA.

Bouchard, T. J., Jr. (1997). Genetic influence on mental abilities, personality, vocational interests and work attitudes. In C. L. Cooper & I. T. Robertson (Eds.), *International Review of Industrial and Organizational Psychology, 12*, 373–395.

Bowman, S. L. (1995). Career intervention strategies and assessment issues for African Americans. In F. T. L. Leong (Ed.), *Career development and vocational behavior of racial and ethnic minorities.* Mahwah, NJ: Lawrence Erlbaum Associates.

Brislin, R. W., Lonner, W. J., & Thorndike, R. M. (1973). *Cross-cultural research methods.* New York: Wiley.

Brown, M. T. (1995). The career development of African Americans: Theoretical and empirical issues. In F. T. L. Leong, *Career development and vocational behavior of racial and ethnic minorities.* Mahwah, NJ: Lawrence Erlbaum Associates.

Campbell, J. P. (1996). Group differences and personnel decisions: validity, fairness and affirmative action. *Journal of Vocational Behavior, 49*, 122–158.

Carter, R. T., & Swanson, L. J. (1990). The validity of the Strong Interest Inventory with Black Americans: A review of the literature. *Journal of Vocational Behavior, 36*, 195–209.

Chu, P. H. (1975). Cross-cultural study of vocational interests measured by the Strong-Campbell Interest Inventory. *Acta-Psychologica-Taiwanica, 17*, 69–84.

Crites, J. O. (1997, May). *Definition of interests.* Paper presented at the meeting of The Society for Vocational Psychology, Bethlehem, PA.

Cronbach, L. J. (1961). *Essentials of psychological testing.* New York: Harper & Row.

Edwards, J. R. (1991). Person-job fit: A conceptual integration, literature review, and methodological critique. In C. L. Cooper & I. T. Robertson (Eds.), *International Review of Industrial and Organizational Psychology, 6*, 283–357.

Elton, C. F, & Rose, H. A. (1981). *Retention revised: With congruence, Differentiation and consistency.* Unpublished Manuscript, University of Kentucky, Lexington.

Fouad, N. A., Cudeck, R., & Hansen, J. C. (1984). Convergent validity of the Spanish and English forms of the Strong-Campbell interest inventory for bilingual Hispanic high school students. *Journal of Counseling Psychology, 31,* 339–348.

Fouad, N. A., & Dancer, L. S. (1992). Cross-cultural structure of interests: Mexico and the United States. *Journal of Vocational Behavior, 40,* 129–143.

Gati, I. (1979). A hierarchical model for the structure of vocational interests. *Journal of Vocational Behavior, 15,* 90–106.

Gati, I. (1991). The structure of vocational interests. *Psychological Bulletin, 109,* 309–324.

Hansen, J. C. (1986). Strong Vocational Interest Blank/Strong-Campbell Interest Inventory. In W. B. Walsh & S. H. Osipow (Eds.), *Advances in vocational psychology* (Vol. 1, pp. 1–29). Hillsdale, NJ: Lawrence Erlbaum Associates.

Hansen, J. C. (1987). Cross-cultural research on vocational interests. *Measurement and Evaluation in Counseling and Development, 19,* 163–176.

Hansen, J. C. (1992). Does enough evidence exist to modify Holland's theory to accommodate the individual differences of diverse populations? *Journal of Vocational Behavior, 40,* 188–193.

Hansen, J. C., & Campbell, D. P. (1985). *Manual for the SVIB-SCII* (4th edition). Stanford, CA: Stanford University Press.

Hener, T., & Meir, E. I. (1981). Congruency, consistency and differentiation as predictors of job satisfaction within the nursing occupation. *Journal of Vocational Behavior, 18,* 304–309.

Hesketh, B., & Rounds, J. (1995). International cross-cultural approaches to career development. In W. B. Walsh & S. H. Osipow, *Handbook of vocational psychology: Theory, research and practice* (2nd ed., pp. 367–390). Mahwah, NJ: Lawrence Erlbaum Associates.

Hofstede, G. (1994). *Culture and organization: Intercultural cooperation and its importance for survival.* Hammersmith, London: Harper & Collins.

Holland, J. L. (1972). *Professional Manual for the Self-Directed Search.* Palo Alto, CA: Consulting Psychologists Press, 1972.

Holland, J. L. (1973). *Making vocational choices: A theory of careers.* Englewood Cliffs, NJ: Prentice-Hall.

Holland, J. L. (1985a). *Professional manual for the Self-Directed Search.* Odessa, FL: Psychological Assessment Resources.

Holland, J. L. (1985b). *Making vocational choices: A theory of vocational personalities and work environments.* Odessa, FL: Psychological Assessment Resources.

Holland, J. L. (1994). *The Self-Directed Search.* Odessa, FL: Psychological Assessment Resources.

Holland, J. L. (1996a). Exploring careers with a typology. *American Psychologist, 51,* 397–406.

Holland, J. L. (1996b). *Self-Directed Search (SDS) Form E: 4th edition - English Canadian.* Odessa, FL: Psychological Assessment Resources, 1997.

Holland, J. L. (1997a, May). *Interests and personality.* Paper presented at the meeting of the Society for Vocational Psychology, Bethlehem, PA.

Holland, J. L. (1997b). *Making vocational choices: A theory of vocational personalities and work environments* (3rd ed.). Odessa, FL: Psychological Assessment Resources.

Holland, J. L., & Gottfredson, G. D. (1990). *An annotated bibliography for Holland's theory of vocational personalities and work environments.* Johns Hopkins University.

Holland, J. L., & Gottfredson, G. D. (1992). Studies of the hexagonal model: An evaluation (or, The perils of stalking the perfect hexagon). *Journal of Vocational Behavior, 40,* 158–170.

Hunter, J. E. (1986). Cognitive ability, cognitive aptitude, job knowledge, and job performance. *Journal of Vocational Behavior, 29,* 340–362.

Jensen, A. R. (1986). g: Artifact or reality? *Journal of Vocational Behavior, 29,* 301–331.

Johansson, C. B. (1986). *Career Assessment Inventory: The enhanced version.* Minneapolis, MN: National Computer Systems.

Karayanni, M. (1987). The impact of cultural background on vocational interest. *The Career Development Quarterly, 36,* 83–90.

Khan, S. B., Sabir, A. A., Shaukat, N., Hussain, M. A., & Baig, T. (1990). A study of the validity of Holland's theory in a non-western culture. *Journal of Vocational Behavior, 36,* 132–146.

Kuder, F. (1970). Some principles of interest measurement. *Educational and Psychological Measurement, 30,* 205–226.

Kuder, F. (1988). *Kuder E General Interest Survey, General Manual.* Chicago: SRA/Pergamon Press.

Leong, F. T. L. (Ed.). (1995). *Career development and vocational behavior of racial and ethnic minorities.* Mahwah, NJ: Lawrence Erlbaum Associates.

Lykken, D. T., Bouchard, T. J. Jr., McGue, M., & Tellegen, A. (1993). Heritability of interests: A twin study. *Journal of Applied Psychology, 78,* 649–661.

Marsella, A. J., & Leong, F. T. L. (1995). Cross-cultural issues in personality and career assessment. *Journal of Career Assessment, 3,* 202–218.

Meir, E. I. (1968). *Structural elaboration of Roe's classification of occupations.* Jerusalem: Israel Program for Scientific Translations.

Meir, E. I. (1973). The structure of occupations by interests: A smallest space analysis. *Journal of Vocational Behavior, 3,* 21–31.

Meir, E. I. (1975). *Manual for the Ramak and Courses Interest Inventories*. Tel Aviv University, Department of Psychology.

Meir, E. I. (1989). Integrative elaboration of the congruence theory. *Journal of Vocational Behavior, 35*, 219–230.

Meir, E. I. (1990). Halimat Ha'Kariera Ha'Mikzoit Ve'Halimat Ha'Seviva [Career congruence and environmental congruence]. In K. Benyamini, A. Dolev, M. Amir, E. Cohen, & I. M. Schlesinger (Eds.), *Theory and application in psychology* (pp. 247–259). Jerusalem: Magnes.

Meir, E. I., Bar, R., Lahav, G., & Shalhevet, R. (1975). Interest inventories based on Roe's classification modified for negative respondents. *Journal of Vocational Behavior, 7*, 127–133.

Meir, E. I., & Ben-Yehuda, A. (1976). Inventories based on Roe and Holland yield similar results. *Journal of Vocational Behavior, 8*, 269–274.

Meir, E. I., & Gati, I. (1981). Guidelines for item selection in inventories yielding score profiles. *Educational and Psychological Measurement, 41*, 1011–1016.

Meir, E. I., & Melamed, S. (1986). The accumulation of person-environment congruences and well-being. *Journal of Occupational Behavior, 7*, 315–323.

Meir, E. I., Melamed, S., & Abu-Freha, A. (1990). Vocational, avocational, and skill utilization congruences and their relationship with well-being in two cultures. *Journal of Vocational Behavior, 36*, 153–165.

Meir, E. I., Melamed, S., & Dinur, C. (1995). The benefits of congruence. *The Career Development Quarterly, 43*, 257–266.

Meir, E. I., Rubin, A., Temple, R., & Osipow, S. H. (1997). Examination of interest inventories based on Roe's classification. *Career Development Quarterly, 46*, 48–61.

Meir, E. I., Sohlberg, S., & Barak, A. (1973). A cross-cultural comparison of the structure of vocational interests. *Journal of Cross-Cultural Psychology, 4*, 501–508.

Meir, E. I., & Stauffer, E. (1980). Strukturelle Messung der Berufsinteressen [Structural measurement of vocational interests]. *Diagnostica, 26*, 85–92.

Melamed, S., Meir, E. I., & Samson, A. (1995). The benefits of personality-leisure congruence: Evidence and implications. *Journal of Leisure Research, 27*, 25–40.

Osipow, S. H. (1991). Developing instruments for use in counseling. *Journal of Counseling and Development, 70*, 322–326.

Peiser, C., & Meir, E. I. (1976). A Spanish version of the Ramak interest inventory. *Interamerican Journal of Psychology, 10*, 9–15.

Peiser, C., & Meir, E. I. (1978). Congruency, consistency and differentiation of vocational interests as predictors of vocational satisfaction and preference stability. *Journal of Vocational Behavior, 12*, 270–278.

Prediger, D. J., & Vansickle, T. R. (1992). Locating occupations on Holland's hexagon: Beyond RIASEC. *Journal of Vocational Behavior, 40*, 111–128.

Roe, A. (1956). *The Psychology of Occupations*. New York: Wiley.

Roe, A. (1957). Early determinants of vocational choice. *Journal of Counseling Psychology, 4*, 212–217.

Rounds, J., & Tracey, T. J. (1993). Prediger's dimensional representation of Holland's RIASEC circumplex. *Journal of Applied Psychology, 78*, 875–890.

Rounds, J., & Tracey, T. J. (1996). Cross-cultural structural equivalence of RIASEC models and measures. *Journal of Counseling Psychology, 43*, 310–329.

Spokane, A. R. (1985). A review of research on person-environment congruence in Holland's theory of careers. *Journal of Vocational Behavior, 26*, 306–343.

Strong, E. K. (1943). *Vocational interests of men and women*. Stanford: Stanford University Press.

Subich, L. M. (1992). Holland's theory: "Pushing the envelope". *Journal of Vocational Behavior, 40*, 201–206.

Super, E. K., & Crites, J. O. (1962). *Appraising Vocational Fitness*. New York: Harper.

Tracey, T. J., & Rounds, J. (1993). Evaluating Holland's and Gati's vocational interest models: A structural meta-analysis. *Psychological Bulletin, 113*, 229–246.

Tracey, T. J., & Rounds, J. (1994). An examination of the structure of Roe's eight interest fields. *Journal of Vocational Behavior, 44*, 279–296.

Tranberg, M., Slane, S., & Ekeberg, S. E. (1993). The relation between interest- congruence and satisfaction: A metaanalysis. *Journal of Vocational Behavior, 42*, 253–264.

Walsh, W. B., & Osipow, S. H. (Eds.). (1986). *Advances in Vocational Psychology*. Hillsdale, NJ: Lawrence Erlbaum Associates.

Waller, N. G., Lykken, D. T., & Tellegen, A. (1995). Occupational interests, leisure time interests, and personality: Three domains or one? Findings from the Minnesota Twin Registry. In D. L. Lubinski & Dawis, R. V. (Eds.), *Assessing individual differences in human behavior: New concepts, methods, and findings* (pp. 233–259). Palo Alto, CA: Davies-Black.

Chapter 7

Cross-Cultural Perspective on Super's Career Development Theory: Career Maturity and Cultural Accommodation

Frederick T. L. Leong
Felicisima C. Serafica
The Ohio State University

As the 21st century approaches, the population of the United States is becoming increasingly diverse. It is projected that by 2000, 71.8% of the population will be of European descent whereas 12.2% will be African Americans, 11.4% Hispanics, 3.9% Asian and Pacific Islander Americans, and 0.7% Native Americans (U.S. Bureau of Census, 1998). By 2010, European Americans will decrease further to 68% whereas all other groups will increase with Hispanics comprising 13.8%, African Americans 12.6%, Asian/Pacific Islander Americans 4.8%, and Native Americans 0.8% (U.S. Bureau of Census, 1998). Projections of the resident population by age and race in the year 2000 indicate that the potential entrants into the labor force, those aged 18–24, will represent 9.2% of European Americans but 11.8% of Native Americans, 11.7% of Hispanics, 11.2% of African Americans, and 10.3% of Asian/Pacific Islanders (U.S. Bureau of Census, 1998). Greater proportions of ethnic minority groups than the majority group will enter the labor force. "Most new entrants to the labor force will be non-White, female, or immigrants" (Hudson Institute, 1987, p. 95). Thus, the ethnic composition of the civilian labor force will change substantially.

The implications of the changing demographics of the workplace has not been lost on behavioral and social scientists who study career development. As far back as the 1970s, Osipow (1975) expressed concern that the extant career theories might not adequately represent how the careers of special groups (e.g., women and minorities) evolve and function in the real world as it appears to these individuals. More recently, Osipow and Littlejohn (1995) noted that increasing numbers of ethnic minorities are entering the labor force at a time when the economy and the workplace are less stable and subject to rapid and abrupt changes. No longer willing "to accept a society and an economy that relegates them to second- or third-class employment" (Osipow & Littlejohn, 1995, p. 252), members of ethnic minority groups are seeking promising careers within a global economy that has brought about less job security and greater competition for jobs and advancement.

Given the challenges facing ethnic minorities as they enter the work-force in increasing numbers, Osipow and Littlejohn (1995) called for a supportive database and the creation of a cross-cultural theory of career development. In this chapter, we examine recent progress in developing a scientific database and formulating a theory that can "account for the career development of and behavior of all people" (Osipow & Littlejohn, 1995, p. 252). We also identify the problems attendant to these endeavors and assess the prospects for a cross-cultural psychology of career development. The current chapter is framed within a developmental–contextual perspective (Vondracek, Lerner, & Schulenberg, 1986). The first section attempts to synthesize the research on career maturity of ethnic minority adolescents within a developmental framework, and the second section proposes a cultural accommodation approach to improving Super's (1990) theory by incorporating culture-specific variables, including contextual factors. For more comprehensive recent reviews of research on career development of ethnic minorities, the interested reader is referred to Arbona (1991), Hoyt (1989), Koegel, Donin, Ponterotto, and Spitz (1995), Leong (1995), and London and Greller (1991).

CAREER MATURITY IN ETHNIC MINORITY ADOLESCENTS: A DEVELOPMENTAL ANALYSIS

The interests, abilities, and skills that eventually form the basis of a vocational choice usually emerge and develop during childhood, but it is not until adolescence that they become integrated and focused toward a particular career goal. Achieving this integration and focus is one of the central developmental tasks of adolescence. Responding to both internal (e.g., a growing sense of self) and external (e.g., societal expectations) pressures, adolescents become increasingly aware that they have to make a vocational choice. Aspirations and expectations, often vague and unacknowledged even to one's self, must now be articulated and defined more sharply, and eventually, an occupation is chosen from an array of possible choices.

The scientific study of career choice crystallization or how the adolescent arrives at a vocational choice has been approached from a variety of theoretical perspectives (Osipow & Fitzgerald, 1996) that have focused on different aspects of the process and emphasized different constructs. Because of space limitations, this selective review of ethnic minority adolescent career development will focus solely on the construct career maturity. This construct was chosen because of (a) its centrality in theories and research on adolescent career development, (b) the availability of theoretical propositions regarding its development, (c) empirical evidence of developmental trends in career maturity among European-American adolescents and last but not least, (d) the lack of a clear and coherent description of career maturity development among ethnic minorities despite the availability of research articles and reviews.

This section describes career maturity development during early to late adolescence among ethnic minorities, based primarily on studies reported from 1970–1998 in two journals devoted exclusively to career development: *Career Development Quarterly* and its predecessor, *Vocational Guidance Quarterly*, and the *Journal of Vocational Behavior*. The review begins with studies published in 1970 because it was around this time that marked changes in the educational and occupational opportunities for women and ethnic minorities began to form a critical mass, a consequence of court-ordered school desegation, the Civil Rights Movement, the Women's Movement, and Affirmative Action policies (Bergman, 1996; Gallegos & Kahn, 1986; Hughes, Gordon, & Hillman, 1980). Because of these expanding opportunities, the career development context for cohorts of ethnic minorities who came of age around 1970 and beyond would be altered in important ways from that of their counterparts in prior decades.

Research on career development of ethnic minorities has been severely criticized for its methodological shortcomings (e.g., Koegel et al., 1995) but to dismiss it out of hand because of these limitations would be tantamount to throwing the baby out with the bathwater. There may be lessons to be gained from the data available, as long as we keep in mind the limitations of the research that produced these findings and guard against similar weaknesses when designing future studies. At the very least, we can learn what is known to date about the development of career maturity in this population. The review is organized around the following questions: What are the quantitative and qualitative changes in career maturity during adolescence? Within a particular group, does the rate or sequence of development vary as a function of gender, social class, or ethnicity? What are the factors that influence the development of career maturity? Can the development of career maturity be facilitated through intervention?

Developmental Trends

As conceptualized by Super (1953, 1990), career maturity is a multidimensional construct representing an individual's readiness to cope with the vocationally related developmental tasks at a particular period of the life-span. Its development during adolescence involves changes in the adolescent's awareness that he or she has to make an occupational choice and his or her attitudes toward this task. There are also changes in the competencies (i.e., knowledge, abilities, and skills) that facilitate making and implementing a career choice effectively, especially career exploration, decision making, and planning. Hence, career maturity is often conceptualized as having an attitudinal dimension and a cognitive dimension. In a stimulus-organism-response (S-O-R) paradigm for studying career maturity, these attitudes and competencies serve as the intervening variables (Savickas, 1985). The successful evolution of career maturity during adolescence is expected to culminate in career choice crystallization and commitment.

In studying the development of career maturity, investigators have chosen to conceptualize change in quantitative terms, that is, as increases in the attitudinal and cognitive dimensions that are operationalized differently in various measures of career maturity (Savickas, 1985). Quantitative changes in cognitive maturity in American adolescents of European descent have been amply documented in cross-sectional studies (e.g., Wallace-Broscious, Serafica, & Osipow, 1994) and a few longitudinal studies (e.g., Super, Starishevsky, Matlin, & Jordaan, 1963). Similar studies conducted among ethnic minority adolescents were not found. The few available studies of career maturity among ethnic minorities used either only one age grade or combined adolescents varying in age or grade into a single group. Only one of these studies examined the role of grade level in career maturity. Dillard and Perrin (1980) were unable to test for grade differences in their study of ethnic minority students in ninth through twelfth grade but they managed to show through regression analyses that school grade level accounted for a statistically significant portion (5%) of the variance in career maturity that was not already explained by gender, socioeconomic status, or their interactions. Regression coefficients indicating that students in higher grades tended to obtain higher career maturity scores also suggest that career maturity changes over time during adolescence.

Differential Rates of Development

Several studies of high school students have explored whether the development of career maturity varies as a function of ethnicity. In a study of high school students representing three ethnic groups from western New

York, Dillard and Perrin (1980) reported that the mean score on career maturity attitudes of the European American high school students was significantly higher than that of their African American peers. The career maturity level of the Puerto Ricans did not differ significantly from those of the other two groups. Westbrook and Sanford (1991) also found ethnic group differences when they compared the responses of African American and European American ninth graders to the Counseling Form of the Career Maturity Inventory (CMI)Attitude Scale. European Americans scored significantly higher than their African American peers on Involvement, Independence, and Compromise in Career Decision Making. The validity of these findings was questioned by Westbrook and Sanford (1991) because the same study also failed to show in African Americans a significant relationship between the CMI Attitude Scale subscales and a measure of appropriateness of career choices. They suggested that separate analyses of career maturity scores should be carried out for different ethnic groups.

In another study of ninth graders, Lundberg, Osborne, and Miner (1997) found that European Americans had significantly higher mean scores than Mexican Americans on Decision Making (DM) and World of Work Information (WWI) from the Career Development Inventory (CDI) Cognitive Scale. The two ethnic groups did not differ significantly, however, on Career Exploration (CE) and Career Planning (CP) which comprise the CDI Attitude Scale nor on the CDI Knowledge of Preferred Occupation (PO) Scale. The only study of career maturity in Native Americans yielded by the literature search was a study conducted in the state of Montana. Martin, Dodd, Smith, White, and Davis (1984) compared non-Indian urban high school students with Indian reservation high school students on three indices of knowledge of work: (a) past work experience, (b) knowledge of vocational training required for various jobs, and (c) self-estimates of capabilities to attain various occupations. The non-Indian adolescents had significantly higher mean scores on past work experience and knowledge of vocational training required for various jobs than their peers who lived and went to school on the reservations. They had held more jobs and were more knowledgeable about the amount of vocational training time required for various occupations. There was no significant group difference, however, in their self-estimates of capabilities to attain various occupations. Both groups of adolescents expressed confidence in their capabilities to attain a wide range of occupations, irrespective of the extent of their work experience or knowledge of occupations. If one considers self-estimates of capabilities to attain various occupations as an index of self-efficacy rather than of career maturity, then the results reported by Martin et al. (1984) might be re-interpreted as showing that Indian adolescents on the reservation score lower on a cognitive dimension of career maturity than their non-Indian urban peers.

Among college students, Leong (1991) found that Asian Americans had significantly lower scores than European Americans on career maturity attitudes also as measured by the CMI. This finding was later confirmed in Luzzo's (1992) study of Asian-, African-, European-, Filipino-, and Hispanic-American college students. European Americans had significantly higher scores on career decision-making attitudes than either the Asian Americans (mainly of East Asian descent) and Filipinos (who are also classified as Asian Americans).

At face value, these ethnic group differences in career maturity observed in both high school and college students give the impression that the development of career maturity occurs at a slower rate in ethnic minority adolescents than it does among European Americans. Researchers, however, have questioned this interpretation and attributed the observed ethnic differences to the use of instruments that are not valid for specific ethnic minority groups, the use of ethnic groups that are not comparable with respect to socioeconomic status (SES), geographic location that affects career-related experiences, English language proficiency, work values, and other cultural norms that might affect the definition and measurement of career maturity (e.g., Leong, 1991; Luzzo, 1992; Martin et al., 1984; Westbrook & Sanford, 1991). It is even possible that when responses from students differing in age are combined for purposes of statistical analysis, group differences in age composition may affect the group mean scores. For example, if the European-American group includes many more seniors than the ethnic minority group, its mean career maturity score is likely to be higher than that of the latter.

From a developmental perspective, comparative studies of career maturity in ethnic minority groups may be premature because normative developmental trends for ethnic minorities have not yet been established. Furthermore, because descriptive studies of normative development do not require a control group, the emphasis on comparative studies in career development research on ethnic minorities suggests an implicit acceptance of European-American career developmental trends as the norm, a questionable assumption. Ethnic comparisons are appropriate for such purposes such as verifying the generalizability of a developmental sequence, examining differential rates of development, or exploring the differential effects of contextual factors but what seems needed at this phase in the evolution of career development research on ethnic minorities is a careful description of the phenomenon or set of phenomena. Description has to precede explanation for the adequacy of explanatory theories rests in part on careful description of the phenomenon or set of phenomena to be explained. Describing "career development as it *is* and not as we think it *should* be might produce more powerful career concepts for *all* kinds of people" (Osipow & Littlejohn, 1995, p. 256). Toward this end, it may be more helpful to delineate career developmental trends for a particular group and document within-group differences in these trends instead of making ethnic group comparisons, thereby formulating a empircally based description of early career development for a particular ethnic group or subgroup.

The importance of examining within-group differences was emphasized by Osipow (1975) because he thought that the mixed results of research on validity of career development theories may be partly explained by their having been applied to varied populations under a variety of conditions. As he saw it, the challenge for career development scientists would be to differentiate among the subgroups that they study and identify those who do or do not meet the underlying assumptions of career development theories regarding (a) perceived and actual availability of choice for individuals, and (b) individuals being strongly motivated toward interest satisfaction. Identification of this subgroup requires that research reports include a careful description of sample characteristics. In response to this challenge, the remainder of this section will be devoted to trying to understand the development of career maturity by examining within-group differences in a specific ethnic group.

Gender Differences

Several studies of high school students compared examined gender differences in career maturity. All but one study failed to find a significant gender difference. A significant difference in the maturity of career attitudes held by males versus females did not emerge in a sample of African-American twelfth graders attending an integrated senior high school (Lawrence & Brown, 1976) nor in a sample of low-socioeconomic status African-American seniors in a high school located within a large metropolitan city in New York state (Smith, 1976). There was also no significant difference in the career maturity mean scores of males versus females recruited from an academically heterogeneous high school student population in an urban area of western New York (Pound, 1978). A similar finding was revealed by a study of high school students from ninth through twelfth grade representing three ethnic groups living in western New York state (Dillard & Perrin, 1980). In contrast, in a study with the primary aim of investigating sex differences (Brown, 1997) among African Americans attending midwestern urban high schools, girls scored significantly higher than boys on the Attitude Scale and the Competence Test from the abbreviated CMI (Crites, 1995).

Two studies that used the nonabbreviated CMI (Crites, 1973) with college samples also did not yield gender differences. Luzzo (1992) did not find differences in the attitudinal dimension of career maturity in a sample of college students that included five ethnic groups. Neither did Leong (1991) in his study of Asian- and European-American college students.

To date, almost all of the studies have reported that African-, Asian- and Hispanic-American males and females do not differ in their levels of career maturity. In the absence of cross-sectional or longitudinal studies, however, it cannot be stated conclusively that the rates of development for career maturity remain the same throughout adolescence for males and females. Also, the fact that the only study to find a significant gender difference was conducted only recently raises a question regarding the potential effect of changes in gender socialization on career maturity development of females.

Social Class Differences

The effect of social class on career maturity of ethnic minorities has been of interest to career developmental scientists for at least two reasons. First, social class has implications for the availability of educational and career experiences that facilitate career development. Second, there is concern that observed ethnic group differences in career maturity may be due to the confounding of ethnicity and social class. Dillard (1976) investigated the effects of SES on African-American male sixth graders' scores on the CMI Attitude Scale. Using the Hollingshead (1957) Two Factor Index of Social Position as a measure of SES, he found that the suburban middle-class group had the highest career maturity scores, followed by the urban middle and, last, the urban lower class. This pattern of SES differences remained even after career maturity scores were subjected to an analysis of covariance with reading achievement test scores as a covariate. The pattern remained robust despite findings that the two middle SES groups had significantly higher mean reading scores than the lower SES urban group and that, for the total sample, reading achievement and socioeconomic status were significantly related. Perhaps, the robustness of SES might be explained by a finding from the multiple regression analysis showing that reading (besides socioeconomic status, residence, family intactness) accounted for only 2.1% of the variance in career maturity scores in this study, which made adjustments (combined use of tape-recorded and printed versions of the CMI) in the test administration for potential differences in reading ability. Subsequently, Dillard and Perrin (1980) reported that SES significantly accounted for an additional 5% of the variance in career maturity scores of their multiethnic sample of high school students.

Among studies of college students, the only study that assessed the effect on career maturity of socioeconomic status, operationalized as the Duncan

Socioeconomic Index (SEI), did not yield a significant SES effect for a multiethnic sample (Luzzo, 1992). It is conceivable that college samples are not as representative of the ethnic minority population as high school samples are. Ethnic minority college students may come from predominantly middle class families or upwardly mobile lower class families that foster the development of career maturity. Studies are needed to further explore the role of social class in career maturity of ethnic minority college students, including how they interact to influence college retention.

Correlates and Predictors. Although scientists who study career maturity in ethnic minority populations have not appeared interested in identifying developmental sequences, they have been quite active in exploring its correlates and predictors. One such study explored the relationship between reference group perspective and career maturity. Smith (1976) contended that attributing low vocational maturity scores of African-American youth to their SES, a conclusion reached in many studies, overlooks significant within-group differences among members of the lower class. She proposed that reference group perspectives might account for variations in vocational maturity among individuals of the same socioeconomic status. This hypothesized relationship between reference group perspectives and career maturity was confirmed in a sample of urban African-American high school seniors from families with low socioeconomic status, as indexed by the Hollingshead Scales (Hollingshead, 1957). Reference Group Perspective (RGP) scores and total CMI scores were positively correlated, significantly so. Lower socioeconomic African-American seniors with a middle-class orientation tended to have higher CMI scores. Significant relationships among CMI, RGP, and post high-school plans were also found. Students with high CMI and RGP scores were more likely to be bound for college. Among these students from low socioeconomic backgrounds, the reference-group perspectives of the college bound were more oriented to the middle class whereas those of their work-bound peers were more oriented to the lower class. Furthermore, students who expressed an open view of the opportunity structure in America were more oriented toward the middle class than students who held a closed view of the opportunity structure. Interestingly, CMI and RGP scores did not vary as a function of whether the student came from an intact or broken family background.

Lawrence and Brown (1976) investigated the role of intelligence, self-concept, socioeconomic status, race, and gender in predicting career maturity of African-American as well as European-American twelfth graders. The measures included both the Attitude Scale and the Competence Test of the CMI (Crites, 1973), the Tennessee Self-Concept Scale (TSCS), and the Otis–Lennon Mental Ability Test. For the total sample, the best set of predictors for the Attitude Scale (ATT) score was made up of Intelligence Quotient (IQ), Self-Concept (SC), and Race. Only IQ contributed significantly to the prediction of ATT in African-American males, whereas IQ and SES made up the best set of predictors for African-American females. Also for the total sample, the best set of predictors for Self-Appraisal included IQ, Gender, SC, and Race. None of the predictors added significantly to the prediction of Self-Appraisal in African-American males and only IQ contributed significantly to the prediction of Self-Appraisal for females. For the total sample, IQ, Gender, Race, and SC emerged as the best set of predictors of Occupational Information. For African-American males, IQ and SES were the best set of predictors whereas only IQ was a significant contributor to the prediction of Occupational Information in females. For the total sample, IQ, gender, SC, and race comprised the best set of predictors for Goal Selection. None of the variables added significantly to the prediction of Goal Selection for African-American males and only IQ contributed significantly to its prediction in African-American females. For the total sample, the best set of predictors of Planning were IQ, race, and gender. Only IQ contributed significantly to the prediction of Planning for both African-American males and females. Finally, IQ and gender were the best predictors of problem solving for the total sample but only IQ contributed significantly to the predictability of problem solving in the subgroups. These findings might be summarized as indicating that among African Americans, only IQ appeared in this study to be the most consistent predictor of various dimensions of career maturity, for both males and females. Although African-American males and females did not differ significantly in their mean scores on each cognitive aspect of career maturity, gender differences characterized the extent to which various predictors contributed significantly to the prediction of the different cognitive dimensions. Finally, it is noteworthy that contrary to expectations, self-concept was not found to be a significant predictor of career maturity in African Americans. Lawrence and Brown (1976) suggested that Super's (1953) self-concept theory may have more validity for White males than females or for African Americans in general.

Given the questions raised (Lawrence & Brown, 1976) about the validity of Super's (1953, 1963) self-concept theory of career development for African Americans, Pound (1978) sought to clarify the role of self-concept in the development of career maturity by using multidimensional measures of both self-concept and career maturity. For his total random sample of European- and African-American high-school students, there was a significant positive correlation between total scores on the TSCS (Fitts, 1965) and the Vocational Development Inventory Attitude Scale (VDI-ATT; Crites, 1969). Multiple regression analysis showed that for the

African-American males, Social Self subscale scores contributed significantly to the prediction of career maturity beyond the relationship previously established between the TSCS and VDI-ATT total scores. For African-American females, none of the TSCS subscale scores significantly predicted VDI-ATT. These findings for African Americans were confirmed in a parallel regression analysis. In another parallel regression using only those subscales that contributed significantly to the prediction of career maturity for each subgroup, it was found that the predictive patterns formed by the Personal Self and Satisfaction subscales for the different subgroups were not similar. Further, simple regression analyses for each of the four subgroups revealed that Personal Self, Social Self, and Satisfaction predicted VDI-ATT for all four subgroups, particularly for the African-American sample.

Pound (1978) concluded that self-concept does appear to have a differential impact on career maturity depending upon the race and gender of participants. More specifically, for high-school students in general, Super's (1955, 1963) self-concept theory appears to have more validity for African-American males than for African-American females and European Americans in general. Because the external rather than the internal subscales (Fitts, 1965) emerged as significant predictors of career maturity for African-American males, Pound (1978) hypothesized that their self-evaluations are heavily influenced by external sources whereas African-American females may evaluate self-concept using multidimensional sources that favor neither internal nor external frames of reference. He suggests further that socialization, particularly sex-role stereotyping, may account for the observed gender difference in frames of reference for self-evaluation. Last, based on the results of this study, Pound (1978) asserted that self-concept subscale scores might be more useful than total scores in examining the relationship between self-concept and career maturity. This assertion is strengthened by the failure of McNair and Brown (1983) to find a significant correlation between TSCS Total Positive scores and CMI-ATT scores of the African-American tenth graders in their sample. Not surprising, TSCS Total Positive score did not add significantly to the prediction of CMI-ATT.

Pound's (1978) hypothesis about external sources serving as frames of reference in self-evaluation and its relationship to career maturity raises a question about the role of parents in adolescent career development. Our literature search yielded two studies of parental influence on the career maturity of ethnic minorities. Dillard and Campbell (1981) examined the relationship of career maturity to parents' work values and career aspirations for their children in the multiethnic sample described earlier (Dillard & Perrin, 1980). Neither the parents work values nor their aspirations contributed significantly toward predicting career maturity attitudes of

African-, Puerto Rican-, or European-American high-school students. In contrast, McNair and Brown (1983) found that parental influence, operationalized as students' perception of the degree of mother's or father's encouragement or discouragement of education (Crites, 1969), accounted for a significant portion of the variance in predicting CMI-ATT for African-American male and female tenth-grade students. These investigators interpreted this finding as support for the hypothesis that important models influence career development (Krumboltz, Mitchell, & Jones, 1976). Lee (1984) also explored the relative contributions of self-concept (TSCS total positive score), parental influence (PINF) and socioeconomic status (SES) to prediction of career choice attitudes (CMI-ATT) of African, European-, and Native-American rural high-school students. Both self-concept and parental influence interacted with ethnicity such that different equations were required to predict career choice attitudes for each ethnic group. As expected, self-concept contributed to career choice attitudes of European and African Americans but, surprisingly, was negatively related in Native Americans. Parental influence contibuted more strongly to the prediction of career choice attitudes for both ethnic minority groups than for European Americans. The relative contributions of students' degree of certainty about parental expectations and socioeconomic status to prediction was about the same for both ethnic minority groups.

Finally, the relationship of total or subscale scores on career maturity measures to other career behaviors has been explored. In their study of the relationship between accuracy of self-appraisal and ability to appraise career-relevant capabilities of others in a southern, urban ninth-grade sample, Westbrook, Sanford, Gilleland, Fleenor and Merwin (1988) did not find a significant correlation between CMI Self-Appraisal subtest scores and Accuracy of Self-Appraisal Discrepancy scores for the total sample, nor for either the African- or European-American subgroups. Also, they did not find a significant relationship between CMI Goal Selection subscale scores and Appropriateness of Career Choice Index in a subsequent study of ninth grade rural African- and European-American students (Westbrook, Sanford, & Donelly, 1990). Although these studies did not yield significant ethnic or gender differences, nonsignificant trends led Westbrook et al. (1990) to question the validity of the CMI (Crites, 1978) for students who are not European-American males. One study did find significant relationships between attitudinal and behavioral aspects of career maturity in a sample of urban African-Americans of low SES who were participants in a summer employment program (Fouad & Keeley, 1992). Using subscales from the CMI-ATT Scale and the Youth Competency Evaluation (YCE; Love & O'Hara, 1987), Fouad and Keeley found that of the five CMI subscales, four were significantly correlated with various behavioral competencies. CMI Compromise, a measure of willingness to compromise between needs and reality, was the most effective predictor of behavioral competencies, significantly predicting acceptance of authority, responsibility and self-initiative, getting along with coworkers, and safety. Two other CMI scores, Independence and Task Orientation contributed significantly to the prediction of positive self-image. CMI scores were not significant predictors of attendance, punctuality, quantity of work, or quality of work.

Facilitating Career Maturity Development

Several intervention studies have explored the feasibility of inducing change in career maturity among high-school youth but none of these produced statistically significant effects. Pavlak and Post Kammer (1985) investigated the effect of a short-term career guidance program on the career maturity of African-American and European-American delinquent youth who, on a pretest, showed comparable levels of this construct as measured by the CMI. The intervention did not yield a significant main or interaction effects. Although a review of pre- and posttest mean scores showed that African- and European-American youth who received the intervention obtained higher career maturity scores at the posttest than they did on the pretest whereas those in the control groups attained approximately the same or lower than their pretest scores, the treatment group difference did not reach an acceptable level of statistical significance. Pavlak and Post Kammer attributed the lack of a significant treatment effect to the short duration of the intervention and to the possibility that various depressor variables (e.g., SES) made the procedures inappropriate for this delinquent sample.

Longhead, Liu, and Middleton (1995) examined the effect of PRO-100, a 7-week career development program on inner city, impoverished youth ranging in age from 14 to 18 years. PR-100 had two major components, work experience and a career development curriculum. One of its six goals was to increase career maturity. At pretest, there were no significant differences in any of the target variables as a function of gender or experience. A comparison of pre- and posttest scores on the Counseling Form of the CMI-ATT (Crites, 1978) showed only a trend ($p < .08$) on the Decision making and Compromise subscales of the CMI.

Investigators have explored whether providing systematic experiences would enhance career exploration and planning, two behaviors assumed to contribute to career maturity. Bergland and Lundquist (1975) investigated the effectiveness of the Vocational Exploration Group (VEG; Daane, 1971) in assisting male Mexican-American junior high school students to become more aware of the world of work and its relevance for them. The students were randomly assigned to one of three groups: a Vocational

Exploration Group, VEG without interaction, and a control group. Following treatment, they were given a Career Exploration Questionnaire. Although treatment group means were higher than that of the control group, these group differences were not significant. No differences between treatment groups emerged on the Career Exploration Questionnaire and another questionnaire that assessed their reactions to the treatment experience.

Career planning has proven to be more responsive to intervention. The effect of an intervention, school busing, on career planning was examined by Gable, Thompson, and Iwanicki (1983) in a survey of the post high-school occupational attainments of students who participated in an urban–suburban school busing experiment in which they were randomly assigned to an experimental group or to a comparison group of nonparticipants. The survey return rates were 87% for the participants (including graduates and dropouts) and 63% for nonparticipants, a statistically significant difference. Based on responses to questions dealing with job/career choice, work history, and post high-school education activities, the career pattern for each respondent was classified as: consistent, inconsistent, or mixed. A consistent career pattern was one in which the occupational choice (particularly the 5 years in the future choice) was reinforced by work history or postsecondary education that would likely lead to the attainment of the occupational choice. Compared to the nonparticipants, a significantly higher percentage of both the graduates and dropouts exhibited consistent career planning and progression. Gable et al. (1983) interpreted this finding as suggesting that participation in Project Concern facilitated the development of more consistent career planning patterns. In PR-100, the intervention study on career development among inner-city, impoverished youth reported earlier (Longhead et al., 1995), the intervention had significant effects on career planning and job search skills. These two variables had a high and statistically significant correlation ($r = .83$) so they may be measuring the same constructs.

The only career maturity intervention study with college students (Rodriguez & Blocher, 1988) yielded by the literature search involved Puerto Rican women who, through a special admissions program, were in their first semester of college. These students were randomly assigned to one of three treatment groups: a modified Adkins Career Choice Modular program, a career development program formulated for this particular study, and a placebo control, the regular college orientation program. Career maturity was assessed through the Knowledge (CDK) and Attitude (CDA) scores on the College and University Form of the CDI (Super, Zelkowitz, & Thompson, 1979), and scores on the Adult Vocational Maturity Assessment Interview (AVMAI; Manuele, 1983), a measure of vocational maturity designed for use with disadvantaged adults. Treatment had a significant effect on the attitudinal component of career maturity but not on knowledge. With pretest scores as covariants, the analysis showed that at posttest, students in Treatment 2, the career development program, had a significantly higher mean CDA score than students in Treatment 3, the placebo control group. A one-way ANOVA on AVMAI total scores from the postintervention produced a statistically significant treatment effect ($p < .011$) but Scheffe post hoc comparisons showed only a significant trend. Students who received Treatments 1 and 2 had higher scores than students in the Treatment 3 group ($p < .10$), but the effects of Treatments 1 and 2 did not differ significantly from one another.

Enhancing career maturity levels or facilitating its development in either high school or college students has proven to be a quite a challenge for investigators. Among high school students, significant gains have been made only when specific career behaviors (e.g., career planning) are targeted. In college students, intervention significantly affected only the attitudinal dimension of career maturity. Stability over time of these meager gains were not assessed. Aside from the methodological limitations of the studies, there are conceptual issues that have yet to be addressed in intervention research. In the absence of data concerning the sequence of development for career maturity, the important transition points are unknown. Yet such information is vital because developmentally based approaches to intervention have demonstrated that it is when individuals are in transition from one level to the next in the development of a specific process that intervention is most effective. Furthermore, as best as it could be ascertained, the intervention programs were not informed by what the research to date has revealed about the factors that influence career maturity development.

Problems and Prospects

Two major problems were identified in this review of research on career maturity in ethnic minority populations. First, career development research is not developmental and the second, with some rare exceptions, it is not contextual. The lack of cross-sectional or longitudinal studies is a serious omission for in this vacuum, developmental norms for other ethnic groups (e.g., European Americans) end up being used as the standard by which career maturity development among ethnic minorities is evaluated. Furthermore, lacking normative data and knowledge of the factors that contribute significantly to career maturity development, it is difficult to predict when adolescents who appear to be making slower progress than their peers will catch up and how they may be assisted in this process.

The emphasis on quantitative changes in career maturity albeit heuristic has to be complemented by attempts to understanding the process of development. For example, although exploration, decision making, and planning are sometimes construed as steps, as well as processes or behaviors in career maturity development, their exact ordering in the developmental sequence has never been clearly established. It has never been empirically determined that there is a progression from career exploration to decision making to planning. Nor have the sequential changes in each of these been explored. For example, how do the number and type of career exploration strategies change over time? Also, how do career attitudes and competencies influence one another over time in the development of career maturity. As competencies increase, do attitudes toward career choice crystallization become more positive or vice versa? Or is there a changing reciprocal interaction over the course of adolescence? How is the development of career maturity related to other important developmental processes taking place during adolescence? These are but a few of the research questions that might be explored in a truly developmental research on career maturity.

By its very nature, career development is context bound, yet there is very little research into the contextual factors underlying the development of career maturity. Although these contextual factors (e.g., opportunity structure, exposure to different careers) are acknowledged, research on context has not gone beyond an examination of parental influences and socioeconomic status. Even attempts to unpackage SES end up with what is essenatially an organismic variable (e.g., reference group perspective). The affordances offered by the school environment (e.g., career education programs, career counseling), peers (e.g., support for career-related activities), and the work environment (e.g, career role models, diversity of work experiences) have yet to be explored in a meaningful way in career maturity research.

Research on career development of ethnic minorities tends to favor an etic approach. At this phase in its evolution, it would benefit from the added use of an emic approach, alone or combined with etic approaches. Studies employing an emic approach can yield insights into the cultural meanings of career constructs and culturally congruent ways of measuring them. Emic approaches are discussed more fully in the second section of this chapter.

Considering the substantial increase in reviews and theoretical articles on culture and career development that have been published since 1970, all dealing with how research in this area can be improved, conceptually and methodologically, the paucity of empirical studies on ethnic minority career development is surprising, particularly on such a central construct as career maturity. More research simply needs to be done. The prospects for doing so are definitely improving. The representation of ethnic minorities among Ph.D. graduates is increasing. There is greater interest in ethnic minority research expressed by majority as well as minority behavioral scientists. The changing demographics of the workplace creates a demand for a cross-cultural scientific database on career development. Very likely, funding for research on career development of ethnic minorities will be made available to meet this demand. For that to happen sooner than later, career development scientists have to become more active in influencing funding priorities of public and private funding agencies. They have been slow to become involved in public policy yet only by doing so can they take advantage of the emerging opportunities for increased research on career development of ethnic minorities. In the past, the legislative and executive branches of government have proven responsive to recommendations from the National Institutes of Health and professional organizations for funding to support normative research on ethnic minority children. They might prove likewise responsive to requests for funding to support normative research on career development of ethnic minority adolescents.

Based on this review of research, there remains a need for a longitudinal study that would test the hypothesis that there are age or grade-related changes in the attitudinal and cognitive dimensions of career maturity in adolescents from a particular ethnic group. Previous research does not provide evidence for predicting stability or change in these dimensions in each year from ninth to twelfth grade, but those need to be assessed so the developmental curves can be plotted. Furthermore, the interrelationships among these dimensions at different grades have to be examined in order to depict the changing structure of career maturity during adolescence. Finally, the relationships between career maturity and other developing processes such as planning and decision-making have to be explored.

Based on prior studies, career maturity is not likely to vary as a function of gender but it might as a function of socioeconomic status. The research reviewed also indicated a need for studies that will attempt to "unpackage" SES as a variable. Smith's (1976) work on reference group perspectives is a start but other efforts are needed.

The relationship between self-concept and career maturity still needs to be resolved. The inconsistent findings are due partly to differences in operationalization of the construct, self-concept. Studies of European-American samples have yielded more consistent findings when the self has been operationalized as identity, particularly as occupational identity (e.g., Wallace-Broscious, Serafica, & Osipow, 1994).

Most importantly, the role of contextual factors in career maturity development has to be explored. For example, previous research indicating a relationship between career maturity and parental encouragement–discouragement of education suggests that there would be a positive relationship between parental support for career-related activities and career maturity. This is certainly worth exploring, but it behooves researchers to first ascertain some culture-specific variables such as the implicit norms regarding career maturity development held by parents from a particular ethnic group and how they conceptualize the parent's role in adolescent career development.

These are but a few of the research questions from a developmental perspective that merit priority in any program of research on normative career development of ethnic minority adolescents. Others from a contextual perspective are discussed in the next section.

FROM CULTURAL CRITIQUES
TO CULTURAL ACCOMMODATION

Donald Super's (1955, 1976, 1990) career development theory has been a major theory in mainstream vocational psychology since the 1960s. Despite this dominant position, it has been consistently criticized regarding it's applicability to cultural and ethnic minorities. For example, Leong and Brown (1995) identified four major and interrelated criticisms that have plagued current career choice theories and have led some scholars either to dismiss them as models for understanding the career behavior of diverse groups or to call for rearticulations that would render them more cross-culturally relevant (cf. Brooks, 1991; Smith, 1983): (a) they are based on either a restricted range of persons; (b) they are based on assumptions of limited scope; (c) when cross cultural perspectives are introduced, they confuse or inappropriately define terms such as *race, ethnicity, minority*; and (d) they tend to ignore or limitedly address the sociopolitical, socioeconomic, social psychological, and sociocultural realities of cross-cultural individuals. Many of these criticisms apply to Super's career development theory.

Leong and Brown (1995) also observed that most theories of career choice make five assumptions, the validity of which appear particularly suspect when considered from a cross cultural perspective: (a) career development is continuous, uninterrupted, and progressive; (b) decision makers possess the psychological, social, and economic means of affecting their choices; (c) there is dignity in all work; (d) there exists a free and open labor market; and (e) most career choices flow essentially from internal (viz., personality) factors. Most of these assumptions are also contained within Super's theory.

This section of the chapter moves the field beyond simply identifying cross-cultural criticisms to Super's career development theory to actually using a cultural accommodation approach in expanding the theory to make it more culturally relevant for racial and ethnic minorities. The proposed cultural accommodation approach involves three steps: (a) identifying the cultural gaps or cultural blindspots in an existing theory that restricts the cultural validity of the theory, (b) selecting current culturally specific concepts and models from cross-cultural and ethnic minority psychology to fill in the cultural gaps and accommodate the theory to racial and ethnic minorities, and (c) testing the culturally accommodated theory to determine if it has incremental validity above and beyond the culturally unaccommodated theory.

Before presenting this cultural accommodation approach in relation to Super's theory, it would be useful to review several related conceptual issues. First, the concepts of cultural validity and cultural specificity as they relate to career theories as articulated by Leong and Brown (1995) is quite important in understanding cultural accommodation. In reviewing the literature in cross-cultural psychology and cross-cultural counseling, particularly as they pertain to the career development and vocational behavior of culturally different individuals in this country, Leong and Brown (1995) observed cultural validity and cultural specificity are two dimensions that can serve as components of a unifying theoretical framework for cross-cultural career development. According to Leong and Brown (1995), cultural validity is concerned with the validity of theories and models across other cultures in terms of the construct, concurrent, and predictive validity of these models for culturally different individuals (e.g., Holland's concept of congruence has been found to be predictive of job satisfaction among White Americans; Does this prediction also hold for African Americans, Asian Americans, and so on?). Cultural specificity is concerned with concepts, constructs, and models that are specific to certain cultural groups in terms of its role in explaining and predicting behavior (e.g., colorism or level of melanin in skin of African Americans as a variable in vocational behavior).

The concepts of cultural validity and cultural specificity are also embedded in a larger model of cross-cultural counseling and psychotherapy developed by Leong (1996). Leong (1996) has recently proposed a multidimensional and integrative model of cross-cultural counseling and psychotherapy. In that model, using Kluckhohn and Murray's (1950) tripartite framework, Leong (1996) proposed that cross-cultural counselors and therapists need to attend to all three major dimensions of human personality and identity, namely the Universal, the Group, and the Individual dimensions. The Universal dimension is based on the knowledge base generated by mainstream psychology and the "universal laws" of human behavior that have been identified (e.g., the Universal "fight or flight" response in humans to physical threat). The Group dimension has been the domain of both cross-cultural psychology, as well as ethnic minority psychology and the study of gender differences. The third and final dimension concerns unique Individual differences and characteristics. The Individual dimension is more often covered by behavioral and existential theories where individual learning histories and personal phenomenology are proposed as critical elements in the understanding of human behavior. Leong's (1996) integrative model proposes that all three dimensions are equally important in understanding human experiences and should be attended to by the counselor in an integrative fashion.

Leong (1996) used a famous quote from Kluckhohn and Murray's (1950) influential article on "Personality Formation: The Determinants" published in their book *Personality in Nature, Society, and Culture,* as the beginning point for his integrative model. In the quote, "Every man is in certain respects: (a) like all other men, (b) like some other men, and (c) like no other man," Kluckhohn and Murray pointed out that some of the determinants of personality are common features found in the genetic makeup of all people. This addresses the biological aspect of the biopsychosocial model generally used in today's medical sciences. For certain features of personality, Kluckhohn and Murray (1950) state that most men are like some other men, showing the importance of social grouping, whether that grouping is based on culture, race, ethnicity, gender or social class. Lastly, they say that "Each individual's modes of perceiving, feeling, need, and behaving have characteristic patterns which are not precisely duplicated by those of any other individual" (p. 37). Each person's individuality, often the focus of social learning theories and models, is thus expressed in the last part of the quote. It accentuates the fact that all persons have distinct social learning experiences which can influence their values, beliefs, and cognitive schemas.

According to Leong (1996), the Universal component of personality is reflected in Kluckhohn and Murray's (1950) observation that "all persons are like all other persons" in some respects (p. 35). This statement accentuates the idea that all human beings share some characteristics, whether they are physical or psychological. There is much evidence to support this notion, as all humans develop physically in similar fashions, learn to talk in similar fashions, and learn to think in similar fashions (e.g. Piaget's conservation experiments). This notion has been thoroughly accepted by the medical community, as group and individual differences are often not seen as important in medical treatment. It has also been accepted by many in the psychological community, however. This is seen in models such as the common factors model (Frank, 1961) which points out that the effective aspects of counseling and psychotherapy are shared by many cultures. In their search for universal laws of human behavior, psychologists are looking for these universal elements of human personality. The concept of cultural validity as articulated by Leong and Brown (1995) is concerned with these universal principles. Each psychological construct or model needs to be examined with regard to its cultural validity. Until its cultural validity is evaluated, cross-cultural extentions and applications of a construct or model beyond the cultural population upon which it has been developed needs to proceed cautiously. As pointed out by Leong and Brown (1995), much of the work of cross-cultural psychology is concerned with the assessment of the cultural validity of psychological constructs and models which have been developed primarily within the Western cultural context.

On the other hand, simply focusing on the universal dimension, however, completely ignores the group and individual components that are absolutely necessary for a complete understanding of human behavior. While the universal dimension in counseling is very important to the integrative model, it is necessary but not sufficient (Leong, 1996). According to Leong (1996), the Group component of human personality is equally important as the Universal component. These groupings may be based on culture, race, ethnicity, social class, occupation, or even gender. All persons in one group will share some type of bond with other members of the group, and at the same time, this bond will distinguish the group members from all other groups. It is further believed that belonging to a group will be a major determinant of a person's personality.

Membership in a group can affect an individual in many ways, and these ways can become the focus of counseling and psychotherapy. For example, persons who have suffered from oppression because of their religion or race will need to address these feelings. They will no longer be speaking from a universal perspective, as their experiences have not been shared by all persons. A therapist who tries to relate to these types of clients on a universal level will be doing a disservice, and this will most likely lead to premature termination of the therapeutic relationship.

Another aspect of the group dimension is the existence of different types of societies, such as Individualistic versus Collectivistic societies. Individualistic societies are seen as those where the needs of the individual are put before the needs of the group. Western societies are traditionally seen as being Individualistic. Collectivistic societies generally put the needs of the group before the needs of the individual. Eastern societies are seen as Collectivistic in nature (Hofstede, 1980). Depending on which type of society one is raised in affects many aspects of a person's life, including the manner in which one communicates, what life choices one makes, and how one copes with stress. All of these are extremely pertinent in counseling situations, and if not attended to may lead to premature termination.

The group component of personality is especially important when discussing cross-cultural counseling and psychotherapy. There have been many models of racial identity that focus on the group component. Other important constructs related to the group dimension include racial/ethnic identity, acculturation, and value preferences. A competent counselor must be able to look at all these variables from the standpoint of his or her client, especially if the client is a member of a different group. Not doing so would make it impossible to accurately conceptualize the psychological state the client is in, which in turn would make effective therapy impossible.

There has been much research looking at the experiences of different groups. There are many dynamics that must be taken into consideration in counseling situations involving a client and therapist of different cultural backgrounds. Each must have some awareness of the experiences of the other in order to be able to form a relationship. This is especially true for the therapist. A therapist operating only at the universal level may alienate his/her client. Although the two may not have shared experiences in their backgrounds, the counselor must be able to address issues that involve groups other than his or her own. Leong (1996) pointed out that using only the Universal dimension to understand people or clients is severely limited due to the importance of cultural differences. Indeed, Leong and Brown (1995) proposed that when problems occur in establishing the cultural validity of a construct or model, cultural specificity, expressed in the use of culture-specific (often referred to as "indigenous" in cross-cultural psychology circles) variables can add greatly to our understanding of human behavior. It is important to note here that human behavior always occurs within a specific cultural context. In other words, the integrative combination of the universal and group dimensions of human personality provides a richer model with which to understand human beings. This in turn requires us to examine both cultural validity and cultural specificity issues in advancement of career developmental theories.

Finally, there is the Individual component of human personality within Leong's (1996) integrative model. Although it is true that we all share some commonalities, as seen by looking at the universal component, no two persons are indentical in every way. The medical community can look at humans from a genetic perspective in order to show how all humans are completely alike. Psychologists, on the other hand, can look at persons from an environmental perspective to show how no two humans are completely alike. Kluckhohn and Murray (1950) said "Each individual's modes of perceiving, feeling, need, and behaving have characteristic patterns which are not precisely duplicated by those of any other individual" (p. 37). Kluckhohn and Murray have referred to an idea akin to the concept of the "psychological environment" (Lewin, 1951). Lewin was trying to show that although two people may share the same physical space, they may not share the same psychological space. The individual component of human personality is equally as important as the universal or group components, but it will not be dealt with directly here inasmuch as we are concerned primarily with the issues of cultural validity and cultural specificity.

The integrative model of cross-cultural counseling proposed by Leong (1996) has as one of its fundamental bases the notion that the individual client must exist at three levels, the universal, the group, and the individualistic. The problem with much of the past research done in the field of cross-cultural counseling is that the focus has only been on one of the three levels, ignoring the influence of the other levels in the counseling situation. Leong's (1996) integrative model includes all three dimensions of personality as well as their dynamic interactions, and, thus, will have better incremental validity than any model that only focuses on one of the three levels. The integrative model for cross-cultural counseling and psychotherapy was conceived to provide a more complex and dynamic conception of human beings.

Using Leong's (1996) integrative model of cross-cultural counseling as a theoretical foundation and incorporating the concepts of cultural validity and cultural specificity (Leong & Brown, 1995), we move from a discussion of the cultural accommodation approach to Super's (1990) career development model. According to Super (1990), there are three concepts that are particularly important for understanding a person's career development, namely, self-concept, vocational developmental tasks, and career maturity. A person tends to select a career as "an implementation of his or her self-concept." For example, if a person sees herself as a great debater who can win most arguements and also enjoys competitive and adversarial activities, she is likely to gravitate toward a career as a criminal lawyer. On the other hand, if another person sees himself as a compassionate, caring, and religious person, he may choose to be a priest or minister. Super proposed that the selection and implementation of a career that follows the individual's self-concept is a developmental process that occurs throughout the lifespan in predictable stages. These four stages include growth, exploration, estabishment, and disengagement. Each stage has a specific set of vocational developmental tasks that the individual needs to master. For example, during the exploration stage, the individual needs to crystallize his or her career interests and then specify a particular career choice that then needs to be implemented. As with any developmental theory, there is a maturational dimension to Super's model that accounts for individual variation across the stages. Just as children acquire the ability to walk or talk at different ages, they are exhibiting variations in the maturational dimension. Within Super's model, this maturational dimension is captured by the concept of vocational or career maturity. A person who successfully masters the developmental tasks within his or her developmental stage is considered to exhibit career maturity whereas the individual who does not is classified as suffering from career immaturity. Career maturity is an important concept because it implies a readiness to transition to the next stage and tackle the developmental tasks and challenges of that stage. Obviously, the nature and type of career counseling provided to the career-mature individual and the career immature individual will necessarily be different. As such, Super's model emphasizes the accurate assessment of an individual's career developmental stage and his or her level of career maturity. Cross-cultural issues related to career maturity have been discussed earlier.

The major cultural gap or cultural blindspot in Super's model, as outlined earlier, is that his model was developed and based on White middle-class persons. The model is culturally valid for the majority of Americans who are White and middle class. However, the model's cultural validity is suspect when applied to cultural and racial or ethnic minorities in the United States. This does not mean that we should automatically conclude that Super's theory is not culturally valid for non-White European Americans simply because the model was developed on White European Americans. Instead, what is needed is an examination of Super's model to determine its cultural validity for other cultural groups. In that process, where problems are found in the level of cultural validity for a particular group, culture-specific constructs and models from that group may enrich Super's theory. More importantly, we need to examine Super's model in light of the psychology of culturally different groups and culturally accommodate his model to these cultural differences.

When applying a cross-cultural perspective in analyzing psychological theories, including Super's model of career development, such theories can be classified as belonging to one of three approaches. The first is the universalist approach where culture is considered to be an unimportant and nuisance variable that needs little or no attention. The cultural variable is essentially ignored. This is the dominant approach in mainstream psychology and represents the Universal dimension within Leong's (1996) integrative model. As Leong pointed out (1996), this approach is necessary but not sufficient in understanding the experiences and behaviors of individuals given the importance of the Group dimension (e.g., gender, race/ethnicity, socioeconomic status, and so on). The second is the culture assimilation approach where cultural differences are recognized but minimized with the assumption that racial and ethnic minority groups should assimilate to mainstream American culture (i.e., Western European culture). With a strong belief in the "melting pot" concept, and to the extent that these racial and ethnic minority persons assimilate, then these psychological theories and models will work equally well with these groups. The third is the culture accommodation approach being proposed in this chapter where the culturally unique experiences of racial and ethnic minority groups are considered major factors in understanding their behavior. These culture-specific factors are identitied and added to the existing theories and models to enrich them and increase their relevance and utility to racial and ethnic minority groups.

To return to Leong's (1996) integrative model where he argued that a model that integrates the universal, group, and individual dimensions of human personality will be a better model than one in which only one dimension is salient, we are proposing that the culture accommodation approach will be superior to either the universalist or the culture assimilation approach to psychological theories. In ignoring the cultural dimension, the universalist approach will be culturally valid for the original group on which the theory was developed (i.e., White European Americans) but of limited cultural validity for racial and ethnic minority groups. In minimizing the role of cultural factors, those who proposed models based on a culture assimilation approach will also have their theories be of limited values cross-culturally and when applied to racial and ethnic minority groups. Both the universalist and culture assimilation aproaches suffer from many cultural gaps and blindspots.

Identifying Cultural Gaps and Cultural Blindspots

In order to identify the cultural gaps and blindspots in Super's (1990) model, we provide a brief overview of his developmental model. For our current purposes we limit ourselves to only the second and third stages within Super's (1990) career development model. According to Super (1990), the Exploration stage of career development which ranges from ages 15 to 25 years, requires that individuals acquire occupational information, choose career alternatives, decide on careers, and start to work. The stage includes three substages: crystallizing, specifying, and implementing. During the crystallizing substage, people begin to clarify what it is they want to do. They learn about entry-level jobs that may be appropriate for them and learn skills that are required for jobs that interest them. Work experience and work knowledge help the person narrow down his choices. During the specifying substage, which occurs for most people during their college years (the early 20s), people seek employment directly after high-school graduation or select additional education for their chosen career. As these young people must choose different full-time jobs or graduate training, they are required to specify their preferences, so they may find an employer or an appropriate graduate training program. In the Implementing substage, people make plans to build the career objectives they have chosen. They may be starting to network by meeting people who can help them get a job. Many are also talking to counselors in a university career planning and placement office as part of this phase. Writing resumes, arranging job interviews, and deciding between potential employers are all part of this substage that is the final one before people beginning working.

The Exploration stage is followed by the Establishment stage that generally ranges from ages 25 to 45 for most people. In general, Establishment refers to getting established in one's work by starting in a job is likely to mean the start of working life. It means settling down to a particular career or type of work and using one's talents and skills to achieve whatever career or work goals they have set for themselves (e.g., earning a good enough salary to buy a home and have an annual vacation with the family or advancing in one's career until one becomes president of the company). The substages of stabilizing, consolidating, and advancing refer to career behaviors that take place once working life has started.

During the Stabilizing substage (late 20s to early 30s), most people begin a job and stay at it for a least a few years. Stabilization is concerned with settling down into a job and being able to meet those job requirements that will ensure job continuity. Entry into a job and organization usually involves a certain amount of anxiety and apprehension. As people learn the skills required for the job and the rules (both formal and informal) that govern their work place, they become more comfortable and begin to consolidate their position during the consolidating substage. Consolidation is considered to be taking place when the person starts to become more comfortable with his job and wishes to be known by others as a competent and dependable worker. Having consolidated their position, workers generally feel more secure and begin working on their advancement to higher positions in their organizations.

Occurring anytime in the Establishment stage, but usually after stabilizing and consolidating have taken place, the advancement substage usually involves moving ahead into a position of more responsibility with higher pay. In some organizations, particularly in large corporations, there is concern with advancing to positions of higher authority. This involves planning how to get ahead and how to who improve the chances of been promoted. This next step requires that their superiors know that they can do well and are capable of handling the greater responsibility and challenges that will come with the higher positions.

According to Leong's (1996) integrative model, it is important to examine the universal, group, and individual dimensions of human personality in understanding any psychological theory. In other words, it would be useful to evaluate the cultural validity and cultural specificity in Super's (1990) developmental theory. More specifically, what aspects of Super's (1990) theory can be considered culture-general and extend to other cultural groups beyond White European Americans. Conversely, what elements in Super's (1990) theory is culture-specific to White European Americans and do not generalize readily to other racial and ethnic minority groups. Additionally, what experiences of racial and ethnic minority groups, when represented as culture-specific constucts, are not captured within Super's theory. Furthermore, these issues of cultural validity and cultural specificty are best considered within a person–environment model where the cultural context of the environment is also examined. Using this person–environment model, which has been spearheaded by Vondracek and his colleagues as the development–contextual model of career development, we can now illustrate the process of cultural accommodation for Super's (1990) theory. It is important to note here that we are only able to illustrate the cultural accommodation approach in this chapter. A complete model would require an entire textbook.

In both the Exploration and Establishment stages of Super's (1990) theory, the development and implementation of the self-concept (Who am I? What do I enjoy doing? What am I good at?) is a central developmental task. As mentioned earlier, the major problem with this formulation is that it is the self-concept of White European-American youth who have served as the template for delineating this developmental sequence. What is not included in Super's formulation is the important role of cultural and ethnic identity that is so central to racial and ethnic minority youth. Cultural and ethnic identity is a major construct in our understanding of the experiences of racial and ethnic minorities and it should play a major role in career developmental theory. A second major gap in Super's theory concerns contextual factors. The importance of the contextual factor to career developmental theory is best represented by the developmental–contextual perspective of Vondracek, Lerner, and Schulenberg (1986). For our purposes, it is the *neglect* of the cultural context within Super's career developmental theory that is central. Furthemore, cultural identity and cultural context have a complex and reciprocal relationship to each other, and it is essential that Super's (1990) theory accommodate for these two major contructs in order to be a viable and useful theory for the culturally diverse population within the United States.

Cultural Accommodation

Beginning with the person side of the P × E equation, Leong and his colleagues (Hartung, Vandiver, Leong, Pope, Niles, & Farrow, 1998) have proposed that a sixth dimension be incorporated into Super's C-DAC model. The C-DAC model emerged from the life-span, life-space theory of careers (Super et al., 1996). According to Hartung et al. (1998), "Although the C-DAC model currently contains elements (e.g., values and role salience assessment) that implicitly tap cultural variables, it could be strengthened and made more relevant by explicitly specifying this culturally sensitive dimension. Adding this sixth dimension, then, would (a) make cultural identity a core component of the C-DAC model, (b) foster cultural relevance in implementing each step of the model, and (c) specify culturally sensitive assessments and counseling interventions as part of the core C-DAC assessment battery and counseling process" (p. 280).

Cultural identity as a core C-DAC component involves taking account of cultural differences that may overlay each of the other components and influence individual career development and vocational behavior. Including cultural identity as a core C-DAC element also prompts career counselors to be equally aware of their own attitudes about clients who are culturally different from themselves. Just as the C-DAC model emphasizes understanding clients' life narratives, it seems equally important for counselors to recognize their own life narratives when working with culturally different clients. This extends to counselors perhaps reviewing their own career development in terms of the C-DAC model and taking a C-DAC battery of instruments. They might also reflect on their own realities of growing up in America relative to that of their culturally different clients. Creating such a parallel process might enhance a counselor's ability to understand and support the career process of a culturally different client. Failing to address personal cultural attitudes may sustain high levels of counselor ethnocentrism or cultural encapsulation (Wrenn, 1962) in using the C-DAC model (Hartung et al., 1998).

A major perspective on cultural identity, especially for Asian Americans, Hispanic Americans, and American Indians involves the concept of Acculturation. In applying Leong's (1996) integrative model within the C-DAC model, counselors need to recognize how acculturation links the group and individual dimensions as it moderates cultural and individual differences. At the group or cultural level, for example, Asian Americans (e.g., Chinese-, Japanese-, and Korean-Americans) may share certain cultural values, norms, and beliefs. Concurrently, as individuals, Asian Americans differ from each other. Acculturation helps the counselor to understand how each Asian American (or other minority group member) differs from another. Step one of the C-DAC model, then, should incorporate assessing the client's acculturation level. This, in turn, would guide the counselor in determining whether and how to modify subsequent steps (e.g., in terms of selecting, sequencing, and interpreting assessment instruments). Major issues related to ethnic minority vocational behavior and career development relative to their acculturation levels include occupational segregation, stereotyping, discrimination, prestige, mobility, attitudes, aspirations and expectations, stress, satisfaction, choice, and interest (Leong, 1985; Leong & Serafica, 1995).

A second important dimension of cultural identity concerns cultural values. Hartung et al. (1998) pointed out that value orientations serve as a major dimension for understanding group or cultural differences affecting the C-DAC process. Of the various values that have been examined, Individualism–Collectivism has received the most research attention during the last 2 decades. Individualism–collectivism represents a value orientation that plays a potentially significant role in career development and vocational behavior (Hartung, Speight, & Lewis, 1996; Leong, 1993). Individuals from groups with more collectivistic value orientations (e.g., Asian Americans, Hispanic Americans, and Native Americans) may conceive of the *self* as interdependent, whereas persons from individualistic cultures view the self as independent (Markus & Kitayama, 1991). Such a self-conception may make career decision making a much more interpersonal process for collectivists than for individualists. For the latter, career decision making may be an individual matter based mainly on personal interests, values, and aspirations (Hartung et al., 1996). Such value differences can easily lead counselors to culturally inappropriate counseling process and work towards culturally inappropriate goals when using the C-DAC model with collectivists. Therefore, also assessing the client's cultural value orientation in step one would further guide culturally sensitive use of the C-DAC model. Specific suggestions on how to apply the cultural identity dimension to the C-DAC model can be found in Hartung et al. (1998).

The major thesis of this section is that Super's theory lacks cultural validity for racial and ethnic minorities because it does not account for significant and highly salient experiences of these minority groups. In order to be relevant and useful for racial and ethnic minorities, Super's (1990) model needs to culturally accommodate for these culture-specific variables. On the person side of the person–environment equation, cultural identity represents one of many such culture-specific variables in this accommodation process. By accommodating person-variables such as acculturation level, individualism–collectivism, self-construal, ethnic identity, cultural mistrust, and a whole host of other culture-specific variables, Super's (1990) theory can become more useful for racial and cultural minorities. However, the value of the cultural accommodation approach will have be examined by conducting empirical research. For example, to what extent, does cultural identity as represented by either acculturation level or ethnic identity, influences the process and outcomes outlined by Super (1990) during the Exploration or Establishment stages.

To the extent that acculturation level is an important component of cultural identity, some possible relationships between career variables and acculturation for Asian Americans has already been delineated by Leong and Chou (1994). In providing an overview of the research and theoretical literature in Asian American ethnic identity and acculturation, Leong and Chou (1994) proposed an integration of those two areas of inquiry: ethnic identity and acculturation. They argued that although labeled as an acculturation model, Berry's (1980) model actually deals more directly with cultural identity. According to Berry's model, individuals who hold positive views of both their own culture and the host culture are Integrationists who attempt to have the best that both cultures have to offer. Assimilationists, the second possible acculturation outcome, hold a positive view of the host culture, but a negative view of their own culture (Berry, 1980). Individuals who view their host culture negatively and their own culture positively are Separationists (Berry, 1980). Finally, Berry's model includes a group which is not recognized by the other models. Berry's (1980) Marginal person holds a negative view of both host and own culture. Leong and Chou (1994) proposed that we needed to make explicit the link between Berry's acculturation model to ethnic identity models. To undetake this linkage, they recommended adding the term *identity* to the end of each acculturation outcome, that is, Integrationist Identity (II), Assimilationist Identity (AI), Separationist Identity (SI), and Marginalist Identity (MI).

Using this integrated model of cultural identity, Leong and Chou (1994) further proposed significant relationships between Asian Americans' cultural identity (e.g., Assimilationist identity) and various career variables such as occupational segregation, stereotyping, discrimination, prestige, mobility, attitudes, aspirations and expectations, stress, satisfaction, choice, and interest (see Leong, 1985; Leong & Serafica, 1993). For example, they proposed that Asian Americans with Separationist Identity (i.e., less acculturated or Traditionalist persons) are more susceptible to occupational segregation, while those with Assimilationist Identity (i.e., more acculturated persons) are less susceptible to occupational segregation. This pattern could be the result of the cultural background (Fong, 1973) of less acculturated Asians or stereotyped tracking of Asians by the majority-dominated working world. They also proposed that occupational stereotyping would follow the pattern of occupational segregation for Asian Americans. Leong and Serafica (1993) explained that stereotypes of Asian Americans suggest they are more qualified in the physical, biological, and medical sciences and less qualified or likely to be successful in verbal, persuasive, or social careers. They proposed that Asians who are more strongly ethnically identified (Separationist) may believe occupational stereotypes to be more valid. On the other hand, strongly ethnically identified Asians may be subject to occupational stereotyping more. Assimilationists and Integrationists, on the other hand, will be more resistant to such stereotypes and are therefore more likely to enter non-traditional career fields (e.g., law, sales, and social work).

Leong and Chou (1994) also proposed that Assimilationist (i.e, least ethnically identified) Asian Americans will perceive and experience the least amount of occupational discrimination (e.g., existence of glass ceilings) because they will tend to attribute lack of success of Asians to individual lack of ability and not to discrimination. In addition, they proposed that more acculturated Asian Americans (Assimilationists and Integrationists) will view their job in much the same way European Americans do (e.g., as more of a virtue in and of itself) and, thus, choose occupations based on what they enjoy (Leong & Tata, 1990), and less acculturated Asian Americans (Separationists) will view careers more as a means to an end (e.g., financial security). However, for Assimilationists there may be more of a tendency to choose traditionally closed occupations to *prove* to European Americans they are not stereotypically Asian.

Finally, they proposed that Asian Americans who are less acculturated (Separationist Identity) may exhibit less self-efficacy in career choice, interest, or expectations because of the strong reverence and respect of parental authority in Asian cultures. These individuals may choose their careers based more on family desires or needs than on their own desires or interest. Therefore, these individuals may experience more stress (Padilla, Wagatsuma, & Lindholm, 1985) and less job satisfaction. Recent research is beginning to find support for Leong and Chou's (1994) proposition that acculturation or cultural identity is a significant factor in understanding the career behavior of Asian Americans. For example, Tang, Fouad, and Smith (1999) applied a path model to 187 Asian-American college students career choice and found that acculturation plays a significant role in influencing career self-efficay and career choice.

With regard to the Environment side of the P × E equation, there are also culture-specific elements in the social experiences of racial and ethnic minorities that are not accounted for in Super's (1990) model. We need to accommodate for these variables in order to extend and increase the utility and value of Super's (1990) model. Within Super's (1990) theory, the importance of role models and mentors during both the crystallization and specification stage is quite important. Observing a role model engage in a rewarding career can motivate individuals to follow that role model in pursuing the same career. At the same time, having a mentor in high school or colleage can help an individual with their career decision making process. Indeed, it can be argued that role models and mentors represent universal dimensions within Super's theory. Role models and mentors should be important to the career decision-making and implementation for persons from any culture. The relative importance of role models and mentors may vary from culture to culture, but these "career influencers" would play a central role across many, if not all, cultures. However cultural gaps exist within Super's theory because of culture specific factors that differentiate White European Americans from other racial ethnic minority groups experience of role models and mentoring. Due to the dominance of White European Americans within the occupational structure in the

United States, particularly in the higher authority positions, racial and ethnic minorities do not have the same experience of role models and mentors in schools and in the workplace. Research on the availability of same-race role models or mentors have demonstrated that racial and ethnic minorities simply do not have equal access to role models and mentors as White European Americans. Factors such as institutional racism, prejudice, and ethnocentricism contribute to this differential experience for ethnic minorities in the United States. Ethnocentricism, which is universal to all cultures, ensures that we are most comfortable and socialize (mentor or serve as role models) with those in our environment who are most similar to us culturally. At the same time, prejudice and institutional racism restricts the number of non-European Americans from entering significant sections of the workforce (e.g., number of CEOs in companies or number of full professors in universities).

Due to these and other factors, racial and ethnic minority youth simply have a different experience during the crystallization and specification substage than their White European counterparts. The fact that disproportionate numbers of racial and ethnic minority youth enter low-end and low-paying jobs, compared to White European youths, illustrates this point. It would be safe to say that these racial and ethnic minority youth chose these occupations because their "crystallization and specification" experiences were severely constrained by many factors, of which the lack of race-appropriate role models and mentors is only one. White European Americans, in crystallizing and specifying their career choices, simply do not face these problems of racism, prejudice, and limited numbers of role models and mentors. In order to be useful and culturally valid and relevant to racial and ethnic minorities, Super's theory needs to culturally accommodate for these factors. Racism, prejudice, and lack of role models, actively and qualitatively influences the career development experiences for racial and ethnic minorities. Chronic experiences with ethnocentricism, racism, and prejudice will in turn produce cultural mistrust among racial and ethnic minority groups. For many racial and ethnic minority individuals, cultural mistrust will become a central component in their cultural identity. Recent research on cultural mistrust had shown that variable to play a significant role in attitudes towards counseling and help-seeking behavior. Failure to accommodate for the effects of these culture specific factors across the various stages will result in a lack of cultural validity in Super's (1990) theory.

In conclusion, we proposed that it is time to move from cultural critiques of Super's theory to a cultural accommodation approach whereby we evaluate the cultural validity of Super's theory to identify cultural gaps and blindspots. These gaps can often be reduced by incorporating culture-specific variables into Super's model to make it more relevant and useful for racial and cultural minorities. By using Leong's (1996) integrative model of examining universal, group, and individual dimensions of human personality, we can increase the cultural validity of Super's theory by making it more culturally relevant and culturally appropriate for other racial and cultural groups. Furthermore, the cultural accommodation approach needs to recognize the importance of using the person-environment interaction model rather than just focusing on the person and ignoring the cultural context variables that are such a central factor in the lives of racial and ethnic minorities.

The value of the proposed cultural accommodation approach will be determined by future research. Two major lines of research on the value of cultural accommodation approach consist of (a) showing that the culture specific variables (e.g., cultural identity) can account for signficant amounts of variance in the vocational behavior (see Tang et al., 1999, findings in support of Leong and Chou's, 1994, formulations) of racial and ethnic minority individuals, and (b) demonstrating incremental validity where culture specific variables account for additional variance above and beyond those accounted for by the variables in the original model (e.g., Super's model).

REFERENCES

Arbona, C. (1990). Career counseling research with Hispanics: A review of the literature. *The Counseling Psychologist, 18,* 300–323.

Atkinson, D. R., Morten, G., & Sue, D. W. (1989). *Counseling American minorities: A cross cultural perspective* (3rd ed.). Dubuque, IA: William C. Brown.

Bergland, B. W., & Lundquist, G. W. (1975). The vocational exploration group and minority youth: An experimental outcome study. *Journal of Vocational Behavior, 7,* 289–296.

Bergman, B. R. (1996). *In defense of affirmation action.* New York: Basic Books.

Berry, J. W. (1980). Acculturation as varieties of adaptation. In A. Padilla (Ed.), *Acculturation: Theory, models and some new findings.* Boulder, CO: Westview Press.

Bingham, R. P., & Ward, C. M. (1996). Practical applications of career counseling with ethnic minority women. In M. L. Savickas & W. B.Walsh (Eds.), *Handbook of career counseling theory and practice* (pp. 291–314). Palo Alto, CA: Davies-Black.

Bowman, S. L. (1995). Career intervention strategies and assessment issues for African Americans. In F. T. L. Leong (Ed.), *Career development and vocational behavior of racial and ethnic minorities.* Mahwah, NJ: Lawrence Erlbaum Associates.

Brooks, L. (1991). Recent developments in theory building. In D. Brown, L. Brooks, & Associates, *Career choice and development* (2nd ed.). San Francisco: Jossey-Bass.

Brown, C. (1997). Sex differences in the career development of urban African American adolescents. *Journal of Career Development, 23,* 295–304.

Brown, D., & Brooks, L. (1991). *Career counseling techniques.* Boston: Allyn & Bacon.

Crites, J. O. (1969). *Vocational psychology: The study of vocational behavior and development.* New York: McGraw-Hill.

Crites, J. O. (1973). *Career Maturity Inventory*. Monterey, CA: CTB/McGraw Hill.

Crites, J. O. (1978). *Theory and research handbook for the Career Maturity Inventory*. Monterey, CA: CTB/McGraw Hill.

Crites, J. O. (1995). *Abbreviated Career Maturity Inventory*. Boulder, CO: Crites Career Consultants.

Cross, W. E., Jr. (1995). The psychology of nigrescence: Revising the Cross model. In J. G. Ponterotto, J. M. Casas, L. A. Suzuki, & C. M. Alexander (Eds.), *Handbook of multicultural counseling*. Thousand Oaks, CA: Sage.

Daane, C. (1971). A trip with vocational exploration in groups. *Hawaii Personnel and Guidance Association, 1*, 13–16.

Dillard, J. M. (1976). Socioeconomic background and the career maturity of Black youths. *Vocational Guidance Quarterly, 25*, 65–70.

Dillard J. M., & Campbell, N. J. (1981). Influences of Puerto Rican, Black, and Anglo parents career behavior on their adolescent children's development. *Vocational Guidance Quarterly, 30*, 139–148.

Dillard, J. M., & Perrin, D. W. (1980). Puerto Rican, Black, and Anglo adolescents career aspirations, expectations, and maturity. *Vocational Guidance Quarterly, 29*, 313–321.

Fitts, W. H. (1965). *Tennessee self concept scale manual*. Nashville, TN: Counselor Recordings and Tests.

Fitzgerald, L. F., & Betz, N. E. (1994). Career development in cultural context: The role of gender, race, class, and sexual orientation. In M. L. Savickas & R. W. Lent (Eds.), *Convergence in career development theories: Implications for science and practice* (pp. 103–117). Palo Alto, CA: Consulting Psychologists Press.

Fong, S. L. M. (1973). Assimilation and changing social roles of Chinese Americans. *Journal of Social Issues, 29*(2), 115–127.

Fouad, N. A. (1993). Cross-cultural vocational assessment. *Career Development Quarterly, 42*, 4–13.

Fouad, N. A., & Keeley, T. J. (1992). The relationship between attitudinal and behavioral aspects of career maturity. *Career Development Quarterly, 40*, 257–271.

Frank, J. D. (1961). *Persuasion and healing*. Baltimore, MD: Johns Hopkins University Press.

Gable, R. K., Thompson, D. L., & Iwanicki, E. F. (1983). *Vocational Guidance Quarterly, 32*, 230–239.

Gallegos, G. E., & Kahn, M. W. (1986). Factors predicting success of underprivileged youths in Job Corps training. *Vocational Guidance Quarterly, 34*, 171–177.

Harmon, L. W., & Borgen, F. H. (1995). Advances in career assessment and the 1994 Strong Interest Inventory. *Journal of Career Assessment, 3*, 347–372.

Harmon, L. W., Hansen, J. C. Borgen, F. H., & Hammer, A. L. (1994). *Strong Interest Inventory applications and technical guide*. Stanford, CA: Stanford University Press.

Hartung, P. J., Speight, J. D., & Lewis, D. M. (1996). Individualism-collectivism and the vocational behavior of majority culture college students. *Career Development Quarterly, 45*, 87–96.

Hawks, B. K., & Muha, D. (1991). Facilitating the career development of minorities: Doing it differently this time. *Career Development Quarterly, 39*, 251–260.

Helms, J. E. (1984). Towards a theoretical explanation of the effects of race on counseling: A Black and White model. *The Counseling Psychologist, 12*, 153–165.

Helms, J. E. (1995). An update of Helms's White and people of color racial identity models. In J. G. Ponterotto, J. M. Casas, L. A. Suzuki, & C. M. Alexander (Eds.), *Handbook of multicultural counseling*. Thousand Oaks, CA: Sage.

Highlen, P. S., & Sudarsky-Gleiser, C. (1994). Co-essence model of vocational Assessment for Racial/Ethnic Minorities (CEMVA-REM): An Existential Approach. *Journal of Career Assessment, 2*, 304–329.

Hofstede, G. (1980). *Culture's consequences: International differences in work-related values.* Beverly Hills, CA: Sage

Hollingshead, A. B. (1957). *Two Factor Index of Social Position.* Unpublished manuscript. Yale University, New Haven, CT.

Hoyt, K. B. (1989). The career status of women and minority persons: A 20-year retrospective. *Career Development Quarterly, 37,* 202–212.

Hudson Institute (1987). *Workforce 2000: Work and workers for the twenty-first century.* Indianapolis, IN: Author.

Hughes, L. W., Gordon, W. M., & Hillman, L. W. (1980). *Desegregating America's schools.* New York: Longman.

Jackson, G. C., & Healy, C. C. (1996). Career development profiles and interventions for underrepresented college students. *Career Development Quarterly, 44,* 258–269.

Koegel, H., Donin, I., Ponterotto, J. G., & Spitz, S. (1995). Multicultural career development: A methodological critique of 8 years of research in three leading career journals. *Journal of Employment Counseling, 32,* 50–63.

Kluckhohn, C., & Murray, H. A. (1950). Personality formation: The determinants. In C. Kluckhohn & H. A. Murray (Eds.), *Personality in nature, society, and culture* (pp. 35–48). New York: Knopf.

Krumboltz, J. D., Mitchell, A., & Jones, G. B. (1976). A social learning theory of career selection. *The Counseling Psychologist, 6,* 71–81.

Lawrence, W., & Brown, D. (1976). An investigation of intelligence, self-concept, socioeconomic status, race, and sex as predictors of career maturity. *Journal of Vocational Behavior, 9,* 43–52.

Lee, C. C. (1984). Predicting the career choice attitudes of rural Black, White, and Native American high school students. *Vocational Guidance Quarterly, 33,* 177–185.

Lewin, K. (1951). *Field theory in social science: Selected theoretical papers.* New York: Harper & Row.

Leong, F. T. L. (1985). Career development of Asian-Americans. *Journal of College Student Personnel, 26,* 539–546.

Leong, F. T. L. (1991). Guest Editor's Introduction: Special issue on career development of racial and ethnic minorities. *Career Development Quarterly, 42,* 196–198.

Leong, F. T. L. (1991). Career development attributes and occupational values of Asian American and White American college students. *Career Development Quarterly, 39,* 221–230.

Leong, F. T. L. (1993). The career counseling process with racial/ethnic minorities: The case of Asian Americans. *Career Development Quarterly, 42,* 26–40.

Leong, F. T. L. (1995). *Career development and vocational behavior of racial and ethnic minorities.* Hillsdale, NJ: Lawrence Erlbaum Associates.

Leong, F. T. L. (1996). Toward an integrative model for cross-cultural counseling and psychotherapy. *Applied and Preventive Psychology, 5,* 189–209.

Leong, F. T. L. (Ed.). (1995). *Career development and vocational behavior of racial and ethnic minorities.* Hillsdale, NJ: Lawrence Erlbaum Associates.

Leong, F. T. L., & Brown, M. (1995). Theoretical issues in cross-cultural career development: Cultural validity and cultural specificity. In W. B. Walsh & S. H. Osipow (Eds.), *Handbook of vocational psychology* (pp. 143–180, 2nd ed.). Hillsdale, NJ: Lawrence Erlbaum Associates.

Leong, F. T. L., & Chou, E. L. (1994). The role of ethnic identity and acculturation in the vocational behavior of Asian Americans: An integrative review. *Journal of Vocational Behavior, 44,* 155–172.

Leong, F. T. L., & Gim, R. H. C. (1995). Career assessment and intervention with Asian Americans. In F. T. L. Leong (Ed.), *Career development and vocational behavior of racial and ethnic minorities* (pp. 193–226). Hillsdale, NJ: Lawrence Erlbaum Associates.

Leong, F. T. L., & Hartung, P. (1997). Career assessment with culturally-different clients: Proposing an integrative-sequential conceptual framework for cross-cultural career counseling research and practice. *Journal of Career Assessment, 5*, 183–202.

Leong, F. T. L., & Leung, S. A. (1994). Career assessment with Asian Americans. *Journal of Career Assessment, 2*, 240–257.

Leong, F. T. L., & Serafica, F. (1995). Career development of Asian Americans: A research area in need of a good theory. In F. T. L. Leong (Ed.), *Career development and vocational behavior of racial and ethnic minorities* (pp. 67–102). Hillsdale, NJ: Lawrence Erlbaum Associates.

Leong, F. T. L., & Tata, S. P. (1990). Sex and acculturation differences in occupational values among Chinese American children. *Journal of Counseling Psychology, 37*, 208–212.

London, M., & Geller, M. M. (1991). Demographic trends and vocational behavior: A twenty-year retrospective and agenda for the 1990s. *Journal of Vocational Behavior, 38*, 125–284.

Longhead, T. A., Liu, S., & Middleton, E. B. (1995). Career development for at-risk youth: A program evaluation. *Career Development Quarterly, 43*, 274–284.

Love, K. G., & O'Hara, K. (1987). Predicting job performance of youth trainees under a Job Training Partnership Act Program (JTPA): Criterion validation of a behavior-based measure of work maturity. *Personnel Psychology, 40*, 323–340.

Lundberg, D. J., Osborne, W. L., & Miner, C. U. (1997). Career maturity and personality preferences of Mexican-American and Anglo-American adolescents. *Journal of Career Development, 23*, 203–213.

Luzzo, D. A. (1992). Ethnic group and social class differences in college students' career development. *Career Development Quarterly, 41*, 161–173.

Manuelle, C. A. (1983). The development of a measure to assess vocational maturity in adults with delayed career development. *Journal of Vocational Behavior, 23*, 45–63.

Markus, H. R., & Kitayama, S. (1991). Culture and the self: Implications for cognition, emotion, and motivation. *Psychological Review, 98*, 224–253,

Martin, W. E. (1991). Career development and American Indians living on reservations: Cross-cultural factors to consider. *Career Development Quarterly, 39*, 273–283.

Martin, W. E., Jr., Dodd, J., Smith, H., White, H., & Davis, H. (1984). *A preliminary look at the need for a temporal component in vocational training.* Paper presented at the annual convention of the Montana Council for Exceptional Children, Helena, MT.

McNair, D., & Brown, D. (1983). Predicting the occupational aspirations, occupational expectations, and career maturity of black and white male and female 10th graders. *Vocational Guidance Quarterly, 32*, 29–36.

Morrison, R. F. (1977). Career adaptivity: The effective adaptation of managers to changing role demands. *Journal of Applied Psychology 62*, 549–558.

Nevill, D. D., & Calvert, P. D. (1996). Career assessment and the Salience Inventory. *Journal of Career Assessment, 4*, 399–412.

Nevill, D. D., & Kruse, S. J. (1996). Career assessment and the Values Scale. *Journal of Career Assessment, 4*, 383–398.

Nevill, D. D., & Super, D. E. (1986). *Salience Inventory: Theory, application, and research.* Palo Alto, CA: Consulting Psychologists Press.

Niles, S. G., & Goodnough, G. E. (1996). Life-role salience and values: A review of recent research. *Career Development Quarterly, 45*, 65–86.

Niles, S. G., Lewis, D. M., & Hartung, P. J. (in press). Using the Adult Career Concerns Inventory to measure task involvement. *Career Development Quarterly.*

Osipow, S. H. (1975). The relevance of theories of career development to special groups: Problems, needed data, and implications. In J. S. Picou & R. E. Campbell (Eds.), *Career behavior of special groups* (pp. 9–22). Columbus, OH: Charles E. Merrill.

Osipow, S. H., & Littlejohn, E. M. (1995). Toward a multicultural theory of career development: Prospects and dilemmas. In F. T. L. Leong (Ed.), *Career development and vocational behavior of racial and ethnic minorities* (pp. 251–261). Hillsdale, NJ: Lawrence Erlbaum Associates.

Osipow, S. H., & Fitzgerald, L. (1996). *Theories of career development* (4th ed.). Needham Heights, MA: Allyn & Bacon.

Padilla, A. M., Wagatsuma, Y., & Lindholm, K. J. (1985). Acculturation and personality as predictors of stress in Japanese and Japanese-Americans. *The Journal of Social Psychology, 125*(3), 295–305.

Parsons, F. (1909). *Choosing a vocation*. Boston: Houghton-Mifflin.

Pavlak, M. F., & Post Kammer, P. (1985). The effects of a career guidance program on the career maturity and self-concept of delinquent youth. *Journal of Vocational Behavior, 26*, 41–54.

Pomales, J., Claiborn, C. D., & LaFramboise, T. D. (1986). Effects of Black students' racial identity on perceptions of White counselors varying in cultural sensitivity. *Journal of Counseling Psychology, 34*, 123–131.

Pound, R. E. (1978). Using self-concept subscales in predicting career maturity for race and sex subgroups. *Vocational Guidance Quarterly, 27*, 61–70.

Prince, J. P. (1995). Influences on the career development of gay men. *Career Development Quarterly, 44*, 168–177.

Richardson, M. S. (1993). Work in people's lives: A location for counseling psychologists. *Journal of Counseling Psychology, 40*, 425–433.

Rodriguez, M., & Blocher, D. (1988). A comparison of two approaches to enhancing career maturity in Puerto Rican college women. *Journal of Counseling Psychology, 35*, 275–280.

Savickas, M. L. (1985). Career maturity: The construct and its measurement. *Vocational Guidance Quarterly, 32*, 222–231.

Savickas, M. L. (Ed.). (1993). Special section: A symposium on multicultural career counseling. *Career Development Quarterly, 42*(1), 3–55.

Savickas, M. L. (1995). Current theoretical issues in vocational psychology: Convergence, divergence, and schism. In W. B. Walsh & S. H. Osipow (Eds.), *Handbook of vocational psychology: Theory, research, and practice* (2nd ed., pp. 1–34). Mahwah, NJ: Lawrence Erlbaum Associates.

Savickas, M. L. (1997). Career adaptability: An integrative construct for life-span, life-space theory. *Career Development Quarterly, 45*, 247–259.

Savickas, M. L., & Hartung, P. J. (1996). The Career Development Inventory in review: Psychometric and research findings. *Journal of Career Assessment, 4*, 171–188.

Savickas, M. L., & Walsh, W. B. (Eds.). (1996). *Handbook of career counseling theory and practice*. Palo Alto, CA: Davies-Black.

Sharf, R. S. (1997). *Applying career development theory to counseling* (2nd ed.). Pacific Grove, CA: Brooks/Cole.

Smith, E. J. (1976). Reference group perspectives and the vocational maturity of lower socioeconomic Black youth. *Journal of Vocational Behavior, 8*, 321–336.

Stillwell, W. E., & Thoresen. C. E. (1972). Social modeling and vocational behaviors of Mexican-American and Non-Mexican-American adolescents. *Vocational Guidance Quarterly*, 279–286.

Stout, S. K., Slocum, J. W., & Cron, W. L. (1987). Career transitions of superiors and subordinates. *Journal of Vocational Behavior, 30*, 124–137.

Super, D. E. (1957). *The psychology of careers*. New York: Harper and Row.

Super, D. E. (1983). Assessment in career guidance: Toward truly developmental counseling. *Personnel and Guidance Journal, 61*, 555–562.

Super, D. E. (1990). A life-span, life-space approach to career development. In D. Brown & L. Brooks (Eds.), *Career choice and development* (pp. 197–261). San Francisco, CA: Jossey-Bass.

Super, D. E., & Nevill, D. D. (1985a). *Salience inventory*. Palo Alto, CA: Consulting Psychologists Press.

Super, D. E., & Nevill, D. D. (1985b). *Values scale*. Palo Alto, CA: Consulting Psychologists Press.

Super, D. E., Osborne, L., Walsh, D., Brown, S., & Niles, S. G. (1992). Developmental career assessment in counseling: The C-DAC Model. *Journal of Counseling and Development, 71*, 74–80.

Super D. E., Savickas, M. L., & Super, C. M. (1996). The life-span, life-space approach to careers. In D. Brown & L. Brooks (Eds.), *Career choice and development: Applying contemporary theories to practice* (3rd ed., pp. 121–178). San Francisco, CA: Jossey-Bass.

Super, D. E., Starishevsky, R., Matlin, N., & Jordaan, J. P. (1963). *Career development: Self-concept theory*. New York: CEEB Research Monograph No. 4.

Super, D. E., Thompson, A. S., Lindeman, R. H., Jordaan, J. P., & Myers, R. A. (1979). *Career Development Inventory: School form*. Palo Alto, CA: Consulting Psychologists Press.

Super, D. E., Thompson, A. S., Lindeman, R. H., Jordaan, J. P., & Myers, R. A. (1981). *Career Development Inventory: College form*. Palo Alto, CA: Consulting Psychologists Press.

Super, D. E., Thompson, A. S., & Lindeman, R. H., Myers, R. A., & Jordaan, J. P. (1988). *Adult Career Concerns Inventory*. Palo Alto, CA: Consulting Psychologists Press.

Super, D. W. (1953). A theory of vocational development. *American Psychologist, 8*, 185–190.

Super, D. W. (1963). The definition and measurement of early career behavior: A first formulation. *Personnel and Guidance Journal, 41*, 775–779.

Super, D. W., Zelkowitz, R. S., & Thompson, A. S. (1979). *Career Development Inventory, College and University Form*. Palo Alto, CA: Consulting Psychologists Press.

Tang, M., Fouad, N. A., & Smith, P. (1999). Asian Americans' career choices: A path model to examine factors influencing their career choices. *Journal of Vocational Behavior, 54*, 142–157.

U.S. Bureau of Census (1998). *Statistical abstract of the United States: 1998*. Washington, DC: U.S. Government Printing Office.

Vacha-Hasse, T., Walsh, B. D., Kapes, J. T., Dresden, J. H., Thomson, W. A., Ochoa-Shargey, B., & Camacho, Z. (1994). Gender differences on the Values Scale for ethnic minority students. *Journal of Career Assessment, 2*, 408–421.

Vondracek, F. W., & Fouad, N. A. (1994). Developmental contextualism: An integrative framework for theory and practice. In M. L. Savickas & R. W. Lent (Eds.), *Convergence in career development theories: Implications for science and practice* (pp. 207–214). Palo Alto, CA: Consulting Psychologists Press.

Vondracek, F. W., Lerner, R. M., & Schulenberg, J. E. (1986). *Career development: A life-span developmental approach*. Hillsdale, NJ: Lawrence Erlbaum Associates.

Wallace-Broscious, A., Serafica, F. C., & Osipow, S. H. (1994). Adolescent career development: Relationships to self-concept and identity status. *Journal of Research on Adolescence, 4*, 127–150.

Walsh, W. B. (Ed.). (1994). Special feature: Career assessment with racial and ethnic minorities. *Journal of Career Assessment, 2*(3).

Ward, C. M., & Bingham, R. P. (1993). Career assessment of ethnic minority women. *Journal of Career Assessment, 1*, 246–257.

Westbrook, B. W., & Sanford, E. E. (1991). The validity of career maturity attitude measures among black and white high school students. *Career Development Quarterly, 39*, 199–208.

Westbrook, B. W., Sanford, E. E., & Donnelly, M. H. (1990). The relationship between career maturity test scores and appropriateness of career choices: A replication. *Journal of Vocational Behavior, 36*, 20–32.

Westbrook, B. W., Sanford, E. E., Gilleland, K., Fleenor, J., & Merwin, G. (1988). Career maturity in Grade 9: The relationship between accuracy of self-appraisal and ability to appraise the career-relevant capabilities of others. *Journal of Vocational Behavior, 32,* 269–283.

Wrenn, C. G. (1962). The culturally encapsulated counselor. *Harvard Education Review, 32,* 444–449.

Chapter 8

Women's Career Development: A Postmodern Update

Louise F. Fitzgerald
Lenore W. Harmon
University of Illinois—Urbana-Champaign

In the literature on vocational psychology, it has become trite to observe that the mid-20th century entry of women into the world of work represents one of the major social phenomena of our time. Women now constitute the majority of the American workforce, their presence taken for granted by employers, social and economic policy makers, the general public, and women themselves. Not surprisingly, the study of women's career development is arguably the most vibrant and productive area in vocational psychology today (Fitzgerald, Fassinger, & Betz, 1995).

From our current perspective, when the phrase "turn of the century" is about to take on an entirely new meaning, it is sometimes difficult to recall that not only was it not always thus but, even as recently as 25 years ago, it wasn't thus at all. In 1970, the majority of American women did not work outside the home, and those who did constituted only about one third of the national workforce. Almost completely absent were married women with children, especially small children, and the literature abounds with studies of the effects of female employment on marital satisfaction (particularly the husband's) and the deleterious consequences of maternal employment for children. The message was clear: "[T]he . . . basic assumption was that men had careers and women (did) not" (Osipow, 1975, p. 3).

In the fall of 1973, Osipow conducted a seminar on women's careers, a seminar culminating in 1975 in the publication of *Emerging Woman: Career Analysis and Outcomes*. This edited volume, the first comprehensive treatment of the vocational psychology and career development of women, foreshadowed a subsequent explosion of scholarship, framing the issues in a manner that 25 years later still provides a viable model for organizing and understanding the complex relationship between women and work. The chapters produced by Osipow and his students provided scholarly reviews of topics such as demographic and social factors in women's work lives, parental, individual, and marital influences, the role of gender stereotyping, and other barriers to women's career development. It outlined women's growing contributions to the economy, debunked the myth that we have no real vocational interests, and highlighted the influence of external social factors on our involvement in the workforce.

As we celebrate Osipow's contributions to the field of vocational psychology and career development, it seems fitting that we revisit these issues, exploring their status in light of the social and theoretical developments of the past quarter century. We begin with a brief overview of the major developments since 1975, noting that, although most of the issues identified by Osipow remain central, the nature of career development itself and the way we view gender at the end of the 1990s is fundamentally different than when *Emerging Woman* appeared. This is due to the changing relationship of women and work. We then explore the implications of these changes for the career psychology of women in the future, comparing these issues with those Osipow outlined in 1975. Essentially, we aspire to apply the pioneering spirit this extraordinary man brought to the study of women's career development in the 1970s to the issues of the 21st century, thus creating a postmodern extension of his ideas.

THE CHANGING FACE OF THE FEMALE WORKFORCE

In 1973, less than 44% of all women were employed, constituting only 38% of the total workforce. In contrast, by March 1996, more than half the U.S. workforce was female, and nearly 60% of American women were employed. Even this figure is a considerable underestimate, including as it does women younger than 24 and older than 55, age groups for whom labor force participation is historically low for reasons generally unrelated to gender. In 1966, fully 75% of women between ages 25 and 55 were employed, an increase of more than 70% since 1973.

Even more remarkable is the fact that the greatest proportion of this increase is accounted for by women with children, traditionally the group least likely to be working. Historically, the presence and age of children is by far the most important predictor of a woman's workforce participation, far outweighing her skills, education, or socioeconomic level (Betz &

Fitzgerald, 1987). As noted in *Emerging Woman*, only 27% of women with children under age 3 were in the labor force in 1971; rates for mothers of 3- to 5-year-olds and school-age children (6 to 17 years) were 38% and 52%, respectively. In contrast, data from 1996 indicate that 62% of mothers of preschool children were presently employed; for mothers of school-age children, the labor force participation rate was an incredible 77.2% (Hayghe, 1997).

The impact of these changes cannot be overestimated. Female employment is critical to buffering thousands of families, particularly racial and ethnic minority families, from poverty (Cattan, 1998). In addition, female employment has been shown to increase women's decision-making power in the marital relationship (Ferber & O'Farrell, 1991), an effect that has far reaching consequences, including many for the nature of work organizations and career development itself. Finally, as Osipow (1975) predicted, the sheer magnitude of this shift has stimulated changes of the most profound nature in Western and, to some degree, global, social, and political institutions. Such changes are dynamic in nature, influencing each subsequent generation of young women and men, creating individual possibilities and social patterns unknown and even unimagined only 50 years ago. Women have changed, and with them, the world as we knew it; it is from this vantage point that we examine what Osipow and his collaborators first explored in *Emerging Woman*.

INTERESTS

Research and observational data do suggest that women have vocational interests . . .
—*Emerging Woman*, p. 153

Appearing on the eve of the great interest measurement debates of the 1970s and 1980s, *Emerging Woman* foreshadowed those issues with considerable prescience. Writing at a time when interest inventories still came in separate versions for men and women, contributors to this volume noted that women's inventories reflected fewer options and offered mainly sex-stereotyped occupations for consideration. Possibly most striking to a current reader is the opening to Peoples' (1975) chapter on this topic, which began by posing the question of whether women had real vocational interests at all. Although she concluded firmly that they did, the fact that it was necessary to pose the question vividly evokes the profoundly different world that existed barely 25 years ago.

In 1974, Campbell pioneered the Strong–Campbell Interest Inventory (SCII), the first "combined sex" version of the venerable Strong Vocational Interest Blank (SVIB). In addition to a single form for both sexes, the

SCII incorporated for the first time Holland's (1992) theoretical framework, provided combined scores on all occupational scales for both men and women, and in general ushered in a new generation of interest measurement. These and other changes, designed to take into account recommendations proposed by the Association for Measurement and Evaluation in Guidance Task Force (Harmon, Cole, Wysong, & Zytowski, 1973) and Harmon (1973), arose as the steadily increasing numbers of work and professionally oriented women rendered the old instruments increasingly obsolete.

Throughout the 1970s, concerted attempts were made to revise or delete gender stereotyped items from most inventories, occupational scales were developed in areas previously considered non-traditional for women, scales were normed for both sexes (National Institute of Education, 1974; Diamond, 1975), and supporting career exploration materials were substantially revised. Many of these changes are chronicled in Harmon, Cole, Diamond, and Zytowski (1977).

A number of stubborn problems remained, however, and ink continued to be spilled in these controversies well into the 1980s. For example, the practice of norming and scoring male and female occupational scales for both sexes met the letter of the law with respect to gender equity, but proved cumbersome in practice. Individuals' scores often differed considerably on the male and female versions of a scale, probably because of baserate gender differences in the respective comparison groups (i.e., the "In General" group) on which item selection was based. Explaining such discrepancies to puzzled test takers and clients was awkward, complicating the process of test interpretation and the use of interest measures in general.

The controversy over the appropriate comparison groups has proven a durable one, continuing to some degree today. Although same-sex norms presented the fewest technical problems, they proved difficult to construct for the numerous occupations in which women were relatively rare. Supplementation with cross-sex comparison groups presented a number of interpretive problems; not only were there often discrepancies between scores on male and female scales for the same occupation, but it was unclear whether cross-sex scales actually possessed predictive validity, the traditional *raison d'etre* for interest inventories per se. Finally, the very existence and presentation of separate sex norms could be criticized for underscoring occupational differences between the sexes.

Johansson and Harmon (1972) and Harmon and Webber (1978) were among the first to advocate developing *combined sex norms*, that is, building occupational scales based on a single group comprised of occupational members of both sexes. Arguing against this approach, Campbell (1974) noted in the manual for the first "merged" form of the SCII that a number of items showed large sex differences, an argument reiterated until the 1985 revision (Hansen & Campbell, 1985). Although the most recent manual (Harmon, Hansen, Borgen, & Hammer, 1994) emphasizes that such items rarely appear on occupational scales, the Strong (and Kuder) continue to employ separate occupational scales. Campbell's *Career Interest and Skills Survey* (CISS) (1995) and Johansson's *Enhanced Career Assessment Inventory* (1986) have successfully developed combined-sex occupational groups and, in the most recent contribution to this perennial problem, Harmon (in preparation) demonstrated that it is possible to build combined scales from items differentiating both men and women from their respective comparison groups.

An entirely different approach was taken by the theory-based inventories, which eschewed the thorny issue of occupational scales altogether, providing instead scores reflecting respondents' resemblance to the broad categories of Holland's (1992) occupational typology. This approach has become considerably more popular in the years since Osipow, *Emerging Woman*, in large part due to its ease of administration and interpretation. Like the Strong–Campbell Inventory, however, typological measures continue to reflect the stubborn (if declining) gender differences in interest baserates. For example, the most recent manual for the Self-Directed Search (SDS; Holland, Fritzsche, & Powell, 1994) still reports large gender differences for some of the types; other inventories have adopted similar typologies with similar results. The UniACT explicitly set out to minimize gender differences at the item level, but was only partially successful (Hanson & Rayman, 1976, Rayman, 1976).

The various typological inventories differ in how they treat such problems, with most employing separate sex norms in some form or other. Some instruments, most notably Holland's SDS, are not normed at all. Holland's use of raw scores generated considerable controversy, with opponents arguing that such procedures reinforced and perpetuated existing gender differences in occupational distribution. The argument over whether to use raw or normed scores, and what type of norms should be used, preoccupied vocational psychologists throughout much of the 1970s. Prediger and Lamb (1979) described the aspects of this controversy well, citing data indicating that hit rates (accuracy of classification) for several norming approaches are similar, although in general more accurate for males. There appear to be no definitive answers to these questions at present, and the various approaches are still used and defended by their respective devotees.

The importance of these issues for women's career development in the 21st century depends largely on how one conceptualizes the notion of career. We believe that women (and men) will develop increasingly nonlinear work lives, marked by coherent but largely unpredictable changes in position, employer, working conditions, and even occupation. Such flexibility will increasingly be required in response to the financial and familial realities of their lives, the rapidly changing nature of technology, and, in particular, the global economic situation. Good person–environment "matches" will still be very desirable, of course, but interests are only one part of that matching. Other aspects of work are increasingly important as well to both men and women, and systems that allow consideration of all important aspects of a position (Gati, 1998; Gati, Garty, & Fassa, 1996) are probably more useful than interest measurement alone. Job characteristics change much more rapidly today than in the past and will likely continue to do so, rendering one position a better "fit" at one time than another; simultaneously, individual life circumstances will also be changing. Issues of person–environment fit must, thus, be not only conceptualized more broadly than heretofore, but embedded in their dynamic context. It is this changing state of affairs that we expect will give women's career development an increasingly nonlinear character in the years to come.

PARENTAL INFLUENCES

Like mother, like daughter

—Old proverb

The chapter in *Emerging Woman* by Sorensen and Winters (1975) focused mainly on the facilitating effects of maternal role models, maternal identification, and socioeconomic status on women's career development. The importance of the maternal role model to this generation of theorists is vividly reflected in their writing, and they concluded that women whose mothers were employed were more likely to work than daughters of homemakers. They noted as well that parental identification was related to the type of career plans pursued, and that socioeconomic status affected knowledge of options, as well as the possibilities that were realistically available (pp. 46–47).

From the perspective of today, when the majority of women are employed and very few are brought up by stay-at-home mothers, the critical influence of maternal modeling has lost much of its power to explain women's life choices. It would be wrong to conclude, however, that parental influences have become irrelevant to this process; rather, current thinking emphasizes somewhat different aspects of such influence, generally characterized by attention to *relationship* rather than *status* variables.

Betz and Fitzgerald (1987) suggested that a woman's attitudes toward career involvement may be less related to her mother's actual employment than to her mother's attitudes toward her work. The earliest theoretical model of women's career development (Farmer, 1976, 1980, 1985) considered parental support for women working as an important environmental influence; Farmer (1985) found this variable directly influenced girls' long-term career motivation. Testing the Betz, Fitzgerald, and Fassinger model (Betz & Fitzgerald, 1987, Fassinger 1985, 1990), O'Brien and Fassinger (1993) incorporated aspects of the mother–daughter relationship (including mother-independent activities, mother-independent beliefs, and mother attachment) in a structural equation model predicting career orientation and career choice, and reported that the maternal relationship construct was indeed related to career orientation. Although neither Farmer (1985) nor O'Brien and Fassinger (1993) incorporated parental variables in a way that allowed differential examination of maternal and paternal influences, they did confirm that a woman's perceptions of her parents' support is an important facilitator of her career development.

Contemporary researchers have begun to argue that related concepts, based in the identity and attachment literature, explain important aspects of career development more generally. For example, Blustein, Walbridge, Friedlander, and Palladino (1991) found that adolescents who were securely attached to their parents but conflictually independent from them were less likely to foreclose their career choices. Blustein, Prezioso, and Schultheiss (1995) suggested that secure attachments to parents foster exploratory behavior in the career realm and provide support for the inevitable risks involved in making career choices. They also hypothesized that secure attachments promote greater mastery of work tasks. Clearly, the perception that there is a supportive family behind the career decision maker should facilitate the best choices and achievement. Harkening back to early discussions of the positive and negative effects of maternal employment, these authors suggest that it is important to examine how "shifting gender roles in contemporary Western society influence the accessibility of attachment figures in one's early life and the function of attachment relationships in one's contemporary career life" (p. 428).

This innovative application of the attachment literature provides a link between early discussions of parental influence and Bandura's (1977) notion of self-efficacy; indeed, if secure attachment predisposes individuals to greater exploration and risk taking, the connection seems clear. Individuals who are secure enough to explore and take risks should certainly, according to the theory, have greater self-efficacy. And, a style of parenting that supports secure attachments seems likely to share aspects of two powerful facilitators of self-efficacy: modeling and persuasion (Bandura, 1977). Following up women participants in Farmer's (1985) study, Farmer, Wardrop, Anderson, and Risinger (1995) found that parental support measured in 1980 predicted math self-efficacy in 1990, which, in turn, predicted persistence in math, science, and technology careers.

O'Brien and Fassinger (1993) assessed the concept of agency with confidence or self-efficacy and found that it predicted both career orientation and career choice; the authors interpreted their data as providing support for the importance of the attachment–individuation balance in young women. Research aimed at articulating more clearly the differential relationship of parental attachment and adolescent individuation to self-efficacy for various tasks would be helpful in understanding these relationships more fully.

Before leaving this section, it is worth noting that most of the writing on women's career development, both early and late, reflects a number of assumptions concerning the relative desirability of various career choices. Given social conditions at the time *Emerging Women* was written, it is not surprising that it focused primarily on women's access to careers that had previously been closed to them; that is, those in which men had traditionally earned considerable prestige and money. Twenty-five years later, we propose that examination of career facilitators such as parental support, secure attachments, career self-efficacy and the like are best rooted in the recognition that any choice that is realistic and satisfying for the individual is a good one. Rather than encouraging one-time choices in prestigious and financially advantageous careers, parents (and vocational psychologists) may be best encouraged to support a *process* of discovery that encourages young women to explore themselves and their options in a lifelong search for challenge and satisfaction on whatever level they may find them.

INDIVIDUAL FACTORS

To the degree that classical vocational psychology considered women at all, it typically treated them as a homogeneous group, as if the sheer fact of their sex was the most important thing about them. By the early 1970s, this was beginning to change, if only because researchers faced the task of understanding which women would seek employment outside the home and which would not. Thus, the chapter in *Emerging Woman* by Winters and Sorensen examined individual factors related to female career orientation, noting that these should prove valuable in the vocational education and counseling of individual women. Reviewing such traditional individual difference variables as ability, personality, and values, they noted that the career-oriented woman appeared to be characterized by high ability, need for achievement, and nontraditional (i.e., "masculine") role orientation. Once again presaging the career self-efficacy literature, they noted "How a woman views herself—her self-concept—is apparently a potent variable. *A woman who views herself as desiring and capable of high achievement is more apt to seek and be committed to employment*" (p. 60; italics added).

Revisiting this literature some 2 decades later, Fitzgerald, Fassinger, and Betz (1995) traced its development from roots in studies comparing homemakers with employed women, through subsequent examination of traditional versus nontraditional career choices, to more contemporary studies of the degree to which women choose careers in the sciences and mathematics (Betz, 1991; Fox, Brody, & Tobin, 1985; Hollinger, 1983; Humphreys, 1982; National Science Foundation, 1984; Pfafflin, 1984). They noted the shift from viewing choice traditionality as an outcome variable to more sophisticated formulations in which it is seen as moderating other relationships, such as interest–field congruence (Wolfe & Betz, 1981; Betz, Heesacker, & Shuttleworth, 1990). Finally, they observed that the home–career dichotomy that occupied earlier researchers has given way to more nuanced examinations of multiple role planning (e.g., Weitzman, 1994; Weitzman & Fitzgerald, 1996; McCracken & Weitzman, 1997), but caution "the history of women's traditional roles as homemaker and mother continues to influence every aspect of their career choice and adjustment" (Fitzgerald et al., 1995, p. 72), typically in the direction of placing limits on what can be achieved.

Such comments highlight one of the most intransigent conditions affecting women's career development; that is, the dramatic increase in their work participation implies that they are now expected to cope simultaneously with two full-time jobs—one outside the home and the other within it (Scarr, Phillips, & McCartney, 1989). Rather than "having it all," the literature suggests instead that many women are now "doing it all," and the cost to women, their families, and society is increasingly clear.

Reflecting on the changes of the last 25 years, we are struck by how—in this particular area—so much has remained the same. It is now generally recognized that, like men, women have "traits and factors" as well as gender, that most will work outside the home for most of their lives, and that career orientation is not a dichotomous variable. What seems to us ironic is that this focus on women's variability, their individual strengths and characteristics, may obscure what most of us continue to have in common; that is, full responsibility for childrearing, a task we are expected to accomplish with virtually no institutionalized societal support, whether we are scientists, physicians, factory workers, or welfare mothers. In this vein, we read with chagrin the words of Winters and Sorenson (1975):

> . . . [C]omplex, yet prepotent, reality factors . . . necessarily limit a woman's vocational options. Inadequate child care facilities; lack of support from industry in the areas of day care, part-time employment, and job sharing; the variable, yet universally inadequate systems of allotting public aid to mothers of dependent children; . . . the relative availability of appropriate jobs; and the availability of transportation are all external factors, generally

beyond the individual woman's control . . . (T)o speak meaningfully to the career development of women, researchers *must* consider the importance of these external factors. (p. 64; italics added)

THE ROLE OF MARRIAGE

. . . it is important to point out that woman's role as a childbearer makes her the keystone of the home, and therefore gives homemaking a central place in her career.
—Super, 1957

Although the traditional assumption that women would not work outside the home[1] was beginning to change by the time *Emerging Woman* appeared, the effects of traditional expectations set much of the agenda for subsequent research. For example, many studies examined what was typically termed the "consequences" women's employment would have on their marriages and the wellbeing of their children. As Miyahara (1975) noted in her chapter, "Some apprehension has been expressed over the increasing numbers of women entering the labor force as a potential threat to the institutions of marriage and the family" (p. 70).

Miyahira's chapter in *Emerging Woman* summarized what was known about these topics at that time. In her summary, she noted that the issues were complex, the questions not easy, and the answers mainly unclear; she did, however, outline a few tentative conclusions. She noted that although career-committed women tended to marry later than other women, they were still very marriage-oriented; that the relationship between female employment and the couple's marital satisfaction was not a straightforward one; that the husbands' attitudes and wives' preferences were important moderators of the employment–marital satisfaction relationship; and that the presence of young children tended to inhibit women from working outside the home.

Twenty-five years later, these conclusions are for the large part still valid. It is still the case that professional women marry later than other women, but also still true that the great majority eventually do marry and bear children. Possibly one of the most important developments in this

---

[1]This fiction could be maintained because research in vocational psychology has typically ignored women who were not North American, Caucasian, and, mainly, middle and upper class. A large proportion of the world's women have always labored both within and outside the home, typically at the most menial tasks. In the 20th century United States, African American women have traditionally worked outside the home, and various waves of immigrant families have depended for survival on the wages of their female as well as male members. The notion that one would "choose" between marriage and employment is a bitter joke to the inner city, "under class" women who have neither.

arena has been the recent appearance of research on the career develop-ment of lesbian women (Croteau & Bieschke, 1996). Because lesbians seek committed partnerships and, often, children outside the usual heterosex-ual marital framework, their lives provide a rich opportunity to unpack the relative influences of partnership and childrearing from those of the highly gendered institutions in which they are typically embedded.

Because lesbian relationships are typically more equitable with respect to task-sharing, childcare, and so forth, it may be that we will find that it is not the presence of children per se, but the persistent refusal of most hus-bands to share childrearing equitably that accounts for much of women's "double day." Similarly, the complex relationship of female employment to relationship satisfaction may be substantially clarified when both part-ners to the relationship are women. As Ferber and O'Farrell (1991) noted, the effects of wives' employment continues to depend on a number of fac-tors, and favorable outcomes are most likely to prevail when such employ-ment is consistent with the preferences of both partners (Ross, Mirowsky, & Huber, 1983); it is possible that such consistency will prove more wide-spread when heterosexual assumptions about "breadwinners" are irrele-vant. This line of research is not only exciting in and of itself, but promis-es to cast considerable light on many longstanding questions within women's career development.

In any event, research over the last 2 decades has increasingly demon-strated that concerns for the well-being of children of employed mothers was considerably overblown. Once again, the relationships are more com-plicated than they were originally thought to be. For example, there appears to be no "main effect" for maternal employment. As Ferber and O'Farrell (1991) asserted, "(A) variety of specific factors interact with mother's employment in determining the outcomes. In general, when mothers work by choice and childcare is satisfactory, family stress is not too great and their children are as well adjusted as those with mothers at home" (p. 47).

Fitzgerald and Betz (1983) pointed out some time ago that this peren-nially emotional issue is typically not well framed, as the "consequences" of maternal employment are probably more appropriately thought of as the consequences of inadequate childcare resources. As recent research has shown, when collateral care is adequate, even very young children do well. And, it is consistently the case that maternal employment has a pos-itive influence on daughters in a variety of ways (Betz & Fitzgerald, 1987). As Hoffman (1987) suggested, children whose mothers are employed hold less stereotyped views of gender roles and generally more positive views of themselves and their families.

If female employment has done little damage to the institutions of marriage and motherhood, it is unfortunately still true that the reverse is not necessarily the case. Although the overall relationship of marital–maternal status to women's work behavior has weakened, its relationship to career attainment, commitment, and innovation is still strong. Data continue to confirm substantial inverse relationships between (a) marriage and (b) number of children with virtually every known criterion of career involvement and achievement. This relationship does not exist for men; highly achieving men are at least as likely, if not more likely, as their less successful counterparts to be married and to have one or more children. Such data highlight once more the continuing influence of outdated assumptions concerning female responsibility for family and childcare, and underscore once again the lack of societal support for women's dual roles as one of the most stubborn barriers to their career development. It is to this topic that we now turn.

BARRIERS

In conclusion, women's career development is laden with numerous barriers.
—*Emerging Woman*, p. 137

That women's vocational development is complicated by numerous factors not salient for men[2] has been recognized since women first began to work outside the home. Mishler's (1975) chapter in *Emerging Woman* reviewed a number of these considerations, including possible gender differences in abilities, gender-role stereotyping, educational constraints, the influence of masculine preferences and prejudices, and the ubiquitous assumptions concerning women's role as wife and mother. To these, she added formal and informal discrimination, and environmental constraints of various types. To our knowledge, this work was the first to cast these issues as barriers, thus conveying that female aspiration and motivation was not absent or deficient, but blocked. This formulation was more fully articulated by Farmer (1976) and subsequently by Betz and Fitzgerald (1987) and Betz (1993).

One of the most interesting developments since Mishler's (1975) chapter was published has been the change in the nature, if not the existence, of the barriers that are thought to be most salient. Perhaps most striking is the degree to which concern about internal psychological factors (e.g., role conflict, fear of success) has given way to discussion of the more durable impediments imposed by society. Although gender discrimina-

---

[2]At least, not White Anglo Saxon Protestant men. The history of this country is unfortunately rife with discrimination against African-American men, as well as various groups of ethnic immigrants.

tion was formally prohibited in 1964 and had all but disappeared by the time *Emerging Woman* appeared in 1975, it was and is not the case that women are necessarily welcomed as colleagues nor treated as equals. Indeed, informal discrimination can often be sufficiently invidious to violate the law. For example, Ann Hopkins sued and won when Price-Waterhouse denied her a partnership, believing that she was too aggressive and insufficiently feminine—characteristics presumably prized in their male employees (*Hopkins vs. Price-Waterhouse*, 1987). Similarly, Eveleth Taconite Mines hired Lois Jenson and three other women to integrate its all male workforce, when the company stood by as they were physically and sexually harassed by male coworkers who believed that women had no place in the mines, the women sued and won (*Jenson, et al., vs. Eveleth Taconite Mines, et al.*, 1993).

Traditional beliefs about women's roles have been specifically identified as factors facilitating discrimination and sexual harassment (Fiske, Bersoff, Borgida, & Deaux, 1991; Fiske & Glick, 1995). Although the law requires full access to all jobs regardless of sex, old ways die hard, and attitudes cannot be legislated. Women may have formal access to careers traditionally closed to them, but once on the job, they face numerous barriers (what Crites, 1976, labeled "thwarting conditions") to achieving success and satisfaction. For example, between 40% and 60% of women will experience some form of sexually harassing behavior from supervisors or coworkers. Recent research demonstrates that such experiences have significant consequences for women and organizations alike (Schneider, Swan, & Fitzgerald, 1997; Faley, Knapp, Kurtis, & Dubois, 1999). Decrements in job satisfaction and organizational commitment; elevated levels of job withdrawal and work withdrawal; increased symptoms of anxiety and depression; and higher incidence of stress-related illness are just some of the ways that women and organizations are affected by this largely gender-specific stressor.

WHAT IS MISSING FROM THIS PICTURE?

Another major set of external barriers arises from organizations' slowness to provide adequate structures and resources to employees—mainly women—with significant family responsibilities (Ferber & O'Farrell, 1991). Resources include such things as on-site or subsidized child care and elder care, paid parental or family leave, and spousal relocation programs. Structures include the availability of flextime, job sharing, telecommuting, and the like. Although the Family Medical Leave Act (FMLA) has since 1993 mandated a limited amount of unpaid leave for family reasons, this benefit is only guaranteed to those employed by organizations beyond a certain size. And, it is also true that 6 weeks without a paycheck is a benefit the majority of women cannot afford.

Women are often employed in the secondary labor market or even the "invisible economy" (e.g., paid housework, child care) in which benefits are minimal or nonexistent. Finally, federal and state welfare policies have traditionally provided financial incentives to poor mothers to stay out of the labor market. Although this appears to be changing, as policy initiatives emphasize "workfare" and the "end of welfare as we know it," the lack of resources devoted to critical support structures such as childcare raise concerns that such policies may yield a net loss for the women they are designed to benefit. In summary, it seems fair to say that it is still the case, as Mishler (1975) asserted, that "women's career development is laden with numerous barriers" (p. 137).

THE EMERGING WOMAN IN THE YEAR 2000

Consider Fig. 8.1, taken from Osipow's introduction to *Emerging Woman*. According to this framework,[3] women's career development is a function of individual and social factors, as well as a set of moderating influences. Individual factors include attitudes, abilities, interests, and knowledge of opportunity, whereas social factors include family and significant others; the influence of school, church, and the media; and societal stereotypes of both gender and occupations. These influences are moderated by internal barriers such as fear of success, role conflict, and role overload, as well as the external ones of discrimination (either formal or indirect) and the limitations of space and time. This set of influences yields outcomes of various quality in a number of domains, including the combination of career and marriage; level of achievement; utilization (of abilities and interests); and, importantly, social change.

Now, consider Fig. 8.2, which represents our revised conceptualization of Osipow's framework, extended in light of changing social circumstances, as well as the current state of our knowledge concerning women and work. The first modification that appears is the title, which we have recast as "Factors Influencing American Women's Vocational Behavior at the Beginning of the 21st Century." Far from being a "millennium conscious" cosmetic change, this designation is intended to capture a number of important current insights. First, by grounding the framework in its cultural (i.e., Western, North American) and temporal (i.e., postindustrial,

---

[3]Figure 8.1, prepared by Susan A. Mishler, a graduate student in the original seminar and author of one of the chapters in *Emerging Woman*, was inspired by Senesh and Osipow's figure "Fundamentals of Career Education" in Senesh (1973).

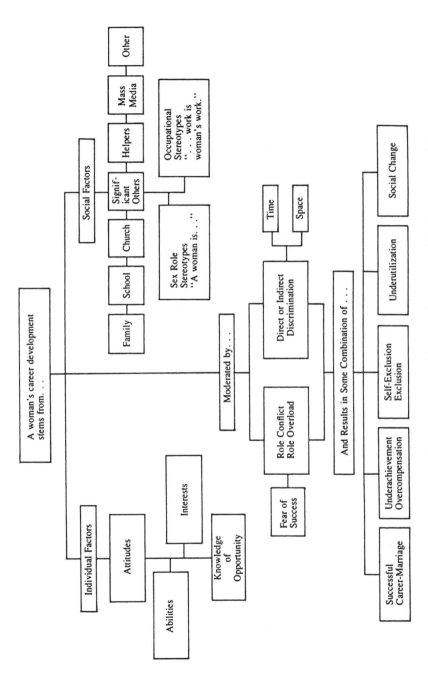

Fig. 8.1. Psychological aspects of women's career development. This figure, prepared by Susan A. Mishler, was inspired by Senesh and Osipow's table "Fundamentals of career education" in Senesh (1973).

221

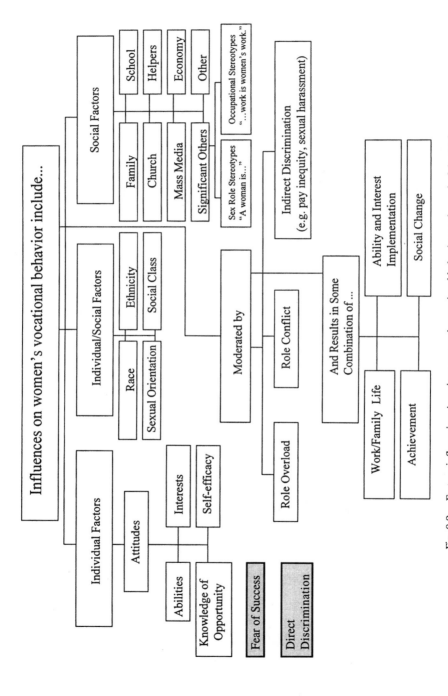

Fig. 8.2. Factors influencing American women's vocational behavior at the end of the 20th century.

late 20th century) specifics, we avoid reifying women as an abstract homogeneous group, and also acknowledge the destabilizing influence of social change across time. Second, shifting the focus from aspects of women's career development to the factors influencing their (our) vocational behavior further weakens the implication that there exists something inherent about women that is implicated here, and challenges the applicability of the term development (at least in its traditional sense) and thus career (with which it is linked) to work life in current American society.

Turning to the two major facets of the framework, we acknowledge the continuing importance of the traditional triad of individual factors (interests, abilities, attitudes–values) as well as awareness of opportunity. To these, we would add the concept of career self-efficacy, arguably the most important theoretical advance of the last 25 years. With respect to social factors, we de-emphasize the role of occupational stereotyping, recognizing that although the tails of the job–gender distribution remain stubbornly sex-segregated (e.g., coal mining on the one hand; secretarial work on the other), such pockets are far less common now than in 1975; jobs that occupy such pockets are declining in the face of technological changes; and, in general, the majority of fields are considerably more gender-integrated than any of us might have foreseen. Indeed, we would argue that occupational segregation in the United States at the turn of our century is predominantly an issue of level, not field.

With respect to the other societal influences identified by Osipow, (1975), we would argue that the role of the mass media has increased exponentially, whereas that of the church has generally declined. In addition, the critical influence of the economy, both its nature and state of health, as well as technology and its advances must be acknowledged in any comprehensive attempt to account for women's vocational behavior.

Finally, and importantly, we would add an additional macro-variable to the two already discussed; that is, a reciprocal Individual–Social Factor that includes such stimulus variables as race, ethnicity, sexual orientation, and social class. With the exception of social class, it is fair to say that such variables—now the focus of a burgeoning literature—were virtually unknown when *Emerging Woman* appeared. The criticism accorded to the abstract concept "woman" in feminist and the "minority" approaches to vocational psychology is well-enough known to avoid repeating here.

With respect to moderators, we would eliminate fear of success, arguing that it has little descriptive or explanatory power for women's behavior today; likewise, formal discrimination is virtually extinct. Other variables (i.e., role conflict, geographical restrictions), although arguing exerting less influence than formerly, continue as salient issues in women's lives, whereas the barriers imposed by role overload and the less formal, less institutionalized forms of discrimination (e.g., pay inequity, sexual harassment)[4] appear as intractable as ever.

Finally, we suggest that the outcomes produced by these combined influences are more positive, at least for middle-class White women, than at any time previously. It is now more possible (although still difficult) for a woman to combine what the Marxists call "production" (Jagger, 1988) and family life[5] than at any time since the Industrial Revolution first separated them; although in now way as widespread as they need to be, spousal hiring and relocation programs, coordinated transfer policies, dual career programs, flextime and (to a lesser degree) job sharing have helped make multiple roles a "do-able" norm. More women are successfully achieving in more domains, including those (e.g., sports, the judiciary, and higher levels of the military and diplomatic services) in which they were previously almost nonexistent. And, it is arguably true that high-ability women are less likely to underutilize their talents and abilities, although like the other outcomes we cite, this class remains almost certainly at least half empty. Finally, we emphasize once again that Osipow's most perceptive insight concerning women's vocational behavior was his inclusion of social change as an outcome of their participation in the world of work.

ISSUES FOR THE 21ST CENTURY

Historically, feminists have been concerned with two major issues related to women's vocational behavior: *entrance* and *equality* (which are another way of thinking about choice and adjustment). At the time *Emerging Woman* was written, strong social assumptions about appropriate behavior for women kept most of them from entering many occupations and from persisting in the world of work, particularly in combination with marriage and motherhood. It was primarily these issues of entrance and persistence that Osipow and his colleagues addressed in their book. The world has changed considerably since then and with it many basic assumptions about the fabric of social life in the United States. It is probably fair to say that most Americans assume that most women will have meaningful work involvement throughout their lives. Similarly, it is now generally accepted

---

[4]It is possible to argue that the extremely widespread nature of these problems suggest that they are more institutionalized than not. We would not necessarily quarrel with that argument, but rather intend to convey that, unlike the separate hiring policies of yesterday, they are at least normatively unacceptable.

[5]We employ the term *family life*, as opposed to marriage, to acknowledge the multiple forms of commitment and responsibility that characterize late 20th century life.

that they (we) can do any job, and the old beliefs about "appropriateness" appear well on their way to extinction. When entrance to educational or career opportunities is limited, it is often because decision makers give lip service to the concept of equal access but find ways not to afford it to specific women or minority group members. Although this is profoundly unjust, it is a far cry from the days of "men only" job advertisements and the systemic, normative, and socially acceptable discrimination of the past.

Thus, we now find ourselves more concerned with issues of equality rather than entrance, issues that more or less took a back seat when *Emerging Woman* was written. Specially, we refer to the social factors that include persistent inequality in pay, promotion, and perquisites; sexual harassment; and the perennial and stubborn fact that the working woman is still considered to be the primary caregiver for young children. The transformation of the American family, most often for the better, as well as of the American workforce resulting from women's integration into that workforce has not been matched or often even adequately recognized by employers and social policy makers.

POSTMODERN INFLUENCES ON WOMEN'S VOCATIONAL BEHAVIOR

One of the most profound differences between earlier and postmodern society is the dramatic change in the type of workforce needed. Not only are technological changes profound, but the nuclear family requires many more services from society than it did when mothers provided virtually all of those services at home, for free. Service workers now comprise a larger share of the workforce than ever before and have assumed many of the tasks traditionally provided by women in the home. Unfortunately, they are rarely paid adequately or compensated with benefits such as health care, sick and family leave, or retirement earnings. Not surprisingly, most of the individuals providing these services are women. Thus, the hard won entry of some women into professional career tracks has opened for others a revolving door to low level service occupations, and it is debatable whether this represents an improvement in the lives of the latter group. A major challenge for social policy makers of the 21st century is to find ways to compensate and train critically needed service workers, such as childcare providers and those who care for the elderly, that can provide them decent quality of life as well as pride and satisfaction with their positions. Complicating this problem is the need to integrate these goals with the profit motive of the corporations that administer such services. That many of the expanding opportunities are in jobs providing services formerly seen as "women's work," that the individuals who now perform them for pay are overwhelmingly women, and that many of these positions are devalued and exploitative in nature are not unrelated issues. Rather, they represent the postmodern equivalent of the historical belief that women's work is unskilled, unpaid, and unimportant. These issues rank high on the hierarchy of those that must be solved if women are to take an equal place in society.

Other, somewhat different, sectors of the workforce that have experienced profound changes since *Emerging Woman* was written include technology and financial services, in the past clearly considered "men's" careers. Along with the professions, these areas have seen large increases in women's participation, with some (a few) reaching high levels of authority. At the same time, these fields are changing so rapidly that individuals are often hired to do a specific project, rather than to serve for years and years. Consequently, the workforce is considerably more fluid and tenure less predictable than it was 25 years ago; career planning is now a lifetime task rather than simply a matter of a good initial choice. Today's workers must be able to track where the next opportunity will arise and prepare for it by continued education and new types of on-the-job training, implying that today's worker must be even more involved in her career than previously. Yes, if she is the primary caregiver or has primary responsibility for planning, implementing, and quality control for the care of her children or the elderly, how free can she be to prepare herself for the inevitable changes today's world will require? On the other hand, the fluidity of today's world is an exciting challenge, carrying an opportunity to try out new skills, interests, and aspects of the self. The individual who has the most freedom to do so will have the most fun . . . but in the majority of cases, will not be female.

THE CHANGING/LESS/NON/GENDERED NATURE OF LIFE IN THE 21ST CENTURY

It should be clear that we believe life is, in many ways, less gendered than it was in the 1970s, in that women have greater involvement, entrance, and opportunities in the world of work, and that this involvement has at least modulated the balance of responsibilities in many families. Nevertheless, there are still ways in which life and its opportunities are partially controlled by gender stereotypes, and the greatest of these have to do with responsibility for care of children and the elderly.

How can we, in our postmodern society, effect the changes needed to allow women to achieve success and fulfillment in their work? Although there are doubtless many answers to that question, one of the most critical is to achieve a fundamental shift in our view of the tasks necessary to a successful society (not that ours is necessarily very successful, that's a story for another day). We have traditionally called some of the most important tasks in society "women's work" and compensated them on the same level that we do parking lot attendants. This anomaly escaped serious scrutiny when such tasks were most often performed by women in the home. Now that it is no longer free, we are beginning to see just how critically important "women's work" has been to the functioning of society. Yet, we still remain the only developed country in the world without a national child care policy, and the often heart-rending problems associated with elder care in this country are yet to be addressed in any serious manner.

If women are ever to be able to participate as full and equal members of society, we must begin to face these issues squarely and search for meaningful answers, answers that neither push women back into the home, exploit those who have taken on the care of others for pay, nor ignore the nurture we owe our children or the care that is due our elderly. It is only then that the promise of Osipow in *Emerging Woman* will be fulfilled.

ACKNOWLEDGMENT

The authors would like to thank Linda L. Collinsworth of the University of Illinois for her assistance with the preparation of the manuscript.

REFERENCES

Bandura, A. (1977). Self-efficacy: Toward a unifying theory of behavioral change. *Psychology Review, 84*, 191–215.

Betz, N. (1993). Women's career development. In F. L. Denmark & M. A. Paludi (Eds.), *Psychology of women: A handbook of issues and theories* (pp. 627–684). Westport, CT: Greenwood Press.

Betz, N. E. (1991). *What stops women and minorities from choosing and completing majors in science and engineering*. Washington, DC: Federation of Behavioral, Psychological, and Cognitive Sciences.

Betz, N. E., & Fitzgerald, L. F. (1987). *The career psychology of women*. New York: Academic Press.

Betz, N. E., Heesacker, R. S., & Shuttleworth, C. (1990). Moderators of the congruence and realism of major and occupational plans in college students. *Journal of Counseling Psychology, 37*, 269–276.

Blustein, D. L., Prezioso, M. S., & Schultheiss, D. P. (1995). Attachment theory and career development: Current status and future directions. *The Counseling Psychologist, 23*, 416–432.

Blustein, D. L., Walbridge, M. M., Friedlander, M. L., & Palladino, D. E. (1991). Contributions of psychological separation and parental attachment to the career development process. *Journal of Counseling Psychology, 38*, 39–50.

Campbell, D. P. (1974). *Manual for the Strong-Campbell Interest Inventory*. Stanford, CA: Stanford University Press.

Cattan, P. (1998). The effect of working wives on the incidence of poverty. *Monthly Labor Review, 121(3)*, 22–29.

Crites, J. O. (1976). A comprehensive model of career development in early adulthood. *Journal of Vocational Behavior, 9*, 105–118.

Croteau, J. M., & Bieschke, K. J. (1996). Beyond pioneering: An introduction to the special issue on the vocational issues of lesbian women and gay men. *Journal of Vocational Behavior, 48*, 119–124.

Diamond, E. E. (Ed.). (1975). *Issues of sex bias and sex fairness in interest measurement*. Washington, DC: U. S. Government Printing Office.

Faley, R. H., Knapp, D. E., Kustis, G. A., & Dubois, C. L. Z. (1999). Estimating the organizational costs of sexual harassment: The case of the U.S. Army. *Journal of Business & Psychology, 13*, 461–484.

Farmer, H. S. (1976). What inhibits career and achievement motivation in women? *The Counseling Psychologist, 6*, 12–14.

Farmer, H. S. (1980). Environmental, background, and psychological variables related to optimizing achievement and career motivation for high school girls. *Journal of Vocational Behavior, 17*, 58–70.

Farmer, H. S. (1985). Model of career and achievement motivation fo women and for men. *Journal of Counseling Psychology, 32*, 363–390.

Farmer, H. S., Wardrop, J. L., Anderson, M. Z., & Risinger, R. (1995). Women's career choices: Focus on science, math, and technology careers. *Journal of Counseling Psychology, 42*, 155–170.

Fassinger, R. E. (1985). A causal model of college women's career choice. *Journal of Vocational Behavior, 27*, 123–152.

Fassinger R. E. (1990). Causal models of career choice in two samples of college women. *Journal of Vocational Behavior, 36*, 225–248.

Ferber, M. A., & O'Farrell, B. (Eds.). (1991). *Work and family: Policies for a changing work force*. Washington, DC: National Academy Press.

Fiske, S. T., Bersoff, D. N., Borgida, E., & Deaux, K. (1991). Social science research on trial: Use of sex stereotyping research in Price Waterhouse v. Hopkins. *American Psychologist, 46*, 1049–1060.

Fiske, S. T., & Glick, P. (1995). Ambivalence and stereotypes cause sexual harassment: A theory with implications for organizational change. *Journal of Social Issues, 51*, 97–115.

Fitzgerald, L. F., & Betz, N. (1983). Issues in the vocational psychology of women: In W. B. Walsh & S. H. Osipow (Eds.), *Handbook of vocational psychology* (pp. 83–159). Hillsdale, NJ: Lawrence Erlbaum Associates.

Fitzgerald, L. F., Fassinger, R., & Betz, N. E. (1995). Theoretical advances in the study of women's career development. In W. B. Walsh & S. H. Osipow (Eds.), *Handbook of vocational psychology* (2nd ed., pp. 67–109). Hillsdale, NJ: Lawrence Erlbaum Associates.

Fox, L. H., Brody, L., & Tobin, D. (1985). Women and mathematics: The impact of early intervention programs upon course-taking and attitudes in high schools. In S. F. Chipman, L. R. Brush, & D. M. Wilson (Eds.), *Women and mathematics*. Hillsdale, NJ: Lawrence Erlbaum Associates.

Gati, I. (1998). Using career-related aspects to elicit preferences and characterize occupations for a better person-environment fit. *Journal of Vocational Behavior, 52*, 343–356.

Gati, I., Garty, Y., & Fassa, N. (1996). Using career-related aspects to assess person-environment fit. *Journal of Counseling Psychology, 43*, 196–206.

Hansen, J. C., & Campbell, D. P. (1985). *Strong Interest Inventory Manual, 4th edition*. Palo Alto, CA: Consulting Psychologists Press.

Hanson, G. R., & Rayman, J. (1976). Validity of sex-balanced interest scales. *Journal of Vocational Behavior, 9,* 279–291.

Harmon, L. W. (1973). Sexual bias in interest testing. *Measurement and Evaluation in Guidance, 5,* 496–501.

Harmon, L. W., Cole, N. S., Diamond, E. E., & Zytowski, D. G. (1977). A case history of change: A review of the responses to the challenge of sex bias in career interest inventories. (Association for Measurement and Evaluation in Guidance Commission on Sex Bias in Measurement) *Measurement and Evaluation in Guidance, 10,* 148–152.

Harmon, L. W., Cole, N. S., Wysong, E., & Zytowski, D. (1973). AMEG commission report on sex bias in interest measurement. *Measurement and Evaluation in Guidance, 6,* 171–177.

Harmon, L. W., Hansen, J. C., Borgen, F. H., & Hammer, A. C. (1994). *SII Applications and Technical Guide.* Palo Alto, CA: Consulting Psychologists Press.

Harmon, L. W., & Webber, P. (1978). The reliability and concurrent validity of three types of occupational scales for two occupational groups: Some evidence bearing on handling sex differences in interest scale construction. In C. K. Tittle & D. G. Zytowski (Eds.), *Sex-Fair Interest Measurement: Research and Implications.* Washington, DC: National Institute of Education.

Hayghe, H. V. (1997). Developments in women's labor force participation. *Monthly Labor Review, 120,* 41–46.

Hoffman, L. (1987). The effects on children of maternal and paternal employment. In N. Gerstel & H. E. Gross (Eds.), *Families and work* (pp. 362–395). Philadelphia: Temple University Press.

Holland, J. L. (1992). *Making vocational choices: A theory of vocational personalities and work environments.* Odessa, FL: Psychological Assessment Resources.

Holland, J. L., Fritzsche, B. A., & Powell, A. B. (1994). *Self-Directed Search Technical Manual.* Odessa, FL: Psychological Assessment Resources.

Hollinger, C. L. (1983). Self-perception and the career aspirations of mathematically talented female adolescents. *Journal of Vocational Behavior, 22,* 49–62.

Hopkins v. Price Waterhouse, 825 F.2d 458, 473, 44 FEP Cases 825 (D.C. Cir. 1987).

Humphreys, S. M. (1982). *Women and minorities in science: Strategies for increasing participation.* Boulder, CO: Westview Press.

Jaggar, A. M. (1988). *Feminist politics and human nature.* Totowa, NJ: Rowman & Littlefield.

Jenson v. Eveleth Taconite Co. (1993). 824 F. Supp. 847, 61 FEP Cases 1252 (D. Minn.).

Johansson, C. B. (1986). *Career Assessment Inventory; The Enhanced Version.* Minneapolis, MN: National Computer Systems.

Johansson, C. B., & Harmon, L. W. (1972). The Strong Vocational Interest Blank: One form or two? *Journal of Counseling Psychology, 19,* 404–410.

McCracken, R. S., & Weitzman, L. M. (1997). Relationship of personal agency, problem-solving appraisal, and traditionality of career choice to women's attitudes toward multiple role planning. *Journal of Counseling Psychology, 44,* 149–159.

Mishler, S. A. (1975). Barriers to the career development of women. In S. H. Osipow (Ed.), *Emerging woman: Career analysis and outlooks* (pp. 117–146). Columbus, OH: Merrill.

Miyahira, S. D. (1975). Marriage and the employment of women. In S. H. Osipow (Ed.), *Emerging woman: Career analysis and outlooks* (pp. 69–90). Columbus, OH: Merrill.

National Institute of Education (1974). *Guidelines for assessment of Sex Bias and Sex-Fairness in Career Interest Inventories.* Washington, DC.

National Science Foundation. (1984). *Women and minorities in science and engineering.* Washington, DC: Author.

O'Brien, K. M., & Fassinger, R. E. (1993). Career orientation and choice of women. *Journal of Counseling Psychology, 40,* 456–469.

Osipow, S. H. (Ed.). (1975). *Emerging woman: Career analysis and outlooks.* Columbus, OH: Merrill.

Peoples, V. Y. (1975). Measuring the vocational interest of women. In S. H. Osipow (Ed.), *Emerging woman: Career analysis and outlooks* (pp. 23–36). Columbus, OH: Merrill.

Pfafflin, S. M. (1984). Women, science and technology. *American Psychologist, 39*, 1183–1186.

Prediger, D. J., & Lamb, R. R. (1979). The validity of sex-balanced and sex-restrictive vocational interest reports: A comparison. *Vocational Guidance Quarterly, 28(1)*, 16–24.

Rayman, J. R. (1976). Sex and the single interest inventory: The empirical validation of sex-balanced interest inventory items. *Journal of Counseling Psychology, 23*, 239–246.

Ross, C. E., Mirowsky, J., & Huber, J. (1983). Dividing work, sharing work, and in-between: Marriage patterns and depression. *American Sociological Review, 48*, 809–823.

Scarr, S., Phillips, D., & McCartney, K. (1989). Working mothers and their families. *American Psychologist, 44*, 1402–1409.

Schneider, K., Swan, S., & Fitzgerald, L. F. (1997). The job-related, psychological, and health-related outcomes of sexual harassment. *Journal of Applied Psychology, 82*, 401–415.

Senesh, L. (1973). *New paths in social science curriculum design.* Chicago: Science Research Associates, 1973.

Sorensen, J., & Winters, C. J. (1975). Parental influences on women's career development. In S. H. Osipow (Ed.), *Emerging woman: Career analysis and outlooks* (pp. 37–50). Columbus, OH: Merrill.

Super, D. E. (1957). *The psychology of careers.* New York: Harper and Row.

Weitzman, L. M. (1994). Multiple-role realism: A theoretical framework for the process of planning to combine career and family roles. *Applied & Preventive Psychology, 3*, 15–25.

Weitzman, L. M., & Fitzgerald, L. F. (1996). The development and initial validation of scales to assess attitudes toward multiple role planning. *Journal of Career Assessment, 4*, 269–284.

Winters, C. J., & Sorensen, J. (1975). Individual factors related to career orientation in women. In S. H. Osipow (Ed.), *Emerging woman: Career analysis and outlooks* (pp. 51–68). Columbus, OH: Merrill.

Wolfe, L. K., & Betz, N. E. (1981). Traditionality of choice and sex role identification as moderators of the congruence of occupational choice in college women. *Journal of Vocational Behavior, 19*, 61–77.

Chapter 9

Career Assessment: Changes and Trends

Judy M. Chartrand
Consulting Psychologists Press

W. Bruce Walsh
The Ohio State University

Samuel Osipow anticipated and helped to create several trends in our field, including the convergence of vocational theories, the expanded study of women's career development and the measurement of career decision making, occupational stress, and task-specific occupational self-efficacy. Founding the *Journal of Vocational Behavior* is further evidence of his penchant for establishing the cutting edge of our field. On several occasions, he has been asked to speculate and write about trends in our field, and his predictions have been quite accurate (see e.g., Osipow 1980; 1991). Osipow's (1980) approach to forecasting the future was "to review the data and try to extrapolate" (p. 18) and to ground himself with empirical evidence. In this chapter, Bruce Walsh and I pay homage to the vision and spirit of Osipow's work by reviewing the data and by trying to extrapolate changes and trends in career assessment. To determine our chapter focus we looked at the impact of demographic shifts, the global economy, and technological advances. Both work and the workforce are being transformed and, as a result, both the content and the delivery of career assessment services are changing and evolving.

Career assessment has always been a staple part of counseling psychology, but it has never been more widely accepted than it is today. Career assessment instruments and interpretations can readily be found in computer systems located in community centers, schools, public libraries, career resource centers at large corporations, and on the Internet. Current applications are different than early characterizations of career assessment, which included the benevolent expert counselor and the studious client (Williamson, 1939) and criticisms of a myopic "test and tell" approach that was popularized by the phrase "three interviews and a cloud of dust" (Crites, 1981, p. 49). The Information Age has led to many changes in our society, which are reflected in the practice of career assessment.

In this chapter, we discuss career assessment in relation to societal and technological evolution. Some changes have been gradual, such as changes in the workplace and in the workforce, developments in educational–career guidance, the evolution of testing standards, and advances in the field of psychological measurement. Other changes have been more rapid, such as the advent of computer-based assessment and computer-assisted interpretation. Finally, we engage in a bit of speculation about how these changes will coalesce to influence the practice of career assessment and related basic research domains (e.g., interest measurement).

Our focus on the contemporary evolution of career assessment is only one of several possible ways in which to review the topic. Our intent was to compliment recent reviews and publications devoted to career assessment. Readers who would like a critical synthesis of career assessment are referred to Hackett and Watkins (1995) and Betz (1992). Reviews and descriptions of individual instruments are available in *The Journal of Career Assessment*, which has been published since 1993, Kapes and Mastie (1988), and Watkins and Campbell (1990). Further, a thorough description of how to effectively use career assessment instruments in counseling is provided by Seligman (1994). Spokane (1991) offers an integrated model that includes career theory, assessment, and intervention. Portions of Leong's (1995) book address multicultural assessment and intervention issues. This written cadre offers excellent resources for learning and refining one's knowledge of career assessment. Although career assessment does not necessarily involve the use of psychometric instruments, testing is typically an important feature. Therefore, this chapter covers psychometric measures and associated issues as they affect career assessment. Further, we use the word *testing* in a broad sense to include performance measures, preference inventories, and attitude scales.

CAREER ASSESSMENT: DEFINITIONS AND STAKEHOLDERS

Although career assessment can be defined in different ways, most authors agree that *assessment* is a process used for counseling or selection, and that its *purpose* is to provide information. The process of assessment involves collecting information to help people understand and cope with problems (Walsh & Betz, 1995, p. 17). The purpose of career instruments, such as interest inventories, is to facilitate career development or informed-career decision making (Holland, 1985). At a more general level, the *Standards for Educational and Psychological Testing* (1985) state that testing devices are used to inform decisions. Spokane (1991) eloquently elaborated the purpose of career assessment in terms of actuarial and applied utility. He referred to career assessment as unearthing congruent career possibilities, discovering leading edge interests, confirming congruence, assessing conflicts or problems, motivating constructive behavior, acquiring a cognitive structure for evaluating career alternatives, clarifying expectations and planning interventions, and establishing ability range. Career instruments are also the measurement component of research, and as such, they play an important role in furthering our understanding of career development and decision making.

In summary, there are two applied goals that drive career assessment. The first, and primary goal, is to gather information that will help people make career decisions. The second goal is to gather information that will help counselors to work more effectively with their clients. Ideally, these goals converge, as exemplified in narrative assessment, where the counselor and client together develop a picture that is personally meaningful to the client (Borgen & Harmon, 1995). Further, testing is a major component, but not the only component, of career assessment. Contextual aspects are paramount in understanding assessment results: the individual's background and current situation, the nature of the relation between counselor and client, the testing situation, and the nature of the test itself. Finally, career assessment furthers our basic knowledge of career development and decision making.

Rogers (1995) describes four major groups or stakeholders who have a vested interest in the testing enterprise. His categories also represent the major parties who are involved in career assessment. First, are the primary beneficiaries of career assessment information: the student, the client, the employee, and the self-learner. Career assessment is typically described from the perspective of counselor–client relationships. With a few important exceptions, like John Holland, many career professionals have been slow to acknowledge that people often engage in self-directed assessment. Today, it only takes a few key strokes or mouse clicks on the Internet to find self-assessment measures of various types and quality. Later, we discuss changes in service delivery, including a trend toward self-directed assessment and computer assessment and interpretation.

The second stakeholder group is professionals who use career assessment in their professional activities: the counselor, the psychologist, the educator, and the human resource professional. Responsibility for accurate and ethical application of career assessment falls to these professionals because they are in a position to shape the decisions of others. Professionals need to be aware of the costs and benefits of use (including over and underuse) and misuse of career assessment materials. Further, this group is responsible for adherence to current testing–assessment standards and the evaluation of instrument quality. Often the aforementioned issues are interconnected, such as the need to understand differential item functioning (a psychometric concept) to evaluate whether or not an item is gender or racially biased. Later, we discuss standards for testing and measurement advances that are pertinent to professional competency.

The third group is comprised of career assessment producers: the authors and publishers. Although we devote little attention to this group, it is important to acknowledge their role in creating career assessment materials for multiple users and in generating standards for testing.

Rogers (1995) labeled the fourth group *society*, within which we would like to highlight educational and vocational institutions. For example, within the United States, legislation (e.g., the School-to-Work Initiative, welfare reform) and recommendations from the Department of Labor (e.g., the report written by the Secretary's Commission on Achieving Necessary Skills; SCANS Report) are driving needs for career assessment. In addition, changes in the workplace are creating different needs with respect to career assessment. For example, it is now common to examine teamwork style and skills in the context of career assessment. In the next section, we look at some of these workplace changes in more detail.

TRANSFIGURATION OF WORK AND THE WORKFORCE

In many parts of the world, technological and economic factors are changing the way we work and the way we describe work. Companies and organizations have become more interested in understanding organizational culture and the impact it can have on productivity, policies, and work satisfaction. Shifting demographics, including greater ethnic and immigrant representation and an aging population, create a different workplace and a workforce whose needs are different from those of the workforce of previous generations. Change is pervasive, and it is occurring worldwide. Kanter's (1991) cross-cultural study of world managers suggested that change was occurring across country, culture, and corporation. Career counselors need to fully understand these changes, so that they can effectively select and use career assessment tools with clients. In this section, we discuss some of the fundamental changes in the nature of work and describe how those changes are having an impact on career assessment research and practice. We also discuss the new workforce and touch upon some of the values changes that are creating different needs among clientele who use or benefit from career assessment tools. Career counselors will need to understand these techniques to enhance culturally sensitive assessment practice and research.

Changing Nature of Work

As we move from the Industrial Age to the Information Age, we are experiencing a fundamental transformation of work (Rifkin, 1995), and secure jobs are giving way to more transitional and temporal positions. Service occupations are growing rapidly (Saveri, 1991) along with a customer oriented philosophy, which creates a need for employees with interpersonal skills. Many manufacturing firms are adopting new approaches, such as Just-In-Time manufacturing, which emphasizes efficiency and speed. They are also implementing new manufacturing technology that creates a need for workers with technological skills. Across industries there is a trend toward self-managed teams and flattened hierarchical structures, which, in turn, creates a need for effective team players and people who can work in a self-directed manner. The increase in job telecommuting and job sharing gives employees greater flexibility but require better communication and planning skills. In general, there is an emphasis on creating environments that possess diversity, decentralization, and the generation of ideas and knowledge. Employees are being encouraged to generate ideas and to solve problems. In addition, the stakes are higher in the job market as positions become increasingly polarized in terms of education and skill (Saveri, 1991). Because of these changes, there is a need for career assessment that addresses skills for the current workplace, interpersonal style, and problem solving style.

The relationship between employees and employers has also changed. The assumption that companies will reward performance with job security is no longer valid. With the advent of downsizing, delayering, right sizing, and restructuring, the long-term employee–employer relationship has given way to a new alliance. Employers want employees who can quickly and flexibly respond to changing business needs. Employees need, and employers need to foster, self-reliant workers who can continually assess their interests, values, temperaments, interpersonal style, and skills. From the corporate side, companies need to help employees update and benchmark their skills, so that they are actively learning and can make informed decisions about their career development (Waterman, Waterman, & Collard, 1994). In high school and postsecondary settings, counselors and teachers need to prepare students for the demands of work and the practice of lifelong learning.

Describing the New Work Environment. These changes have both sweeping and subtle implications for research in vocational psychology. Vocational psychology has traditionally studied and described the work environment in terms of occupations and occupational clusters. For example, E. K. Strong's (1927) pioneering work on interests (Strong Vocational Interest Blank) used occupations as core indicators, and the *Dictionary of Occupational Titles* (DOT; U.S. Department of Labor 1991), a mainstay in career libraries, is organized by occupations. However, job titles as descriptors are becoming less useful, and jobs tasks or skills as descriptors are becoming more useful. John Holland (1996) noted that if the predicted trends come true, career theories may lack phenomenon to explain.

In the future, job tasks and skills or competency requirements will become more prominent as taxonomic descriptors. For example, O-NET (The Occupational Information Network), which is being developed by the Department of Labor to replace the DOT, will use a skill-based framework. The shift away from occupational titles as a common denominator can also be seen in vocational research. Recently, Day and Rounds (1997) argued that basic interests, which fall between general occupational themes and occupational titles in level of generality, best reflect the nature of the emerging vocational environments. They note that basic interests provide meaningful dimensions in the interpretation of career inventories and may be more optimal cognitive categories than other levels of classification. Rounds and Day (1999) summarized research on the structure of interests and presented a circumplex model in which Holland's RIASEC themes—R [Realistic], I [Investigative], A [Artistic], S [Social], E [Enterprising], and S [Social], known as RIASEC, and basic interests are both plotted around the circumference, with the later representing greater specificity than the former. If this type of research is translated into practice, then basic interests would play a more prominent role in interest assessment. Further, the utility of occupational titles, which are a major component in most major interest inventories (e.g., Career Assessment Inventory, Johansson, 1986; Kuder Occupational Interest Survey, Kuder & Zytowski, 1991; Strong Interest Inventory, Stanford University Press, 1994), may need to be reconsidered. In the past, counselors (ourselves included) have used occupational titles to help clients identify interest patterns. Because of project-based jobs, continual skill acquisition, and a generalist job philosophy, concepts such as basic interests and job tasks may become the anchors for person–environment career assessment.

Skills Critical for the New Work Environment. A second implication of change is the heightened focus on the so-called "soft" skills necessary for surviving in a shifting work environment—personality traits, temperament, and self-management skills that foster compatibility and adaptability in the work environment (Harkness, 1997). Personality research is not new, but it has not always been thought of as a core part of career assessment research. For example, reviews of career assessment research have been organized by individual difference variables, such as aptitude–ability, interest, and values measures, but not personality measures (e.g., Betz, 1992; Hackett & Watkins, 1995). It is now essential that vocational researchers study personality characteristics and qualities, such as flexibility, adaptability, and self-control. Interpersonal skills are necessary in work environments that are using teams drawn from increasingly diverse groups of employees. Because of the shift to information–oriented work, teams will be the primary work unit rather than individuals (Drucker, 1994). As Zuboff noted, "the virtuoso in interpersonal skills is the corporate future" (cited in Goleman 1994, p. 149). Finally, cognitive style characteristics, such as creativity and effective problem solving are needed to facilitate self-managed groups and to respond to the work environment demands of what has been labeled the "nanosecond nineties" (Peters, 1992). Cognitive style research that bridges the areas of cognition and personality is promising for predicting school and work performance (Sternberg & Grigorenko, 1997).

Goleman's (1994) work on emotional intelligence is a compelling example of the so-called soft skills needed in today's workplace. He referred to abilities such as self-control, zeal, persistence, and ability to motivate oneself as emotional intelligence. He also emphasized emotional and social qualities, such as empathy and ability to relate to others. In a chapter on emotional intelligence and the workplace, he cited a study (Kelley & Caplan, 1993) in which star performers were differentiated from average performers at a prestigious research lab. The results indicated that the groups differed little on standard cognitive and personality measures, but they did differ on internal and interpersonal strategies used to get their work done. "Star" performers were more likely to develop rapport and key relationships, so that they had reliable networks that they could use to handle unexpected problems or crises.

The increased emphasis on personality and emotional intelligence has implications for the study of vocational psychology and the practice of career assessment. First, we need to better understand (including better construct definitions) concepts such as emotional intelligence or practical intelligence (Neisser, 1979) and how they relate to personality measures, cognitive ability, knowledge of a given domain (job knowledge), decision making, and criterion measures such as job performance. The conceptualization of intelligence as more than what is proposed by traditional hierarchical theories of intelligence is evident in a recent issue of the *American Psychologist* (Sternberg, 1997a), which was devoted to intelligence and life-long learning. Sternberg (1997b) called for a broad understanding of what is meant by intelligence and a "principled way of determining just what criteria an ability must pass to be viewed as part of intelligence" (p. 1036). At one level, practical intelligence measures can be used in addition to traditional cognitive measures and personality measures to predict job performance in areas such as business management and sales (Wagner, 1997). At another level, the domains of intelligence, personality, and interests can be explored to better understand their relatedness and overlap (Ackerman & Heggestad, 1997; Waller, Lykken, & Tellegen, 1995). Within vocational psychology, a few attempts have been made to link domains (e.g., personality and interests; Borgen & Harmon, 1995; Gottfredson, Jones, & Holland, 1993; Holland, Johnston, & Asama, 1995; Tokar & Swanson, 1995). However, more effort is needed in this area (cf. Hackett & Watkins, 1995). Perhaps the development of new instruments, such as the BarOn Emotional Quotient-Inventory (BarOn EQ-I; Bar-On, 1996) will facilitate such efforts.

To keep pace with a continually shifting work environment, clients will need to know how their personality, interests, and abilities relate. As a result, there is likely to be more integration across assessment batteries. Good career counselors have always helped clients to synthesize results across instruments, and interdomain assessment models are certainly not new (e.g., Lowman, 1993). However, integrated interpretive reports are relatively new and are likely to become more common in the future. In addition, it is likely that more professionals will want to create a tailored battery by selecting relevant scales from personality, interest, and intelligence tests. This tailored testing raises validity issues that require careful study. However, cross-instrument assessment efforts have been reported in the area of cognitive testing (Daniel, 1997).

The heightened interest in soft skills coincides with the popular view of human's as agentic beings. The cognitive shift in psychology has greatly influenced vocational research and the subsequent development of cognitive measures and career cognitions measures (Hackett & Watkins, 1995). It has also influenced the development of dynamic assessment, which focuses more on cognitive processing and the teachability of those processes than on the structure of abilities (Daniel, 1997). Essentially, the focus is on learning. Collectively, the trend toward conceptualizing humans as active, information processors suggests that more attention will be given to cognitive processing (e.g., self-efficacy measures) and process-oriented assessment.

Changing Nature of the Workforce

The workforce is becoming more diverse as racial and ethnic minority and cross-cultural representation increase across companies within the United States and multinational corporations increase across the world. Similar demographic shifts are also evident in educational institutions. Issues such as cultural sensitivity and sexual harassment have become more salient in the workplace and issues such as balance between home and work have become more salient to the workforce. Several recent publications discuss the impact of diversity in the workplace and how to better address and understand the career needs of different groups of people (Jackson &Associates, 1992; Leong, 1995; Savickas & Walsh, 1996; Triandis, Kurowski, & Gelfand, 1994; Walsh & Osipow, 1995).

Cross Cultural Transportability. One fundamental issue that impacts multicultural career assessment is cross-cultural applicability. Within cross-cultural research, there are two differing perspectives: cross-cultural psychology and cultural psychology (e.g., Greenfield, 1997; Leong & Brown, 1995). Cross-cultural psychology is concerned with discovering universals and cross-cultural variability, whereas cultural psychology questions these goals. For example, in an article on the cross-cultural applicability of ability assessments, Greenfield contrasts the two perspectives with the summary phrases "you can take it with you" and "you can't take it with you," respectively (p. 1115). From a cultural psychology perspective, assessment transportability rests on the standard of universality across values and meaning, knowing, and communication. If the standard is not met, then the test is not transportable across cultures. This view is associated with caution or even a reluctance to translate an instrument developed in one culture to another. From this perspective, a preferable alternative would be the development of an instrument by a team whose members represent the cultures in which the instrument would be used (Greenfield, 1997). Cross-cultural instrument development is an excellent idea that hopefully will appeal to those who have the resources to engage in such an endeavor.

In a practice that is more consistent with the cross-cultural psychology perspective, the reliability and validity of instruments and models developed in one culture have been examined in other cultures. Several key issues need to be examined when evaluating the cross cultural adequacy of instruments. Fouad (1993) discussed functional and conceptual equivalence of language, behaviors queried, and theoretical constructs. In addition, cultural and linguistic factors that might influence test administration and interpretation, such as differential response to counseling professionals or inadequate norms, need to be considered. Further, the impact or consequences of instrument use also needs to be evaluated. For example, the issue of adverse impact is a societal concern that extends well beyond psychometric equivalence.

With these considerations in mind, the utility and validity of numerous instruments have been examined across age, gender, and racial groups within the Unites States as well as across countries. It is not possible to provide a comprehensive summary in this chapter, but career counselors should refer to instrument manuals, as well as resources that summarize career research that is relevant to their clientele (e.g., Leong, 1995). Later in this chapter, we discuss measurement techniques that can and should be used in instrument development to better address issues of cross-cultural adequacy.

Workforce Values.   The changing nature of the workforce is also creating changes in the content of career assessment. For example, career assessment content that focuses exclusively on the work setting is often insufficient. Many people want to examine their values across multiple life roles. There also appears to be a heightened interest in finding a sense of meaning, balance, and spirituality through work (e.g., Bloch & Richmond, 1997). Retirement issues are becoming more salient for workers who are a part of the large baby boomer generation.

Within the work setting, the need and desire for diversity training has increased as the representation of people of different colors, cultures, ages, and sexual orientation have increased. For many people, topics such as respect for cultural differences and flextime are important considerations in evaluating a work environment, and contemporary work values assessment should represent current topics. Although not necessarily a function of the changing workforce, people are experiencing more stress (Rifkin, 1995), and this too is an important topic in career assessment (Osipow & Spokane, 1984). Violence in the workplace has also become a more salient issue (Davis, 1997), and instruments aimed at identifying violence potential or reducing violence are needed.

The changing workforce generates a full agenda for vocational researchers. The cultural and cross-psychology perspectives can inform instrument development and guide research on cross-cultural patterns in instrument administration and interpretation. Integrative research on racial identity development and career development and counseling would be informative, as would research that applies a multiple role perspective to individual difference variables, such as interests and values. Cross-disciplinary research that centers on spirituality and meaning in work and life could enhance our understanding of how vocational and theological concerns intersect. Further work on occupational stress and coping could improve our understanding of stress and how people react to it in the workplace. Finally, interdisciplinary collaboration could improve our understanding of career and human development, particularly older adult development.

TESTING STANDARDS, ETHICAL RESPONSIBILITIES

A number of detailed and well written professional standards serve as reference for professionals who engage in career assessment. The ethical codes of professional organizations whose members include career counselors (e.g., American Psychological Association, American Counseling Association) touch on issues of competent assessment practice. Further, guidelines such as *Standards for Educational and Psychological Testing* (1985), the National Career Development Association Standards (National Career Development Association, 1991), and *Responsible Test Use* (Eyde et al., 1993) have been specifically developed to address quality test development and competent use. Multidisciplinary organizations, such as the Fair Access Coalition to Testing, also advocate competency as the primary standard for determining test user qualification. Clearly, there is no shortage of written material or standards to guide professionals who practice assessment. However, criticism about test misuse continues, and because of the numerous tests and inventories now being published in popular magazines and on the Internet, confusion about propriety and criticism could escalate.

Anastasi (1992) articulated several reasons why tests are misused, including a desire for simple solutions and inadequate or outdated knowledge of testing and interpretation. She noted several common assessment hazards that can lead to misuse, including: acceptance of a single score, without considering the impact of error; acceptance of results from a single time period, without considering the impact of change; acceptance of a single indicator, without considering convergent evidence; and acceptance of precision, without considering evidence of reliability and validity. Career counselors need to be particularly aware of these hazards because they often encounter situations where these problems can occur. Such situations include group work that involves dealing with multiple people at once, personnel testing, and the use of narrative reports to facilitate interpretation. Collectively, these circumstances can lead to an over reliance on single scores or support materials whose development may not be fully understood. Professionals who engage in the practice of career assessment need a solid background in measurement theory. However, they may not be getting it. A survey of graduate programs found that emphasis on and training in measurement have declined considerably over the last 20 years (Aiken, West, Sechrest, & Reno, 1990). An academic degree may not be a sufficient indicator of assessment competence.

Anastasi (1992) ended her article on psychological assessment with the quote, "Just as old scores in the test taker's file need to be updated, so do old courses in the test user's educational history" (p. 614). Career counselors need continuing education. Although we could discuss a number of topics that impact competent career assessment, we focus on three areas where advances have generated a particular need to stay abreast of current knowledge: advances in measurement models and analyses, multicultural diversity, and proliferation of computer-based assessment.

EMERGING COMPETENCIES
AND QUANTITATIVE ADVANCES

Psychological testing is undergoing a significant change as many measurement specialists move from using classical test to modern test models. Classical test theory has been used to guide test development for decades, and it is often still the primary theory taught in measurement courses. However, modern test theory (sometimes referred to as item response theory or latent trait theory) offers a number of advantages over classical test theory (Hambleton & Slater, 1997; Mellenbergh, 1994), and in some instances, the rules of one theory do not apply to the other. Embretson (1996) describes why "old rules," which many of us learned in measurement class (e.g., the standard error of measurement applies to all scores in a particular population, longer tests are more reliable than shorter tests) are not applicable in modern test theory. These differences and the complexity of modern test theory make it difficult for many practitioners to effectively evaluate instruments developed using modern measurement models. Further, these differences may lead researchers to avoid using applications of modern test theory in their work.

The basic concepts of modern measurement theory are worth learning because the theory overcomes some of the shortcomings of classical test theory. In classical test theory, item statistics (e.g., item discrimination) and test information (e.g., reliability and validity) are dependent on the sample from which they were calculated. The confidence with which results can be generalized is dependent on the similarity between the instrument development samples and the intended interpretative samples. Modern test theory overcomes sample dependency, instead relying on mathematical model fitting. Item response theory assumes an item characteristic curve (S shape) relation between respondents at various levels of a psychological characteristic (e.g., intelligence) and the probability of answering an item in an affirmative direction (e.g., answering the item correctly). An item characteristic curve is estimated for each item. Information can be obtained about where an item maximally discriminates along the curve and the level of discrimination. This item information can then be used to develop instruments that provide more information and offer more precision than those developed using classical test theory statistics. The benefit of sample independence is particularly important as assessment tools are being used more frequently with an increasingly diverse population. Although item response theory was initially used almost exclusively in ability test development, applications outside of the ability domain are becoming more prevalent. For example, students' attitudes toward the teaching profession (Yu, 1991), a job interest index (Watanabe & Takahashi, 1994), and personality measures (Harvey & Thomas, 1996; Waller & Reise 1989) have been scaled using item response models.

Perhaps, the greatest applied benefit of modern test theory is that it is the foundation for computer adaptive testing. Computer adaptive testing uses item characteristic information to develop instruments that can be tailored to each individual. Using a branching procedure, individuals are presented with items that provide maximal information for them, thus eliminating the need for all respondents to answer all items. This procedure can considerably shorten the length of a test or inventory, and results can be calculated without delay. Further, computer adaptive testing is particularly useful for longitudinal measurement and determining intra- and interindividual differences (Weiss, 1995). This approach also offers standardized administrative procedures whose effect can easily be studied, as well as accessible items banks that can better address issues such as cross-cultural validity. For example, items that function differently across groups (e.g., racial groups) can be eliminated, thus reducing test bias.

In addition to measurement advances, statistical analyses used in test development are also becoming more sophisticated. For example, confirmatory factor analysis can be used to evaluate item–scale relations, the factor structure of theoretically based instruments, the equivalence of the factor structure across different groups (e.g., men and women), and the equivalence of scales from different instruments. There are also clear advantages to using a confirmatory factor model rather than a multitrait multimethod matrix to estimate validity (Cole 1987). To offer another example, cluster analysis has been used to develop a branching logic that allows for adaptive instrument administration (Laatsch & Choca, 1994). These techniques can improve career assessment and facilitate cross cultural applicability and multi-instrument assessment. However, to properly evaluate psychometric information that is based on techniques such as confirmatory factor analysis or cluster analysis, test users need to understand these methods, the assumptions that underlie the methods, and corresponding fit statistics. Again, level of sophistication is a double edged sword, offering more rigor and better ways to address issues such as validity generalization, but requiring a higher level of statistical literacy. It is somewhat troubling that new professionals are completing less quantitative course work than previous generations (Aiken et al., 1990), when they need more.

EMERGING COMPETENCIES AND MULTICULTURAL DIVERSITY

A second major issue related to career assessment competence is the ability to work effectively with persons from diverse backgrounds. As Fouad (1993) noted, counselors need to understand how cultural diversity affects vocational issues at all points in career development. Career assessment can play an important role in enhancing career development and the work environment, but counselors will need to be skilled in multicultural assessment. Ward and Bingham (1993) developed a multicultural career counseling checklist that counselors can use to assess their level of awareness when working with clients who are ethnically or racially different than themselves. Meara (1996) wrote about the importance of making implicit assumptions explicit. Healy (1990) emphasized the importance of collaborating with clients and suggested ways that would make traditional career appraisal a more collaborative endeavor. Over the last 10 years, standards for multicultural assessment have been published to guide counselor practice. One useful resource for counselors is an article, "Multicultural Assessment Standards: A Compilation for Counselors" (Prediger, 1994), which integrates multicultural assessment standards from several resources. As noted previously, a number of well-written chapters and articles on the career development of racial and ethnic minorities and multicultural vocational assessment have been published (Fouad, 1993; Leong, 1995; Leong & Brown, 1995; Subich, 1996). Although more research is needed, there are good resources available to career counselors. Further, some of the better manuals for career instruments now include chapters that specifically address cross-cultural research and use (e.g., Strong Interest Inventory; Harmon et al., 1994).

EMERGING COMPETENCIES
AND COMPUTER TECHNOLOGY

Computer applications, including test administration, scoring, and computer-generated feedback, are common in career assessment, and their popularity is growing. Computer technology will impact the practice of career assessment to a greater extent than any other single development over the next 10 years. The phenomenal speed with which the Internet is evolving makes possible what were once futuristic scenarios. For example, it is possible for a counselor to meet with a client via video-conferencing, have the client complete an assessment on-line, receive scored results, send the client narrative interpretative feedback, and discuss the results via videoconferencing. All aspects of this scenario are in use today, though they are not standard practice yet. Many major corporations are moving toward *intranet* (a network within an organization) assessment modules that are coordinated through the corporation's career center. Career counselors work with employees who have the option of completing assessment instruments in the privacy of their own office. Instruments can be scored, and the results accessed by the career counselors who provide interpretation and other needed services.

There are various levels of computer-assisted assessment, which range from test administration, to test scoring, to profile generation, to narrative interpretive report generation, to video disc-based generalized test interpretation (Sampson, 1995). Additionally, there are different levels of services, including *stand alone* computer systems that can be used without other guidance intervention, *supported* systems in which users are seen immediately before or after using the computer system, *incorporated* systems in which the computer system is used within another guidance intervention, and *Internet* applications that are available either to the general public or through restricted access (Sampson, 1997). Sampson (1990b) identified five trends in computer-assisted testing and assessment that are particularly relevant to counseling. These trends include computer-based test interpretation, computer-assisted instruction to guide assessments or interventions, integration of audiovisual media to create a multimedia presentation, adaptive devices to assist persons with disabilities, and computer-assisted research to monitor client responses or delivery of services.

In many ways, the standards for computer-based assessment materials are no different than those for paper-and-pencil materials. The difference is the added complexity associated with computer technology. Similar to paper-and-pencil instruments, the career counselor is concerned with appropriate use: Is this tool appropriate for this client? Will this tool help address the client's needs? Do I have the necessary information and training to use this tool? Counselors also need to weigh the cost of choosing not to use computer-based resources. When used properly, computer resources provide rapid and maximal access to clients, and they can help address the needs of people who might not otherwise be served. Overworked counselors and long waiting lists are barriers to an effective career center.

As a standard practice, psychometric qualities (reliability and validity estimates) need to be established for computer-based tests and inventories. This point seems obvious but is not always followed. Further, possible effects of placing an established paper-and-pencil instrument on a computer should be evaluated, much like a parallel form analysis. Similarly, narrative interpretive reports need to be validated, and the rationale and decision points used in development should be explicitly stated. Applications beyond intended use, such as giving clients narrative reports without benefit of counselor input, are inappropriate unless validated.

Although computer-assisted career guidance systems (CACGS) extend beyond career assessment, they have had a positive impact in the career field. All aspects of CACGS and associated applications need to be described and validated. These systems are complex, and many decisions are involved that relate to the occupational data base, the decision-making process, and conducting an effective computerized dialogue (Gati,

1996). These systems have the image of being faultless and precise (Sampson, 1986), but many human decisions influence what appears on the screen. Gati (1995, 1996) described the dilemmas and problems associated with CACGS, as well as some possible solutions.

A very recent trend is use of the Internet to facilitate career assessment. It is now possible to complete inventories and receive results via the Internet. Some well-known materials and respected inventories can be obtained through reputable publishers who follow guidelines for distribution and use of materials. Other inventories that can be found on the Internet are of questionable origin and validity. We have found instruments on the Internet that were advertised as useful career tools that could be completed and interpreted for a fee (payment via credit card). The quality of the instrument and the training and credentials of the person advertising the materials was often not presented. An attractive Website and instrument presentation can create a very misleading image of propriety and confuse consumers who may not understand the salience of psychometric quality and professional training. Career professionals need to be leaders in the effort to educate the public about inappropriate career assessment applications.

Recently, Sampson, Kolodinsky, and Greeno, (1997) described the possibilities and potential problems in the delivery of counseling services through the Information Highway. The Internet can be used to orient clients to career assessment, administer tests, transfer results to practitioners, and transmit scores, profiles, and interpretive reports to practitioners, or if appropriate, to clients. Self-help materials that address concerns such as career planning, career decision making, dealing with job stress, strategic career planning, dual career families, midlife career transitions, retirement planning, and leadership can be placed on the Internet for general public use. Links between self-help software and additional resources, such as occupational databases, career libraries, additional services, and referral resources, greatly expand the utility of self-help software. Sampson et al. (1997) also note that expert-based systems can be used to identify instances of problematic use, and in those circumstances helpful suggestions to the user can be made.

Relative to current paper-and-pencil assessment procedures, Internet applications offer streamlined processing. Purchases can be made electronically, mailing materials and postage are not necessary, and data collection for research or program evaluation can occur concurrently with administration. Internet applications will improve with technological advances such as the development of Internet2, a system that offers enhanced resolution capabilities and faster processing than the current Internet.

There are concerns about information confidentiality, privacy at the administration site, software validity, inadequate counselor intervention, misuse due to lack of training or knowledge, publisher credentials, inadequate attention to location–specific issues, and equality of access to high technology resources (Sampson et al., 1997; Sampson, 1998). Clearly, these are important issues that will require careful review because of ethical standards and competent practice. Recently, the National Board of Certified Counselors approved standards for counseling over the Internet, which is a controversial position (Morrissy, 1997). From a researcher's point of view, the Internet is an area rich with possibilities. Vocational researchers could apply their expertise in instrument development, psychometrics, assessment, and knowledge of career intervention process and outcome to this new frontier.

In summary, in the career assessment literature, little attention has been given to measurement advances and the impact they have on assessment. The impact of computer technology and resources on career assessment has been presented most extensively by Sampson and his colleagues (Sampson, 1990a, 1990b, 1995; Sampson, Kolodinsky, & Greeno, 1997), but this literature is still relatively small. The growing literature on cognitive career psychology and the career needs of minority groups is welcomed and can be further enhanced by knowledge of measurement and computer advances. There is a need for scholarship that integrates measurement advances with instrument development and assessment of special populations and examines computer advances and their impact on service delivery.

This chapter has identified various areas in which counselors need continuing education to competently perform their job. We now discuss self-directed career assessment, which may appear paradoxical after admonishing counselors about their need to "know more." How can a practice that is becoming more sophisticated also be moving toward increased public accessibility? The notion of career assessment as a public endeavor evokes mixed reactions with concerns about ethical propriety and public welfare on one side and the capability of reaching and benefiting many people on the other. The Internet and computer-assisted guidance systems are evolving, and computer use in homes, offices, schools, and public locations (e.g., libraries) is increasing. People will have more opportunities to engage in career assessment, there will be materials available to them, and there will be cases of abuse and misuse. Change will occur, and career professionals can help guide this evolution. Vocational researchers, career counselors, and test publishers can help to educate the public and legislators about appropriate instrument development, necessary testing standards, guidelines for appropriate use, contraindications for use, benefits and limitations of career assessment, and differences between self-help, psychoeducational, and career counseling interventions.

IMPLICATIONS FOR CAREER ASSESSMENT
AND COUNSELING

The practice of career assessment is at a crossroad. In one direction are career counselors who are trying to synthesize a wealth of information about measurement advances, research, practice relevant to specific populations and new technologies that can facilitate their work. In the other direction is self directed career assessment, which is not new, but is more readily accessible to a population that is more ready than previous generations to use it. This crossroad does not need to be divergent. It simply reflects the emergence of career assessment as a practice that coincides with counseling but is not always is a part of counseling.

Several authors have articulated the importance of integrating career assessment into counseling (e.g., Subich & Billingsley, 1995). At issue is the choice between conceptual models to guide assessment practice, the relationship between counselor and client, and practice behaviors that are sensitive to an increasingly diverse population. Theories of career development and adjustment have changed over the last 10 years. Contextual developmentalism (Savickas, 1989), social cognitive learning theory (Lent, Brown, & Hackett, 1994), and person–environment fit theories (Chartrand, Strong, & Weitzman, 1995) all assume that people actively engage their environments. The cultural context has been granted a much more prominent place in current theories and models than in older ones, though knowledge of contextual constructs is still limited. Basically, many practitioners are informed by theories that subscribe to a philosophy of human agency, acknowledge a broad range of environmental influences that can impact career cognitions and behavior, and acknowledge the importance of development and growth. Both the content and process of career assessment have changed accordingly, such as the development of self efficacy measures and collaborative assessment models (Borgen & Harmon, 1995; Healy, 1990). A growing career literature on ethnic and racial minorities, gay and lesbians, people in midlife and beyond, and people with disabilities can be used to inform administration and interpretation processes. In general, assessment models now emphasize collaborative counselor–client relations and attention to client applicability.

IMPLICATIONS FOR CAREER ASSESSMENT
AND RESEARCH

Test interpretation has a beneficial impact on people. However, Tinsley and Chu (1999) reviewed over 40 years of research on test interpretation outcomes and came to a startling conclusion: There is not a significant body of evidence to support the efficacy of test interpretation. Their conclusion bears some similarity to Eysenck's (1952) challenge of psychotherapy efficacy, and hopefully, it will generate a similar response among researchers. Tinsley and Chu's review of the test interpretation outcome literature revealed relatively few studies and very few methodologically sound studies. They identified a number of methodological problems, such as flawed criteria, only immediate follow-up, lack of random assignment, and lack of a control group. Collectively, these factors limit conclusions that can be drawn from test interpretation outcome studies. The lack of conclusive data that explicitly supports the use of testing in career guidance and counseling is an obvious problem that requires immediate attention. Tinsley and Chu offer a number of useful suggestions to guide future researchers who want to address this understudied domain.

Assessment service delivery models need to be examined in light of the rapid change in career assessment procedures. First, we need to critically examine the effects of career assessment on targeted outcomes. As Tinsley and Chu revealed, we cannot assume that career assessment interventions are effective. With this caveat in mind, there needs to be an examination of different ways in which career assessment can be administered and interpreted (e.g., across different levels of counselor intervention) with different clients (e.g., high vs. low vocational identity). The CACGS have been studied fairly extensively (see Gati, 1996), but other career assessment software and Internet applications have not. At a broader level, program evaluation research, within which career assessment is a major component, is needed. Reardon's (1996) program and cost analysis of a self-directed career decision-making program is a model for this type of research.

Changes within cognitive psychology are impacting career assessment. Theories about intelligence are shifting to include practical and emotional intelligence; measurement efforts are expanding to include cognitive processing (e.g., problem-solving processes, training and skill acquisition). Career professionals need to be aware of the shifts within cognitive psychology and the advancing knowledge that incorporates new constructs in vocational research. Basic questions include construct representation and overlap among interests, personality styles, cognitive styles, and practical intelligence. We need to estimate the degree to which cognitive style and practical intelligence are predictive of educational–work adjustment or performance measures. We need to know whether cognitive constructs can be incorporated to improve theories and further our knowledge within domains such as career readiness or career decision making. We also need to learn how to actively study and measure the cognitive processes that are embedded within career process and outcome research studies.

Research that seeks to understand commonalities across the domains of interests, values, personality, and intellectual capabilities offers a potent paradigm for vocational research. There is clear evidence that commonalities exist and that they can be described within framework that is useful in career assessment. Ackerman and Heggestad (1997) reported that Holland's Social and Enterprising theme scores are associated with personality scales of extroversion, social potency, and well-being. This type of research and level of integration is neither new nor novel (Gottfredson et al., 1993; Holland et al., 1994). However, they also engaged in integrative and meta analytic research and identified four trait complexes that include abilities, interests, and personality traits: Social, Clerical–Conventional, Science–Math, and Intellectual–Cultural. The Intellectual–Cultural complex, for example, includes Investigative and Artistic interests, the personality trait of absorption, and intellectual factors of ideational fluency (crystallized intelligence) and openness (traditional intellectual engagement). This type of effort helps to establish structures within which career relevant factors, such as personality traits and interests, can be studied. This effort should improve prediction of career choice and work adjustment. This type of research may also facilitate efforts to link person and environment measures. For example, occupational choice (often occupational title coded according to Holland type) is an inexact criterion measure. A more precise measure would directly address trait complexes associated with job tasks. Thus, the criterion measures could shift from job title to trait complex-defined job skills–activities. This shift would be consistent with the changing nature of the workplace. Measurement advances within vocational psychology can also draw upon integrative interdomain research and assessment models (Lowman, 1993). Cross instrument multiscale assessment, which could be accomplished via computer adaptive testing, offers test users an efficient way to assess characteristics that are most pertinent for their given situation. In theory, scales from different measures (e.g., interests, personality, ability, and values) could be selected to form an individually–tailored assessment battery. This type of assessment must meet measurement model assumptions and requires careful validation and a better understanding of construct or trait complex relatedness. However, it is a very promising area for future research.

SUMMARY

Career assessment is a popular practice that is evolving to meet changes in the workplace and the workforce. The domains of abilities, interests, values, career decision making and career development continue to be salient. However, these domains are expanding to include multiple role perspectives and "soft" skills language. Personality, cognitive style, and emotional intelligence measures are likely to become more popular. Similarly, more attention will be paid to the cross-cultural applicability these assessment measures.

The career assessment process is filled with questions as the major stakeholders try to determine the appropriate type and level of service delivery for different test users. At a more basic level, the effectiveness of test interpretation for different clientele must be firmly established through well-designed research studies. Emerging computer capabilities are creating a flux within the field of career assessment that will require both ethical and research consideration. Career assessment can be a part of career counseling, but it can also stand alone. There is a trend toward self-directed assessment and the use of career assessment for personal or organizational development. Career professionals have the opportunity to add new roles to their current responsibilities and updated knowledge of measurement advances, cultural diversity, and computer technology will help them develop new skills. At the dawn of the twenty first century, career assessment is an evolving practice that reflects the progress, diversity, and challenges of the Information Age.

REFERENCES

Ackerman, P. L., & Heggestad, E. D. (1997). Intelligence, personality, and interests: Evidence for overlapping traits. *Psychological Bulletin, 121*, 219–245.
Aiken, L. S., West, S. G., Sechrest, L., & Reno, R. R. (1990). Graduate training in statistics, methodology and measurement in psychology. *American Psychologist, 45*, 721–734.
Anastasi, A. (1992). What counselors should know about the use and interpretation of psychological tests. *Journal of Counseling and Development, 70*, 610–615.2.
Bar-On, R. (1996). *The Emotional Quotient Inventory (EQ-I): A test of emotional intelligence.* Toronto, Canada: Multi-Health Systems.
Betz, N. E. (1992). Career assessment: A review of critical issues. In S. D. Brown & R. W. Lent (Eds.), *Handbook of counseling psychology* (2nd ed., pp. 453–484). New York: Wiley.
Bloch, D. P., & Richmond, L. J. (Eds.). (1997). *Connections between spirit & work in career development.* Palo Alto, CA: Davies-Black.
Borgen, F. H., & Harmon, L. W. (1995). Linking interest assessment and personality theory: An example of convergence between practice and theory. In M. L. Savickas & W. B. Walsh (Eds.), *Handbook of career counseling theory and practice* (pp. 251–266). Palo Alto, CA: Davies-Black.
Chartrand, J. M., Strong, S. R., & Weitzman, L. M. (1995). The interactional perspective in vocational psychology: Paradigms, theories, and research practices. In W. B. Walsh & S. H. Osipow (Eds.), *Handbook of vocational psychology: Theory, research, and pracice* (2nd ed., pp. 35–66). Mahwah, NJ: Lawrence Erlbaum Associates.
Cole, D. A. (1987). Confirmatory factor analysis in test validation research. *Journal of Consulting and Clinical Psychology, 55*, 584–594.
Crites, J. O. (1981). *Career counseling: Models, methods, and materials.* New York: McGraw-Hill.
Daniel, M. H. (1997). Intelligence testing: Status and trends. *American Psychologist, 52*, 1038–1045.

Davis, D. A. (Ed.). (1997). *Threats pending fuses burning: Managing workplace violence*. Palo Alto, CA: Davies-Black.

Day, S. X., & Rounds, J. (1997). A little more than kin, and less than kin: Basic interests in vocational research and career counseling. *The Career Development Quarterly, 45,* 207–221.

Drucker, P. (1994). The age of social transformation. *The Atlantic Monthly, 275*(5), 53–80.

Embretson, S. E. (1996). The new rules of measurement. *Psychological Assessment, 8,* 341–349.

Eyde, L. D., Robertson, G. J., Krug, S. E., Moreland, K. L., Robertson, A. G., Shewan, C. M., Harrison, P. L., Porch, B. E., Hammer, A. L., & Primoff, E. S. (1993). *Responsible test use: Case studies for assessing human behavior*. Washington, DC: American Psychological Association.

Eysenck, H. J. (1952). The effects of psychotherapy: An evaluation. *Journal of Consulting Psychology, 16,* 319–324.

Fouad, N. (1993). Cross-cultural vocational assessment. *Career Development Quarterly, 42,* 4–13.

Gati, I. (1995). Computer-assisted career counseling: Dilemmas, problems and possible solutions. *Journal of Counseling and Development, 73,* 51–56.

Gati, I. (1996). Computer-assisted career counseling: Challenges and prospects. In M. L. Savickas & W. B. Walsh (Eds.), *Handbook of career counseling: Theory and practice*. Palo Alto, CA: Davies-Black.

Goleman, D. (1994). *Emotional Intelligence*. New York: Bantam Books.

Gottfredson, G. D., Jones, E. M., & Holland, J. L. (1993). Personality and vocational interests: The relation of Holland's interest dimensions to five robust dimensions of personality. *Journal of Counseling Psychology, 40,* 518–524.

Greenfield, P. M. (1997). You can't take it with you: Why ability assessments don't cross cultures. *American Psychologist, 52,* 1115–1124.

Hackett, G., & Watkins, C. E., Jr. (1995). Research in career assessment: Abilities, interests, decision making, and career development. In W. B. Walsh & S. H. Osipow (Eds.), *Handbook of vocational psychology: Theory, research, and practice* (2nd ed.). Mahwah, NJ: Lawrence Erlbaum Associates.

Hambleton, R. K., & Slater, S. C. (1997). Item response theory models and testing practices: Current international status and future directions. *European Journal of Psychological Assessment, 13,* 21–28.

Harkness, H. (1997). *The career chase: Taking creative control in a chaotic age*. Palo Alto, CA: Davies-Black.

Harmon, L. W., Hansen, J. C., Borgen, F. H., & Hammer, A. L. (1994). *Strong Interest Inventory: Applications and technical guide*. Palo Alto, CA: Consulting Psychologists Press.

Harvey, R. J., & Thomas, L. (1996). Using item response theory to score the Myers-Briggs Type Indicator: Rationale and research findings. *Journal of Psychological Type, 37,* 16–60.

Healy, C. C. (1990). Reforming career appraisals to meet the needs of clients in the 1990s. *The Counseling Psychologist, 18,* 214–226.

Holland, J. L. (1985). *Making vocational choices: A theory of vocational personalities and work environments* (2nd ed.). Englewood Cliffs, NJ: Prentice-Hall.

Holland, J. L. (1996). Exploring careers with a typology: What we have learned and some new directions. *American Psychologist, 51,* 397–406.

Holland, J. L., Johnston, J. A., & Asama, N. F. (1994). More evidence for the relationship between Holland's personality types and personality variables. *Journal of Career Assessment, 18,* 91–100.

Jackson, S. E., & Associates (1992). *Diversity in the workplace: Human resources initiatives*. New York: Guilford Press.

Johansson, C. B. (1986). *Career Assessment Inventory: The enhanced version*. Minneapolis, MN: National Computer Systems.

Kanter, R. M. (1991, May–June). Transcending business boundaries: 12,000 world managers view change. *Harvard Business Review, 69*, 3.

Kapes, J. T., & Mastie, M. M. (Eds.). (1988). *A counselor's guide to career assessment instruments* (2nd ed.). Alexandria, VA: National Career Development Association.

Kelley, R., & Caplan, J. (1993, July–August). How Bell Labs creates star performers. *Harvard Business Review*.

Kuder, F., & Zytowski, D. G. (1991). *Kuder Occupational Interest Survey Form DD general manual* (3rd ed.). Monterey, CA: CTB: Macmillan/McGraw-Hill.

Laatsch, L., & Choca, J. (1994). Cluster-branching methodology for adaptive testing and the development of the adaptive category test. *Psychological Assessment, 6*, 001–007.

Leong, F. T. L. (Ed.). (1995). *Career development and vocational behavior of racial and ethnic minorities*. Mahwah, NJ: Lawrence Erlbaum Associates.

Leong, F. T. L., & Brown, M. T. (1995). Theoretical issues in cross-cultural career development: Cultural validity and cultural specificity. In W. B. Walsh & S. H. Osipow, *Handbook of vocational psychology: Theory, research, and practice* (2nd ed., pp. 143–180). Mahwah, NJ: Lawrence Erlbaum Associates.

Lowman, R. L. (1993). The inter-domain model of career assessment and counseling. *Journal of Counseling and Development, 71*, 549–554.

Meara, N. M. (1996). Prudence and career assessment: Making our implicit assumptions explicit. In M. L. Savickas & W. B. Walsh, *Handbook of career counseling: Theory and practice* (pp. 315–330). Palo Alto, CA: Davies-Black.

Mellenbergh, G. J. (1994). Generalized linear item response theory. *Psychological Bulletin, 115*, 300–307.

Morrissy, M. (1997, November). NBCC webcounseling standards unleash intense debate. *Counseling Today*, p. 6.

National Career Development Association. (1991). National Career Development Association Ethical Standards. *Career Developments, 1*, 18–20.

Neisser, U. (1979). The concept of intelligence. In R. J. Sternberg & D. K. Detterman (Eds.), *Human intelligence: Perspectives on its theory and measurement* (pp. 179–189). Norwood, NJ: Ablex.

Osipow, S. H. (1980). Toward counseling psychology in the year 2000. *The Counseling Psychologist, 8*, 18–20.

Osipow, S. H. (1991). Observations about career psychology. *Journal of Vocational Behavior, 39*, 291–296.

Osipow, S. H., & Spokane, A. R. (1984). Measuring occupational stress, strain, and coping. In S. Oskamp (Ed.), *Applied social psychology annual* (Vol. 5, pp. 67–86). Beverly Hills, CA: Sage.

Peters, T. (1992). *Liberation management*. New York: Fawcett.

Prediger, D. J. (1994). Multicultural assessment standards: A compilation for counselors. *Measurement and Evaluation in Counseling and Development, 27*, 68–73.

Reardon, R. (1996). A program and cost analysis of a self-directed career decision-making program in a university career center. *Journal of Counseling & Development, 74*, 280–287.

Rifkin, J. (1995). *The end of work: The decline of the global labor force and the dawn of the post-market era*. New York: G. P. Putnam's Sons.

Rogers, T. B. (1995). *The psychological testing enterprise: An introduction*. Pacific Grove, CA: Brooks/Cole.

Rounds, J., & Day, S. X. (1999). Describing, evaluating, and creating vocational interest structures. In M. L. Savickas & A. R. Spokane (Eds.), *Vocational interests: Their meaning, measurement and use in counseling*. Palo Alto, CA: Davies-Black.

Sampson, J. P., Jr. (1986). Computer technology and counseling psychology: Regression toward the machine? *The Counseling Psychologist, 14*, 567–583.

Sampson, J. P., Jr. (1990a). Computer-assisted testing and the goals of counseling psychology. *The Counseling Psychologist, 18*, 227–239.

Sampson, J. P., Jr. (1990b). Ethical use of computer applications in counseling: Past, present, and future perspectives. In L. Golden & B. Herlihy (Eds.), *Ethical standards casebook* (4th ed., pp. 170–176). Alexandria, VA: American Association for Counseling and Development.

Sampson, J. P., Jr. (1995). Computer-assisted testing in counseling and therapy. *Eric Digest*. (EDO-CG-95-26).

Sampson, J. P., Jr. (1997). Ethical delivery of computer-assisted guidance services: Supported vs. stand-alone system use. In R. C. Reardon (Chair), *Ethical issues in using computers to deliver career services: Counseling intervention, equality of access, and the Internet*. Paper presented at the National Career Development Association Conference, Daytona Beach, FL.

Sampson, J. P., Jr. (1998). The Internet as a potential force for social change. In C. C. Lee & G. R. Walz (Eds.), *Social action: A mandate for counselors* (pp. 213–225). Greensboro, NC: University of North Carolina at Greensboro [ERIC Clearinghouse on Counseling and Student Services].

Sampson, J. P., Jr., Kolodinsky, R. W., & Greeno, B. P. (1997). Counseling on the information highway: Future possibilities and potential problems. *Journal of Counseling and Development, 75*, 203–212.

Saveri, A. (1991). The realignment of workers and work in the 1990s. In J. M. Kummerow's *New directions in career planning and the workplace: Practical strategies for counselors* (pp. 117–154). Palo Alto, CA: Davies-Black.

Savickas, M. L. (1989). Annual review: Practice and research in career counseling and development, 1988. *Career Development Quarterly, 38*(2), 100–134.

Seligman, L. (1994). *Developmental career counseling and assessment* (2nd ed.). Thousand Oaks, CA: Sage.

Spokane, A. R. (1991). *Career intervention*. Englewood Cliffs, NJ: Prentice-Hall.

Standards for Educational and Psychological Testing. (1985). Washington, DC: American Psychological Association.

Strong Interest Inventory (1994). Stanford University. Palo Alto, CA: Consulting Psychologists Press.

Sternberg, R. J. (1997a). Introduction to the special issue on intelligence and lifelong learning. *American Psychologist, 52*, 1029.

Sternberg, R. J. (1997b). The concept of intelligence and its role in lifelong learning and success. *American Psychologist, 52*, 1030–1037.

Sternberg, R. J., & Grigorenko, E. L. (1997). Are cognitive styles still in style? *American Psychologist, 52*, 700–712.

Strong E. K., Jr. (1927). *Vocational Interest Blank*. Stanford, CA: Stanford University Press.

Strong Interest Inventory. (1994). Stanford University. Palo Alto, CA: Consulting Psychologists Press.

Subich, L. M., & Billingsley, K. D. (1995). Integrating career assessment into counseling. In W. B. Walsh & S. H. Osipow (Eds.), *Handbook of vocational psychology: Theory, research, and practice* (2nd ed., pp. 261–294). Mahwah, NJ: Lawrence Erlbaum Associates.

Subich, L. M. (1996). Addressing diversity in the process of career assessment. In M. L. Savickas & W. B. Walsh (Eds.), *Handbook of career counseling: Theory and practice* (pp. 277–291). Palo Alto, CA: Davies-Black.

Tinsley, H. E. A., & Chu, S. (1999). Research test and interest inventory interpretation outcomes. In M. L. Savickas & A. R. Spokane (Eds.), *Vocational interests: Their meaning, measurement, and use in counsleing*. Palo Alto, CA: Davies-Black.

Tokar, D. M., & Swanson, J. L. (1995). Evaluation of the correspondence between Holland's vocational personality typology and the five-factor model of personality. *Journal of Vocational Behavior, 46*, 89–108.

Triandis, H. C., Kurowski, L. L., & Gelfand, M. J. (1994). Workplace diversity. In H. C. Triandis, M. D. Dunnette, & L. M. Hough (Eds.), *Handbook of industrial and organizational psychology, 4* (2nd ed., pp. 769–827). Palo Alto, CA: Consulting Psychologist Press.

U.S. Department of Labor, Employment and Training Administration. (1991). *Dictionary of occupational titles* (4th ed.). Washington, DC: U.S. Government Printing Office.

Wagner, R. K. (1997). Intelligence, training, and employment. *American Psychologist, 52,* 1059–1069.

Waller, N. G., Lykken, D. T., & Tellegen, A. (1995). Occupational interests, leisure time interests, and personality: Three domains or one? Findings from the Minnesota Twin registry. In D. Lubinski & R. V. Dawis (Eds.), *Assessing individual differences in human behavior: New concepts, methods, and findings* (pp. 233–260). Palo Alto, CA: Davies-Black.

Waller, N. G., & Reise, S. P. (1989). Computerized adaptive personality assessment: An illustration with the absorption scale. *Journal of Personality and Social Psychology, 57,* 1051–1058.

Walsh, W. B., & Betz, N. E. (1995). *Tests and assessments* (3rd ed.). Englewood Cliffs, NJ: Prentice-Hall.

Walsh, W. B., & Osipow, S. H. (1995). *Handbook of vocational psychology: Theory, research, and practice.* Mahwah, NJ: Lawrence Erlbaum Associates.

Ward, C. M., & Bingham. R. P. (1993). Career assessment of ethnic minority women. *Journal of Career Assessment, 1,* 476–486.

Watanabe, N., & Takahashi, K. (1994). *A development of a job interest index by item response theory: Based on Japanese samples.* Paper presented at the 23rd International Congress of Applied Psychology, Madrid, Spain.

Waterman, R. H., Jr., Waterman, J., & Collard, B. (1994, July/August). "Toward a Career-Resilent Workforce." *Harvard Business Review.*

Watkins, C. E., Jr., & Campbell, V. L. (Eds.). (1990). *Testing in counseling practice.* Hillsdale, NJ: Lawrence Erlbaum Associates.

Weiss, D. J. (1995). Improving individual differences measurement with item response theory and computerized adaptive testing. In D. Lubinski & R. V. Dawis (Eds.), *Assessing individual differences in human behavior: New concepts, methods, and findings* (pp. 49–80). Palo Alto, CA: Davies-Black.

Williamson, E. G. (1939). *How to counsel students.* New York: McGraw-Hill.

Yu, J. (1991). Developing a professional attitude scale for teachers, school students. *Proceedings of the International Academic Symposium on Psychological Measurement,* Peking, China.

Chapter 10

Career Counseling:
The Evolution of Theory

Linda Mezydlo Subich
Kelly Simonson
The University of Akron

In 1994, in his role as a discussant for the career theory and convergence project, Osipow noted the need in vocational psychology for a theory (or multiple theories) of career counseling. He stated that the practice of career counseling would be advanced with the creation of such theory. In 1996, in a similar commentary on the convergence of career theory and practice, Osipow suggested that some progress had been made in this endeavor, but that the difficulty inherent in trying to define and research career counseling may stand in the way of real progress for some time to come. In these two commentaries, Osipow highlighted the essential dilemma that confronts the practitioner of career counseling—what is to guide one's practice?

In the past, practitioners relied on career development theory. For example, in the 1973 edition of his classic text entitled *Theories of Career Development*, Osipow discussed the role of theory in vocational psychology practice and suggested that practitioners operating without an explicit theoretical orientation are handicapped in their ability to plan and carry out effective interventions for their clients. In this text, however, no theories of career counseling were provided, only brief sections at the end of each theory which outlined ideas regarding that theory's implications for practice. The conclusion to be drawn from this structure was that counselors would find traditional career development theories useful in their practice. In revisions of this text, Osipow (1983) and Osipow and Fitzgerald (1996) expanded the practice focus of the text by including a chapter

257

that consisted of a piecemeal presentation of the research literature on the components of career counseling practice and outcome, rather than presentation of a coherent theory of career counseling.

If one does not consider the "after the fact" implications for practice that characterize the ends of chapters in many career theory texts, such piecemeal approaches (at times termed *technical eclecticism*) are perhaps the most common approach taken by vocational psychologists to conceptualizing career counseling practice (e.g., Phillips, 1992). In a review of the literature on career counseling, Phillips identified five components of the "ideal" situation of "problem-free choosing" and then presented relevant theory and practice literature for each component in an attempt to guide intervention. Although she cautioned at the outset that the components are likely interwoven in practice, her presentation facilitated discrete thinking about them. Unfortunately, however, no coherent theory of career counseling was available to Phillips to serve as a framework for presentation of the literature.

As the issue of how to integrate career theory and practice has been debated at conferences and in print (e.g., Savickas & Walsh, 1996), it has become clearer that many professionals believe that trying to adapt current theory to practice does not serve adequately the purposes of the field in terms of either science or practice. The call for the development of theories of career counseling has become the anthem of the field. In this chapter, we trace the evolution of some early models of career counseling, outline three newly proposed theories of career counseling, and sketch out the possibilities for the future refinement of the latter based on postmodern critiques and recent research. Our differentiation between early models and emergent theories of career counseling is based on what we interpret to be differences in linearity and the extent of focus on environmental/social/emotional factors, diagnosis, counseling process and client empowerment. Emergent theories are those that suggest a potentially nonlinear process of career counseling and development and that recognize the importance of environmental/social/emotional factors, counseling process and client empowerment.

MODELS OF CAREER COUNSELING

Since the 1980s, a number of models of career counseling have been proposed. Typically, they are presented as chapters in textbooks or edited volumes, and they represent a logical synthesis of accepted wisdom regarding effective career counseling techniques. A representative selection of these models is presented and reviewed here.

Crites' (1981) Comprehensive Career Counseling Model

An early model of career counseling is that of John Crites (1981). In his book, Crites summarized career counseling interventions from various approaches and then proposed his own Comprehensive Career Counseling approach, which draws from five other orientations. His Comprehensive approach begins with diagnostic testing and interviews. Through diagnosis, the counselor seeks to identify the discrepancies between a client's career choice and his or her aptitudes and interests. Indecision and unrealism are seen as the two main sources of discrepancy, which Crites referred to as the *differential diagnosis*. The counselor then seeks to identify the causes of the problem (the *dynamic diagnosis*). The client's career maturity is also assessed (the *decisional diagnosis*).

Crites proposed that the counselor and the client next work together at the task of problem clarification and specification. The collaborative aspect of this work is intended to counteract the dependence of the undecided client and the defensiveness of the unrealistic clients. Crites' Comprehensive approach includes three main career counseling methods or areas of focus. The first method is *interviewing* in which problem exploration is best facilitated by a non-directive counselor who later interprets client responses in an effort to clarify the causes of the client's problem. In the end stages of counseling, interviewing may involve the counselor using trait-factor and behaviorist approaches of reviewing solutions and reinforcing choices made. The second counseling method is *test interpretation* which helps diagnose the client's problem. When tests are interpreted to the client, Crites emphasized that they should be communicated within the client's frame of reference and should not use psychometric jargon. The third focus is *occupational information* which Crites felt often was ignored in other approaches. Clients are made responsible for gathering occupational information outside of the counseling sessions. This model was presented by Crites as a first approximation of a system of career counseling designed to be applicable to all possible combinations of clients and counselors in both individual and group counseling situations.

Yost and Corbishley's (1987) Eight-Stage Process of Career Counseling

A few years later, Yost and Corbishley (1987) proposed a composite of current decision making models and career counseling processes to describe an eight stage process of career counseling. The authors stated that most clients complete the stages in order, but at times stages may shift position or overlap. Different clients also were conceptualized as moving through stages at their own rate. With these parameters as context, Yost and Corbishley termed the first stage the *initial assessment*. It is characterized by the counselor explaining career counseling and the client's role in the process. Information is gathered about the client's personal and employment history. Then, the client and counselor collaborate to develop a feasible career counseling goal and possibly decide upon a time frame for reaching this goal.

At the second stage, *self-understanding*, the client explores personal values, interests, experiences, and abilities that he or she feels relate to his or her goal. Assessment of psychological issues that may affect career counseling is done at this point. Then, the information that has been gathered is synthesized into a coherent set of statements about the client's desired outcomes for a career choice, termed *making sense of self-understanding data*. These statements are used as a reference point for future stages of counseling. Personal and environmental barriers to pursuing the client's desired career also are summarized.

The fourth stage is labeled *generating alternatives*. A list of possible career alternatives is developed. Judgments about the value of the alternatives are withheld at this point. At the fifth stage *obtaining occupational information*, an informed choice is made. The client learns as much as possible about each career alternative, and he or she narrows the list of career options. He or she then *makes a choice* concerning career options. This choice may be difficult, and it is recognized that various psychological problems may arise and need to be dealt with before effective counseling can continue.

The seventh stage is termed *making plans*. As the client makes plans to reach his or her career choice goal, contingency plans also may be made. Finally, the client takes the action necessary to achieve the selected career goal, *implementing plans*. Yost and Corbishley (1987) present no data to support the validity or utility of this model, but both may be inferred by the fact that the various stages are derived from prior literature on components of effective career decision making.

Peterson, Sampson, and Reardon's (1991) Cognitive Information Processing Model

In 1991, Peterson, Sampson, and Reardon took an information-processing approach and proposed a seven-step counseling sequence to guide clients through career-related problem solving and decision making. The initial interview comprises their first step; in it, the counselor gains qualitative information about five different aspects of the context of the client's career problem. First, the "gap," or dissonance between the perception of an existing state of reality and the mental representation of an ideal state (i.e., the difference between what exists and what ought to exist), is assessed. Next, the "complexity of the ambiguous cues" surrounding the career problem is determined; clients must clarify and differentiate between the cognitive and affective states that may complicate their career problems. Recognition that there is no one right answer is termed *interdependent courses of action*, and this is a third contextual characteristic of career problems that is examined. Given that there is no one right career choice for every client, "uncertainty of the outcome" of career counseling must be acknowledged by counselor and client; change can happen, but the career counseling process involves taking risks and making an effort. Finally, choices may be deemed optimal at the time of a decision, but may become less so at a subsequent vantage point; thus, clients' "problem solving and decision-making skills" provide a final important background factor to assess.

Subsequent to the previous contextual assessment is the second step of "preliminary assessment" that involves the client completing a screening instrument that gives the counselor quantitative information about client problems such as vocational identity, career maturity, indecision, career beliefs, decision-making style, or occupational certainty. This is followed by a third step of "defining the problem and analyzing causes" in which a preliminary understanding is gained of the client's problem in terms of the gap between the client's reality and ideal state, as well as possible causes for the gap.

Next, the counselor and client together develop a set of attainable counseling goals to remove the gap (i.e., *formulate goals*) and an "individual learning plan (ILP)" is developed. The goals help the client develop the ILP and help identify resources and activities necessary for the client to attain these goals. The ILP is flexible and is modified with the addition of any new data. The ILP is used to monitor and guide the career counseling process. For each counseling goal, the counselor lists planned activities and their purpose and then prioritizes them. Many learning activities in the ILP are in the form of instructional modules that may include a set of objectives, a self-administered diagnostic test and progress assessments, alternative learning activities, and a self-administered summary assessment.

The sixth step is to "execute the ILP." This is done with the counselor providing encouragement, information, clarification, reinforcement, and planning for future experiences. Information processing domains of *knowledge* (i.e., self-knowledge of interests, abilities, and values and occupational knowledge about individual occupations and the structural relationships among occupations); *decision skills* (i.e., problem awareness, analysis of the problem cause, synthesis of all possible courses of action, elimination of obviously inconsistent options, evaluation and prioritization of courses of action according to its likelihood of success or failure and its probable impact on self and others and execution of a course of action); and *executive processing* (i.e., metacognitions of self-talk, self-awareness, and control and monitoring) are assessed to formulate and execute effectively a client's ILP and counseling goals. Step seven involves a "summative review and generalization" during which the counselor and client discuss the client's progress toward meeting the counseling goals. If the goals were met, they discuss applying this problem-solving approach to future career problems. If the goals were not met, they go back to Step three and redefine the problem and formulate goals. This complex process incorporates much of the content mentioned in previous models but embeds it in an information-processing framework that provides explanatory power for understanding how the process occurs. That framework also provides a research base for this model.

Spokane's (1991) Career Intervention Process

Taking a very different approach, Spokane (1991) presented a career counseling model with three major phases (beginning, activation, and termination) and eight subphases (opening, aspiring, loosening, assessment, inquiry, commitment, execution, and follow-through). The *beginning phase* consists of the *opening*, *aspiring*, and *loosening* subphases. The *opening* subphase's main therapeutic tasks involve establishing the therapeutic context, including setting expectations and providing some structuring about what will and will not occur in counseling. The *aspiring* subphase uses fantasy to help clients rehearse their career aspirations, dreams, and goals. During the *loosening* subphase, clients begin to uncover or identify conflicts that their aspirations create and may relive previous painful compromises or old hurts and failures. Clients may come to realize the full complexity and intractability of their career problem. As assessment procedures continue, the incongruence between the client's interests, abilities, and aspirations and the demands of a client's current job become clearer, and the client may become anxious as he or she sees that counseling may require a difficult realignment of his or her past beliefs about what is appropriate or possible to achieve.

Spokane's (1991) "activation phase" consists of the *assessment*, *inquiry* and *commitment* subphases. During this phase, the counselor becomes more active and cognitive in order to help the client see incongruencies between interests, abilities, and personality and the requirements of specific jobs. Counselor support is important during this phase, especially given that clients' anxiety levels tend to increase, and traditional career counseling models tend to become less structured. At the *assessment* subphase, the client receives feedback from assessment inventories and begins to form hypotheses about what jobs may fit him or her and may be accessible. The principal therapeutic task is to help the client form a cognitive structure that allows him or her to evaluate explored occupations. The *inquiry* subphase involves both the counselor and the client engaging in hypothesis testing and changing based on behavioral changes seen in the client. Finally, during the *commitment* subphase, the client must compromise unrealistic aspirations and prepare for the execution of an interim career choice. A substantial reduction in state anxiety level is necessary before this subphase can be successfully completed. Anxiety may peak as conflicts or environmental barriers become apparent, and clients fear they will be unable to execute a reasonably fitting option for themselves. At that point, counselors may have to admit that some of the client's fears about barriers may be valid but then must attempt to engage the client in constructive behaviors to overcome external barriers.

The last phase is the *completion phase* and includes the *execution* and *follow-through* subphases. Spokane (1991), however, does not describe these subphases. The completion phase begins when the client has resolved his or her presenting conflicts sufficiently to engage in constructive emotions, attitudes, and behaviors leading to a satisfactory career choice. Spokane notes that some clients may resist termination and engage in resistant behaviors and these issues must be addressed by the counselor. Spokane's model focuses more on the emotional experience of clients with career issues and the process of career counseling than previous ones. He incorporates these foci into a model that also attends to more traditional career counseling foci (e.g., occupational aspirations, assessment, information).

Isaacson and Brown's (1993) Career Counseling Model

Finally, Isaacson and Brown (1993) described the career counseling process in five stages. The first stage is defined as "establishing and structuring a relationship." The client and counselor develop an open trusting relationship based on mutual respect. The relationship is structured by giving the client a clear statement about the counseling process, including goals, procedures used, the risk to the client, limitations of the process, information about confidentiality policies, possible outcomes, and possible costs and fees (Yost & Corbishley, 1987). The counselor's expectations of the client, especially his or her responsibilities, also are discussed. Subsequently, *assessment* is undertaken to offer the client an increased awareness of his or her interests, values, aptitudes, personality traits, and decisional style. These authors urge that counselors continuously test and retest hypotheses about clients. The end result of the assessment is a diagnosis of the client's problem by the counselor, which is then shared with the client.

Stage three, "goal setting," involves identification of the problems to be resolved and the areas of self-improvement desired. The counseling goals formulated are specific, feasible, desired by the client, and not dictated by the wishes of others. The goals also must be compatible with the skills of the counselor. Multiple goals are identified and prioritized prior to the fourth stage of "intervention." At this stage, occupational information is gathered to clarify alternatives; to generate new alternatives or eliminate some alternatives; to familiarize clients with jobs and eliminate stereotypical perceptions of those jobs; to motivate clients to make career choices; and to help with reality testing by exposing clients to the skills, aptitudes, and training required for certain jobs. The counselor and client also identify transferable skills to help people see their general skills and competencies in terms of job skills. Checklists, card sorts, and activity logs may be used to help the client organize activities into clusters or patterns. Two types of aids may be used to facilitate decision making: lateral and balance sheet decision-making aids. Lateral decision-making aids are designed to increase the quantity and quality of information available. The authors cite de Bono's (1985) "six thinking hats" as an example. Another intervention would be to improve client's time perspective by helping him or her to have a future orientation through techniques such as a birth-to-death lifeline or guided fantasy. Homework is developed collaboratively to extend the learning outside of the counseling setting. The fifth stage of career counseling, "evaluation," is listed but never described. Although Isaacson and Brown's (1993) model is traditional, it focuses more on the counseling relationship than previous models.

SUMMARY

Overall, these models share common emphases on diagnosis, assessment, and intervention (often emphasizing the role of information seeking) to resolve a client's particular career-related issue(s). They also illustrate a progression from an early focus on traditionally accepted career decision making and counseling "steps" that later was expanded to include affective issues and interpersonal processes of counseling as well. Crites (1981), Yost and Corbishley (1987), and Peterson, Sampson, and Reardon (1991) presented models that included relatively little attention to counseling and relationship process issues beyond notations that the process was a collaborative one. Spokane (1991) and Isaacson and Brown (1993) devoted more attention to relational aspects of career counseling. Further, Spokane's model is unique in its emphasis on the importance of anxiety in the career development and counseling process, as is the cognitive information-processing perspective of Peterson et al.

The previously described models also illustrate a progression from linear thinking about the career counseling process to more cyclical thinking. Early models (e.g., Crites, 1981; Yost & Corbishley, 1987) began with an initial assessment, moved through standard decision-making practices, and ended with a decision or action plan to implement. Peterson et al. (1991), Spokane (1991), and Isaacson and Brown (1993), however, included some sort of generalization, follow-through or evaluation step which had the potential to recycle the person through the process. These later models, thus, were somewhat more dynamic and flexible. Finally, although mention is made of barriers (e.g., Yost & Corbishley), compromises (e.g., Spokane), and counselor-client collaboration (e.g., Crites, 1981), these constructs generally received little direct focus. It also bears mention that although each of the models was based on prior theoretical and empirical literature on career development and career counseling, subsequent empirical investigation of their validity was rare and indirect. These models, however, set the stage for subsequent developments.

EMERGING CAREER COUNSELING THEORIES

Although Swanson (1996) argued convincingly that "the theory is the practice" in her discussion of trait–factor and person–environment fit career counseling, other authors have proposed theories of career counseling that are separate from established theories of career choice and development. In recent years, three such theories (Chartrand, 1996; Fouad & Bingham, 1995; Krumboltz, 1996) have been introduced into the literature to move the field beyond the previously described models of career counseling. Each of the three takes a somewhat different approach, but all provide a more comprehensive and coherent statement about career counseling than do prior models and literature. It can be seen, however, that these emergent theories are informed by the previously documented evolution of career counseling models, as well as other vocational research literature.

Fouad and Bingham's (1995) Culturally Appropriate Career Counseling Model

Fouad and Bingham (1995) listed five assumptions that inform their theoretically-based model of career counseling. Their first assumption is that all effective career counseling takes place within a cultural context which must be recognized at the initiation of the career counseling process. Their second and third assumptions are that the variables to be considered in career counseling are different for members of different cultures and that established models may not explicate satisfactorily the career behavior of racial and ethnic minorities. Fourth, they emphasize the importance of considering culture in vocational assessment. Finally, they assume that cultural differences are considered within a context of diversity, not deficit, and clients are assisted to make "culturally appropriate" choices. Fouad and Bingham argued that in order to do cross-cultural career counseling, counselors must first become skilled in cross-cultural counseling; a culturally aware counselor knows his or her own biases and attitudes, has knowledge of different cultures, and has developed specific intervention strategies for working with culturally diverse clients.

Attention to culture is an important contextual factor in Fouad and Bingham's emergent (1995) theory. They suggest that cultural variables may be especially important to consider in clients' career decision-making processes. Clients grow up with different world views, and these are expressed in their interests, attitudes, and values. As such, individuals' loci of control and responsibility are particularly likely to vary in accordance with world view. Current career counseling interventions, however, generally are influenced by a European world view that focuses on the individual to the exclusion of the needs of the group—thus setting up the potential for cultural conflicts. Relatedly, Fouad and Bingham note that a client's current stage of racial–ethnic identity development may have implications for career decisions. Counselors' understanding of their own stage of identity development also may be important for establishing rapport in counseling. Finally, Fouad and Bingham highlight the fact that minority persons may be over- and underrepresented in some occupations because they may be more likely to compromise their career aspirations due to external circumstances. Even clients' approaches to compromise may be explained by differing world views. Consequently, a client's career decision-making processes likely will be most adaptive if she or he evaluates realistically obstacles while at the same time remaining aware of self-efficacy issues that may restrict choices.

Fouad and Bingham (1995) identify culture as a critical variable whose consideration should enter into every part of the career counseling process. Their "culturally appropriate career counseling model" may be conceptualized as an emergent theory that extends the work of Bingham and Ward (1994) and consists of seven steps. Prior to the first step, however, is what Fouad and Bingham term *preparation for counseling*. In order to prepare for counseling culturally different clients, they suggest that counselors need to be culturally sensitive—for example, being open to their clients' experiences and letting clients know their experiences are valued and accepted. The counselor also must be knowledgeable about cultural groups and the cultural strengths that clients bring to counseling. In addition, counselors should be open to utilizing clients as cultural teachers, be aware of their own world view, know their own stage of racial–ethnic identity development, understand the impact of socioeconomic status (SES), be aware of their political views, and know what assumptions they make about the role of work in their clients' lives.

Subsequent to this preparation, the first step in Fouad and Bingham's (1995) model is the "establishment of rapport in a culturally appropriate relationship." Relationships are very important to many racial and ethnic minorities, and thus, it may be important to pay particular attention to developing rapport. Culturally appropriate relationships may differ across cultures, but the most critical aspects of establishing a relationship are flexibility, suspension of stereotypes and assumptions, and attention to the counselor role desired by the client.

Next is the step of "identification of career issues." The authors suggest that it is important to take a broad approach to the issues troubling a client who presents with career issues; emotional, cognitive, behavioral, and environmental issues also may be present. It is important to identify what is within the client's control and what is not since this model differentiates between environmental issues, which are any concerns clients may have about the working environment, and external barriers, which clients experience as being outside of their control. Fouad and Bingham (1995) indicate that it may be relevant to use Sue and Sue's (1990) model of locus of control and locus of responsibility.

The third step is "assessment of effects of cultural variables." Fouad and Bingham (1995) outline a sphere of influence of cultural variables. At the core are immutable characteristics of the individual. The next layer is gender, which shapes the child's behavior almost from birth. Gender shapes the individual's sense of self and perception of appropriate career choices. The layer beyond gender is family. It may be essential to know who is the "head of the family" because this person may influence the client's career decision. Desires of the family may supersede desires of the individual in many cultures. The fourth sphere of influence is the racial–ethnic group. Stage of racial–ethnic identity development of both the client and the counselor may affect counseling. The final influence is the dominant culture. Racial and ethnic minority persons may get messages from the dominant culture about their roles in the culture and careers that are acceptable. All these influences may be more or less powerful depending on the ethnic group. The counselor may need to help the client work toward decreasing the influence of those spheres that are overly influential or maladaptive to him or her in choosing a career. The strength of the various spheres can be used to help set goals for counseling as the counselor needs to consider those spheres that are most relevant when making a culturally appropriate intervention.

"Setting culturally appropriate counseling process and goals" is the fourth step in the career counseling process, and "using culturally appropriate counseling interventions" is the fifth step. It is important to consider issues of cultural values, functional and linguistic equivalence, translation, test bias, and norms when using assessment instruments in cross-cultural counseling. Interventions should be tailored to meet the client's need rather than the counselor's comfort with particular techniques, strategies, or instruments.

"Decision making" and "implementation and follow-up" are the last two steps of the counseling process. Counselors must be aware that not all clients see decision making as a rational, linear process; some may cycle back through the career counseling process when they have clarified their issues. Counselors also must be certain that the client's plan is consistent with his or her world view and should encourage the client to return to counseling if the need arises. This may be difficult if the client interprets the need to return to counseling as a failure, a special concern if the client has attributed an expert role to the counselor.

This emergent theory covers some traditionally emphasized areas (e.g., decision-making processes), but also introduces a number of new foci for career counseling. Explicit and extensive attention to the role of culture in the individual's career development and the counseling relationship is one major innovation. Fouad and Bingham (1995) synthesized extant literature on the importance of culture to career development (e.g., Fouad & Arbona, 1994) and counseling process (e.g., Leong, 1993; Sue, Arrendondo, & McDavis, 1992) into a coherent whole. Also, their specific description of the career counseling process as often nonlinear, their overall greater attention to career counseling process, and their inclusion of cognitive, social emotional and environmental factors expand on themes that had begun to emerge in early models. With the publication of their chapter in *Handbook of Vocational Psychology*, Fouad and Bingham advanced a perspective on career counseling that was at a qualitatively different level than other extant models of career counseling.

Krumboltz's (1996) Learning Theory of Career Counseling

Krumboltz's (1996) Learning Theory of Career Counseling, on the other hand, is embedded in the context of his social learning theory of career decision making and incorporates a number of his observations about the evolving nature of the career counseling endeavor. These latter observations are particularly distinctive aspects of the theory. Although he sees Parsons' theory as dominating career counseling, Krumboltz stated that career counseling theories must move beyond such a simplistic perspective. His ideas about this evolution include the argument that a career counseling theory can help identify relationships among the particular characteristics most crucial to the client. Such a theory also may provide a rationale for already existing career counseling practices, as well as stimulate the creation of new counseling techniques and offer criteria for evaluating outcomes.

Career counseling theory also must reflect the current nature of the work world. For example, Krumboltz (1996) pointed out that current interest inventories tend to channel people into fields related to their current interests, rather than encouraging them to explore new activities, hobbies, and occupations. Such an approach is inconsistent with current work world demands that people prepare for changing work tasks, not static occupations; matching individuals to occupations is of limited utility because occupations are no longer static. Consequently, Krumboltz suggested career counseling theory must include attention to work on self-development issues to help people cope with the need for new skills and the associated stresses of a changing work world; people need to be empowered to take action, not merely to be given a diagnosis. Further, Krumboltz indicated that career counselors need to deal with all career problems (not just occupational selection) and need to be open to combining career and personal counseling.

Career counseling from a learning perspective (Krumboltz, 1996) attempts to address some of the previously mentioned issues. It is based in the social learning theory of career decision making which proposes that people have learning experiences as a result of their genetics, social, cultural, and economic circumstances. These are then synthesized into self-observation generalizations and task approach skills that guide people's thinking about career decisions and actions. Occupational choices are attributed to a lifelong sequence of learning experiences that are either instrumental, as a consequence of a behavior, or associative, from observing others. Consequently, the goal of career counseling is to facilitate the learning of skills, interests, beliefs, values, work habits, and personal qualities that enable people to create a satisfying life within a constantly changing work environment. The counselor's task is to promote client learning and to emphasize that all of these skills, interests, and values are likely to change as a result of further learning experiences. These learning activities are intended to promote clients' abilities to create satisfying lives for themselves, however they define that for themselves at a point in time.

The role of assessment in this emergent career counseling theory is to make inferences about how a client might match with educational or occupational environments *and* to suggest new learning experiences. Krumboltz (1996) stated that most counselors emphasize the first role at the expense of the second. Skill assessments often are interpreted as aptitudes that are unchangeable instead of targets for new learning, partly because the test results often are norm-referenced rather than criterion-referenced scores. He argued that tests and counseling need to emphasize how a client may improve his or her performance and pinpoint new learning goals. Given that interests are learned and that it is difficult to be interested in something to which one has never been exposed or about which one knows little, it is important not to be bound by the limits of current interests. Assessment tools may be used to identify and dispel harmful false beliefs, as well as to confirm and reinforce facilitative beliefs. Similarly, values and personality are viewed by Krumboltz as open to change and should be assessed and discussed from this perspective.

Intervention, then, also needs to be dynamic and proactive according to Krumboltz (1996). Developmental and preventative interventions (e.g., career education, school-to-work initiatives, job club programs, study materials, and simulations) are especially important in facilitating client growth. Tailored and remedial interventions (e.g., goal clarification, cognitive restructuring, countering a troublesome belief, cognitive rehearsal, narrative analysis, exploration bibliotherapy, role playing, desensitization, using paradoxical intention to discover disconfirming evidence, transmitting metamessages, using humor for perspective, investigating assumptions to discover disconfirming evidence) are useful in circumventing blockages and specific problem areas.

Desired outcomes of career counseling from a learning perspective are more expansive than those from traditional theories. Traditionally, success in career counseling has been measured by a reduction in indecision or by an increase in congruence between occupational goals and measured characteristics according to Krumboltz (1996). In his theory, however, indecision is a necessary and desirable quality to motivate learning activities; thus, indecision may be better labeled openmindedness. Further, congruence is no longer a sufficient criterion for measuring the success of career counseling given the reality of rapidly changing occupations and the fact that many people with very different characteristics are successful in many occupations despite not looking exactly like their coworkers. In his theory, tentative decisions to try out alternatives are encouraged to stimulate more learning and to help reduce feelings of guilt and failure for the client. Krumboltz argued that process and product outcomes should be evaluated to see if counseling is meeting its goal of creating a more satisfying life for the client. Process outcomes might be termed career exploratory behavior. Product outcomes would be desired changes in client's skills, interests, beliefs, and values assessed psychometrically or anecdotally or more subjective measures of satisfaction.

This theory is assumed to work equally well for all people because it is dependent on basic learning principles. Specific learning goals for individuals might be different for people from different cultures and some assessment devices might need to be adapted in terms of language or cultural customs. Krumboltz (1996) stressed, however, the importance of not losing sight of the individual in favor of what is known about specific cultures. That said, practical implications for career counselors are the use of assessment instruments to stimulate new learning, the use of more educational interventions, learning outcomes as criteria for success, and integrating career and personal counseling. Practical implications for the career development profession are making career counseling a national priority for which career counselors assume leadership.

This theory, too, broke new ground for the field. Krumboltz's (1996) attention to the dynamic, changing nature of work and the need to proactively approach this issue with clients is especially notable. In addressing these issues, he incorporates the postmodern perspectives of Savickas (1993) and Richardson (1993) into a learning theory of career counseling. Further, like Fouad and Bingham (1995), Krumboltz includes culture as an important variable in career development and counseling, and like Spokane (1991), he emphasizes the importance of client affect. Finally, Krumboltz builds on prior work with his attention to environmental barriers (e.g., Fouad & Bingham, Spokane) and the dynamic nature of the career counseling process (e.g., Fouad & Bingham).

Chartrand's (1996) Sociocognitive Interactional Model for Career Counseling

Chartrand (1996) proposed the third emergent theory of career counseling—a sociocognitive interactional approach. She argued for the need to develop career counseling frameworks that integrate theories of vocational development and adjustment with knowledge of counseling process. Such models would facilitate the connection of theory to practice.

Chartrand's (1996) work is based on Lent, Brown and Hackett's (1994) sociocognitive model of career choice but incorporates it into an interactional career counseling framework that describes social cognitive and interactional processes. The social cognitive component is the "what to focus on" and the interactional component addresses the "how to" within a counseling context. The sociocognitive components are used to explain individual differences in readiness to process and use information gained in career counseling.

Underlying assumptions of Chartrand's (1996) theory are that sociocognitive processes are hierarchically structured. Core cognitive constructs (metacognitions) are tacit organizational principles central to cognitive organization, and contain beliefs fundamental to a person's sense of self. They are useful in understanding thematic unity among thoughts, feelings, and behavior. Also, core constructs shape lower-level or peripheral constructs which are less central to the self and can be modified without serious modification of the core constructs. In contrast, efforts to change core constructs often result in anxiety which must be reduced.

Sociocognitive career counseling, then, requires that counselors understand both core and peripheral cognitive constructs and assess both levels; career-relevant cognitions can involve core cognitions, peripheral cognitions, or both. Chartrand (1996) argued that cognitive intervention from a sociocognitive perspective is best done at the core level as intervention at the peripheral level is ineffective if these beliefs diverge from core beliefs.

According to Chartrand (1996), relevant core cognitions may be metacognitions (i.e., core constructs pertaining to fundamental sense of self) or career-specific cognitions. Metacognitions merit special attention as they are part of a metacognitive-affective-behavioral dynamic which results in relatively stable response styles that guide career-related behavior. For example, persons' cognitive themes regarding the basis of their self-worth (e.g., competence versus love and respect from others) may interact with their affective tendencies toward positive or negative affectivity and behavioral approach to problem solving to produce a particular approach to life and career issues. This approach or style may be important to explore and address in career counseling. Career-specific cognitions are more circumscribed (e.g., self-efficacy and outcome expectations), but similarly important to understand and address in career counseling. In exploring core cognitions, Chartrand indicated certain cognitive themes, affective reactions and behavioral response modes are common, often involving dysfunctional beliefs regarding love and competence.

Chartrand (1996) noted that interpersonal factors often are neglected in career assessment literature and consequently suggested the importance of specifying an interactional component in any career counseling framework. Some of her reasons for attending to interpersonal style included that interpersonal functioning is becoming more important to successful work adjustment as employers focus more on teamwork and cooperation, and that interpersonal process is key to effective treatment and successful career counseling. Chartrand's emergent theory includes detailed analyses of how the interaction of sociocognitive and interpersonal factors may impact career counseling process.

Chartrand's (1996) conceptualization of career counseling, then, is based on the assumed importance of the previously described sociocognitive and interactional factors. The "beginning phase" of career counseling involves the counselor gathering information and developing rapport. As part of this phase, there may be assessment of standard career information, as well as metacognitive–affective–behavioral response styles and core cognitive processes. Examination of automatic thoughts and dysfunctional beliefs may be especially useful in this early phase of counseling.

In the "middle phase" of counseling, the counselor helps the client frame or reframe his or her vocational self-concept. Also, identification of obstacles to career development may be important. In this working phase, monitoring discrepancies between counselor intentions and client reactions is crucial to the quality of the process. In so doing, the counselor may have to move back and forth between career cognitions and metacognitive–affective–behavioral responses.

Finally, the "closing phase" of counseling involves client information synthesis, implementation actions, and termination activities such as those identified by Spokane (1991). Chartrand (1996) highlighted the importance of the fact that the interpersonal process of counseling changes as the goals of counseling evolve and change, but that client response styles identified as salient in consideration of client reactions to career problems also may be salient when considering the counseling process.

Chartrand's (1996) Sociocognitive Interactional Model for Career Counseling further accentuates and develops themes found in early models of career counseling regarding the importance of cognitions (e.g., Peterson et al., 1991), environmental barriers (e.g.,Yost & Corbishley, 1987), affect (e.g., Spokane, 1991) and interpersonal processes (e.g., Isaacson & Brown, 1993), as well as the importance of the social–cognitive processes highlighted in the theory of Lent et al. (1994). In particular, her linkage of theory and practice by suggesting parallel foci on traditional career decision-making tasks (e.g., occupational assessment, information gathering) and the dynamics of the counseling process was innovative and effective. Additionally, her treatment of metacognitions and response styles and their role in career processes and counseling extended current models and theory. Finally, her emphasis on the importance of interpersonal factors in the changing work world echoed the observations and postmodern perspectives of Richardson (1993) and Savickas (1993).

SUMMARY

Each of these three emergent theories advances qualitatively the level of theorizing about career counseling. These authors each draw from prior career counseling models and then extend them to address with more sophistication issues of the importance of culture, the changing work world, the role of cognitive mechanisms, and the dynamic interaction that is career counseling. All three emergent theories describe a nonlinear career counseling process in which the importance of environmental–social–emotional factors is highlighted, and diagnosis is attenuated. Each emergent theory also describes explicitly a particular perspective on the nature of the career counseling process (although all assume it to be collaborative) and each sketches out an approach to intervention that serves to empower the client. This empowerment takes various forms including acknowledgment of the role of the client's cultural heritage and differentiation of environmental issues from external barriers (Fouad & Bingham, 1995), facilitation of the client's acquisition of new skills, interests or work habits in service of the creation of a more satisfying life (Krumboltz, 1996) and consideration of the cognitive constructs brought to counseling by the client (Chartrand, 1996).

Contributing to the sophistication of these emergent theories is the fact that each is grounded in a broader theoretical perspective which guided the authors' thinking. In the case of Fouad and Bingham (1995), the perspective was that of multicultural theory. In contrast, Krumboltz (1996) drew from social learning theory and Chartrand (1996) drew from social cognitive theory. The depth and richness of these contexts contributes to these emergent theories' potential explanatory power. It also contrasts with the more pragmatic origins of earlier and less theoretically based models of career counseling.

Finally, in each of these emergent theories, the lines between career and personal counseling are blurred. Client affect, general response styles and other life issues and circumstances are recognized as relevant to career counseling. This implicit assumption of the seamless blending of career and personal counseling is notable. Although there has been some consensus regarding the appropriateness of such a perspective (see the 1993 special issue of *Career Development Quarterly* and the chapter by Blustein & Spengler in the 1995 *Handbook of Vocational Psychology* on this topic), the question continues to be raised (e.g., Hackett, 1993).

CONCLUSIONS AND IMPLICATIONS

Over the last two decades, it can be seen that early models of career counseling have evolved and engendered more sophisticated and "theoretical" writings about career counseling. Authors have incorporated into their thinking new foci and developments from vocational psychology (e.g., attention to barriers and counseling process), as well as from more general areas of psychology and sociology (e.g., the importance of emotion and its effects on decision making, the significance of the social environment to human behavior). Further, transformational ideas regarding the roles of culture and cognition in human behavior, and the changing nature of work have been adapted for use in career counseling. Current emergent theories of career counseling are poised to guide research and stimulate further theorizing as the field moves into the new millennium.

It is also important not to lose sight of the fact, however, that for the most part the newer perspectives on career counseling also have affirmed the value of prior work by building on that base. For example, Fouad and Bingham's (1995) attention to the client's cultural context was perhaps foreshadowed by Crites' (1981) recommendation that the client's frame of reference be considered in career counseling. Similarly, Krumboltz's (1996) emphasis on the importance of interests, skills, values, and beliefs in career counseling reaffirms most prior models while adding the dimension of the counselor's facilitation of their development and expansion. Similarly, Chartrand's (1996) incorporation of interpersonal theory seems a logical outgrowth of prior models which had begun to attend to counseling process issues (e.g., Isaacson & Brown, 1993; Spokane, 1991). Overall, the current emergent theories of career counseling represent the steady evolution of prior models in response to societal changes, as well as professional developments; as such, they suggest a promising future for the endeavor of developing a theory of career counseling.

As Osipow (1996) noted, however, the vocational psychology field likely will continue to encounter some difficulties as theorists, practitioners and researchers struggle to agree on a common definition of career counseling and to maintain clarity as to the difference between career counseling methods and outcomes. He observed that theorists, practitioners, and researchers must continually attend to these issues if they hope to make progress in understanding the career counseling endeavor.

Osipow (1996), along with Swanson (1995) and Walsh and Savickas (1996), also raised the issue of the woefully inadequate empirical base for our career counseling models and theories. They noted that it is all too common for models and theories to be derived initially from perfectly legitimate empirical work, but then never subsequently to be tested for their validity. In particular, empirical research on the validity of newly emergent theories is critical. Field and case-based research are viewed by the authors as difficult, but important, methods by which to probe the accuracy and utility of emergent models and theories. Qualitative approaches may be another important research venue for such investigations.

As a result of the gaps in the research base of career counseling models and theories, those who engage in career counseling are left in the disconcerting situation of knowing that career counseling is effective (e.g., Oliver & Spokane, 1988; Whiston, Sexton, & Lasoff, 1998), but not knowing how or why. Some relatively recent research on career counseling and career classes, for example, suggests clients and students attach significant importance to affective interventions (Gold, Kivlighan, Kerr, & Kramer,

1993; Kivlighan, Johnson & Fretz, 1987) and view as less desirable counselor note-taking in career counseling sessions (Miller, 1992), but in general, there is little known about the mechanisms and processes of change
which contribute to the efficacy of career counseling. An additional difficulty inherent in such efficacy research is the need to determine what con-
structions of outcome are appropriate or important to study; they may
vary with clients and situations.

Finally, in attempting to expand the theory and research base of our
understanding of career counseling, it may be valuable to follow Walsh's
(1996) suggestion to consider what may be learned from the psychotherapy process literature. He presented a number of ideas as to how accepted principles discussed in this literature may have relevance for the
endeavor of constructing a career counseling theory. By taking this perspective, Walsh evidenced an assumption of the importance of thinking
about career counseling in terms of process, as well as content and technique. Perhaps more than any other innovation, this perspective represents the extent to which career counseling theories have evolved in
recent years. Indeed, to different degrees, it can be seen that Fouad and
Bingham (1995), Krumboltz (1996) and Chartrand (1996) each incorporated ideas mentioned by Walsh (e.g., a focus on the counseling interaction as a change mechanism, the importance of counseling relationship
quality, the function of learning in change). Further elaboration of these
ideas seems profitable and warranted.

REFERENCES

Bingham, R. P., & Ward, C. M. (1994). Career counseling with ethnic minority women. In W. B.
    Walsh & S. H. Osipow (Eds.), *Career counseling with women* (pp. 165–195). Hillsdale, NJ:
    Lawrence Erlbaum Associates.
Chartrand, J. M. (1996). Linking theory with practice: A sociocognitive interactional model
    for career counseling. In M. L. Savickas & W. B. Walsh (Eds.), *Handbook of career counsel-
    ing theory and practice* (pp. 121–134). Palo Alto, CA: Davies-Black.
Crites, J. O. (1981). *Career counseling: Models, methods, and materials.* New York: McGraw-Hill.
de Bono, E. (1985). *Six thinking hats.* Boston, MA: Little, Brown.
Fouad, N. A., & Arbona, C. (1994). Careers in a cultural context. *Career Development Quarter-
    ly, 43,* 96–104.
Fouad, N. A., & Bingham, R. P. (1995). Career counseling with racial and ethnic minorities.
    In W. B. Walsh & S. H. Osipow (Eds.), *Handbook of vocational psychology: Theory, research,
    and practice* (2nd ed., pp. 331–365). Mahwah, NJ: Lawrence Erlbaum Associates.
Gold, P. B., Kivlighan, D. M., Kerr, A. E., & Kramer, L. A. (1993). The structure of students'
    perceptions of impactful, helpful events in career exploration classes. *Journal of Career
    Assessment, 1,* 145–161.
Hackett, G. (1993). Career counseling and psychotherapy: False dichotomies and recom-
    mended remedies. *Journal of Career Assessment, 1,* 105–117.

Isaacson, L. E., & Brown, D. (1993). *Career information, career counseling, and career development* (5th ed., pp. 379–386). Boston, MA: Allyn & Bacon.

Kivlighan, D. M., Johnson, B., & Fretz, B. (1987). Participant's perception of change mechanisms in career counseling groups: The role of emotional components in career problem solving. *Journal of Career Development, 14*, 35–44.

Krumboltz, J. D. (1996). A learning theory of career counseling. In M. L. Savickas & W. B. Walsh (Eds.), *Handbook of career counseling theory and practice* (pp. 55–80). Palo Alto, CA: Davies-Black.

Lent, R. W., Brown, S. D., & Hackett, G. (1994). Toward a unifying social-cognitive theory of career and academic interest, choice and performance. *Journal of Vocational Behavior, 45*, 79–122.

Leong, F. T. L. (1993). The career counseling process with racial-ethnic minorities: The case of Asian Americans. *Career Development Quarterly, 42*, 26–40.

Miller, M. J. (1992). Effects of note-taking on perceived counselor social influence during a career counseling session. *Journal of Counseling Psychology, 39*, 317–320.

Oliver, L. W., & Spokane, A. R. (1988). Career intervention outcome: What contributes to client gain? *Journal of Counseling Psychology, 35*, 447–462.

Osipow, S. H. (1973). *Theories of career development* (2nd ed.). Englewood Cliffs, NJ: Prentice-Hall.

Osipow, S. H. (1983). *Theories of career development* (3rd ed.). Englewood Cliffs, NJ: Prentice-Hall.

Osipow, S. H. (1994). Moving career theory into the twenty-first century. In M. L. Savickas & R. W. Lent (Eds.), *Convergence in career development theories: Implications for science and practice* (pp. 217–224). Palo Alto, CA: Consulting Psychologists Press.

Osipow, S. H. (1996). Does career theory guide practice or does career practice guide theory? In M. L. Savickas & W. B. Walsh (Eds.), *Handbook of career counseling theory and practice* (pp. 403–409). Palo Alto, CA: Davies-Black.

Osipow, S. H., & Fitzgerald, L. (1996). *Theories of career development* (4th ed.). Boston: Allyn & Bacon.

Peterson, G. W., Sampson, J. P., & Reardon, R. C. (1991). Individual career counseling: A case study. In *Career development and services: A cognitive approach* (pp. 231–257). Pacific Grove, CA: Brooks/Cole.

Phillips, S. D. (1992). Career counseling: Choice and implementation. In S. D. Brown & R. W. Lent (Eds.), *Handbook of counseling psychology* (2nd ed., pp. 513–548). New York: Wiley.

Richardson, M. S. (1993). Work in people's lives: A location for counseling psychologists. *Journal of Counseling Psychology, 40*, 425–433.

Savickas, M. L. (1993). Career counseling in the postmodern era. *Journal of Cognitive Psychotherapy: An International Quarterly, 7*, 205–215.

Savickas, M. L., & Walsh, W. B. (1996). Introduction: Toward convergence between career theory and practice. In M. L. Savickas & W. B. Walsh (Eds.), *Handbook of career counseling theory and practice* (pp. xi–xvi). Palo Alto, CA: Davies-Black.

Spokane, A. R. (1991). The process of career intervention. In *Career intervention* (pp. 23–49). Englewood Cliffs, NJ: Prentice-Hall.

Sue, D. W., Arrendondo, P., & McDavis, R. J. (1992). Multicultural counseling competencies and standards: A call to the profession. *Journal of Multicultural Counseling and Development, 20*, 64–88.

Sue, D. W., & Sue, D. (1990). *Counseling the culturally different: Theory and practice* (2nd ed.). New York: Wiley.

Swanson, J. L. (1995). The process and outcome of career counseling. In W. B. Walsh & S. H. Osipow (Eds.), *Handbook of vocational psychology: Theory, research, and practice* (2nd ed., pp. 217–259). Hillsdale, NJ: Lawrence Erlbaum Associates.

Swanson, J. L. (1996). The theory IS the practice: Trait-and-factor/person-environment fit counseling. In M. L. Savickas & W. B. Walsh (Eds.), *Handbook of career counseling theory and practice* (pp. 93–108). Palo Alto, CA: Davies-Black.

Walsh, W. B. (1996). Career counseling theory: Problems and prospects. In M. L. Savickas & W. B. Walsh (Eds.), *Handbook of career counseling theory and practice* (pp. 267–275). Palo Alto, CA: Davies-Black.

Walsh, W. B., & Savickas, M. L. (1996). Integrating career theory and practice: Recommendations and strategies. In M. L. Savickas & W. B. Walsh (Eds.), *Handbook of career counseling theory and practice* (pp. 417–431). Palo Alto, CA: Davies-Black.

Whiston, S. C., Sexton, T. L., & Lasoff, D. L. (1998). Career-intervention outcome: A replication and extension of Oliver and Spokane (1988). *Journal of Counseling Psychology, 45,* 150–165.

Yost, E. B., & Corbishley, M. A. (1987). *Career counseling: A psychological approach* (pp. 21–23). San Francisco, CA: Jossey-Bass.

Chapter 11

Career Services Within the University

Jane L. Winer
Texas Tech University

As an academic dean of the College of Arts and Sciences at Texas Tech University, I routinely interact with the academic, administrative, and student services personnel. As a faculty member, I have met the publication and teaching requirements for tenure and promotion to full professor within a department of psychology, for which I was the designated career psychology professor in its APA-accredited counseling psychology doctoral training program. In that role, I interacted closely with the university's counseling center. My experience in the applied, academic, and administrative realms has given me a perspective that I share with my counseling psychologist colleagues to better prepare others who find themselves in this situation. I am proud to be a student of Samuel Osipow, and I hope that my thoughts on career services will help safeguard Osipow's contributions for future generations of students.

CAREER COUNSELING SERVICES FROM THREE PERSPECTIVES

Applied Perspective

Dean and Meadows (1995) traced the roots of college counseling in vocational counseling, mental health counseling, and student personnel counseling. College counseling is made up of a number of professions within student affairs and is a specialty within the counseling profession. For a professional in university career counseling services, students are the central client population, and other student service offices (e.g., residence halls, ethnic- or gender- or sexual orientation-focus service units) are the primary source of professional colleagues with whom one interacts. Interaction with faculty is comparatively infrequent except for faculty in discipline-related areas (e.g., those with joint appointments in a department of psychology or educational psychology and a student services unit). Students and their concerns are increasingly demanding, a phenomenon that has been reported not only in the professional literature (e.g., Stone & Archer, 1990) but also in the general professional press, such as *The Chronicle of Higher Education*. Geraghty (1997, p. A32), for example, reported that as many as one in five students are receiving counseling of all types, about twice as many as 5 years ago.

Academic Perspective

Professors who teach and conduct research may appreciate the services provided by their professional colleagues in the career and counseling services, or they may have a vague, stereotyped, negative, or no understanding of the contributions made by these professionals. Faculty may not know that university career counseling services exist or may not recognize these services' relevance to their own work. Some take a negative view because they did not use career counseling services themselves when they were students. Having pursued a single field through the terminal degree and having become and remained professors, they may not appreciate the career-decision problems of their students, or they may appreciate the problems but not recognize their amelioration as an academic responsibility. They may question the employment of professionals whose mission they do not perceive as clearly and directly the support of the faculty's activities in teaching and scholarship. They may identify counseling professionals as employees tangential to the university's missions and, not recognizing counselors as scholars, identify them as illegitimate competitors with faculty for university resources.

Professors who teach, conduct research, and supervise applied work in the area of counseling psychology in general, and career counseling psychology in particular, may demonstrate the full range of attitudes toward their counselor colleagues. Some may identify positively with counselors whose work is the application of the faculty member's focus of research. Some may function as natural allies with counselors in university debates and conflicts over the allocation of resources. Others may manifest the negative views that would be more understandable among faculty with no ties of education or experience with counseling psychology or career counseling.

Pursuing further the work done by Fitzgerald and Osipow (1988), Heppner, O'Brien, Hinkelman, and Flores (1996) attempted to deterimine the reasons behind a decreasing identification with career counseling among counseling psychologists. Heppner et al. surveyed 290 counseling psychology graduate students from 12 APA-approved counseling psychology training programs. Their results indicated that "trainees' most negative experiences were disparaging remarks about career counseling from faculty and supervisors and their formal course work in career development" (p. 105). Presumably, a professor's opinions as expressed in the classroom are similar to those expressed to his or her colleagues. If the contribution of counseling faculty to campus debates on allocation of resources to counseling services is negative, the effect may be more destructive than that of negative opinions expressed by faculty from other fields who would be assumed not to value counseling services in the first place. If the faculty whose own academic focus is counseling or career development do not manifest the value of career counseling to their own students, then they are unlikely to be effective in making a case for counseling services to university decision makers.

Administrative Perspective

Academic deans come from the faculty, where they established their credentials in teaching and scholarship, but they are administrators who authorize college expenditures, influence university allocations of resources, and have responsibility for ensuring the delivery of appropriate educational experiences and services to students. They hear from faculty and need to be sensitive to the faculty's expressed views about the relative value of prospective recipients of university resource allocation. They also hear from students, students' parents, students' attorneys, legislators, and other constituents of the university, which means that the information they receive is disproportionately weighted on the dysfunctional side of the faculty's and staff's interactions with students. They hear that students should receive more and better service and that faculty should provide more attention to a greater range of student needs. They know that faculty are not able to meet all student service needs but that various constituents believe that faculty should meet all of these needs. They know that faculty are not necessarily supportive of providing funds to other personnel who might meet identified student needs, unless the need is central to the faculty's view of the university's mission.

THE CONTEXT

The Power Discrepancy Between Faculty
and Other Campus Professionals

Professors who teach and conduct research, who have full-time academic appointments, and who have tenure possess power within the university. Other professionals, regardless of their titles, educational background, assignments, or activities, do not. The power of faculty relative to that of professionals who are not faculty extends to their respective administrators. An example is Stone and Archer's (1990) description of vice presidents for student affairs: "Because they represent support services, they are often the least powerful executive in the system and are sometimes forced to operate in a defensive, reactive mode" (p. 580).

From the faculty perspective, stereotype, or prejudice, even doctoral-level counseling staff may have inadequate educational backgrounds, deficient in the liberal arts or in science or both, and insufficient research and teaching backgrounds to be considered one of the true faculty or to be considered equal to the faculty in the governance of the university. Counseling center personnel may not be considered truly faculty even if they have teaching and research responsibilities. They may not be represented in the faculty governing body. They may not be paid as much, or from the same source, as faculty. If they are similar to faculty in all of these ways, their assignments differ sufficiently that they may be perceived not only as different but of lesser status. Counseling center staff may not be eligible for faculty promotions, and their own work environments, being minimally hierarchical, do not provide promotion opportunities (Stone & Archer, 1990). Furthermore,

> the low salaries for many counseling center psychologists provide a rather graphic statement to them of their lack of importance and centrality to the mission of the institution. The feeling of not being valued contributes greatly to staff burnout. . . . The core problem . . . is the 'in between' status that most counseling centers experience. Centers are usually part of the student affairs division which is composed of professional student personnel workers. Staff in the departments in student affairs are typically among the lowest paid professionals at the college or university and salaries of counselors, even though they often have doctoral degrees and are similar to faculty in some ways, reflect their membership in student affairs. (p. 576)

In his response to Reardon's (1996) analysis of the cost of career counseling, Rayman (1996, p. 286) pointed out that Reardon had not appreciated the difference between paraprofessionals and professionals in providing services, in particular, the difference between career advising and

individual career counseling involving psychological content within a relationship between client and counselor. Reardon's purported lack of appreciation reflects the more comprehensive lack of appreciation for counseling personnel held by many faculty. From their perspective, all providers
of student services are paraprofessionals and, by definition, are not equivalent to faculty in status or power. Stone and Archer (1990) identified the
problem staff counselors have of being generalists in a university environment in which faculty are rewarded for specialization. Counselors do not
have the time or the environmental support to pursue a major research
program and to become an expert in one area of scholarship, a professional circumstance that creates them forever unequal to the faculty.
Hotelling (1990) addressed the status problems of staff counseling psychologists who are "often viewed as, and take on the role of being, less
important to the mission of universities than our academic counterparts"
(p. 621). June (1990), contrasting the current status of counseling centers
with that of the past, observed that "today, counseling centers are not
called on to carry out an integral role in the overall present or future
agenda of many universities and colleges, as was the case in times past.
Often they seem to be taken for granted" (p. 624).

The continuing dialogue between scientists and practitioners within the
counseling psychology profession is a particular case of the conflicts
between the scientists and practitioners within the university. Counseling
psychologists trained in APA-accredited programs may be closer than most
to the image required for full acceptance by university faculty, as the scientist–practitioner is similar to the scientist–teacher, but there remains a perceived difference in status. Mintz (1992) acknowledged that early in the
career of a tenure-track assistant professor in counseling psychology, one is
exposed to a perceived status heirarchy in which the counseling psychology academicians disparage the counseling psychology practitioners:

> Counseling psychologists know that different individuals are better suited to
> different careers based on such factors as interests, abilities, and values. Nev-
> ertheless, it seems that many academicians ignore this information when deal-
> ing with students and colleagues. Instead, the attitude portrayed is that 'the
> best and the brightest' choose academic careers, perhaps despite practice
> interests and abilities. Indeed, academic departments often measure their suc-
> cess by the number of graduates who pursue academic careers. (p. 41)

Competition for Resources

University counseling services have experienced chronic financial problems within an environment of increased cost and demand. Services have
been downsized, privatized, merged, or submerged within other campus
entities, such as health services.

Stone and Archer (1990) described the 1970–1982 period in the development of counseling centers' roles and functions as one in which the campus became the client. Their thoughtful analysis of the role of counseling centers in the current decade was based on three assumptions: "The ethnic, racial, national, and experiential background of students will change. . . . The psychological health, safety, and financial needs of students will increase. . . . Competition for resources in higher education will increase" (pp. 542–543). The third of these assumptions was elaborated as follows:

> As colleges and universities try to define their market niche, focus their strengths, upgrade their technology, research facilities, physical plants, and athletic complexes, create centers of excellence, and recruit a diverse and renowned faculty, the search for new resources will be intense. Increased economic development and international activities, renewed partnerships with external constituencies, and fund-raising will become the top priority of many university administrators. Accountability will have increasing importance in the life of the university as it struggles with economic issues and tough decisions regarding priorities. (p. 543)

Bishop (1995) reviewed issues pertinent to funding problems in supporting counseling services, including fees, outsourcing, and cost-benefit studies; the question of service entitlements, with particular emphasis on establishing limits to individual counseling sessions; and personnel issues. Waehler, Hardin, and Rogers (1994) conducted research on the role of fee-for-service in students' decisions to seek counseling, research that would have been irrelevant in an earlier era in which free counseling services, or services already financed by general fees, were a student entitlement. Reardon (1996) developed a procedure for the cost-benefit analysis of a self-directed career decision-making program, emphasizing salary costs. Whatever the differences in emphasis and definition, in a higher education environment in which cost-benefit analyses are increasingly required by participants in the competition for resources, there is merit in having addressed the relative cost and value of services of different types.

UNACKNOWLEDGED PROBLEMS AND UNRECOGNIZED SOLUTIONS

Safeguarding Counseling Services Within the University: Student Emphasis

Stone and Archer (1990) recommended that the profession develop an empirical literature demonstrating the cost-effectiveness of counseling services based on the cost to the institution of various student problems, such as failing to continue to enroll, substance abuse, and campus disruption. Bishop (1995) also recommended such a strategy:

> It is legitimate for any educational institution to ask how the activities of a college or university counseling center relate to the educational mission of the school. Institutions of higher education are not mental health organizations. It is important, therefore, for counseling centers to describe and to evaluate their activities from the educational perspective of the entire campus. Counseling centers that have data demonstrating their impact on the campus are obviously in a stronger strategic position compared with those that do not. Contributions to retention efforts, consultative relationships with other campus units, and teaching and training activities are all examples of counseling center work that can be viewed as central to an institution's overall missions and goals. (p. 37)

Within this context, Bishop's review of the literature suggested that counseling centers in general have not done well in strategically planning for their inclusion and centrality in the university, and all too often have left upper administrators unaware of the importance of their activities.

The importance of the arguments by Stone and Archer (1990) and Bishop (1995) cannot be overstated. Support for the case made to university decisionmakers need not be limited to local data, although local data, financial and qualitative, are crucial. Supporting arguments from the outside, especially those that appear in prestigious, refereed academic journals with high rejection rates, have more than typical impact in a university in which research-oriented faculty are central to governance. The report of Wilson, Mason, and Ewing (1997) is an example of this type of supporting argument. Wilson et al. evaluated the impact of receiving personal counseling on student retention, defined as graduated or still enrolled after two years, and found a statistically significant retention advantage for those who were counseled. Wilson et al.'s methods were judged sufficiently rigorous to permit the report's publication in the *Journal of Counseling Psychology*, a fact that should be underscored in presenting this article to a university president, as I did.

Wilson et al.'s (1997) report provides reassurance that the investigation was not simply self-serving to mental health interests: "Counseling centers exist to serve the mission and purpose of the university, and therefore evaluation should be tied to educational outcomes that lie at the core of the university mission, such as academic success or attrition" (p. 316). Similarly, a section of a response by Levy (1990) would serve as reassurance to administrators suspicious of funding requests by counseling entities:

> A college campus or college community is not a therapeutic environment. It is an intentional community where the intent is education—cultural, liberal, vocational, or professional. Developmental tasks and responsibilities

should be directed toward the objective of education. If a person is not able to function effectively within that community and requires support systems and programs specific to that person's needs beyond what the college can realistically provide, then the person may not belong in the community. Thus a counseling center tailors its projects and its programs to addressing real needs of real people, but more likely in a global fashion and in a limited way. The priority is short-term intervention therapy, not long-term commitments. (pp. 614–615)

In Stoltz-Loike's (1995) review of practice and research in career development and counseling, she concluded that career centers were being compelled to articulate their goals and to use new approaches to achieve their goals. In particular, counseling personnel have learned to rely on university faculty to support services, such as student mentoring programs and panel discussions, as a strategy in getting the work of counseling centers done on campus.

Pace, Stamler, Yarris, and June (1996) proposed an extension of the counseling service model developed by Morrill, Oetting, and Hurst (1974) which should be helpful in meeting the challenge of winning support for counseling. Morrill et al. (1974) described four targets of intervention, three purposes of intervention, and three methods of intervention, all graphically depicted in a cube. Pace et al.'s (1996) extension describes an interdependent university community, in which a counseling center would interact with students, faculty, administration, and other support offices in the service of common goals and in which "institutional issues and concerns rather than the structure of the counseling center drive the work that needs to be done" (p. 322). Pace et al. did not provide many examples of how faculty and others in the university would work together and did not directly address how decisions are made in a university, but the concept of an interdependent whole should suggest examples to the interested reader.

Developing the data to demonstrate the value of counseling services to students is an approach that is available to every counseling center. In addition to this direct method, I recommend that counseling services attempt to manipulate the power base of the university by meeting the needs of the faculty.

Safeguarding Counseling Services Within the University: Faculty Emphasis

Stone and Archer (1990) suggested the importance of counseling services' garnering political support on campus. In particular, integrating counseling services with educational services provided by other departments, including academic departments, is a worthwhile strategy, as is including counseling personnel on policy-making committees of the university. "Working relationships with faculty and administrators create an opportunity for them to observe counselors' work and value counselors' activities" (p. 594). Stone and Archer's strategy is focused on developing an appreciation among faculty and administration of counseling services' contributions to students. The extension of this focus to faculty and administrators themselves is the next necessary step.

In the ideal, university faculty have perfect jobs. They have great freedom of choice in content of work and in time allocation. They can choose whether to work alone or in collaboration. They can express almost any view. But no job is fully understood from the outside. The ideal aspects of the faculty job, in which many thrive, can function as extreme stressors to many others. Osipow (1986) observed that:

> A given objective environmental event may not have the same impact on different people. For example, one worker may find constant deadlines oppressive and stressful, whereas a colleague in the same environment with the same deadlines may thrive on the situation. Thus, Spokane and I (Osipow & Spokane, 1983) have taken the approach that occupational stress is affected by the perceptions individuals have of their work environment and is buffered by individual coping resources. Thus, the degree to which people experience strain or disruption is a function of the occupational stress that they perceive. . . . Job demands influence and are influenced by family demands; in addition, they are moderated by a variety of personal attributes. In particular, the job demands are ameliorated or exacerbated by the degree to which individuals possess personal, environmental, family, and social resources. These resources serve as buffers. (p. 159)

Academic positions support front-loading careers, which create a top-heavy occupational environment. Osipow (1992) observed, "New professionals in academia must, by necessity, be so aware of the tenure clock that they design their scholarship accordingly; they are always looking over their shoulder and ahead of themselves" (p. 106). In the early years of their careers, new faculty set and reach major professional goals: tenure, promotion to associate professor, and promotion to professor. After that, there is no obvious next goal to reach within the university. Within psychology faculties, from 1973 to 1991, the proportion of full professors increased from 34.0% to 41.5%, with associated declines in proportion of assistant and associate professors (Pion et al., 1996, p. 521). As in other disciplines, individuals holding lower ranks are promoted to higher ranks, remain in position, and need not retire, given the abolition of a mandatory retirement age. If financial contingencies prevent the university from increasing the number of faculty, the faculty becomes an increasingly static group.

Stone and Archer (1990) described student needs in terms that can be applied to faculty needs:

> The need for psychologically oriented career counseling is great. Students in the 1990s who will be strongly influenced by materialism and careerism, will need career counseling that offers them a balanced and broader view of career and life satisfaction. They should be able to connect their vision of a career and life-style with an understanding of their own interests, personality, and values. (p. 550)

The problem of materialism and careerism is not new, but it is suppressed in the debate about faculty wellbeing. An insight from an investigation from the 1930s provided by Crites (1969) may still apply:

> Professional people, i.e., physicians, lawyers, and college professors, wanted to compete for social status with persons far above them in income, e.g., business executives. Consequently, even though they were at a high income level, they were disproportionately dissatisfied. (Centers & Cantril, 1946, cited by Crites, 1969, p. 513)

Faculty may want to live at the same level as business leaders, but their financial compensation does not permit it.

An academic who receives his or her last promotion at a relatively young age may feel that he or she has reached a career plateau without an end. The resulting many middle years are filled with despair. The manifestations of professional despair include all of the human problems with which counseling psychologists deal routinely. In the academic world, the include another, which is described euphemistically as lack of collegiality. Hilt (1986) described the problem at the group and at the individual level:

> Rare is the department not affected to some degree by internecine fighting. By training and temperament, we professors are inclined to quibble and argue points. We bring the wrong tools to solve problems with our neighbors; what stood us in good stead in graduate school—the ability to dissect an issue, to compete with others, to quantify and criticize—simply does not work in interpersonal situations. (p. A80)

Wilson (1997) reported on Arizona State University's referral of dysfunctional academic departments to professional counseling. The counselors were identified as faculty from psychology or educational psychology departments. The individual identified as the intervener appears to function also as a one-person employee assistance program. The successful contribution of counseling psychologists to this type of intervention would secure faculty gratitude and esteem on almost any campus.

Kjos (1995) provided examples of how an understanding of the interactions of personality disorders or abnormal personality with career development can inform career counseling:

> Many factors associated with personality disorders play a part in career development. These include the inability to make decisions, to take criticism, to get along with others, and to be assertive. Characteristics such as self-defeating behaviors, anxiety, hypersensitivity, extreme vigilance, impulsiveness, and inconsistency are also related to specific personality disorders. Effectiveness in career counseling is enhanced by the counselor's ability to (a) recognize the particular traits and groups of traits that make up personality styles and personality disorders that, in turn, may inhibit or enhance career development; (b) develop a treatment plan that is cognizant of career development issues and will complement individual client style; and (c) work with clients who exhibit these traits to maximize the strengths inherent in specific personality disorders. (p. 592)

Kjos notes that of the ten personality disorders recognized by the American Psychiatric Association (1994), nine are linked with "occupational difficulties or impairment in occupational functioning" (Kjos, 1995, p. 592).

Blustein (1992) proposed an emphasis on occupational mental health (i.e., a focus on the psychosocial and vocational concerns of employees) as a means of enhancing vocational counseling psychology as a profession. Stone and Archer (1990) predicted that:

> Faculty and staff may also emerge as new recipients of center services. Many centers are involved in newly developed Employee Assistance Programs (EAPs). In the *1989 Counseling Center Survey* (Gallagher, 1989), 138 schools reported having EAP programs ($N = 248$) and 22 of these programs were administered by counseling centers. Of the others, 56 used the counseling center for some role in the program. (p. 555)

In many universities, faculty may be referred to EAPs if they are dysfunctional, and they may have health insurance that supports mental health services to some extent. But the concept of faculty personnel services is far less well-developed than that of student personnel services. .

By serving the needs of the university faculty, counseling professionals can manipulate their power-discrepant relationship with the faculty into one in which they are empowered in specific areas of mutual interest. In order to safeguard services to students, and to ensure that these services continue to be provided competently by professional staff, professional counseling personnel need the political support of the faculty. By being recognized as support personnel for faculty, counseling personnel are more likely to have faculty advocates who will endorse the administrative allocation of scarce campus resources to counseling services. Peterson, Sampson, and Reardon (1991) predict that the traditional role of the career counselor (i.e., individual counselor and test-administrator and interpreter) will be supplemented (not supplanted) by three other roles: teacher-educator, designer-developer-evaluator, and strategic planner. The career counselor as strategic planner:

> Focuses on the contribution of career counseling services to the good of the organization and the community. . . . As a strategic planner, the counselor becomes proactive in promoting the career service by constantly entertaining the possibility for extending the services made available to the organization. . . . The strategic planning role also requires that career counselors possess a strong belief in the worth of their profession for enhancing the quality of life. (p. 422)

Taking their services to the faculty should constitute a significant part of any counseling service's strategic plan.

THE LARGER CONTEXT

Can there be a productive integration of the three perspectives, applied, academic, and administrative, within a context of power discrepancy and competition for resources, to advance the interests of counseling services in the university? The literature would suggest that the answer is yes, if the counseling interests on campus take the challenge seriously and take the initiative. The challenge for counseling centers and counseling personnel is to demonstrate the importance of their activities to the decision makers for university expenditures, given that their direct representation among decision makers likely always will be low.

Although addressing the establishment of a women's studies program rather than the maintenance of counseling services, the leading career theorist, Lenore Harmon, revealed an acute understanding of how those without power might get things done on a university campus. "We chose not to become an academic department, not to become a student services department, but to be a resource department for both faculty and students who wanted to learn more about the scholarship associated with women's studies" (Fouad, 1997, p. 104). This option is open to those who are establishing new entities. For those with established units, the manipulation of the existing power structure is the more realistic approach.

In a power-discrepant relationship, why should the participant with less power help the participant with more power? Ultimately, when the faculty loses its power within the university, they will be better allies with the staff as the entire institution of higher education loses power relative to more powerful social institutions. Counseling psychologists' contributions to faculty interests can include typical occupational mental health issues such as stress, violence, harassment, and discrimination, but they also can include helping faculty deal with change in the social contract of their workplace. Helping faculty deal with threats to tenure and to the traditional permanence in employment that faculty have enjoyed will help forge a working alliance between faculty and staff that may prove useful in a larger arena of conflict. Although many current faculty will live their whole careers without a reduction in their own employment security, more junior faculty are less likely to have full-time permanent positions for all of their professional lives. Their conditions of work, and their power, will become more similar to that of other professionals in the university community. Holland's (1996) prediction for nonprofessional workers will hold for more and more professional workers, including staff and, finally, faculty in universities:

> Large proportions of the population must learn to cope with transient and unpredictable work opportunities. Among other things, the need for a sense of personal identity will greatly increase, for the stable employment structures of the past have reduced the need for personal identity and independent planning. Many people will have to create their own structure for combining incompatible work with a more satisfying social and recreational life. To deal with this need, what has been seen as career counseling may become life counseling, in which work is an important facet of creating a more satisfying life. (p. 404)

The university needs people who understand that career counseling is life counseling. The people who provide counseling services in universities and the people who conduct the research and teach the next generation of professionals need to work together to meet the needs of the students, the staff, and the faculty. Those with less power need to be perceived as critically important by those with more power in order to secure the place of career psychology in the university.

The abstract for the article version of Levinson's (1994) Distinguished Professional Contributions to Knowledge award address is as follows:

> The failure of many American corporations to adapt to changed economic circumstances has become a major social concern. Many reasons have been alleged for those catastrophes. These allegations describe the ostensible reasons, but they do not explain adequately. The explanations are fundamentally psychological, significantly having to do with individual and organizational narcissism, unconscious recapitulation of family dynamics in the organization, exacerbating dependency, psychologically illogical organiza-

tion structure and compensation schemes, inadequate management of change, and inability to recognize and manage cognitive complexity. To deal more effectively with such problems calls for greater psychological sophistication among boards of directors and senior executives. (p. 428)

Levinson's address did not mention universities among the organizations that have fallen, but a university counseling psychologist reading this industrial–organizational analysis will observe many points relevant to university dysfunction. Dealing more effectively with the psychological experience of the people who make a university function well or poorly calls for greater psychological sophistication among the faculty and the administration. The counseling staff could help those who constitute the power structure of the university function more effectively to the benefit of all, safeguarding not only the provision of counseling services to students but helping to save the institution from itself.

REFERENCES

American Psychiatric Association (1994). *Diagnostic and statistical manual of mental disorders* (4th ed.). Washington, DC: Author.
Bishop, J. B. (1995). Emerging administrative strategies for college and university counseling centers. *Journal of Counseling and Development, 74*, 33–38.
Blustein, D. L. (1992). Toward the reinvigoration of the vocational realm of counseling psychology. *The Counseling Psychologist, 20*, 112–123.
Centers, R., & Cantril, H. (1946). Income satisfaction and income aspiration. *Journal of Abnormal and Social Psychology, 41*, 64–69.
Crites, J. O. (1969). *Vocational psychology: The study of vocational behavior and development.* New York: McGraw-Hill.
Dean, L. A., & Meadows, M. E. (1995). College counseling: Union and intersection. *Journal of Counseling and Development, 74*, 139–142.
Fitzgerald, L. F., & Osipow, S. H. (1988). We have seen the future, but is it us? The vocational aspirations of graduate students in counseling psychology. *Professional Psychology: Research and Practice, 19*, 575–583.
Fouad, N. A. (1997). Lenore White Harmon: One woman's career development. *The Counseling Psychologist, 25*, 96–115.
Gallagher, R. P. (1989). *Counseling center survey and directory.* Pittsburgh: University of Pittsburgh Counseling Center.
Geraghty, M. (1997, August). Campuses see steep increase in students seeking counseling. *The Chronicle of Higher Education, 43*(47), A32–A33.
Heppner, M. J., O'Brien, K. M., Hinkelman, J. M., & Flores, L. Y. (1996). Training counseling psychologists in career development: Are we our own worst enemies? *The Counseling Psychologist, 24*, 105–125.
Hilt, D. (1986, April). More collegiality could foster civilized behavior in academe. *The Chronicle of Higher Education,* A80.
Holland, J. L. (1996). Exploring careers with a typology: What we have learned and some new directions. *American Psychologist, 51*, 397–406.
Hotelling, K. (1990). Taking the lead. *The Counseling Psychologist, 18*, 619–622.

June, L. N. (1990). Challenges and limits: A provocative but limited view. *The Counseling Psychologist, 18,* 623–627.

Kjos, D. (1995). Linking career counseling to personality disorders. *Journal of Counseling and Development, 73,* 592–597.

Levinson, H. (1994). Why the behemoths fell: Psychological roots of corporate failure. *American Psychologist, 49,* 428–436.

Levy, S. R. (1990). Challenges and limits: A view from a chief student affairs office. *The Counseling Psychologist, 18,* 614–618.

Mintz, L. B. (1992). Assistant professor: Paranoid or self-preserving. *The Counseling Psychologist, 20,* 39–46.

Morrill, W. H., Oetting, E. R., & Hurst, J. C. (1974). Dimensions of counselor functioning. *Personnel and Guidance Journal, 53,* 354–359.

Osipow, S. H. (1986). Career issues through the life span. In M. S. Pallak, & R. O. Perloff (Eds.), *Psychology and work: Productivity, change, and employment* (pp. 137–168). Washington, DC: American Psychological Association.

Osipow, S. H. (1992). Adjustment to career entry: Issues for new counseling psychologists. *The Counseling Psychologist, 20,* 103–106.

Osipow, S. H., & Spokane, A. R. (1983). *Manual for the occupational environment scales, personal strain questionnaire, and personal resources questionnaire.* Columbus, OH: Marathon Consulting and Press.

Pace, D., Stamler, V. L., Yarris, E., & June, L. (1996). Rounding out the cube: Evolution to a global model for counseling centers. *Journal of Counseling and Development, 74,* 321–325.

Peterson, G. W., Sampson, J. P., Jr., & Reardon, R. B. (1991). *Career development and services: A cognitive approach.* Pacific Grove, CA: Brooks/Cole.

Pion, G. M., Mednick, M. T., Astin, H. S., Iijima Hall, C. C., Kenkel, M. B., Keita, G. P., Kohout, J. L., & Kelleher, J. C. (1996). The shifting gender composition of psychology: Trends and implications for the discipline. *American Psychologist, 51,* 509–528.

Rayman, J. R. (1996). Apples and oranges in the career center: Reaction to R. Reardon. *Journal of Counseling and Development, 74,* 286–287.

Reardon, R. (1996). A program and cost analysis of a self-directed career decision-making program in a university career center. *Journal of Counseling and Development, 74,* 280–285.

Stolz-Loike, M. (1996). Annual review: Practice and research in career development and counseling—1995. *Career Development Quarterly, 45,* 99–140.

Stone, G. L., & Archer, J., Jr. (1990). College and university counseling centers in the 1990s: Challenges and limits. *The Counseling Psychologist, 18,* 539–607.

Waehler, C. A., Hardin, S. I., & Rogers, J. R. (1994). College students' perceptions of the relationship between fee and counseling. *Journal of Counseling and Development, 73,* 88–93.

Wilson, R. (1997, August). Universities turn to psychologists to help dysfunctional departments. *The Chronicle of Higher Education, 43*(47), A10–A11.

Wilson, S. B., Mason, T. W., & Ewing, M. J. M. (1997). Evaluating the impact of receiving university-based counseling services on student retention. *Journal of Counseling Psychology, 44,* 316–320.

Chapter 12

Toward a Comprehensive Theory of Career Development: Dispositions, Concerns, and Narratives

Mark L. Savickas
Northeastern Ohio Universities College of Medicine

One of Osipow's major contributions to the fields of vocational psychology and career counseling continues to be his efforts to describe, evaluate, and compare theories of career choice, development, and adjustment. Osipow's interest in this topic spans his career in counseling psychology. He began his reading and reflection on career theory when, as a graduate student at Syracuse University in the late 1950s, he wrote a term paper on the topic. After completing his doctoral studies, Osipow worked in the Counseling Center at Pennsylvania State University (1961–1967) which was directed by Donald Ford who had written a book on theories of counseling and psychotherapy (Ford & Urban, 1963). Osipow's relationship with Ford, along with the intellectual climate at Penn State, nurtured Osipow's ambition to expand his term paper into a textbook that organized and explained the theories of career development. That book, *Theories of Career Development*, first published in 1968, is now in its fourth edition (Osipow & Fitzgerald, 1996). Osipow's (1968) book along with Crites' book on *Vocational Psychology* (1969) helped crystallize vocational psychology as basic science discipline, distinct from the applied psychology of career counseling. Furthermore, *Theories of Career Development* became the standard textbook for generations of graduate students enrolled in career counseling courses.

In the preface to the first edition, Osipow (1968) explained that he wrote *Theories of Career Development* to examine and evaluate current theories and pertinent empirical findings as well as to compare similarities and differences in the theories. "A further purpose of this book is to attempt to synthesize some general theoretical statements which might integrate the more useful and effective constructs of the various theoretical positions, as well as to identify the ingredients common to most of the theories" (p. viii). Osipow's enduring interest in identifying and synthesizing common elements in career theories, in due course, resulted in a landmark article written to celebrate the 20th anniversary of the *Journal of Vocational Behavior*, which he founded. In this article, entitled "Convergence in theories of career choice and development: Review and prospect," Osipow (1990) examined the convergence in four major career theories that had remained central in vocational psychology and career counseling for at least the life of the journal he founded: trait-and-factor (Holland, 1997), social learning (Krumboltz, 1994), developmental (Super, Savickas, & Super, 1996), and work adjustment (Dawis, 1984). Osipow explained that these four theories now resemble each other in important ways, prompting him to examine the possibility of theory unification. This seminal article induced vocational psychologists to consider the possibility of theory integration (e.g., Borgen, 1991; Super, 1992; Hackett, Lent, & Greenhaus, 1991), which in due course led to a national conference and subsequent book on *Convergence in Theories of Career Development* (Savickas & Lent, 1994).

PROBLEMS IN CONVERGENCE FROM PERSPECTIVE OF LIFE-SPAN, LIFE-SPACE THEORY

The convergence in career theories strongly influenced the prevailing presentation of life-span, life-space theory (Super, Savickas, & Super, 1996). The life-span, life-space approach to comprehending careers evolved over a 50-year period as Super used the functionalist approach to empirically integrate existing knowledge. He synthesized what had been learned by researchers and scholars into conceptual models that allowed him and others to note contradictory findings, locate gaps in research, and attempt explanatory efforts. Thus, the current life-span, life-space model includes four distinct theory segments: individual differences (including vocational interests and abilities), development (including life stages and career maturity), self-concept (including dimensions and their implementation), and context (including life roles and their salience). Each segment was developed independently, and during a different historical epoch, with the hope that someday the segments would be conceptually and empirically integrated into a comprehensive description of career development.

In preparing the most recent presentation of the theory, I tried to integrate as tightly as possible the four segments. The time seemed right for such an attempt because of the interest in theory unification. Furthermore, any success in such a unification would have heuristic implications for further converging life-span, life-space theory with other major career theories. As I worked toward integrating the segments of life-span, life-space theory, I concluded that each distinct segment was internally consistent yet weaving them together into a coherent whole was difficult. One of the major stumbling blocks was the core construct of career maturity, a hallmark of the developmental segment in life-span, life-space theory. This predicament prompted an article (Savickas, 1997a) raising the possibility that further advances in career development theory might require replacing maturity with a new construct, one that would allow tighter integration with the other three theory segments. In that article, I proposed that "adaptability" could replace maturity. After thinking about adaptability and maturity, I have come to some new realizations and I must thank Crites (1997) for the motivation to pursue this line of thinking and Vondracek (1997) for specific ideas that elaborated my thinking.

In the first half of this chapter, I interrogate the vitality of career maturity as a life-span construct by enumerating 12 reasons why career development theories, and their unification, might benefit from redefining or replacing the construct of maturity. I use these criticisms to prescribe a dozen criteria that must be met by any replacement for career maturity. In the second half of the chapter, I describe a framework for more completely comprehending careers, one that allows consideration of vocational personality dispositions, career concerns, career narratives, and developmental processes. A second goal for the chapter is to examine contemporary theorizing in personality, motivational, and developmental psychology to identify potential ways to integrate the segments of life-span, life-space theory and then link this theory to other major theories of career, development, personality, and motivation.

Vitality of Career Maturity for Future Theorizing

Career maturity has long been the principal construct in the developmental theory of vocational behavior. Originally, it was conceived of as readiness to make educational and vocational choices. In a short period of time, choice readiness became vocational maturity, and in due course, career maturity. The construct of career maturity was generalized across the life-span to denote a readiness to deal with the vocational development tasks appropriate to an individual's life stage. Having held center stage in career development theory for 40 years, career maturity has garnered an impressive amount of empirical support concerning its operational definition, nomological network, and construct validity. Unfortunately, some critics have shown that conceptualizations of career maturity have not remained current with advances in life-span, developmental psychology. Prompted by an interest in unifying the four distinct segments within life-span, life-space theory and then converging it with other career development theories, I have become concerned about 12 limitations inherent to the career maturity construct that may weaken its viability and vitality for future theorizing about careers.

1. Career Maturity Fosters a Function-Centered Theory but Hinders a Life-Span Theory

Baltes, Lindenberger, and Staudinger (1996) differentiated between two metatheoretical strategies for developing a life-span theory. They called the first strategy a *person-centered or holistic* approach. This strategy for theory construction emphasizes the longitudinal study of lives, in fact, a life is the very unit of study. Age periods, states, and stages are connected into "one overall, sequential pattern of lifetime individual development" (p. 3). Vocational psychologists think of this as the biographical study of lives and refer to it as *life-course psychology*. Theories familiar to vocational psychologists include Erikson's (1950) ontogenetic theory of psychosocial development and Buehler's (1933) life stages. When Super (1954) decided to study careers, he adopted Buehler's five stages in designing the Career Pattern Study (CPS). As originally conceived, this longitudinal study was to follow careers from ninth grade through age 35. CPS researchers accumulated tremendous amounts of data on 100 ninth-grade boys. While waiting for career patterns to unfold, CPS researchers concentrated on using this data to characterize the vocational developmental tasks and coping behaviors of the exploration stage in a career. This concentration on vocational maturation during adolescence represented a switch away from a life-course perspective, a switch that would prevail for about 20 years.

The research on adolescents in the exploration of their careers represents what Baltes, Lindenberger, and Staudinger (1996) identified as the second strategy for advancing life-span psychology. This *function-centered* strategy focuses on a category of behavior, such as initial choice of an occupation by adolescents, and examines the processes and mechanisms involved. The function-centered approach typically produces an *age-specialized* developmental theory. Of course, Super (1942, p. 135) and his colleagues knew that eventually they would have to characterize the life course with career patterns and a model of maturity specific to each career stage—at each period conceptualizing a new structure and mechanisms. Taken together, career patterns across the life course and a developmental sequence of stage-focused models and mechanisms of maturity would portray the overall landscape of career development theory. Unfortunately, this never happened because Super spent the majority of his own career studying adolescents and young adults.

2. Scant Empirical Evidence Exists Concerning the Predictive Validity of Career Maturity Relative to Subsequent Career Stages

If a researcher is primarily interested in one segment of the life course, as Super was, that segment must eventually be related to later segments in the life course (Brown, 1990; Osipow & Fitzgerald, 1996; Swanson, 1992). This is major problem with career maturity; researchers have rarely related adolescent career maturity to its sequella and long-term consequences. Of course, vocational psychologists relied on Havinghurst's developmental maxim as they argued that people who do not choose a viable and suitable occupation would later encounter significant problems in implementing and stabilizing these choices. Unfortunately, there is little empirical evidence that adolescent career maturity predicts adult occupational adjustment. Some evidence exists (Savickas, 1993) but evidence also exists that shows maturity makes no difference (Noeth, 1983), or even that more mature people may be more likely to change occupations (Gribbons & Lohnes, 1982). This is a complicated issue that can only be resolved through longitudinal research that examines connections between earlier developmental processes and later developmental processes and outcomes.

3. Maturity Denotes a Linear and Unidirectional Movement Toward Higher Levels of Functioning

Career maturity represents a unidirectional, linear, and hierarchical model. As such, it describes a universal and cumulative sequence of increased functioning aimed at a single end state, namely, work adjustment. The original conceptions of career maturity followed the biological concepts of growth and maturation articulated by Werner (1948), Beilin (1955), and Harris (1957). Although vocational maturity seems to loosely fit the conceptual needs of the growth and exploration stages, it certainly does not fit the needs of subsequent stages. Maturation privileges the exploration stage as the most important period in a career. Establishment, maintenance, and decline do not necessarily involve linear increases. For example, Super characterized the establishment stage with five coping behaviors, only two of which are positive: instrumentation and stabilizing. The other three are negative in connotation: drifting, floundering, and stagnating. The maintenance stage obviously involves little growth. As its name implies, maintenance denotes a period of holding on at worst and updating at best. In fact, the maintenance substages articulated by Super are not developmental; instead, they reflect distinct styles of maintaining oneself in an occupational position. Decline or disengagement is not growth, and one would be hard pressed to stretch the construct of maturity to describe this final stage in a career.

4. Maturity has Inadvertently Encouraged a Reliance on Age as the Developmental Indicator

Physical maturation is an age-based process, so many researchers implicitly or explicitly use age as an indicator of maturation. Thus, age becomes a proxy for development. For example, in constructing the Vocational Development Inventory, Crites (1965) selected only items that showed a monotonic increase with age, arguing that this relationship was a necessary yet not sufficient condition for an operational definition of career maturity. However, career maturity should not be treated as an age-based process similar to physical maturation. Researchers need to attend more closely to developmental organizers other than age. These organizers should reflect the ontogenetic processes involved in continuity and change across a career. The concept of development should still be used to organize the evidence about life-long adaptive processes, yet it should be operationally defined by variables such as identity, self-concept, and coping mechanisms.

5. Development Includes Losses as Well as Gains

An open and plastic system that does not rely on age as a developmental indicator would account for losses as well as gains. Growth denotes an increase in adaptive functioning whereas development denotes improvement. Whereas growth connotes increase following gain, development can follow gain, decrease, or loss. Thus, development is not linear; it comes in fits and starts. Therefore, life-course psychologists and sociologists assert that a life-span theory must comprehend loss, as well as growth. For example, Baltes, Lindenberger, and Staudinger (1996) argued that any truly life-span theory needs to comprehensively address issues of gain, loss, and resilience. Each life stage has some combination of all three and should be characterized by a different proportions of growth, resilience, and loss. This means that in career development theory, the stages of growth and exploration could be characterized primarily by growth, yet some attention should be paid to loss and resilience. For example, as adolescents become more independent (and therefore more career mature), they lose some amount of affective and instrumental dependence on their parents. As a teenager moves from a group of chums to partner with a friend of the other sex, she or he loses the sense of identity anchored in the former clique. The balance of gains and losses may be an a heuristic way to characterize the school-to-work transition (Savickas, 1997c). The establishment and maintenance stages may involve more resilience and renewal than growth and, certainly as one progresses through them, losses will accumulate. When viewing the declines of the disengagement stage, regulation of loss is predominant, yet growth and recovery from loss are more or less possible depending upon an individual's biological state and cultural resources. Career development theory needs more complexity than provided by viewing maturation only as a progression of advances and gains.

6. Career Maturity Models Are Structural Not Developmental

The existing models of career maturation are structural not developmental. For example, Super's model structures career maturity in adolescence using four dimensions. Two attitudinal dimensions deal with response tendencies for foresight and curiosity: attitudes toward career planning and career exploration. Two cognitive dimensions deal with fund of information and rational decision making: knowledge about occupations and about decision making. These four dimensions are operationally defined by the Career Development Inventory. Notice that the model does not conceptualize maturation as improvement following recursive cycles of differentiation and integration like Neimeyer's (1988) developmental model. Rather, it is structural in defining maturation as increases on four trait-like dimensions. Crites has pointed out, however, that development in structure can be noted by increasing differentiation of the structure with increased age.

7. The Processes of Career Maturation Are Poorly Defined

The actual processes and mechanisms of career maturation are insufficiently described. Processes are mechanisms of action; they are distinct from the developmental tasks that prompt them and the attitudes and competencies that condition them. The construct of maturation, with its connotation of unfolding, does not encourage researchers to examine the actual processes that unfold career development. Career maturity models have been criticized because they generally ignore the learning and decisional processes that foster development (Brown, 1990; Hackett & Lent,

1994; Krumboltz, 1994). Certainly, developmental researchers could study, at a microlevel of analysis, the learning and decisional processes involved in life-span career development.

8. Some Dimensions of Career Maturity Privilege Traits More Highly Valued at Midcentury Than Now

The traits that compose career maturity may be less adaptive now than they have been in the past. In effect, the career maturity model takes the cardinal developmental task of adolescence, choosing a vocation, and outlines how to cope with that task in a planful, systematic, and rational manner. The maturity model privileges dimensions such as future orientation, emotional independence, systematic exploration, fund of information, rational decision making, and linear planning. With the advent of constructivist epistemologies, some scholars have attacked career maturity by deconstructing these dimensions and arguing for interdependence, other-than-rational decision making, and a focus on work rather than career. Taking the posture of "reconstructive postmodernism" allows researchers to consider new alternatives to these traditional either/or constructs. For example, rather than independence being the goal, maybe the goal should be interdependence or the judicious expression of dependence and independence contingent upon the situation.

9. Careers Today Do Not Follow a Fixed Course

At midcentury, vocational psychologists could be confident that dynamics between biology and culture prefigured pathways of development and forged an agenda of adaptive challenges called vocational development tasks. The tasks are really social expectations. Super weaved these expected tasks or anticipated developments into a script that can be called a grand narrative of career. The story expresses Western Christian values and middle-class attitudes, with little acknowledgment of cultural and personal diversity. This grand narrative of career rests in unalterable school curricula and predictable status passages, as well as a social opportunity structure that too often assigns developmental pathways based on gender, race, and ethnicity. The story of the stages articulated by Super and others tells a grand narrative about psychosocial maturation in a stable and predictable work world. Maybe no one individual ever lived all of it, yet the narrative, written at midcentury, portrays the then current societal expectations for a life, especially a male life. Today, society is revising the grand narrative, but the new storylines for contemporary lives are far from being clear, coherent, and complete. Today, in an unstable and rapidly changing society, individuals must create their own futures in various contexts. The new narratives will emphasize self-organization and self-regulation that advance individuals into an open and plastic tomorrow. Counselors might no longer talk about developing a career; instead, they may talk about managing a career.

10. Career Maturity May Manifest Some Aspects of Social Class

Holland once criticized career maturity as being interchangeable with the outcomes of growing up in a middle-class home. Postmodern and feminist critics implicate the normative and hierarchical position inherent in career maturity when it suggests that something is more grown, more mature, more developed than something else. Accordingly, it is important to examine whether the dimensions of career maturity rest on arbitrary grounds that consciously or unconsciously unfairly advantage some people. In other words, psychologists must ask whether the construct of career maturity is an objective variable or a manifestation of social class and cultural hegemony.

11. The Concentration on Maturity has Caused Career Development Theory to Isolate Itself From Person–Environment Fit Theory

Developmental and differential career psychology have evolved from two perspectives on the same behavior into two distinct discourse communities. Articles on career development theory and person–environment theory tend to appear in different journals and different graduate training programs emphasize one over the other. Clashes between the two research camps hinder advances in their common goal of researching and developing careers (Savickas & Lent, 1994). This bifurcation between differential and developmental approaches to career has not promoted the conceptual integration required by a life-span psychology of careers. Theorists must move beyond the antagonism caused by contrasting stability-oriented and change-oriented approaches to a position from which researchers can study the ontogenesis of both general commonalities in development and unique individual difference, as well as specify their age-related interplay. In collaboration, differentialists and developmentalists can create a comprehensive career theory that has as its primary substantive focus, the structure, sequence, and dynamics of the entire life course. For example, vocational psychology could benefit from a comprehensive theory about the development of interests. Such a theory might explain the origins and development of Holland's (1997) six vocational interest types (also known as RIASEC types) by integrating works that view the development of interests from the perspectives of aspirations (Gottfredson, 1981), ego-strength (Crites, 1960), intrinsic motivation (Blustein & Flum, 1999), personal meaning (Savickas, 1995), and cognition (Barak, 1981; Lent, Brown, & Hackett, 1994).

12. The Concentration on Maturity has Caused Career Development Theory to Ignore Advances in Developmental Psychology

Concentrating on maturity, which at midcentury was part of mainstream developmental psychology, seems to have caused career psychology to divert from contemporary developmental psychology that now focuses much more on interaction than unfolding and on contextual particulars rather than universal principles (Vondracek, Lerner, & Schulenberg, 1986). Developmental psychologists no longer rely on maturity as the central construct for conceptualizing human development. Accordingly, I propose that vocational psychologists retire the name "career maturity" and return to its original name "career choice readiness," that is, readiness for making educational and vocational choices during adolescence. This will allow life-span, life-space theory to retain its impressive conceptual and empirical literature on choice readiness while at the same time circumscribing its use to the career exploration stage. Rather than stretch career maturity beyond its range of convenience, educational/vocational choice readiness can retain its status as a heuristic stage-specific, function-centered construct and a noteworthy contribution to life-span developmental psychology.

What Next?

With the retirement of the career maturity construct, life-span, life-space career theory requires a new general theory of ontogenetic development from growth through disengagement. In response, researchers must construct new career development theories that, as their primary substantive goal, focus on the structure, sequence, and dynamics of the entire life course. Following from the twelve criticisms of career maturity as a central construct in life-span, life-space theory, I wish to propose a list of requirements for this new theorizing. Life-span, life-space developmental constructs must:

1. Serve both life-course theorizing and stage-specific, function-centered theorizing.
2. Emphasize connections between earlier and later developmental processes.

3. Allow an open and plastic construction of career development.
4. Not rely on age as a developmental organizer.
5. Comprehend gains as well as losses.
6. Avoid unique structural models for each stage.
7. Specify mechanisms of development for microlevel analysis.
8. Be bipolar and culturally sensitive.
9. Attend to the particular contexts that constrain individual developmental pathways.
10. Avoid normative and hierarchical connotations that privilege certain groups.
11. Reintegrate the developmental and differential perspectives on vocational behavior.
12. Exploit conceptual and empirical advances in developmental psychology and life-course sociology.

This list enumerates the criteria for a framework that integrates the theory segments of life-span, life-space among themselves and with other career theories. Such a framework does not currently exist, yet advances in personality, developmental, and motivational psychology suggest an outline for an initial framework. One such outline could be articulated by adapting a conceptual framework such as the one proposed by McAdams (1995) to describe personality theories. The second half of the present chapter attempts an initial effort to transpose McAdam's tripartitie model of personality theories to the vocational realm.

LEVELS OF PERSONALITY AND CAREER THEORY

McAdams (1995) advanced the idea that "personality descriptors encompass at least three independent levels: (a) dispositional traits, such as the Big Five (McCrae & Costa, 1990); (b) contextualized concerns, such as developmental tasks and personal strivings (Cantor & Zirkel, 1990); and (c) integrative narratives of the self." McAdams asserts that a full description of personality requires all three levels: dispositional traits, personal concerns, and life stories.

Each level of personality description has a particular range of convenience, with its own models. methods, and materials. Theory and research pertinent to each of these three levels "requires its own indigenous nomenclatures, taxonomies, theories, frameworks, and laws" (McAdams, 1995, p. 365). As postmodern scholarship instructs, theory is never neutral or objective because it shapes the very system of observations. Thus, a theory channels the data that is chosen for observation and the categories used to organize this data. McAdams (1995) conceptualized the levels of personality theories to link the theories, rather than continue epistemic wars about which theory is best and force scholars to join distinct discourse communities.

I believe that vocational psychologists interested in the unification of career theories and the eventual construction of a comprehensive theory can benefit from transporting McAdams' (1995) analysis of personality theories to the realm of vocational psychology. A full description of vocational behavior and career development, similar to a full description of personality, may also require at least three distinct levels of analysis. The remainder of the chapter examines this possibility, and then broaches the possibility of supplementing McAdams' tripartite conceptualization with a fourth level of analysis that concentrates on a construct which is indispensable to career development theory, namely, mechanisms of development.

Level I: Vocational Personality Types

The career theory that parallels McAdams' Level I dispositions, with an emphasis on the Big Five, appears to be Holland's (1997) typology of vocational personalities. Vocational personality types and Big Five dimensions both differ from traits in that they are dispositions. Traits attribute recurring uniformities in a person's social behavior to personality structure. Behavioral continuity reflects personality traits. A collection of traits into syndromes and dispositions constitute a type. Holland's conceptual framework provides a broad band tool for organizing phenomenon into type categories. Types represent abstract syndromes that emerge from concrete trait patterns. In fact, types are at a rather high level of abstraction despite being composed of a broad variety of concrete experiences. Types show a dispositional signature and include skills, interests, and abilities for dealing with life roles. Types can be thought of as blueprints, tools, guidelines, or preferences for adaptation to life tasks. As an abstraction of the thematic properties that form a generic, loose adaptive strategy, types constitute the content of personality. Furthermore, dispositional types have an organizing influence that affects how individuals construe reality and their core roles. Thus, dispositions represent a self-organization of core structure that influences construing and interpreting the world. Holland's (1997) RIASEC model of personality types offers a practical structure for identifying the personological and vocational results of an individual's efforts at self-organization.

Similar to the personality dispositions in McAdams' Level I, the six RIASEC personality types are decontextualized and relatively nonconditional constructs that describe syndromes of traits. The trait syndromes or vocational personality types provide extremely useful comparative dimensions for conducting a vocational appraisal of individuals because RIASEC dimensions have proven social and career significance. Furthermore, the types demonstrate cross-situational consistency and longitudinal stability. They are relatively nonconditional, meaning that they are recurrent theme across diverse situations under different conditions and in manifold contexts. Their longitudinal stability may eventually prove to involve a genetic component. For example, recent research suggests that genetic factors may explain as much as 40 or 50% of the variance in vocational interests (Gottfredson, 1999). There also seems to be strong cross-cultural evidence regarding the usefulness of the RIASEC model (Rounds & Tracey, 1996). In short, similar to personality traits (McAdams, 1995, p. 375), Holland's RIASEC types appear to have two valuable features: comparative dimensions and nonconditionality.

Level II: Career Concerns

Level I descriptors of personality and career concentrate on self-organization and may be viewed as psychological variables. In contrast, Level II descriptors emphasize self-extension into the social environment and may be viewed as psychosocial variables. The psychosocial descriptors are at level II because intrapersonal self-organization precedes interpersonal self-extension. Level II psychosocial variables describe how individuals reach out to integrate with society and regulate their own behavior relative to normative expectations. Level II descriptors provide an orientation to the particular historical time, culture context, life stage, and social role which locates an individual.

McAdams denotes Level II variables as personal concerns. In contrast to Level I dispositions, Level II personal concerns are contingent on contextual factors such as time, place, and role. These noncomparative and highly conditional personal concerns "speak to what people want, often during particular periods in their lives or within particular domains of action, and what life methods people use (strategies, plans, defenses, and so on) in order to get what they want or avoid getting what they don't want over time, in particular places, and/or with respect to particular roles" (McAdams, 1995, p. 376). McAdams operationally defines personal concerns borrowing a sentence from Cantor, Acker, and Cook-Flanagan (1992, p. 644): "those tasks that individual see as personally important and time consuming at particular times in their lives."

In addition to being contingent on life stage and historical era, personal concerns also depend on situational conditions. Conditional patterns (Thorne, 1989) influence behavior in a particular situation. Whereas vocational personality types refer to what people typically have, career concerns refer to what individuals do in a particular time and place. McAdams points out that Level II descriptors account for behavior that "is by and large local rather than general, subject to norms and expectations of a given social place or space" (p. 377). These actions are age-appropriate life adaptations whereas personality dispositions constitute a central structure of the self.

In the vocational realm, personal concern variables have been termed *career concerns*. These Level II descriptors of vocational behavior and career development concentrate on issues of social integration and self-regulation. Career concerns involve the situated use of strategies for effective performance of a specific role in a particular place at a certain time. An individual's career concerns include contextualized strategies, motivational systems, and domain-specific skills for dealing with age-appropriate developmental tasks and social expectations and for pursuing personal projects.

Career concerns have typically been studied by adherents to the developmental perspective on vocational behavior. They have attempted to chart the natural course of career concerns from grade school through retirement. In so doing, they have divided careers into ontogenetic stages and thematic issues denoted by periods of concern about vocational growth, exploration, establishment, maintenance, and decline (Super, 1957). Each of these five periods has been characterized by prototypical developmental tasks; pertinent attitudes, beliefs, and competencies; and relevant coping behaviors. For example, the construct of career maturity discussed in the first half of this chapter has been used to describe the exploration stage during which adolescents make educational and vocational choices. Researchers have characterized this process with developmental tasks of crystallizing and specifying; attitudes toward planning and exploring; beliefs about the work world and succeeding in it; competencies for decision making and problem solving; and coping behaviors.

The temporal context assumed by a life-span view distinguishes the developmental psychosocial perspective on vocational behavior from the differential psychological perspective which emphasizes individual differences in traits and types. Whereas RIASEC types are individual differences used to compare people, career concerns are psychosocial considerations used to compare an individual to himself or herself across developmental eras, as well as to other people.

In addition to addressing the temporal context of career concerns, life-span, life-space theory also addresses the situational context. Accordingly, it explicitly meets McAdams' (1995) suggestion of "seeking information on the most salient settings and environment that make up the ecology of the person's life" (p. 378). Life-span, life-space theory uses the construct of role salience to evaluate an individual's participation in, commitment to, and value expectations for five central life roles: student, worker, citizen, family member, and leisurite. Each role calls for different motivational strivings (i.e., values and goals) and requires different competencies and skills. How these interrelate, and which roles are most salient, strongly shapes career development.

The descriptors used in the life-span, life-space approach to locating career concerns in time and place all focus on self-regulation strategies and goal implementation during a particular ontogenetic period and in a specific social ecology. Thus, career concerns display themes and patterns of social meaning making arising from joint social activity that occurs in a certain cultural context, during a specific life stage, and in a distinct historical era. In short, Level II career concerns are highly contingent on the psychosocial context. In contrast, Level I vocational personality types seem to possess near-universal applicability, generalizing across numerous contexts. This difference may explain why Holland's (1997) RIASEC model and measures such as the Vocational Personality Inventory and the Self-Directed Search have been shown to be more easily transportable to other cultures than models of career concern and measures such as the Career Maturity Inventory and the Career Development Inventory.

McAdams (1995, p. 378) makes an interesting point when he compares Level I and Level II personality descriptors. Level I descriptors are now well-defined and clearly organized in taxonomies such as the Big Five, whereas Level II descriptors are still ill-defined and unorganized. This conclusion certainly extends to the realm of vocational psychology. Level I vocational personality types are well-defined and tightly organized, but Level II career concerns are merely summarized as an accumulation of empirical knowledge loosely organized into segmental theories such as the life-span, life-space approach to careers. A possible reason for this contrast, in addition to the fact that psychologists have studied Level I variables more intensively and for a longer time period, is that Level I variables concentrate on continuity and stability in occupational interests and vocational dispositions, whereas Level II variables emphasize change and development across the life span.

Level III: Career Narratives

Level III personality theories involve self-defining, life stories that are substantive, retrospective narratives about the self and others. These internalized narratives of the self usually include reflective descriptions about how the individual adapted to tasks and traumas. These narratives do more than explain where individuals have been and who they hope to become. By constructing a plot, the narratives address the question of

"Who am I?" The plot explains how they are agentic and to whom they feel connected. These stories of competence and connection impose a narrative structure on lived experience, one that explains the purpose and meaning for a life. The goal is to dramatically portray a dynamic life story and to narrate a theme or secret that makes a whole of an individual's life. For McAdams (1995), it is essential that this life story bring overall unity, purpose, and meaning to a life. Although, narratives explain discrete episodes, as whole they consciously organize and bound together a life. They give a life meaningful continuity over time. In short, the narratives about life path compose a life, that is, they "provide a purposeful self-history that explains how the self of yesterday became the self of today and will become the anticipated self of tomorrow" (p. 382).

Through construction of meaning, life-enhancing narratives foster self-understanding and enrich Level I self-organization and Level II self-extension. McAdams, Diamond, de St. Aubin, and Mansfield (1997) assert that Level III narratives begin to emerge during late adolescence and early adulthood as individuals create a self out of the fabric of their complex and contradictory experiences. They seek "to construct a more-or-less integrative narrative of the self to provide their life with a semblance of unity and purpose" (p. 678). In addition to being unique to adulthood, McAdams and his colleagues hypothesize that life narrative descriptors of personality are germane to modern and postmodern democratic societies that emphasize individuation of the self. "From this standpoint, life stories are jointly constructed by the person whose story it is and the culture within which that story has its constitutive meanings" (McAdams et al., 1997, p. 690). North American cultures foster individualism and, thus, promote stories of uniqueness and identity. Therefore, Level III life narratives are more unique than Level I vocational dispositions or Level II career concerns because these unique stories fully contextualize the self in time, place, and role.

Narrative construction of meaning interprets lived experience by concentrating on a story line that reveals unity and purpose in the self. Obviously, these interpretations include constructs and events that lie outside personality theories of Level I and II. In constructing life narratives, individuals are free to interpret the facts of their life experiences. The narrative explains how individuals interpret the life they have lived and the self they have constructed. Because narratives depend on interpretation of a unique life course, narratives are never as self-evident as dispositional types or the outcomes of developmental and motivational strivings. This is why full knowledge of RIASEC types tells nothing about identity and may be a reason why Holland developed the Vocational Identity Scale to augment his theory of vocational personality types.

In the vocational domain, the counterpart of life narrative descriptions of personality seems to be career; more precisely, subjective career. Level I and II personality theories typically rely on objective conceptions of the individual formed by observers or resulting from personality inventories. In contrast, the subjective life narratives of Level III consist of individuals' conceptions of their personalities from their own point of view as well as the meaning which they give to their lives. These narratives are not composed in terms of psychological traits or psychosocial concerns; instead, they articulate needs and goals, purpose and intentional action, as well as the resultant life patterns—the very stuff of career. Career is how we interpret our work and understand our productive and generative strivings. It embodies dispositional continuity and psychosocial change.

From the objective perspective of society, career is defined as the sequence of occupational positions that an individual holds during her or his life-span. Everyone has an objective career; it is a record of where they have been and what they have done. However, not everyone self-consciously reflects on his or her objective career to construct a life narrative that comprehends it. A subjective career denotes this self-conscious narrative about the vocational past, present, and future. People who do not think about their vocational past, present, and future still demonstrate an objective career yet they do not construct a subjective career. Hughes (1958) appears to be the first social scientist to distinguish between objective and subjective career: "a career consists, objectively, of a series of status and clearly defined offices . . . Subjectively, a career is the moving perspective in which the person sees his [or her] life as a whole and interprets the meaning of his [or her] various attributes, actions, and the things which happen to him [or her]" (p. 63). Miller-Tiedeman and Tiedeman (1985) best articulated the essence of a subjective career when they defined career as "the imposition of direction on vocational behavior."

Postmodern researchers and counselors have been using constructivism as an interpretive science with which to comprehend the narratives that compose a subjective career (Savickas, 1997b). Constructivism embodies a metatheory and epistemic stance that emphasizes the self-conceiving features of human knowing (R. Neimeyer, 1995). Applications of constructivist metatheory to career can be grouped into three categories: personal construct psychology, biographical hermeneutics, and the narrative paradigm. Personal construct approaches (G. Neimeyer, 1992) make meaning of vocational behavior by examining the personal constructs that individuals use to anticipate and interpret the role that work plays in their lives. George Kelly (1955) initiated this line of research when, in his monumental *Psychology of Personal Constructs*, he wrote that vocation is "one of the principal means by which one's life role is given clarity and meaning"

(p. 751). A second major constructivist approach to career narratives orig-inated with Super's (1954) life history model for comprehending career patterns. Today, this career pattern approach is subsumed by biographical hermeneutics that concentrates on the psychobiographical construction of careers (Bujold, 1990; Young & Collin, 1988, 1992). The third, and most recent approach to constructing careers integrates personal construct and biographical-hermeneutic approaches into a more comprehensive model with the idea that narration constructs meaning. With regard to the work role, narration forms career as a superordinate construct that guides voca-tional action along thematic lines of development. The work of Cochran (1997) and Jepsen (1992) exemplify the narrative approach to "career as story."

Clearly, Level III personality theories share much in common with the narrative construction of subjective career. Similar to life narratives about identity, career narratives seem germane to modern industrial and post-industrial societies, especially for middle class individuals who have the privilege of charting their career course. Furthermore, career narratives concentrate on creating meaning for the work-role, and their substance integrates individual lives with that of a community in telling about their productive and generative efforts to contribute to and cooperate with a social group.

Level IV: Mechanisms of Development

McAdams (1995) tripartite scheme of dispositional traits, personal con-cerns, and life narratives concentrates on the "content" of personality. He acknowledges that "process" constructs do not fit neatly into the three lev-els. The tripartite model addresses "features of personality that are poten-tial candidates for inclusion within the person's self-concept," that is the self as "me" rather than the ego processes of the "I" (McAdams, 1995, p. 390). In eschewing process while focusing on content, the model ignores variables such as learning, cognition, and decision making. This coincides well with the vocational domain where researchers have generally ignored the actual mechanisms of vocational development. Research on the process of career development should not be mistaken as involving atten-tion to true process variables. Instead, the focus has been on attitudes, competencies, and beliefs that condition these process variables. Attitudes toward and beliefs about career choice and decisional competencies are *not* decision making. Thus, a comprehensive theory about career devel-opment requires attention to a fourth level of descriptors, a category that directly addresses mechanisms of action.

Although vocational psychologists such as Gati (1996), Hackett and Lent (1992), and Krumboltz (1994) have nominated learning and decision making as critical process variables for explaining the actual mechanisms of career development, I prefer the model of selective optimization with compensation (SOC) advanced by Baltes and his colleagues (Baltes & Baltes, 1990; Baltes, Lindenberger, & Staudinger, 1996; Marsiske, Lang, Baltes, & Baltes, 1995) because it could link research in career development directly to a contemporary model in developmental psychology. Furthermore, the SOC model recommends itself to the study of career development because it was constructed to be applied to issues of general ontogenesis and domain-specific issues of adaptation. "Without specifying the substantive goals and outcomes of development, the SOC model is intended to characterize the processes that result in desired outcomes of development while minimizing undesirable ones" (Baltes, Lindenberger, & Staudinger, 1996, p. 42). Thus, the SOC model can be used to comprehend the development of Level I vocational personality types, Level II career concerns, and Level III subjective career.

Selective optimization with compensation is a conceptual model for analyzing changes in the adaptive potential of the self, or more simply, what is gained and what is loss by the person in everyday life. Baltes, Lindenberger, and Staudinger (1996, p. 37) view development as a process of selective adaptation and then define "successful development as the conjoint maximization of gains (desirable goals or outcomes) and the minimization of losses (avoidance of undesirable goals of outcomes)." The central mechanism of development is transactional adaptation to the environment. The actual process of development involves selection and then selective change in adaptive capacity. Thus, the basic component processes for the development of adaptive fitness are selection, optimization, and compensation. Selection and compensation are tools for the optimization of development and means of striving for desired outcomes and goals. Therefore, selection, compensation, and optimization represent fundamental agentic processes of personality that actually constitute the processes for advancing development, operationally defined by improvements in adaptive fitness.

"*Selection* involves goals or outcomes; *Optimization* involves goal related means to achieve success (desired outcomes); and *Compensation* involves a response to loss in goal-relevant means in order to maintain success of desired level of functioning (outcomes)" (Baltes et al., 1996, p. 38). Optimization involves procedural methods and processes that generate and refine means-end resources to achieve selected goals. Because there is no selection without loss, the individual must compensate for these losses. Compensation constitutes the response to loss of resources that were previously available for goal striving. Compensation can mean development of new resources or a change in selected direction. "It is also assumed that in reality the three components are always intertwined, that they form a cooperative (interactive) system of behavioral action or outcome-oriented functioning" (Baltes et al., 1996, p. 42). Selection, optimization, and compensation can be internal or external, conscious or unconscious, and active or passive.

Clearly, the SOC model can be used to comprehend vocational personality types, explain career concerns, and provide a close reading of career narratives. However, applying selective optimization with compensation at these three levels of analysis (psychological, psychosocial, and self) requires the use of different conceptual models, research methods, and assessment materials. Nevertheless, at Level I the SOC model may be useful in explaining the origins and development of vocational personality types. Certainly, selective optimization with compensation can be used to comprehend processes of self-organization and the development of dispositional response tendencies. Adaptive fitness also could help specify the dynamics involved in person-environment congruence. At Level II, adolescent career concerns about selecting educational and vocational paths involve issues of separating from childhood certainties and the comfort of authority rooted in the past while optimizing strivings for uniqueness and compensating for loss of connection to childhood chums. At Level III, the SOC model can be used to give close reading to career narratives. SOC processes can be used to highlight what is considered and selected as individuals become who they are, how choices are implement and optimized, and which regrets people feel about paths not taken and concomitant losses.

TOWARD A COMPREHENSIVE THEORY OF CAREER

Based on my analysis of career maturity and adaptation of McAdams' (1995) tripartite model of personality, I propose a four-level model for comprehending career theories and integrating them into a comprehensive model of careers. A first proposition states that the emergence of a RIASEC structure of personality is a precondition for adaptation. It represents the central structure of personality. The RIASEC model involves self-organization and it explains continuity and coherence in development. Stable RIASEC traits frame how adaptation takes place and influence potential for developmental changes. The adaptive orientation represented by a RIASEC type gives an individual a sense of continuity and coherence, as well as provides coping processes to master developmental changes and to adapt flexibly to changing circumstances.

A second proposition suggests that a secondary system of self-regulatory mechanisms emerges in conjunction with personality self-organization. These mechanisms, which remain generally the same throughout the life-span, meditate successful transactional adaptation. Currently, these mechanisms include concern, control, conviction, competence, and commitment (Super, Savickas, & Super, 1996). Their definitions integrate research findings from the career maturity literature with Erikson's (1950) constructs of psychosocial development. For example, career concern across the life span involves Erikson's trust versus mistrust theme, Super's future time perspective and planful attitudes, Crites' attitudes of orientation and involvement, Tiedeman and O'Hara's anticipation, and other closely related general purpose mechanisms such as optimism and hope.

Career narratives are the focus of the third proposition. Individuals who self-consciously reflect on their objective career can construct a subjective career in the form of a narrative. A career narrative comprehends the vocational self and shapes the further elaboration of this self-conception in the work world. Narratives about subjective career foster self-knowledge and clarify personal goals. A sense of subjective career heightens self-understanding and self-definition. More importantly, subjective career guides adaptation as it negotiates opportunities and constraints, and uses the self-organized personality dispositions to address self-regulatory concerns.

The fourth proposition seeks to specify the actual processes of continuity and change in career adaptation by adopting Baltes and Baltes' (1990) model of selective optimization with compensation. The process of career development involves selection, optimization, and compensation. These three process can be used at the microbehavioral level to specify the actual processes and mechanisms of development for vocational personality types, career concerns, and career narratives.

Taken together, the self-organization of personality dispositions, self-regulatory concerns, self-definitional narratives, and selective optimization processes should be sufficient to portray the landscape of life-span career development. But this raises an important practical question. Should researchers begin reflection and research aimed at linking the levels or just continue examining the variable in usual, separate levels of analysis. McAdams (1995) advises, for the personality domain, against trying to gain order by linking Level I to Level II. Instead, he recommends years of research to let order emerge empirically on Level II. He argues that it would be a mistake to try to explain Level II behavior in terms of Level I constructs; rather he urges researchers to "explore the terrain of Level II directly, without the maps provided by the Big Five" (p. 379). Transposing his argument to the vocational realm means that studying career concerns in disposition terms could be counter-productive, and produce a hierarchy of knowledge that privileges RIASEC traits as explanations of career concerns.

I expect different researchers to respond differently to this issue. On the one hand, some researchers probably will follow McAdams' advice and work to structure Level II concerns and Level III narratives until they are organized by a model as elegant as Holland's (1997) hexagon. Hopefully, the thematic issues of concern, control, convictions, competence, and commitment can someday be formed into a developmental model of recursive career concerns. On the other hand, some researchers will prefer to immediately begin linking variables across the three levels, as has been started by some personologists (e.g., Graziano, Jensen-Campbell, & Finch, 1997). Vocational researchers study, at multiple levels of analysis, how dispositions become situated strategies and goal directed activities. They could investigate improvements in person-environment interaction and movement toward increased congruence between self and situation at any age. Focusing on how improvements in person–environment fit eventuate across the life span requires understanding both continuity and change and should use development and individual differences as two organizers for and indicators of improvements in adaptive fitness. From an applied perspective, researchers could investigate practical problems such how Realistic personality types cope with the career decision-making process and what themes characterize their narratives about subjective career. This seems an intriguing tactic because different personality types probably express their career concerns differently and benefit from different interventions. Something as simple as routine interest inventory interpretations might be formulated and communicated differently for each RIASEC type. Regardless of researchers' preferences for investigation within or between levels of career theory, practitioners should be urged to comprehend clients' dispositional types, vocational concerns, and career narratives. Appropriate models, methods, and materials from each level of career theory should be used to assist clients in their quest for meaningful work and quality lives.

CONCLUSION

This chapter, prompted by Osipow's (1990) article on convergence in career theories, has analyzed problems in integrating the four segments of life-span, life-stage theory. This analysis led to suggestions for improving theorizing about life-span career development by incorporating advances in personality and developmental theory and by integrating differential and developmental perspectives on vocational behavior. Four propositions, emanating from transposing McAdams' (1995) tripartitie model of personality theories to the vocational realm, were advanced to provide an initial framework for research on unifying career theories into a comprehensive description of the structural and mechanism of vocational behavior across the life-span and in relation to other life roles. At a minimum, this framework for conceptualizing career at the levels of personality dispositions, psychosocial concerns, self-construction, and mechanisms of development allows for the systematic comparison of career theories, including each theory's core constructs, their range of convenience, epistemologic assumptions, and research domain. Career counselors are encouraged to continue to comprehend their clients' vocational behavior in terms of dispositions, concerns, and narratives while vocational psychologists work to link these variables into a comprehensive career theory.

REFERENCES

Baltes, P. B., & Baltes, M. M. (1990). Psychological perspectives on successful aging: The model of selective optimization with compensation. In P. B. Baltes & M. M. Baltes (Eds.), *Successful aging: Perspectives from the behavioral sciences* (pp. 1–34). New York: Cambridge University Press.

Baltes, P. B., Lindenberger, U., & Staudinger, U. M. (1996). Life-span theory in developmental psychology. In R. M. Lerner (Ed.), *Theoretical models of human development Volume 1: Handbook of child psychology* (5th ed.), Editor-in-Chief: William Damon. New York: Wiley.

Barak, A. (1981). Vocational interests: A cognitive view. *Journal of Vocational Behavior, 19*, 1–14.

Beilin, H. (1955). The application of general developmental principles to the vocational area. *Journal of Counseling Psychology. 2*, 53–57.

Blustein, D. L., & Flum, H. (1999). A self-determination perspective of exploration and interests in career development. In M. Savickas & A. Spokane (Eds.), *Vocational interests: Their meaning. measurement. and counseling use* (pp. 345–366). Palo Alto, CA: Davies-Black.

Borgen, F. (1991). Megatrends and milestones in vocational behavior: A 20-year counseling psychology retrospective. *Journal of Vocational Behavior, 39*, 263–290.

Brown, D. (1990). Summary, comparison, and critique of the major theories. In D. Brown, L. Brooks, & Associates, *Career choice and development: Applying contemporary theories to practice* (2nd ed., pp. 338–363). San Francisco: Jossey-Bass.

Buehler, C. (1933). *Der menschilche lebenslauf als psychologisches problem*. Leipzig: Hirzel.

Bujold, C. (1990). Biographical-hermeneutical approaches to the study of career development. In R. A. Young & W. A. Borgen (Eds.), *Methodological approaches to the study of career* (pp. 57–69). New York: Praeger.

Cantor, N., Acker, M., & Cook-Flanagan, C. (1992). Conflict and preoccupation in the intimacy life task. *Journal of Personality and Social Psychology, 63*, 644–655.

Cantor, N., & Zirkel, S. (1990). Personality, cognition, and purposive behavior. In L. Pervin (Ed.), *Handbook of personality theory and research* (pp. 135–164). New York: Guilford Press.

Cochran, L. (1997). *Career counseling: A narrative approach*. Newbury Park, CA: Sage.

Crites, J. O. (1960). Ego-strength in relation to vocational interest development. *Journal of Counseling Psychology, 7*, 137–143.

Crites, J. O. (1965). Measurement of vocational maturity in adolescence: 1. Attitude Test of the Vocational Development Inventory. *Psychological Monographs. 79* (2, Whole No. 595).

Crites, J. O. (1969). *Vocational psychology*. New York: McGraw-Hill.

Crites, J. O. (1997, August). The validity of career maturity: Messick's model. In M. L. Savickas (Chair) *Career maturity: The construct's validity, vitality. and viability* (Cassette Recording No. APA 97-1116A-B/Sound Images, Englewood, CO). Symposium conducted at the meeting of the American Psychological Association, Chicago.

Dawis, R. (1984). The theory of work adjustment and person-environment correspondence counseling. In D. Brown, L. Brooks, & Associates, *Career choice and development* (3rd ed., pp. 75–120). San Francisco, CA: Jossey-Bass.

Erikson, E. H. (1950). *Childhood and society*. New York: Norton.

Ford, D. H., & Urban, H. B. (1963). *Systems of psychotherapy*. New York: Wiley.

Gati, I. (1996). Computer-assisted career counseling: Challenges and prospects. In M. L. Savickas & W. B. Walsh (Eds.), *Handbook of career counseling theory and practice* (pp. 169–190). Palo Alto, CA: Davies-Black.

Gottfredson, L. S. (1981). Circumscription and compromise: A developmental theory of occupational aspirations [Monograph]. *Journal of Counseling Psychology, 28*, 545–579.

Gottfredson. L. S. (1999). The nature and nurture of vocational interests. In M. Savickas & A. Spokane (Eds.), *Vocational interests: Their meaning, measurement, and counseling use* (pp. 57–86) Palo Alto, CA: Davies-Black.

Graziano, W. G., Jensen-Campbell, L. A., & Finch, J. F. (1997). The self as a mediator between personality and adjustment. *Journal of Personality and Social Psychology, 73*, 392–404.

Gribbons, W., & Lohnes, P. (1982). *Careers in theory and experience*. Albany: State University of New York Press.

Hackett, G., & Lent, R. W. (1992). Theoretical advances and current inquiry in career psychology. In S. D. Brown & R. W. Lent (Eds.), *Handbook of counseling psychology* (2nd ed., pp. 419–451). New York: Wiley.

Hackett, G., Lent, R., & Greenhaus, J. (1991). Advances in vocational theory and research: A 20-year retrospective. *Journal of Vocational Behavior, 38*, 3–38.

Harris, D. B. (Ed.). (1957). *The concept of development*. Minneapolis: University of Minnesota Press.

Holland, J. L. (1997). *Making vocational choices: A theory of vocational personalities and work adjustment* (3rd ed.). Odessa, FL: Psychological Assessment Resources.

Hughes, E. (1958). *Men and their work*. Glencoe, IL: The Free Press.

Jepsen, D. A. (1992, March). Understanding careers as stories. In M. L. Savickas (chair) *Career as story*. Symposium conducted at the American Association for Counseling and Development, Baltimore, MD.

Kelly, G. A. (1955). *The psychology of personal constructs*. New York: Norton.

Krumboltz, J. D. (1994). Improving career development theory from a social learning perspective. In M. L. Savickas & R. W. Lent (Eds.), *Convergence in career development theories* (pp. 9–31). Palo Alto, CA: CPP Books.

Lent, R. W., Brown, S. D., & Hackett, G. (1994). Toward a unifying social-cognitive theory of career and academic interest, choice, and performance [Monograph]. *Journal of Vocational Behavior, 45*, 79–122.

Marsiske, M., Lang, F. R., Baltes, M. M., & Baltes, P. B. (1995). Selective optimization with compensation: Life-span perspectives on successful human development. In R. A. Dixon & L. Blackman (Eds.), *Compensation for psychological defects and declines: Managing losses and promoting gains* (pp. 35–79). Hillsdale, NJ: Lawrence Erlbaum Associates.

McAdams, D. P. (1995). What do we know when we know a person? *Journal of Personality, 63*, 365–396.

McAdams, D. P., Diamond, A., de St. Aubin, E., & Mansfield, E. (1997). Stories of commitment: The psychosocial construction of generative lives. *Journal of Personality and Social Psychology, 72*, 678–694.

McCrae, R. R., & Costa, P. T. Jr. (1990). *Personality in adulthood*. New York: Guilford Press.

Miller-Tiedeman, A., & Tiedeman, D. (1985). Educating to advance the human career during the 1980's and beyond. *Vocational Guidance Quarterly, 34*, 15–30.

Neimeyer, G. J. (1988). Cognitive integration and differentiation in vocational behavior. *The Counseling Psychologist, 16*, 440–475.

Neimeyer, G. J. (1992). Personal constructs in career counseling and development. *Journal of Career Development, 18*, 163–173.

Neimeyer, R. A. (1995). An appraisal of constructivist psychotherapies. In M. J. Mahoney (Ed.), *Cognitive and constructive csvchotherapies: Theory, research, and practice* (pp. 163–194). New York: Springer.

Noeth, R. (1983). The effects of enhancing expressed vocational choice with career development measures to predict occupational field. *Journal of Vocational Behavior, 22*, 365–375.

Osipow, S. H. (1968). *Theories of career development.* New York: Appleton-Century-Crofts.

Osipow, S. H. (1990). Convergence in theories of career choice and development: Review and prospect. *Journal of Vocational Behavior, 36*, 122–131.

Osipow, S. H., & Fitzgerald, L. F. (1996). *Theories of career development* (4th ed.). Needham Hts., MA: Allyn & Bacon.

Rounds, J., & Tracey, T. J. (1996). Cross-cultural structural equivalence of RIASEC models and measures. *Journal of Counseling Psychology*, 310–329.

Savickas, M. L. (1993). The predictive validity of career development measures. *Journal of Career Assessment, 1*, 93–104.

Savickas, M. L. (1995). Examining the personal meaning of inventoried interests during career counseling. *Journal of Career Assessment, 3*, 188–201.

Savickas, M. L. (1997a). Adaptability: An integrative construct for life-span, life-space theory. *Career Development Quarterly, 45*, 247–259.

Savickas, M. L. (1997b). Constructivist career counseling: Models and methods. In R. Neimeyer & G. Neimeyer (Eds.), *Advances in personal construct psychology: Volume 4* (pp. 149–182). Greenwich, CT: JAI Press.

Savickas, M. L. (1997c, August). Developmental perspective on the transition from school to work. In R. L. Worthington & R. W. Lent (Co-chairs) *Applying vocational psychology theories to the school-to-work transition* (Cassette Recording No. APA 97-2122A-B/Sound Images, Englewood, CO). Symposium conducted at the meeting of the American Psychological Association, Chicago, IL.

Savickas, M. L., & Lent, R. (Eds.). (1994). *Convergence in theories of career development: Implications for science and practice.* Palo Alto, CA: Consulting Psychologists Press.

Super, D. E. (1942). *The dynamics of vocational adjustment.* New York: Harper.

Super, D. E. (1954). Career patterns as a basis for vocational counseling. *Journal of Counseling Psychology, 1*, 12–19.

Super, D. E. (1957). *The psychology of careers.* New York: Harper.

Super, D. E. (1992). Toward a comprehensive theory of career development. In D. Montross & C. Shinkman (Eds.), *Career development: Theory and practice* (pp. 3–64). Springfield, IL: Charles C. Thomas.

Super, D. E., Savickas, M. L., & Super, C. M. (1996). The life-span, life-space approach to careers. In D. Brown, L. Brooks, & Associates. *Career choice and development: Applying contemporary theories to practice* (3rd ed., pp. 121–178). San Francisco, CA: Jossey-Bass.

Swanson, J. L. (1992). Vocational behavior, 1989–1991: Life-span career development and reciprocal interaction of work and non-work. *Journal of Vocational Behavior, 41*, 101–161.

Thorne, A. (1989). Conditional patterns, transference, and the coherence of personality across time. In D. M. Buss & N. Cantor (Eds.), *Personality psychology: Recent trends and emerging directions* (pp. 149–159). New York: Springer.

Vondracek, F. W. (1997, August). The viability of career maturity theory: A developmental-contextualist perspective. In M. L. Savickas (Chair) *Career maturity: The construct's validity, vitality, and viability* (Cassette Recording No. APA 97-1116A-B/Sound Images, Englewood, CO). Symposium conducted at the meeting of the American Psychological Association, Chicago, IL.

Vondracek, F. W., Lerner, R. M., & Schulenberg, J. E. (1986). *Career development: A life-span developmental approach.* Hillsdale, NJ: Lawrence Erlbaum Associates.

Werner, H. (1948). *Comparative psychology of mental development*. New York: International Universities Press.

Young, R. A., & Collin, A. (1988). Career development and hermeneutical inquiry Part I: The framework of a hermeneutical approach. *Canadian Journal of Counselling, 22*, 153–161.

Young, R. A., & Collin, A. (1992). *Interpreting career: Hermeneutical studies of lives in context*. Westport, CT: Praeger.

Author Index

A

Acker, M., 307, 317
Abu-Freha, A., 138, 163, 165
Ackerman, P. L., 124, 125, 127, 130, 238, 250, 251
Adler, N., 93, 94
Aiken, L. S., 241, 243, 251
Aitken, C. J., 88, 89, 94
Ajzen, I., 105, 128
Albert, K., 62, 71, 75
Allalouf, A., 148, 162
Anastasi, A., 241, 251
Anderson, M. Z., 213, 228
Angoff, W. H., 148, 162
Arachtingi, B. M., 36, 51
Arbona, C., 268, 276
Archer, J., Jr., 280, 282, 283, 284, 285, 286, 288, 289, 293
Arrendondo, P., 268, 277
Asama, N. F., 238, 250, 252
Asch, S. E., 103, 125
Assouline, M., 10, 35, 47, 135, 138, 139, 163
Astin, H. S., 287, 293
Aviram, T., 45, 49

B

Baig, T., 152, 164
Baltes, M. M., 313, 315, 317, 318
Baltes, P. B., 298, 300, 313, 314, 315, 317, 318
Bandura, A., 57, 58, 62, 69, 72, 112, 113, 118, 121, 125, 213, 227
Bar, R., 152, 165

Barak, A., 10, 12, 14, 31, 35, 37, 43, 47, 51, 52, 54, 67, 70, 73, 76, 97, 103, 124, 125, 129, 131, 136, 152, 154, 163, 165, 304, 317
Bar-On, R., 238, 251
Bates, G. L., 138, 163
Beach, L. R., 13, 33, 34, 42, 47, 48, 52
Beck. A. T, 114, 118, 119, 125, 126, 127, 131
Beilin, H., 299, 317
Bell, D. E., 11, 41, 48
Benyamini, Y., 34, 48
Ben-Yehuda, A., 152, 165
Berdie, R. F., 101, 103, 126
Bersoff, D. N., 219, 228
Bertoch, M. R., 89, 94
Betz, N. E., 17, 43, 48, 53, 59, 60, 61, 64, 65, 66, 67, 69, 71, 72, 73, 74, 76, 77, 102, 104, 111, 112, 113, 116, 126, 127, 130, 131, 208, 209, 212, 213, 215, 217, 218, 227, 228, 230, 232, 237, 251, 255
Bibby, M., 62, 71, 75
Bieschke, K. J., 61, 62, 71, 75, 113, 126, 217, 228
Billingsley, K. D., 248, 254
Bingham, R. P., 244, 255, 265, 266, 267, 268, 271, 274, 275, 276
Bishop, J. B., 284, 285, 292
Bishop, R. M., 113, 126
Blascovich, J., 57, 73
Blau, S., 110, 126
Bloch, D. P., 240, 251
Blumberg, D., 10, 49
Blustein, D. L., 8, 22, 48, 68, 73

Boggs, K. R., 61, 63, 64, 70, 74, 112, 128
Bordin, E. S., 103, 126
Borg, W. R., 89, 94
Borgen, F. H., 9, 14, 15, 39, 48, 49, 64, 65, 73, 88, 94, 163, 211, 229, 233, 238, 244, 248, 251, 252, 296, 317
Borgida, E., 219, 228
Bouchard, T. J., Jr., 139, 163, 164
Bowman, S. L., 137, 147, 156, 163
Brender, M.,103, 126
Bridges, J. S., 14, 48
Brislin, R. W., 143, 146, 163
Brody, L., 215, 228
Brown, D., 8, 10, 11, 48, 59, 76, 112, 130, 263, 264, 265, 273, 275, 277, 299, 301, 317
Brown, M. T., 147, 163, 239, 244, 253
Brown, S. D., 57, 60, 62-64, 69, 71, 73, 75, 111-113, 116, 118, 120, 121, 122, 124, 126, 128, 129, 271, 273, 277, 304, 318
Brown, S. E., 69, 76
Bruce, R. A., 8, 53
Buboltz, W. C., 89, 94
Buehler, C., 298, 317
Bujold, C., 312, 317
Bunda, M. A., 93, 94

C

Camp, C. C., 10, 48
Campbell, D. P., 10, 53, 102, 106, 126, 127, 146, 163, 209, 210, 211, 228
Campbell, J. P., 135, 163
Campbell, N. K., 70, 74
Campbell, V. L., 102, 131, 232, 255
Cantor, N., 305, 307, 317
Cantril, H., 288, 292
Caplan, J., 237, 253
Carney, C. G., 43, 52, 67, 76
Carson, A., 11, 25, 48
Carter, R. T., 150, 163
Cartwright, G. F., 25, 48
Casas, J. M., 60, 64, 74

Cattan, P., 209, 228
Centers, R., 288, 292
Chang, S. H., 89, 94
Chartrand, J. M., 10, 48, 115, 119, 121, 122, 126, 248, 251, 265, 271, 272, 273, 274, 275, 276
Choca, J., 243, 253
Chu, P. H., 150, 163
Chu, S., 248, 254
Church, A. T, 112, 126
Cochran, L., 93, 94, 312, 317
Colbrow, L., 93, 94
Cole, D. A., 243, 251
Cole, N. S., 210, 229
Collard, B., 235, 255
Collin, A., 312, 320
Cook, L. L., 148, 162
Cook-Flanagan, C., 307, 317
Coon, D. W., 115, 128
Coopersmith, S., 57, 74
Corbishley, M. A., 259, 260, 263, 264, 265, 273, 278
Costa, P. T., Jr., 305, 318
Crites, J. O., 9, 17, 48, 67, 69, 74, 89, 94, 117, 126, 142, 143, 163, 165, 219, 228, 232, 251, 259, 264, 265, 275, 276, 288, 292, 295, 297, 300, 304, 317
Cronbach, J. O., 102, 126
Cronbach, L. J., 150, 160, 163
Croteau, J. M., 217, 228
Cudeck, R., 152, 163
Curley, J. R., 89, 94

D

Daiger, D. C., 67, 74
Dancer, L. S., 152, 156, 163
Daniel, M. H., 238, 251
Darley, J. G., 101, 103, 126, 130
Davis, D. A., 240, 252
Davison, G. C., 118, 127
Dawis, R. V., 9, 10, 13, 14, 16, 35, 48,51, 53, 101, 103, 116, 126, 129, 296, 318

Day, S. X., 115, 126, 236, 252, 253
de Bono, E., 264, 276
de St. Aubin, E., 310, 318
Dean, L. A., 279, 292
Deaux, K., 219, 228
Decker, P. J., 88, 94
DeRubeis, R. J., 118, 119, 126
Diamond, A., 310, 318
Diamond, E. E., 210, 228
Dilley, J. S., 11, 50
Dinur, C., 138, 165
Dorn, F. J., 90, 93, 94, 119, 127
Drucker, P., 237, 252
Dubois, C. L. Z., 219, 228

E

Edwards, J. R., 138, 163
Ekeberg, S. E., 135, 138, 139, 166
Elliott, K. J., 121, 127
Ellis, A., 118, 119, 127
Elton, C. F., 138, 163
Embreston, S. E., 242, 252
Erikson, E. H., 298, 315, 318
Esbaugh, J., 114, 126
Ewing, M. J. M., 285, 293
Eyde, L. D., 241, 252
Eysenck, H. J., 249, 252

F

Faley, R. H., 219, 228
Farmer, H. S., 213, 218, 228
Fassa, N., 13-15, 28, 35, 39, 41, 45,
    49, 117, 127, 212, 228
Fassinger, R. E., 65, 74, 207, 213,
    214, 215, 228, 229
Fauble, M. L., 56, 76
Feldman, S., 111, 124, 125
Ferber, M. A., 209, 217, 219, 228
Ferrin, H. H., 8, 52
Finch, J. F., 316, 318
Fischer, A. R., 69, 76
Fiske, S. T., 105, 127, 219, 228

Fitzgerald, L. F., 9, 52, 56, 76, 79,
    95, 101, 121, 122, 130, 207, 208,
    209, 212, 213, 215, 217, 218, 219,
    227, 228, 230, 257, 277, 281, 292,
    295, 299, 319
Fletcher, F. M., 103, 127
Flores, L. Y., 281, 292
Flum, H., 304, 317
Fogarty, G. J., 88, 89, 95
Foltz, B. M., 69, 74
Ford, D. H., 295, 318
Foss, C. J., 68, 74
Fouad, N. A., 71, 74, 113, 127, 152,
    156, 163, 239, 243, 244, 252, 265,
    266, 267, 268, 271, 274, 275, 276,
    290, 292
Fox, L. H., 215, 228
Freedman, S. M., 91, 94
Freeman, A., 118, 119, 127
Fretz, B., 276, 277
Friedlander, M. L., 213, 227
Fritzsche, B. A., 103, 106, 127, 211,
    229
Fryer, D., 103, 127
Fukuyama, M. A., 68, 74
Funk, D. P., 69, 75

G

Galassi, J. P., 61, 76
Gallagher, R. P., 289, 292
Gardner, J. K., 89, 94
Garty, Y., 13 , 15, 35, 49, 212, 228
Gati, I., 10 , 16, 18, 20, 28, 30, 32,
    35, 39, 41, 43, 45, 46, 48, 49, 51,
    116, 117, 127, 139, 153, 154, 157,
    160, 162, 163, 165, 212, 228, 245,
    246, 246, 249, 252, 312, 318
Gelatt, H. B., 8, 11, 49
Gelfand, M. J., 239, 255
Geraghty, M., 280, 292
Gerhart, B., 106, 127
Givon, M., 16, 40, 49, 116, 117, 127
Glick, P., 219, 228
Goff, M., 124, 127
Gold, P. B., 275, 276

Goleman, D., 237, 252
Good, G., 69, 76, 77
Gore, P. A., Jr., 10, 48, 62, 63, 71, 75, 112, 129
Gottfredson, G. D., 9, 10, 49, 138, 156, 164, 238, 250, 252
Gottfredson, L. S., 14, 35, 40, 49, 304, 307, 318
Gover, M. R., 62, 63, 75
Graziano, W. G., 316, 318
Greenfield, P. M., 239, 252
Greenhaus, J., 296, 318
Greeno, B. P., 25, 53, 246, 247, 254
Gribbons, W., 299, 318
Grigorenko, E. L., 237, 254

H

Ha, Y. W., 26, 50
Haaga, D. A. F., 118, 127
Hackett, G., 57, 59, 61, 64, 70, 72, 73, 75, 111, 113, 116, 118, 120, 121, 124, 126, 127, 129, 232, 237, 238, 252, 271, 273, 274, 276, 277, 296, 301, 302, 304, 312, 318
Hagenah, T., 103, 126
Hambleton, R. K., 242, 252
Hamel, D. A., 42, 50
Hammer, A. C., 211, 229
Hammer, A. L., 14, 39, 49, 241, 244, 252
Hansen, J. C., 10, 14, 39, 49, 53, 102, 127, 133, 134, 146, 147, 150, 152, 156, 157, 163, 211, 228, 229, 244, 252
Hanson, G. R., 211, 229
Hardin, S. I., 284, 293
Harkness, H., 236, 252
Harmon, L. W., 14, 39, 49, 64, 65, 73, 210, 211, 229, 233, 238, 244, 248, 251, 252
Harren, V. A., 8, 11, 12, 14, 43, 50, 52
Harris, D. B., 299, 318
Harrison, P. L., 241, 252
Harvey, R. J., 242, 252

Haushner, O., 31, 47, 70, 73, 104, 109, 110, 111, 113, 118, 124, 125
Hayghe, H. V., 209, 229
Healy, C. C., 244, 248, 252
Heesacker, R. S., 215, 227
Heggestad, E. D., 124, 125, 238, 250, 251
Hener, T., 145, 164
Henly, G. A., 16, 52
Heppner, M. J., 281, 292
Hesketh, B., 8, 50, 133, 136, 145, 164
Higgins, N. C., 91, 94
Hilt, D., 288, 292
Hinkelman, J. M., 25, 50, 281, 292
Hoffman, L., 217, 229
Hofstede, G., 140, 142, 145, 164
Holland, J. L., 9, 10, 14, 35, 39, 49, 50, 53, 56, 58, 63, 64, 66, 67, 74, 101, 104, 106, 109, 110, 112, 127, 135, 137, 139, 144, 147, 148, 151, 153, 155, 157, 162, 165, 210, 211, 229, 233, 236, 238, 250, 252, 291, 292, 296, 303, 306, 309, 316, 318
Hollinger, C. L., 215, 229
Hollon, S. D., 119, 127
Horan, J. J., 117, 129
Hotelling, K., 283, 293
Houminer, D., 14, 45, 49, 117, 127
Huber, J., 217, 230
Hughes, E., 311, 318
Humphreys, S. M., 215, 229
Hunter, J. E., 135, 164
Hurst, J. C., 286, 293
Hussain, M. A., 152, 164
Hyne, S. A., 106, 126

I-J

Iijima Hall, C. C., 287, 293
Ikeda, H., 59, 75
Isaacson, L. E., 263, 264, 265, 273, 275, 277
Ivanevich, J. M., 91, 94
Jackson, D. N., 14, 50, 102, 127
Jackson, M. A., 123, 128

Jackson, S. E., & Associates, 239, 252
Jaggar, A. M., 224, 229
James, M. M., 95
Janis, I. L., 26, 28, 44, 50
Jensen, A. R., 135, 164
Jensen-Campbell, L. A., 316, 318
Jepsen, D. A., 8, 11, 35, 43, 46, 50, 51, 312, 318
Johansson, C. B., 147, 164, 210, 211, 229, 236, 252
Johnson, B., 276, 277
Johnson, C. S., 8, 43, 50
Johnston, J. A., 238, 250, 252
Jones, E. M., 238, 250, 252
Jones, G. B., 57, 70, 74, 106, 122, 128
Jones, J. M., 80, 91, 95
June, L. N., 283, 286, 293
Jungermann, H., 8, 50

K

Kagan (Klein), H., 89, 91, 95
Kagan, N. I., 89, 91, 95
Kahn, S. B., 152, 164
Kahneman, D., 12, 50, 53
Kaldor, D. B., 11, 50
Kanfer, F. H., 119, 128
Kanter, R. M., 234, 253
Kapes, J. T., 232, 253
Kaplan, A., 64, 66, 73
Karayanni, M., 142, 146, 164
Kass, R. A., 8, 50
Kassner, M. W., 106, 128
Katz, M., 11, 16, 20, 31, 39, 42, 46, 50
Kaunitz, N., 89, 95
Keita, G. P., 80, 91, 95, 287, 293
Kelleher, J. C., 287, 293
Kelley, R., 237, 253
Kelly, G. A., 311, 318
Kenkel, M. B., 287, 293
Kerr, A. E., 275, 276, 276
Kibari, L., 33, 49
Kida, T., 33, 52
Kinneir, R. T., 42, 50
Kitson, H. D., 101, 128

Kivlighan, D. M., 275, 276, 276, 277
Kjos, D., 289, 293
Klaynman, J., 26, 50
Klein, K. L., 67, 73
Knapp, D. E., 219, 228
Kohout, J. L., 287, 293
Kolodinsky, R. W., 25, 53, 246, 247, 254
Korman, A. K., 56, 74
Kosaka, T., 89, 90, 96
Kountz, M. R., 89, 95
Kramer, L. A., 275, 276, 276
Krausz, M., 18, 30, 33, 43, 49
Krieshok, T. S., 8, 50
Krug, S. E., 241, 252
Kruglanski, A. W., 105, 128
Krumboltz, J. D., 8, 11, 18, 42, 44, 50, 51, 57, 70, 74, 106, 113, 115, 119, 124, 128, 129, 265, 268, 269, 270, 271, 274, 275, 276, 277, 296, 302, 312, 318
Kuder, F., 102, 131, 143, 148, 150, 162, 164, 236, 253
Kurowski, L. L., 239, 255
Kustis, G. A., 219, 228

L

Laatsch, L., 243, 253
Lagace, R. R., 89, 95
Lahav, G., 152, 165
Lamb, R. R., 211, 230
Lang, F. R., 313, 318
Lang, K., 103, 128
Lapan, R. T., 61, 63, 64, 70, 74, 112, 128
Larkin, K. C., 60, 64, 73, 75, 112, 129
Lasoff, D. L., 275, 278
Layton, P. L., 59, 74
Lee, J. Y., 66, 75
Lenox, R., 63-65, 75
Lent, R. W., 57, 60, 64, 70, 71, 73, 75, 111, 113, 116, 118, 120, 121, 124, 126, 128, 129, 271, 273, 277, 296, 301, 302, 303, 304, 312, 318, 319

Lenz, J. G., 11, 18, 52, 53, 117, 119, 130
Leonard, R. L., Jr., 56, 75
Leong, F. T. L., 8, 50, 140, 147, 150, 161, 162, 164, 232, 239, 244, 253, 268, 277
Lerner, R. M., 304, 319
Levinson, H., 291, 293
Levy, S. R., 285, 293
Librowsky, I., 31, 47, 70, 73, 104, 108, 111, 113, 124, 125
Lichtenberg, J. W., 36, 51
Lindenberger, U., 298, 300, 313, 314, 317
Lissitz, R. W., 89, 95
Locke, E. A., 104, 129
Lofquist, L. H., 9, 10, 13, 14, 16, 35, 48, 51, 53, 101, 103, 116, 126, 129
Lohnes, P., 299, 318
London, M., 121, 129
Long, B. C., 89, 95
Lonner, W. J., 143, 146, 163
Lopez, F. G., 112, 129
Lopez, R. G., 61, 63, 71, 75
Lowman, R. L., 238, 250, 253
Lunnenborg, C. E., 31, 51
Lunnenborg, P. W., 8, 51
Luzzo, D. A., 62, 67, 69, 71, 73, 75, 112, 126
Lykken, D. T., 139, 164, 166, 238, 255

M

Maddux, J. E., 113, 129
Manhardt, P. J., 14, 51
Mann, L., 26, 28, 44, 50
Mansfield, E., 310, 318
Marsella, A. J., 161, 162, 164
Marsiske, M., 313, 318
Martinelli, E., 62, 71, 75
Mason, T. W., 285, 293
Mastie, M. M., 232, 253
Matarazzo, J. D., 13, 15, 51

Mathieu, P. S., 67
Matsui, K., 61, 75
Matsui, T., 59, 61, 75, 89, 90, 95
Matteson, M. T., 91, 94
Matthews, K., 93, 94
Mau, W. C., 8, 35, 43, 51
May, K. M., 88, 95
Mayer, Y., 28, 39, 41, 49
McAdams, D. P., 305, 306, 307, 308, 309, 310, 312, 314, 315, 316, 318
McCartney, K., 215, 230
McCoy, J. F., 138, 163
McCrae, R. R., 305, 318
McCraken, R. S., 215, 229
McDavis, R. J., 268, 277
McGue, M., 139, 164
McNeill, P., 69, 75
McPartland, E. B., 113, 126
McWhirter, E., 117, 129
Meadows, M. E., 279, 292
Meara, N. M., 244, 253
Mednick, M. T., 287, 293
Meichenbaum, D., 109, 118, 129
Meir E. I., 9, 10, 13, 15, 35, 40, 47, 51, 103, 125, 129, 133, 135, 138, 139, 145, 146, 152, 154, 157, 159, 160, 162, 165
Melamed, S., 138, 165
Mellenbergh, G. J., 242, 253
Mendelson, M., 114, 126
Metzler, A. E., 68, 74
Miller, G. A., 7, 18, 51
Miller, M. J., 276, 277
Miller-Tiedeman, A., 7, 51, 311, 318
Mintz, L. B., 283, 293
Mirowsky, J., 217, 230
Mishler, S. A., 218, 220, 229
Mitchell, A. M., 57, 70, 74, 106, 128
Mitchell, L. K., 11, 42, 50, 51, 106, 120, 122, 129
Mitchell, S. L., 59
Miyahira, S. D., 216, 229
Mock, J., 114, 126
Montgomery, H., 26, 28, 44, 51
Moreland, J. R., 8, 50

Moreland, K. L., 241, 252
Morrill, W. H., 63, 64, 70, 74, 112, 128, 286, 293
Morris, J., 8, 50
Morrissy, M., 247, 253
Mowsesian, R., 11, 48

N

Naylor, F. D., 123, 129
Neimeyer, G. J., 11, 14, 51, 68, 74, 122, 129, 301, 311, 318, 319
Neimeyer, R. A., 311, 319
Neisser, U., 237, 253
Nevill, D. D., 67, 68, 74, 75, 122, 129
Nevo, B., 107, 129
Nevo, O., 18, 44, 51, 107, 121, 129
Nichols, C. W., 57, 70, 74, 106, 120, 122, 128
Nieberding, R., 102, 131
Nielson, E. C., 89, 94
Niijer, S. K., 62, 63, 75
Niles, S. G., 67, 75, 88, 95
Nilsen, D. A., 106, 126
Noeth, R., 299, 319
Nord, D., 69, 76, 77
Noy, A., 111, 124, 125

O

O'Brien, K. M., 213, 214, 229, 281, 292
Oetting, E. R., 286, 293
O'Farrell, B., 209, 217, 219, 228
Ohnishi, R., 59, 61, 75
Okev, G., 110, 118, 129
Okon, N. R., 15, 35, 51
Oliver, L. W., 275, 277
Olson, C., 117, 129
O'Neil, J. M., 89, 95
Onglatco, M., 89, 90, 95
Oreshnick, C. A., 69, 76
Oshawa, T., 89, 90, 95

Osipow, S. H., 7, 9, 11, 13, 18, 30, 33, 40, 43, 49, 51, 53, 55, 56, 58, 63, 65, 67, 69, 70, 72, 75, 77, 79, 80, 81, 82, 88, 95, 97, 98, 101, 104, 106, 117, 121, 122, 127, 129, 130, 134, 149, 152, 159, 162-166, 207, 208, 209, 211, 223, 229, 231, 239, 240, 255, 257, 275, 277, 281, 287, 292, 293, 295, 296, 299, 316, 319
Owen, S. V., 89, 95

P

Pace, D., 286, 293
Palladino, D. E., 213, 227
Paquette, L., 33, 52
Parker, H., 138, 163
Parsons, F., 8, 9, 52, 101, 130
Paterson, D. G., 101, 130
Payne, J. W., 32, 52
Pazienza, N. J., 8, 11, 52
Peavy, R. V., 124, 130
Peiser, C., 152, 154, 165
Peoples, V. Y., 209, 230
Peters, T., 237, 253
Peterson, G. W., 11, 18, 52, 53, 117, 119, 130, 260, 264, 265, 273, 277, 290, 293
Peterson, S. L., 68, 76
Pfafflin, S. M., 215, 230
Phillips, D., 215, 230
Phillips, J. S., 91, 94
Phillips, S. D., 8, 11, 14, 22, 48, 52, 116, 130, 258, 277
Pion, G. M., 287, 293
Pithers, R. T., 88, 89, 95
Pitz, G. F., 11, 12, 14, 52
Popma, J., 67, 77
Porch, B. E., 241, 252
Post-Kammer, P., 59, 61, 76, 112, 130
Potter, R. E., 13, 33, 42, 47, 52
Powell, A. B., 103, 106, 127, 211, 229
Powell, T. E., 93, 95
Power, P. G., 67, 74

Prediger, D. J., 31, 34, 35, 52, 115,
130, 145, 165, 211, 230, 244, 253
Prezioso, M. S., 213, 227
Primoff, E. S., 241, 252
Probert, B. S., 68, 74
Probert, B., 122, 129
Pryor, R. G. L., 14, 52
Pugh, S. C., 89, 95

R

Raifa, H., 11, 41, 48
Rayman, J. R., 211, 229, 230, 282, 293
Reardon, R. B., 249, 253, 282, 283, 284, 290, 293
Reardon, R. C., 11, 18, 52, 53, 117, 119, 130, 260, 264, 265, 273, 277
Reise, S. P., 242, 255
Reno, R. R., 241, 243, 251
Resnick, H., 56, 76
Richardson, M. S., 271, 273, 277
Richman, D. R., 121, 130
Richmond, L. J., 240, 251
Rifkin, J., 235, 240, 253
Risinger, R., 213, 228
Robertson, A. G., 241, 252
Robertson, G. J., 241, 252
Rocha-Singe, I. A., 60, 64, 74
Roe, A., 9, 14, 52, 103, 108, 130, 134, 139, 146, 152, 155, 157, 161, 165
Rogers, C. R., 57
Rogers, J. R., 284, 293
Rogers, T. B., 233, 234, 253
Rolfhus, E. L., 124, 130
Rooney, R. A., 63, 65, 76
Rose, H. A., 138, 163
Rose, M. L., 119, 121, 122, 126
Rosenberg, M., 57, 76
Rosenbrook, R., 112, 126
Ross, C. E., 217, 230
Rotberg, H. L., 59, 76, 112, 130
Rounds, J. B., 10, 14, 16, 35, 39, 52, 53, 115, 126, 133, 134, 136, 142, 145, 151, 155, 164, 166, 236, 252, 253, 307, 319

Rubin, A., 134, 152, 159, 162, 165
Rude, S. S., 42, 50
Ryan, N. E., 113, 126

S

Sabir, A. A., 152, 164
Sagiv, L., 8, 53
Saka, N., 33, 49
Sampson, J. P., Jr., 11, 18, 25, 44, 52, 53, 117, 119, 130, 245, 246, 247, 253, 254, 260, 264, 265, 273, 277, 290, 293
Samson, A., 138, 165
Saunders, D. E., 18, 53, 119, 130
Saveri, A., 235, 254
Savickas, M. L., 124, 130, 239, 248, 254, 258, 271, 273, 275, 277, 278, 296, 297, 299, 301, 303, 304, 311, 315, 319
Scarr, S., 215, 230
Schaffer, R. H., 103, 130
Scheid, A. B., 69, 76, 97, 104, 130
Schifano, R., 66, 72, 73, 76
Schlecker, D. I., 67, 75
Schloss, J. A., 88, 89, 94
Schneider, K., 219, 230
Schulenberg, J. E., 304, 319
Schultheiss, D. P., 213, 227
Schutz, H., 8, 50
Schwartz, S., 16, 53
Scott, S. G., 8, 53
Sechrest, L., 241, 243, 251
Seligman, L., 232, 254
Seligman, M., 103, 130
Sells, L., 61, 76
Senesh, L., 230
Sexton, T. L., 275, 278
Shaffer, M., 36, 51
Shalhevet, R., 152, 165
Shaughnessy, P., 61, 70, 74, 112, 128
Shaukat, N., 152, 164
Shaw, T. D., 69, 76
Shenhav, M., 16, 49, 116, 117, 127
Shewan, C. M., 241, 252

Shiloh, S., 31, 47, 70, 73, 104, 108, 111, 118, 124, 125
Shuttleworth, C., 215, 227
Siegel, R. G., 61, 76
Simon, H. A., 14, 40, 53
Sireci, S. G., 148, 162
Slane, S., 135, 138, 139, 166
Slaney, F. M., 9, 53
Slaney, R. B., 9, 11, 53, 68, 74
Slater, S. C., 242, 252
Smith, P. L., 59, 61, 71, 74, 76, 112, 113, 127, 130
Sohlberg, S., 152, 165
Solberg, V. S., 69, 76, 77
Sommer, S. M., 107, 131
Sorensen, J., 212, 214, 215, 230
Sowa, C. J., 67, 75, 88, 95
Spokane, A. R., 9, 10, 35, 53, 80, 82, 88, 89, 95, 114, 131, 138, 165, 232, 233, 240, 253, 254, 262, 263, 264, 265, 271, 273, 275, 277, 287, 293
Stamler, V. L., 286, 293
Staudinger, U. M., 298, 300, 313, 314, 317
Stauffer, E., 153, 165
Sternberg, R. J., 237, 254
Stillson, R. W., 89, 95
Stolz-Loike, M., 286, 293
Stone, G. L., 280, 282, 283, 284, 285, 286, 288, 289, 293
Strang, J., 69, 75
Strein, W. O., 89, 95
Strom, E., 33, 34, 48
Strong, E. K., Jr., 10, 53, 103, 131, 147, 149, 162, 163, 165, 236, 254
Strong, S. R., 248, 251
Subich, L. M., 10, 53, 63, 65, 75, 156, 165, 244, 248, 254
Sue, D. W., 267, 268, 277
Sue, D., 267, 277
Super, C. M., 296, 315, 319
Super, D. E., 13, 15, 17, 37, 53, 55, 56, 77, 104, 112, 113, 116, 117, 131, 142, 143, 165, 216, 230, 296, 298, 308, 312, 315, 319

Swan, S., 219, 230
Swanson, J. L., 93, 95, 150, 163, 238, 254, 265, 275, 277, 278, 299, 319
Szendre, D., 112, 126

T

Takahashi, K., 242, 255
Tanaka, K., 89, 90, 96
Taylor, K. M., 43, 53, 67, 73, 77
Taylor, M., 68, 75
Tellegen, A., 139, 164, 166, 238, 255
Temple, R. D., 65, 66, 76, 77, 134, 152, 159, 162, 165
Teresa, J. S., 112, 126
Thomas, L., 242, 252
Thorndike, R. M., 143, 146, 163
Thorne, A., 307, 319
Tiedeman, D. V., 7, 51, 311, 318
Tikotzky, Y., 34, 49
Tinsley, H. E. A., 8, 50, 248, 254
Tobin, D., 215, 228
Tokar, D. M., 10, 53, 238, 254
Tomaka, J., 57, 73
Tosi, D. J., 8, 13, 52
Tracey, T. J., 10, 52, 53, 109, 131, 133, 134, 142, 151, 155, 165, 166, 307, 319
Tranberg, M., 135, 138, 139, 166
Triandis, H. C., 239, 255
Tsal, Y., 36, 54
Tversky, A., 11, 12, 19, 48, 50, 53

U-V

Urban, H. B., 295, 318
Vansickle, T. R., 115, 130, 145, 165
Vondracek, F. W., 297. 304, 319
Vosvick, M. A., 119, 123, 128
Vroom, V. H., 104, 131

W

Waehler, C. A., 284, 293
Wagner, R. K., 238, 255
Walbridge, M. M., 213, 227

Waller, N. G., 238, 242, 255
Waller, N. J., 139, 166
Walsh, W. B., 7, 9, 11, 13, 52, 53, 56,
75, 97, 102, 115, 130, 131, 149,
163, 164, 166, 232, 239, 255, 258,
275, 276, 277, 278
Ward, C. M., 109, 114, 126, 131,
244, 255, 266, 276
Wardrop, J. L., 213, 228
Ware, W. B., 59, 61, 76, 112, 130
Watanabe, M., 89, 90, 96
Watanabe, N., 242, 255
Waterman, J., 235, 255
Waterman, R. H., Jr., 235, 255
Watkins, C. E., Jr., 102, 131, 232,
237, 238, 252, 255
Watson, M. G., 89, 91, 95
Webber, P., 210, 229
Weishaar, M. E., 118, 119, 126, 131
Weiss, D. J., 16, 52, 243, 255
Weitzman, L. M., 215, 229, 230,
248, 251
Werner, H., 299, 320
West, S. G., 241, 243, 251
Whiston, S. C., 275, 278
Williams, T., 59, 66, 77, 112, 130
Williamson, E. G., 101, 131, 232, 255

Wilson, R., 288, 293
Wilson, S. B., 285, 293
Winer, D., 35, 49
Winters, C. J., 212, 214, 215, 230
Wolfe, L. K., 215, 230
Wysong, E., 210, 229

Y

Yaari, Y., 13, 15, 35, 51
Yanico, B. J., 93, 96
Yarris, E., 286, 293
Yost, E. B., 259, 260, 263, 264, 265,
273, 278
Young, G., 10, 53
Young, R. A., 312, 320
Yu, J., 242, 255

Z

Zakay, D., 12, 14, 36, 54, 119, 131
Zehavi, A. D., 107, 129
Zilber, S. M., 59, 77
Zirkel, S., 305, 317
Zytowski, D. G., 11, 14, 50, 54, 102,
131, 210, 229, 236, 253

Subject Index

A

Ability, 100, 101, 102, 105-111, 112, 116, 119, 120, 122, 123
Acculturation, 188, 194-197
Achievement, 214
Administrators, 279, 281, 282, 284, 285, 286, 287, 290, 292
Adolescent, 213, 214
Adult Vocational Maturity Assessment Interview (AVMAI), 180, 181
American Psychological Association, 279, 281, 283
American Psychological Society, 80
Arizona State University, 288
Aspects
  based approach, 34
  career related, 14, 22, 26, 32, 34, 35, 39, 41, 46
  core aspects, 15, 22, 24, 35, 39
  relative importance, 15, 16, 19-21, 28, 33, 40, 46
Aspiration level, 135-138, 140-141, 147
Assessment, 100, 102, 114-116, 120, 133-134, 146-148, 153, 156
Attachment, 213, 214

B

Barrier, 218, 219, 220
Beck Depression Inventory (BDI), 114
Belief, 99, 105, 111, 116-119, 121-123
Berry's model, 196
Bounded rationality, 14, 40

C

Children, 98-100, 103, 109-110, 111, 207, 208, 216, 217, 218, 225, 226
Cognition, 97, 100, 101, 104-125
Career, 134-135, 138-140, 142-143, 147-148, 150, 156, 212, 213, 214, 215, 218, 220, 225, 226
Career
  adjustment, 215
  assessment, 232-234, 248-250
  choice, 14, 18, 26-30, 31, 32, 34, 38, 42, 44, 45, 67, 101, 104, 105, 112, 116-117, 122, 168, 169
  choice readiness, 304
  comparison of emerging theories of, 273, 274
  concerns, 307-309, 315
  counseling, 9, 25, 43-45, 97, 101, 102, 110, 111, 112, 113, 114-119, 122-123, 214, 279, 280, 281, 283, 286, 288, 289, 291
  decision making, 7, 11-14, 17, 18, 32, 34, 35, 37, 38, 44, 46, 47, 100-102, 112, 119, 122, 280, 284, 289
  development, 208, 209, 213, 215, 217
  difficulties, 18, 43
  emerging theories of, 265
  indecision, 7, 43, 44
  maturity, 67, 167-184, 189, 190, 297-304, 308
  model comparisons, 264, 265
  models of, 258
  models, 8, 43, 46
  narratives, 309-312, 314, 315
  orientation, 214, 215

practice of, 257, 258
preferences, 13, 15, 17-19, 21-23,
   30-35, 37, 38, 40
search efficacy, 69
self-efficacy, 67-69
stages, 17, 18, 44, 46
styles, 7, 8, 35, 41, 43
theories of, 257
theory and practice integration,
   258
theory evolution, 274-276
Career Decision Scale, 72
Career Development Inventory,
   301, 309
Career Interest and Skills Survey
   (CISS), 211
Career Mastery Inventory, 89
Career Maturity Inventory (CMI),
   171-175, 177-179, 309
Career patterns study, 297
Caregiver, 226
CDDQ, 33, 43
Changing nature of work, 235
Chartrand's Socio-Cognitive
   Interactional Model for Career
   Counseling, 271-273
Childcare, 217, 219, 220, 227
Circumscription, 35
Cognitive, 12, 13, 15, 19, 43, 47
Collectivistic societies, 187
Compensation, 313
Compromise, 15, 16, 21, 22, 25, 29,
   31, 32, 35, 37, 44-46
Compensation, 11, 26, 33
Compensatory models, 27, 28, 32,
   36, 41
Computer assisted career guidance
   systems (CACGSs), 8, 12, 13, 15,
   20, 25, 33, 34, 39, 43, 45, 46
Computer technology, 244-247
Congruence, 9, 10, 35, 39, 138-140,
   151, 163-166
Construct validation, 80, 84
Constructivism, 311, 312
Contextual factors, 168, 172, 182,
   183, 193

Convergence in career develop-
   ment theory, 79
Coping resources, 80, 81, 83
   interventions to promote, 90
Counseling center, 282, 283, 284,
   285, 286, 289, 290
Counseling psychologist, 283, 288,
   291, 292
Counseling Psychology, 80, 279,
   280, 281, 283, 289
Counselors, 88, 280, 282, 283, 286,
   287, 288, 289, 290, 292
Courses Inventory, 134, 137, 146,
   152-153, 162, 165
Critesí Comprehensive Career
   Counseling Model, 259
Critical skills, 236-238
Cross-cultural psychology, 133-166,
   168, 185, 187, 188
Cross cultural transportability, 239-
   240
Crystallization, 169, 170, 182, 197,
   198
Cultural accommodation, 167, 184,
   185, 193
Cultural accommodation approach,
   168, 184, 185, 189, 193, 195, 198,
   199
Cultural gap, 190
Cultural gaps, 185, 191, 197, 198
Cultural identity, 193-199
Cultural validity, 185-193, 195, 198,
   199
Cultural specificity, 185, 188, 189,
   192, 193
Culture, 133-166

D

Daughter, 213, 217
Decision making
   models, 8, 11
   styles, 7, 8, 35
   theory, 11
Discover, 68
Discrimination, 218, 219, 223, 224

E

Elderly, 226, 227
Elimination, 25, 26
Emerging competencies, 242-247
Emotion, 97, 101, 104, 105, 107, 114, 116-119
Employee assistance program, 288, 289
Employer, 207
Enhanced Career Assessment Inventory, 211
Ethnic minority groups, 167, 168, 172, 178, 190-193, 197, 198, 209, 223
Expected utility, 11-13, 35, 36, 40

F

Faculty, university, 280, 281, 282, 283, 286, 287, 288, 289, 290, 291, 292
Family, 219, 220, 224, 225, 225
Family Medical Leave Act, 219
Fear of success, 220, 223
Female employment, 209, 217
Feminist, 224
Fouad and Binghamís Culturally Appropriate Career Counseling Model, 265-268
Functional validation, 84
Funding resources, 283, 284, 285, 290

G

Gender, 88, 89, 211, 213, 218
differences, 88, 173, 176, 185
role conflict, 89

H

Health Psychology, 80
Holland themes, 56, 63-65, 70, 72
Holland's theory, 56, 133-166
Hollingshead Scales, 175

H

Homemaker, 212, 215
Hoppock Job Satisfaction Blank, 88
Human Capital Initiative, 80

I

In-depth exploration, 14, 18, 22-26, 29, 30-32, 36, 38, 42, 44, 45
Individual component, 188
Integrative model of cross-cultural counseling, 185, 189
Interests, vocational, 9, 10, 14, 35, 39, 40, 69-72, 97-127, 133-166, 209
Inventories, 209
structure of, 10
Interventions, career self-efficacy, 72
Interventions, math-science self-efficacy, 71-72
Internet, 25
Isaacson and Brown's Career Counseling Model, 263-264

J

Jackson Vocational Interest Survey (JVIS), 102, 115, 127
Japanese OSI, 89, 90
Job sharing, 219

K

Karoshi, 89
Krumboltz's Learning Theory of Career Counseling, 268-271
Kuder Occupational Interest Survey (KOIS), 102, 115, 150
Kuder Preference Record, 56

L

Lesbian, 217
Levels
acceptable, 15, 16, 21, 24
characteristic, 15, 16, 21

optimal, 15, 16, 21, 24, 28, 31, 44, 46
range of acceptable, 16, 21, 46
within aspect, 15, 16, 44, 46
Life-span, life space theory, 296-297

M

Marriage, 216, 217, 218, 220
Maslach Burnout Inventory, 88
Maternal employment, 207, 213
Maternal identification, 212
Maternal role model, 212
Marriage, 224
Marital satisfaction, 207
Mathematics, 215
Mental health status, 88
Minnesota Satisfaction Question-
naire, 88
Modeling, 213
Mother, 209, 212, 213, 215, 217, 218, 224, 225
Motivation, 99, 102-105, 114, 118, 119
Multicultural diversity, 243, 244

N

Needs, 14
New work environment, 235, 236
Norms, 135, 139, 142-144, 148-151, 162, 210, 211
Normative decision theory, 9, 11, 12, 37, 40-42

O

Occupation, 137-140, 144, 151-158
Occupational Environment Scale, 81
Occupational information, 13, 16
Occupational Mental Health, 88
Occupational scales, 210, 211
Occupational Stress Inventory (OCI), 84
model confirmation, 84, 88

interpretive workshops, 90-91
reviews of, 93
user sites, 90
Occupational structure, 152-158, 161, 163
Occupationally induced stress, 89
Organizational commitment, 219
Outcome expectations, 70, 71

P-Q

Parent, 213, 214
Person-environment fit, 9-11, 14, 35, 37, 39, 40, 42, 46
Personal Resources Questionnaire, 81, 82
Personal Strain Scale, 81, 89
Peterson, Sampson and Reardon's Cognitive Information Process-
ing Model, 260-262
Prescriptive models, 11-14, 37
PIC model, 7, 8, 14, 18, 30-32, 36, 37, 39-43, 45
Policy, 207
Postmodern, 207, 208
Power, 282, 286, 289, 290, 291, 292
Prescreening, 9, 14, 18-22, 23, 24, 29-34, 38, 40, 41, 44, 45
Professors, university, 280, 281, 283, 287, 288
Promising alternatives, 10, 18, 19, 21, 22, 24, 25, 30, 34, 36, 38, 40, 42, 45
Psychometric validation, 84, 90
Quantitative advances, 242-243

R

Racial minority, 209
Ramak Inventory, 102, 115, 125, 134, 146, 152-154, 159-162, 165
Raw scores, 211
Realistic self-efficacy, 71, 72
Reinforcement, 109, 123
Role
conflict, 220

overload, 220
salience, 309
strains, 80, 81, 83
stressors, 80, 81, 82, 83
readiness, 17, 18, 30, 43, 44
Roe's theory, 134, 139, 146, 152-155, 157-161

S

Salesmen, 88
Satisfaction, 11, 15, 25, 34, 42, 104, 88, 107-108, 110, 113, 116, 119, 120, 134-135, 137-139, 154, 161, 164-165, 219
Science, 215
Selective optimization, 313
Self-concept theory, 55-56, 176, 177, 214
Self-Directed Search (SDS), 9, 55, 56, 102-103, 106, 127, 137, 152-153, 162-164, 211
Self-efficacy
 beliefs, 111-114, 116, 120, 213, 214, 223
 career, 56
 career decision, 67-69
 career search, 69
 Holland's themes, 63-65
  and vocational interests, 69-72
 mathematics, 61-63
 math-science self-efficacy, 62-63, 71-72
 occupational, 59-60
 scientific/technical, 60-61
 task-specific, 63, 65-67, 72
 theory, 55-56
Self-esteem, 56-57
Sequential elimination, 19-22, 33, 35, 36, 41
Sex differences, 211
Sexual harassment, 219, 224, 225
Sexual orientation, 223
Significant others, 13, 45
Social class, 169, 174, 175, 186, 187
Social cognitive model, 70-71

Social learning theory, 70
Society for Vocational Psychology, 79
Sources of self-efficacy, mathematics, 62-63
Spokane's Career Intervention Process, 262-263
Staff, university, 282, 283, 289, 291, 292
Stereotype, 226
Stress, 80
 identifying sources of, 92
 management interventions, 81
 physical consequences of, 80
 strategies for dealing with, 92
Stress-strain relationship, 80, 89
Strong Vocational Interest Blank (SVIB), 148-150, 209
Strong-Campbell Interest Inventory (SCII), 209
Strong Vocational Interest Inventory (SVII), 102, 115, 209
Students, university, 280, 281, 284, 286, 287, 289, 291, 292
Sudden cardiac death, 89
Suitable alternatives, 25, 26, 29, 44, 45

T

Tennessee Self-Concept Scale (TSCS), 175, 176
Tenure, 282, 283, 287, 291
Testing, 122, 240-241
Texas Tech University, 279
Theory of work adjustment, 10
Trade off, 13, 26
Transfiguration of work, 234-235

U

Uncertainty, 13, 28, 29, 32, 42, 46
Universal dimension, 187, 188, 190, 197
Unstructured information, 16, 17, 22, 24, 45

Utility, 84

V

Vocational behavior, 223, 224
Vocational Development Inventory
    Attitude Scale (VDI-ATT), 176,
    177
Vocational education, 214
Vocational personality types, 306-
    307, 315
Vocational Preference Inventory
    (VPI), 9, 115, 152-153
Vocational psychology, 80, 207, 208,
    214, 216, 223
Vocational teachers, 88

W

Women, 208, 214, 219, 223
Women's career development, 211-
    214, 217, 220, 223
Work, 207, 208, 209, 226
Work values, 14, 240
Workforce, 89, 207, 208, 238-240
World of Work Inventory, 68
World of work map, 10, 34, 47

Y

Yost and Corbishley's Eight Stage
    Process of Career Counseling,
    259-260